HEALTHY
SLOW COOKER
COOKBOOK

2ND EDITION

Also by the American Heart Association

American Heart Association Instant & Healthy

The New American Heart Association Cookbook, 9th Edition

American Heart Association Healthy Fats, Low-Cholesterol Cookbook, 5th Edition

American Heart Association Grill It, Braise It, Broil It

American Heart Association Go Fresh

American Heart Association Eat Less Salt

American Heart Association Quick & Easy Cookbook, 2nd Edition

American Heart Association Low-Salt Cookbook, 4th Edition

American Heart Association Healthy Family Meals

Find the American Heart Association online at heart.org.

American
Heart
Association.

HEALTHY
SLOW COOKER
COOKBOOK

2ND EDITION

**HARMONY
BOOKS**

Steamed Pumpkin
Bread, page 286

Acknowledgments

American Heart Association Consumer Publications

Managing Editor: Deborah Renza Puccio

Content Manager: Roberta Westcott Sullivan

Recipe Developers

Ellen Boeke	Jackie Mills, M.S., R.D.
Janice Cole	Kathryn Moore
Constance Hay	Carol Ritchie
Nancy S. Hughes	Julie Shapero, R.D., L.D.
Annie King	Roxanne Wyss

Nutrition Analyst

Tammi Hancock, R.D.

Mediterranean Fish Stew
with Rouille, page 112

Contents

8   **SLOW COOKING: A Healthy Twist on an Old Favorite**

    10   Enjoying the Benefits of Slow Cooking

    11   Understanding How Slow Cookers Work

    12   Getting the Best from Your Slow Cooker

14   **HEALTHY FOR GOOD™**

    14   Eat Smart.

    15   Add Color.

    16   Move More.

    17   Be Well.

20   **ABOUT THE RECIPES**

---

22   **Appetizers, Snacks, and Beverages**

44   **Soups**

90   **Seafood**

120   **Poultry**

160   **Meats**

202   **Vegetarian Entrées**

242   **Vegetables and Side Dishes**

272   **Sauces and More**

284   **Breads and Breakfast Dishes**

298   **Desserts**

315   **INDEX**

Slow Cooking
A Healthy Twist on an Old Favorite

Slow cookers have been standard equipment in many American kitchens since the original avocado green and harvest gold models were introduced in the 1970s. For decades, cooks turned to their trusty slow cookers when preparing chilis, stews, soups, and hot dips, and the recipes they used usually included the canned soups, fatty meats, and melted cheeses that were so typical of those dishes. These same ingredients, however, are also chock full of harmful sodium, saturated fats, and calories. Today we are looking for a fresh, healthier approach to slow cooking—one that offers new options to create a full range of creative, delicious, and nutritious dishes that make it easy to eat smart.

In *American Heart Association Healthy Slow Cooker Cookbook,* you'll find modern, health-savvy ways to use this popular culinary device. The long, slow simmering of slow cooking is ideal for transforming the leanest meats into tender bites, and it allows the savory flavors in vegetable-rich stews to blend and mellow. Your slow cooker is also capable of gently cooking fish and seafood, steaming breads and desserts, and simmering complex sauces that can make a simple dish outstanding *and* heart healthy.

We understand that there are times when it makes sense to dump everything in the crock and leave it alone for hours—and other times when it's important to take time to attend to a few details. Prepping ingredients, browning meats, layering foods appropriately, preparing pasta or rice separately—these small steps may take a little extra time or effort, but they can make a big difference in your final product, yielding richer flavor and better texture. With this cookbook's wide assortment of recipes from appetizers to desserts and everything in between, you'll discover just how much your slow cooker can do.

In the pages that follow, "Enjoying the Benefits of Slow Cooking" (page 10) discusses the advantages of using a slow cooker for your health, your budget, and your convenience. "Understanding How Slow Cookers Work" (page 11) explains the technical aspects of slow cooking and how the differences in sizes and shapes can affect the process. "Getting the Best from Your Slow Cooker" (page 12) covers the basics of effective slow cookery. These tricks of the trade will help you deliver the best results for your culinary efforts. In this section, you'll also find general slow cooker guidelines and information on flavor development and food safety. "Eat Smart." (page 14) and "Add Color." (page 15) outline how to eat wisely, while "Move More." (page 16) and "Be Well." (page 17) discuss how to adopt an overall heart-healthy lifestyle.

And, finally, the more than 230 recipes starting on page 22 demonstrate the wide variety of dishes you can cook in a slow cooker. The best way to ensure that healthy, mouthwatering food comes *out* of your cooker is to pay attention to the ingredients you put *in* it. When you start with lean proteins, wholesome grains, and vegetables and fruits—without adding a lot of sodium, unhealthy fats, or sugar—you will enjoy both the health benefits and good flavor of the foods you prepare. We invite you to try any of the delicious *and* nutritious recipes in the pages that follow and let the tantalizing aromas from your slow cooker welcome you home tonight.

Enjoying the Benefits of Slow Cooking

Slow cooking offers several significant advantages: It's a great way to turn healthy ingredients into satisfying meals, it's economical, and, of course, it's convenient.

The slow process of cooking with moist heat at low temperatures produces succulent lean meats and poultry of falling-apart tenderness. Nutrition-rich vegetables often cook right in the crock with the protein source, so they're more likely to be part of your regular meal planning instead of being overlooked or a last-minute afterthought. Slow cookers are excellent for cooking legumes such as lentils and dried beans, those heart-healthy essentials that are full of fiber and protein but are often underused in the typical American diet. A slow cooker also makes easy work of preparing homemade broths and long-simmered sauces to use in other recipes, such as soups and pasta dishes. Making your own soups and sauces allows you to control the amount of sodium and other additives in those foods.

By using your slow cooker, you can also save money on both food and energy costs. Because slow cooking breaks down the connective tissue in less-expensive cuts of meat, you won't need to spend an arm and a leg to enjoy a savory stew or roast. Slow cookers can help you go green, since they require less energy than a traditional stove or oven. You can further reduce your kitchen "footprint" by cooking once and eating twice: Make large quantities of your favorite dishes, eat some now, and refrigerate or freeze the rest for a quick meal at another time.

Slow cookers let you enjoy the many benefits of home-cooked meals with a minimum of hands-on attention. Because the heating elements are encased in a protective housing, the slow cooker doesn't need tending. Except in certain cases, you shouldn't stir the food, and you don't need to watch it or worry about it burning. You can simply leave the kitchen—and even the house—while your dinner is cooking. Slow cooking is also great for warmer months when you don't want to turn on the stove and heat up your kitchen.

Understanding How Slow Cookers Work

Slow cookers surround food with low, steady heat, resulting in long, slow cooking without burning. The outside metal housing contains low-wattage electric coils that heat to a designated temperature. As the coils heat, they transmit indirect heat to the inner crock (usually stoneware). Covering the crock with the lid creates a moisture-proof seal that ensures that the heat and steam released by the contents remain in the crock. This seal is important to maintain a steady temperature inside, and it also helps distribute and blend flavors as vapor condenses on the lid and returns to the food in the pot.

TEMPERATURE

Modern cookers have low, high, and warm heat settings. Most cookers set to low heat reach temperatures ranging from 185°F to 200°F, depending on the individual cooker; on high, they reach temperatures between 250°F and 300°F. In actual practice, the internal temperature of different cookers can vary quite a lot from brand to brand; the age of the cooker also can make a significant difference because new models are made to reach higher temperatures than most older ones. (See page 13 for information on how to test the cooking temperature of your slow cooker so you'll know how to best estimate accurate cooking times.) For most recipes in this book, we've provided you the option of cooking on either low or high. Since the low setting can often take up to double the time to cook as the high setting, these options give you choices that work with your schedule. When the recipe calls for only one setting, then the alternate temperature is not recommended for that particular recipe.

SIZE

Today's slow cookers come in several different sizes, each of which has its advantages. It's important to use the right cooker for the recipe you are preparing: The size of the cooker affects not only how much food you can cook but also the timing of your recipe. For effective cooking, the food should fill the crock enough to adequately cover the heating coils embedded in the sides of the cooker. If the cooker is too large, with a lot of empty space left, the food will cook too fast. If the cooker is too small for the total ingredients of your recipe, the crock will be too full and the food will not cook properly. If a recipe in this book requires a specific size for best results, that is noted. Most recipes, however, offer a range of recommended cooker sizes.

SHAPE

The shape of your cooker affects how the heat is distributed, as well as what will fit comfortably in the crock itself. Round cookers are perfect for casseroles, stews, and soups and for recipes cooked in round baking pans. If you want to serve a whole fish, a large chicken or roast, or a recipe that cooks in a longer pan, such as meat loaf or bread, you need an oval cooker long enough to accommodate the food or the pan. When it is important to use a particular shape, it will be indicated in the recipe.

Getting the Best from Your Slow Cooker

When slow cookers were first introduced, most recipes instructed the cook to open a few cans, dump their contents into the crock, and leave the food to cook for about 8 hours. Quick assembly and hands-off cooking still will be your top priority sometimes, but when you put in a little extra effort, your slow cooker will amply reward you.

FOLLOWING A FEW BASIC SLOW COOKER GUIDELINES

The best ways to escalate your slow cooking from so-so to super are to learn a few basic slow cooker do's and don'ts, know how your own cooker works, and observe basic food safety rules.

- Make the cooker work with your schedule. Try prepping a recipe the night before you plan to cook the food. Cover and refrigerate the prepped food in separate airtight containers overnight, fill the crock in the morning, and turn on the heat and, if your cooker has one, the timer.
- Prep foods so they will cook the most efficiently and evenly. For example, take care to cut carrots into pieces of the same approximate size so all the carrots in the dish will be done at the same time.
- Choose the correct size of cooker for the recipe you are preparing, and don't be tempted to substitute sizes. Different sizes make big differences in timing. Ideally, the cooker will be between one-half and two-thirds full of ingredients when you start the cooking process. For best results, use the size guidelines provided in the recipe.

- Resist the urge to stir or sneak a peek. Open the lid only when the recipe directs you to, complete the necessary actions, such as adding ingredients, and re-cover the cooker quickly. Every time you break the seal between the cover and the crock, you lose a lot of heat.
- Follow the recipe directions for how to arrange ingredients in the crock. Placement order and layering can make a big difference in timing and outcome. In general, for recipes that combine meat and vegetables, you'll place fibrous root vegetables at the bottom of the crock and then layer on the meat or poultry; if using tender vegetables as well, you often will be directed to add them on top toward the end of cooking.
- Trim the visible fat from poultry and meats, and in most cases discard the skin before cooking the poultry, both to cut down on unhealthy fats in the finished dish and for more even cooking. (Because fat holds more heat than water does, the more fat a food contains, the faster it will cook.) Some recipes may direct you to leave the skin on a whole chicken while cooking. If so, be sure to discard the skin before serving the chicken.

MAXIMIZING FLAVOR WITH MINIMUM EFFORT

As you prepare meals in your slow cooker, take the time to get the best flavor results. As the recipes developed for this book demonstrate, incorporating a few simple prep steps and knowing when to add ingredients can make the difference between ho-hum and extraordinary. Here are a few flavor tips to keep in mind when using a slow cooker.

- Brown poultry and meats in a skillet before you add them to the cooker when the recipes call for it. (If your slow cooker has the option, brown the food in the crock.) Browning caramelizes the natural sugars, greatly improving the overall flavor and texture of a dish, as well as making it look more inviting.

• Add ground herbs at the beginning of cooking, but add fresh herbs at the end to preserve their taste and appearance.

• Taste your dish for seasoning before serving because the flavors of spices can mellow and dissipate during slow cooking more so than with other cooking methods.

• Perk up flavors by adding fresh ingredients just after you finish cooking the dish. Citrus juice or zest, fresh herbs, vinegars, or spicy peppers will brighten the blended taste of a long-simmered dish.

KEEPING FOOD SAFE

Slow cooking is safe and effective as long as you observe the safety guidelines that are specific to the slow cooker.

• Become familiar with your cooker's temperature range so you can gauge cooking times accurately. Cooking temperatures of units from different manufacturers vary in intensity, and today's cookers tend to cook hotter than the older models; your machine may cook a little hotter or cooler than the norm. If that's the case, the difference may affect not only the success of a recipe but also the safety of the food.

• To test the cooking temperature of your cooker, try this: Fill the crock one-half to two-thirds full of room-temperature water and heat the water, covered, on low for 8 hours. Uncover and immediately test the water temperature with an instant-read thermometer. (Act quickly because the temperature will drop when the lid is raised.) If the temperature is higher than 185°F, your cooker runs hot, and you should cook foods for slightly less time than recommended. If it is lower, foods may not reach an adequate cooking temperature quickly enough for safety. (If your cooker is not heating to a safe temperature, you should consider replacing it.) Altitude will also affect your cooker's performance, so modify your timing according to the manufacturer's instructions.

• Thaw frozen foods, especially meat and poultry, in the fridge or microwave—but not at room temperature—before you put them in the cooker. Frozen ingredients will keep the internal temperature lower than it should be, and the contents of the crock may not reach high-enough temperatures to cook properly.

• Don't leave food on the warm or off setting in your slow cooker for more than 2 hours to prevent harmful bacteria from multiplying.

• If you suspect that your cooker has been off for more than 2 hours because of a power outage, it's safest to discard the food in the cooker.

• Do not reheat slow cooker leftovers in the crock because bacteria can grow in the time it takes for the food to reach a safe temperature. Instead, reheat food in a microwave or on the stove.

• Let your slow cooker favorites cool before you put them in the freezer; you don't want the warm food to thaw surrounding frozen foods.

Healthy For Good™

Healthy For Good is a revolutionary movement built to help you make lasting changes to your health and life, one small step at a time. The approach is simple: *Eat Smart. Add Color. Move More. Be Well.*

Eat Smart.

Eating healthy doesn't have to mean dieting or giving up all the foods you love. You'll learn how to ditch the junk food and give your body the nutrient-dense fuel it needs.

HEALTHY EATING STARTS AT HOME

Cooking more meals at home gives everyone in the family an opportunity to build better eating habits, one plate at a time.

• Sit down and eat as a family to help ensure healthy and balanced meals.
• Build your cooking skills so you can control what ingredients are used and the amount of sodium in your food.
• Keep your kitchen stocked with fruits, vegetables, lean protein, and whole grains to add true nourishment to your life.

TAKE CONTROL OF YOUR PORTIONS

A portion is how much we choose to eat. Portions are 100 percent under our control and learning how to eat smart portions is a big part of eating healthier.

• Read nutrition labels carefully to compare serving size, calories, sodium levels, and added sugars.
• Eat reasonable portions, even when you're served more than you need.
• Prepare and eat more meals at home so you can control the ingredients and portion size.

BUILD A BETTER PLATE

Eating healthy starts with putting the right foods on your plate, in the right amounts. An easy way to have more energy is to make smart food choices.

• Include fruits and veggies, whole grains, beans and legumes, nuts and seeds, lean protein, fat-free/low-fat dairy products, and healthy fats.
• Limit sweets, fatty or processed meats, solid fats such as butter, and salty or highly processed foods.
• Avoid partially hydrogenated oils.

FATS AREN'T ALL BAD

Your body needs fats but some are better than others. Replace bad fats with healthier ones to keep your body nourished.

• Healthier unsaturated fats come from non-tropical liquid oils, nuts and seeds, avocados, and fatty fish.
• Bad fats are solid or saturated fats; they come from animal sources, such as meat and dairy, as well as tropical oils, such as coconut and palm.
• Avoid trans fats and partially hydrogenated oils, found in some processed foods.

A HEALTHY DIET WITHOUT DIETING

Go for a simple, no-fad healthy eating pattern to nourish your body and bring out the best you.

• Concentrate on smaller portions, rather than forcing yourself to eliminate foods you love.
• Add fiber-rich foods that will keep you feeling full, such as whole grains, legumes, vegetables, and fruits.
• Don't buy empty-calorie foods and sugary drinks; if they aren't in your pantry, then you're less likely to indulge.

MAKE HEALTHIER CHOICES WITH THE HEART-CHECK MARK

Hundreds of foods have been certified by the American Heart Association to help you make smart decisions when grocery shopping.

• Foods bearing our Heart-Check mark have been certified to meet an overall healthy diet pattern.
• Look for the mark on packaging in grocery stores.
• Check to see if your favorite brand is certified at heartcheck.org.

Add Color.

An easy first step to eating healthy is to include fruits and vegetables at every meal or snack. All forms (fresh, frozen, canned, and dried) and colors count, so go ahead and add color to your plate—and your life.

EASY ON THE BUDGET

You don't have to break the bank to get fruits and veggies on your plate; just add a little at a time and look for ways to save.

• Many fruits and vegetables cost less than $1 per serving.
• Single-serving fruits and vegetables can be cheaper than vending machine snacks.
• Buying produce in bulk and freezing the excess can help you save in the long run.

EAT COLORFUL FRUITS AND VEGETABLES EVERY DAY

Everyone knows you need to eat a few servings of fruits and veggies, but do you know what a serving means?

• One whole medium-size fruit (like an apple, orange, or banana) is a serving.
• Get a whole serving of most fruits and veggies with just a half cup of fresh, frozen, or canned produce.
• One cup of raw leafy veggies provides you with a full serving.

KNOCK OUT THE ADDED SALT AND SUGAR

Canned, frozen, and dried fruit and veggies are just as nutritious as fresh, but they can come with some unwelcome add-ons.

• Check labels to find options with the lowest amounts of salt and added sugars.

- Choose fruits and vegetables packed in their own juice or water and prepared without heavy syrups or sauces.
- Drain and rinse canned produce.

EAT WITH THE SEASONS
Seasonal fruits and veggies can make adding color more interesting. Be on the lookout for new produce when the seasons change.

- Shop your local farmers' market to find seasonal fruits and vegetables.
- Join a community garden to add diverse color year-round.
- Grow your own fruit and veggie garden.

EAT A RAINBOW
Eat healthier one plate at a time by adding a little color to every meal and snack of the day.

- Look at your plate as a whole each time you eat. If it's looking too beige, add a serving of fruits and veggies.
- Add color to family favorites such as mac and cheese, pasta, and rice by tossing in a handful of veggies.
- Adding color isn't all or nothing; start small, then add more as time goes by.

GO MEATLESS
Salad isn't the only way to be an herbivore. With colorful substitutions, you won't even miss the meat.

- Replace ground beef in any recipe with finely diced mushrooms.
- Choose a vegetarian meal at least once a week, such as Meatless Mondays.
- Omit the meat and double the veggies in a recipe.

Move More.
A good starting goal is at least 150 minutes a week, but if you don't want to sweat the numbers, just move more. Find forms of exercise you like and will stick with, and build more opportunities to be active into your routine.

DON'T SKIP OUT ON THE WARM-UP
Warming up is a critical part of having a safe and efficient workout. Give your body a few minutes of prep time to increase flexibility and prevent injury.

- Five to ten minutes is a good rule of thumb for a sufficient warm-up. The more intense the activity, the longer the warm-up should be.
- Warm up your whole body—not just the muscles you plan on using.

START WALKING
If you're looking for an easy way to add activity to your day, walking could be right up your alley. It's simple, effective, and you can do it almost anywhere.

- Just start walking. Begin with a few minutes each day and add more from there as you get into better shape.
- Find ways to make it fun, whether that's changing your route, inviting a friend, or listening to music.
- If you're too busy to carve out time for a longer walk, split it up into shorter sessions that work for you.

REFUEL AND HYDRATE FOR OPTIMAL EXERCISE

To stay healthy and get the most out of your workouts, your body needs fuel and fluids before, during, and after your sweat session.

• Hydrate with water and fuel up with healthy carbs up to two hours before working out.
• Take small, frequent sips of water during your workout.
• Refuel after your workout with lean protein, healthy carbs, and plenty of water.

MAKE TIME FOR ACTIVITY

Getting more fit can be as simple as adding at least 22 minutes of activity to each day. Carving out time isn't always easy, but it is worth it.

• Break it up into 10- to 15-minute segments at times that are convenient for you.
• Go for a brisk walk during your lunch break.
• Take the stairs as often as possible for an extra boost.

GET THE WHOLE FAMILY MOVING

Adding exercise is easier when it's a shared activity. Bring your family with you for more accountability, time together, and fun.

• Dance your way to fitness with a parents' night out or a fun family dance party.
• Put away the screens and take a walk in your local park.
• Unleash your inner child with fun games such as chase, tag, and kid-friendly obstacle courses.

RECOVER QUICKER WITH A COOL-DOWN

Cooling down after a workout can help your body reset so you can avoid dizziness, reduce lactic acid buildup, and recover a little bit easier.

• Gradually reduce your heart rate by walking for about 5 minutes.
• When your muscles are still warm is the best time to stretch.
• Breathing deeply during your cool-down can also help you relax.

Be Well.

Along with eating smart and being active, real health also includes getting enough sleep, practicing mindfulness, managing stress, keeping mind and body fit, connecting socially, and more.

REST AND RELAXATION FOR THE WIN

• Relaxation is a skill that can be developed. You can take a class to learn new techniques or practice on your own, but the most important thing is to keep it up.
• Practice deep breathing techniques throughout the day by inhaling through your nose and exhaling through your mouth slowly and deliberately.
• Pick up a meditative hobby like walking, painting, gardening, or bird watching.
• Take up tai chi, qi gong, yoga, or guided meditation with an instructor to develop your technique.

TAKE IT SLOW

When you're feeling anxious, stressed out, or angry, take a step back to gather your thoughts and look at the situation objectively.

- In high-anxiety situations, give yourself some space—take a walk and come back later when tensions subside.
- When you're feeling angry or upset with someone, count to ten and take a few deep breaths before you react.
- Take preventive measures to avoid stress, like leaving a few minutes earlier to avoid being late.

LOSING WEIGHT AND KEEPING IT OFF

- Long-term weight loss and maintenance is all about lifestyle and making healthier choices regularly.
- Losing weight is a simple equation: Eat fewer calories than you burn, and you'll see a difference over time.
- Focus on portion control and eating healthy while increasing calories burned with regular activity such as walking.
- Don't fall into the traps of "cheat days." For long-term results, develop a pattern of healthy eating and indulge sensibly on occasion.

KICK STRESS TO THE CURB

How much stress you have in your life as well as how you react to it can play an important role in your overall well-being. Keep stress at bay with positive coping techniques.

- Focus on healthy outlets for your stress, such as taking a walk, journaling, volunteering, or taking up a hobby.

- Add regular exercise and meditation to your routine to help you stay more relaxed under pressure.
- Be sure to get enough sleep and take everything one step at a time, especially when you feel rushed or overworked.

MAKE SELF-CARE A PRIORITY

- Too often we put our own needs aside to get things done for family, work, and other responsibilities. To be your best you, it's important to add a healthy dose of self-care.
- Add calming activities to your day, such as lunchtime walks and yoga, to rejuvenate and refresh.
- Take time out for you; use your vacation days whether it's to go on a big trip or just hang out at home for a staycation.
- Don't overlook your emotional and mental health; get help if you need it to manage stress, anxiety, depression, or grief.

SLEEP YOUR WAY TO WHOLE BODY HEALTH

- Sleep could be the key to unlocking a healthier you. Amount and quality of sleep can influence your eating habits, mood, memory, and more.
- Proper rest allows you to recharge your batteries, so that you're less likely to crave sugary, fatty foods that provide quick energy.
- How much rest you need is personal, but many people require about seven to nine hours of quality sleep each night.
- Be more active, limit caffeine (especially before bed), and establish a bedtime routine to get on track to better sleep.

For more tips, tricks, and recipes, join the movement at heart.org/HealthyForGood.

Kale and Red Quinoa Soup,
page 82

About the Recipes

Understanding the Recipe Icons

We know there are days when you won't have time to do much more than put some ingredients into your slow cooker and let it do its magic. For those hectic times, you'll like that nearly half the recipes in this book require you to do only the usual prep—chopping onions, trimming the fat from the meat—before the slow cooking begins, and maybe do something equally simple during cooking or at the end, such as stirring the food once while it cooks or perhaps sprinkling the finished dish with lemon zest. That's all—no browning onions, preparing dried beans, dry-roasting nuts, or boiling water for rice—to complete the dish. Look through the book for recipes identified with this icon ⏱ when you want to put in minimal effort and get maximum results.

In some recipes, you'll also notice the icon ——— + ——— in the ingredients list. You'll need the ingredients above the symbol right away, but you'll know not to set out the others—especially perishable items—yet. You won't need those for hours, until *after* the slow cooking is complete.

Using the Nutritional Analyses

To help you plan meals and determine how a certain recipe fits into your overall diet, we have provided a nutrition analysis for each recipe in this book. The following guidelines give important details about how the analyses were calculated and products that were used in the recipes. We have made every effort to provide accurate information. Because of the many variables involved in analyzing foods, however, the serving sizes and nutritional values given should be considered approximate.

- Each analysis is for a single serving.
- Garnishes or optional ingredients are not included unless they significantly increase fat, sodium, cholesterol, or sugar content.
- Serving sizes are approximate.
- When more than one ingredient option is listed, the first one is analyzed. When a range of ingredients is given, the average is analyzed.
- Values other than fats are rounded to the nearest whole number. Fat values are rounded to the nearest half gram. Because of the rounding, values for saturated, trans, monounsaturated, and polyunsaturated fats may not add up to the amount shown for total fat value.
- We specify canola, corn, and olive oils in these recipes, but you can also use other

nontropical vegetable oils, such as safflower, soybean, and sunflower.

• Meats are analyzed as lean, with all visible fat discarded. Values for ground beef are based on extra-lean meat that is 95 percent fat-free.

• If meat, poultry, or seafood is marinated and the marinade is discarded, the analysis includes all of the sodium from the marinade but none of the other nutrients from it.

• If alcohol is used in a cooked dish, we estimate that most of the alcohol calories evaporate as the food cooks.

• If a recipe in this book calls for commercial products, wherever possible we use and analyze the ones without added salt (for example, no-salt-added canned beans) or with the least sodium available (for example, soy sauce). (In some cases, we call for no-salt-added and low-sodium products and add table salt sparingly for flavor. The result still has far less sodium than the full-sodium product would.) If only a regular commercial product is available, we use the one with the lowest sodium available.

• If this book includes a recipe that can be used in another recipe, for example, Chicken Broth on page 48 that can be used in Shrimp and Chicken Paella (page 115), we use the data for our own version of broth, rather than a store-bought product, in the analysis and cross-reference the recipe.

• Because product labeling in the marketplace can vary and change quickly, we use the generic terms "fat-free" and "low-fat" throughout to avoid confusion.

• We use the abbreviations "g" for gram and "mg" for milligram throughout.

Appetizers, Snacks, and Beverages

23 Sun-Dried Tomato, Kalamata, and Tuna Tapenade ⏱

24 Pistachio and Pumpkin Seed Snack Mix ⏱

26 Baba Ghanoush

27 Curried Garlic-Bean Spread

28 Smoky Red Bell Pepper Hummus

30 Gingered Pear and Apricot Dip ⏱

31 Smoked Turkey Meatballs

32 Saucy Boneless Chicken "Wings"

34 Pork and Water Chestnut Mini Phyllo Tarts

35 Open-Face Empanadas

36 Artichoke-Spinach "Mini Wraps"

37 Crunchy Barbecue-Flavored Chickpeas ⏱

38 Cajun-Spiced Pecans ⏱

39 Cinnamon-Honey Peanuts ⏱

40 Hot Pomegranate-Cherry Cider ⏱

41 Mulled Pineapple-Citrus Punch ⏱

42 Warm and Spicy Tomato Punch

43 Chai Tea ⏱

Sun-Dried Tomato, Kalamata, and Tuna Tapenade

"Colorful," "chunky," and "pungent" describe this mightily flavored tapenade. Spread it on whole-grain Melba toast, thin slices of toasted whole-grain bread, or even slices of chilled boiled red potatoes.

FAST PREP!

SERVES 12; 3 tablespoons per serving

SLOW COOKER SIZE | SHAPE
3- to 4½-quart | round or oval

SLOW COOKING TIME
3½ to 4 hours ON LOW, **OR**
1 hour 45 minutes to 2 hours ON HIGH

Cooking spray

8 sun-dried tomato halves (about 1 ounce), cut into thin strips

1 cup grape tomatoes, halved

¼ cup finely chopped onion (yellow preferred)

2 tablespoons water

2 medium garlic cloves, minced

———— + ————

1 cup grape tomatoes, halved

¼ cup chopped fresh basil

12 kalamata olives, finely chopped

2 tablespoons olive oil (extra virgin preferred)

1 tablespoon red wine vinegar

3 ounces canned very low sodium albacore tuna, packed in water, rinsed in cold water, drained, and coarsely flaked

1. Lightly spray a 2-cup heatproof glass measuring cup with cooking spray. Put the sun-dried tomatoes, 1 cup grape tomatoes, the onion, water, and garlic in the measuring cup. Place the measuring cup in the slow cooker. Cook, covered, on low for 3½ to 4 hours or on high for 1 hour 45 minutes to 2 hours, or until the sun-dried tomatoes are very soft.

2. Carefully remove the measuring cup from the slow cooker. Pour the mixture into a shallow dish, such as a pie pan. To serve at room temperature, let stand for about 1 hour. To serve chilled, cover and refrigerate for 1 to 2 hours. The tapenade will thicken as it cools.

3. Just before serving, stir in the remaining ingredients except the tuna. Gently fold in the tuna.

PER SERVING
Calories **65**
Total Fat **4.5 g**
  Saturated Fat **0.5 g**
  Trans Fat **0.0 g**
  Polyunsaturated Fat **0.5 g**
  Monounsaturated Fat **3.0 g**

Cholesterol **4 mg**
Sodium **84 mg**
Carbohydrates **5 g**
  Fiber **1 g**
  Sugars **2 g**
Protein **3 g**

Dietary Exchanges:
  1 vegetable, 1 fat

SERVES 12; ⅓ cup per serving

SLOW COOKER SIZE | SHAPE
3- to 4½-quart | round or oval

SLOW COOKING TIME
2 hours ON LOW, **OR**
1 hour ON HIGH

Cooking spray

2 tablespoons canola or corn oil

2 teaspoons smoked paprika

2 teaspoons yellow or Dijon mustard (lowest sodium available)

2 teaspoons Worcestershire sauce (lowest sodium available)

½ teaspoon ground cumin

½ teaspoon garlic powder

⅛ teaspoon chipotle powder or cayenne

3 cups wheat snack-mix-type cereal squares

½ cup unsalted shelled pistachios or slivered almonds

⅓ cup unsalted pumpkin seeds with shells

———— + ————

⅛ teaspoon salt

Pistachio and Pumpkin Seed Snack Mix

Who doesn't like a little something crunchy in the middle of the day? Keep a few single-serving bags of this snack mix in your desk drawer or pack some for a treat in a brown-bag lunch.

1. Lightly spray the slow cooker with cooking spray. Set aside.
2. In a small bowl, whisk together the oil, paprika, mustard, Worcestershire sauce, cumin, garlic powder, and chipotle powder.
3. Put the cereal, pistachios, and pumpkin seeds in a large bowl. Add the oil mixture, stirring until well blended. Transfer to the slow cooker.
4. Cook, covered, on low for 2 hours, stirring every 40 minutes, or on high for 1 hour, stirring every 20 minutes, or just until the cereal is beginning to lightly brown.
5. Spread the mix in a single layer on a baking sheet. Sprinkle with the salt. Let stand for 2 hours (this is very important) so the flavors blend and the mix cools completely and "crisps up." Store the cooled mix in an airtight container for up to two weeks.

PER SERVING
Calories **127**
Total Fat **6.5 g**
  Saturated Fat **1.0 g**
  Trans Fat **0.0 g**
  Polyunsaturated Fat **2.0 g**
  Monounsaturated Fat **3.5 g**

Cholesterol **0 mg**
Sodium **135 mg**
Carbohydrates **15 g**
  Fiber **3 g**
  Sugars **2 g**
Protein **4 g**

Dietary Exchanges:
1 starch, 1 fat

SLOW COOKER SIZE | SHAPE
3- to 4½-quart | round
or oval

SLOW COOKING TIME
3 to 3½ hours ON LOW plus
3 to 3½ hours ON LOW

Cooking spray

2 pounds eggplant
(Japanese preferred)
peeled, seeded if using
large varieties, and cut
into 1-inch cubes

½ cup water

+

¼ cup fresh mint

2 tablespoons tahini

2 tablespoons fresh lime
juice

1 medium garlic clove,
chopped

½ teaspoon smoked
paprika (optional)

¼ teaspoon salt

Pomegranate seeds
(optional)

1 tablespoon olive oil
(extra virgin preferred)
(optional)

Baba Ghanoush

When slow cooked, baba ghanoush (bah-bah gah-NOOSH) has a very
mild flavor. If you want a hint of the smokiness of grilled or roasted
eggplant, simply add a touch of smoked paprika to this Middle
Eastern favorite. Serve it with toasted whole-grain pita wedges or
crudités.

1. Lightly spray the slow cooker with cooking spray. Put the
   eggplant and water in the slow cooker. Cook, covered, on low for
   3 to 3½ hours. Quickly stir once and re-cover the slow cooker.
   Cook for 3 to 3½ hours. Using a slotted spoon, transfer the
   eggplant to a food processor or blender. Discard the cooking
   liquid.

2. Add the mint, tahini, lime juice, garlic, paprika, and salt to
   the eggplant. Process until smooth and creamy. Transfer to a
   serving bowl. Serve garnished with the pomegranate seeds and/
   or drizzled with the oil. Refrigerate any leftovers in an airtight
   container for up to two days.

COOK'S TIP
Tahini is a paste made from sesame seeds. Look for it in the condiment
or ethnic-food sections in the grocery store.

PER SERVING		
Calories **38**	Cholesterol **0 mg**	Dietary Exchanges:
Total Fat **1.5 g**	Sodium **62 mg**	**1 vegetable, ½ fat**
Saturated Fat **0.0 g**	Carbohydrates **5 g**	
Trans Fat **0.0 g**	Fiber **3 g**	
Polyunsaturated Fat **1.0 g**	Sugars **2 g**	
Monounsaturated Fat **0.5 g**	Protein **1 g**	

PER SERVING (with optional ingredients)		
Calories **50**	Cholesterol **0 mg**	Dietary Exchanges:
Total Fat **3.0 g**	Sodium **62 mg**	**1 vegetable, ½ fat**
Saturated Fat **0.5 g**	Carbohydrates **5 g**	
Trans Fat **0.0 g**	Fiber **3 g**	
Polyunsaturated Fat **1.0 g**	Sugars **2 g**	
Monounsaturated Fat **1.5 g**	Protein **1 g**	

Curried Garlic-Bean Spread

Curry and garlic flavor this versatile bean mixture, which can be served warm or at room temperature as a spread on whole-grain crackers or as a dip with fresh vegetables. It's also a great sandwich spread or filling for whole-grain pita pockets.

SERVES 12; ¼ cup per serving

SLOW COOKER SIZE | SHAPE
1½- to 2½-quart | round or oval

SLOW COOKING TIME
4 to 6 hours ON LOW, **OR**
2 to 3 hours ON HIGH

1. Fill a small saucepan three-fourths full of water (not the 3 cups in the ingredients list). Bring to a boil over high heat. Stir in the beans. Return to a boil. Reduce the heat and simmer for 15 minutes. Pour the beans into a colander and rinse.
2. Pour the beans into the slow cooker. Add the remaining ingredients, stirring to combine. Cook, covered, on low for 4 to 6 hours or on high for 2 to 3 hours, or until the beans are tender.
3. Using a slotted spoon, transfer the mixture to a food processor or blender. Process until almost smooth but retaining some texture. Transfer to a medium bowl. If serving at room temperature, let stand for 1 hour. To serve chilled, cover and refrigerate for at least 30 minutes. The spread will keep well for up to three days in the refrigerator.

1 cup dried Great Northern beans (about 8 ounces), sorted for stones and shriveled beans, rinsed, and drained

3 cups water

1 large onion, coarsely chopped

4 large garlic cloves, minced

1½ teaspoons curry powder

1 teaspoon paprika

1 teaspoon ground turmeric

½ teaspoon ground cinnamon

¼ teaspoon pepper

PER SERVING
Calories **54**
Total Fat **0.5 g**
  Saturated Fat **0.0 g**
  Trans Fat **0.0 g**
  Polyunsaturated Fat **0.0 g**
  Monounsaturated Fat **0.0 g**

Cholesterol **0 mg**
Sodium **4 mg**
Carbohydrates **10 g**
  Fiber **3 g**
  Sugars **1 g**
Protein **3 g**

Dietary Exchanges:
  ½ **starch**

SERVES 8; ¼ cup per
serving (plus 4½ cups
chickpeas remaining)

SLOW COOKER SIZE | SHAPE
3- to 4½-quart | round
or oval

SLOW COOKING TIME
10 hours ON LOW

1 pound dried chickpeas,
sorted for stones and
shriveled chickpeas,
rinsed, and drained

6 cups water

+

3 tablespoons sesame
seeds, dry roasted

3 tablespoons fresh lemon
juice

2 tablespoons fat-free plain
Greek yogurt

3 tablespoons water

1 teaspoon olive oil and
1 teaspoon olive oil
(extra virgin preferred),
divided use

2 medium garlic cloves,
minced

2 medium strips of lemon
peel (each about
3 inches by ½ inch)

¼ to ½ teaspoon smoked
paprika

¼ teaspoon salt

1 medium roasted red
bell pepper, quartered,
drained if bottled

Smoky Red Bell Pepper Hummus

Slow cooking the chickpeas results in extra creaminess, so we went ahead and called for cooking a pound of them, even though you need about a third of that for this Middle Eastern spread. Serve the hummus on whole-grain pita wedges or with crudités, then enjoy the bonus chickpeas in soups, stews, and green salads.

1. Fill a large saucepan three-fourths full of water (not the 6 cups in the ingredients list). Bring to a boil over high heat. Stir in the chickpeas. Return to a boil. Reduce the heat and simmer for 15 minutes. Pour the chickpeas into a colander and rinse.

2. Pour the chickpeas into the slow cooker. Pour in the 6 cups water. Cook, covered, on low for 10 hours, adding more water if needed to keep the chickpeas covered. Be sure to quickly add the water and re-cover the slow cooker each time.

3. Measure out 2 cups of the cooked chickpeas for the hummus. Transfer the remaining 4½ cups to an airtight container and refrigerate for up to three days or freeze for up to six months for other uses.

4. To prepare the hummus, process the sesame seeds in a food processor or blender for 30 seconds. Add, in order, the lemon juice, yogurt, remaining 3 tablespoons water, 1 teaspoon oil, garlic, lemon peel, paprika, salt, 2 cups cooked chickpeas, and roasted pepper. Process until smooth. Serve warm or transfer to an airtight container. Cover and refrigerate until serving time. Just before serving, drizzle the hummus with the remaining 1 teaspoon oil.

COOK'S TIPS

Roasted Bell Peppers To prepare roasted bell peppers, preheat the broiler. Spray a broiler pan and rack with cooking spray. Broil the bell pepper on the broiler pan about 4 inches from the heat, turning until the pepper is charred all over. Put the pepper in a small bowl and let stand, covered, for at least 5 minutes. (It won't hurt the pepper to sit for as long as 20 minutes.) Rinse the pepper with cold water, removing and discarding the blackened skin, ribs, seeds, and stem. Blot the pepper dry.

Dry-Roasting Seeds To dry-roast seeds, such as the sesame seeds here, put them in a single layer in a small skillet. Cook over medium heat for about 4 minutes, or until the seeds darken and begin to pop, stirring frequently. Remove them from the skillet so they don't burn.

PER SERVING
Calories **109**
Total Fat **4.5 g**
  Saturated Fat **0.5 g**
  Trans Fat **0.0 g**
  Polyunsaturated Fat **1.5 g**
  Monounsaturated Fat **2.0 g**

Cholesterol **0 mg**
Sodium **80 mg**
Carbohydrates **13 g**
  Fiber **4 g**
  Sugars **3 g**
  Protein **5 g**

Dietary Exchanges:
  1 starch, ½ very lean meat, ½ fat

FAST PREP! ⏱

SERVES 8; ¼ cup per serving

SLOW COOKER SIZE | SHAPE
3- to 4½-quart | round or oval

SLOW COOKING TIME
3 to 3½ hours ON LOW

Cooking spray

2 medium, very firm (unripe) pears, peeled and diced

½ cup all-fruit apricot spread

—————— + ——————

1 teaspoon grated peeled gingerroot

Gingered Pear and Apricot Dip

You're in for a real treat with this dip made of bits of pears swimming in a sweet apricot and fresh ginger sauce. Use banana or pear slices for dipping, or spoon the mixture onto baked sweet potatoes or winter squash.

1. Lightly spray a 2-cup heatproof glass measuring cup with cooking spray. Put the pears in the measuring cup. Spoon the fruit spread on top. Cook, covered, on low for 3 to 3½ hours, or until the pears are just tender.
2. Carefully remove the measuring cup from the slow cooker. Pour the dip into a shallow bowl. Let stand for 1 hour, or until room temperature. Stir in the gingerroot.

COOK'S TIP
If you use ripe pears, the dip will be mushy rather than slightly chunky.

PER SERVING
Calories **66**
Total Fat **0.0 g**
　Saturated Fat **0.0 g**
　Trans Fat **0.0 g**
　Polyunsaturated Fat **0.0 g**
　Monounsaturated Fat **0.0 g**

Cholesterol **0 mg**
Sodium **1 mg**
Carbohydrates **17 g**
　Fiber **1 g**
　Sugars **12 g**
Protein **0 g**

Dietary Exchanges:
　1 fruit

Smoked Turkey Meatballs

Shredded vegetables help moisten the lean ground turkey in these baby meatballs, which are cooked in a maple-sweetened barbecue-like sauce.

1. In a large bowl, using your hands or a spoon, gently combine all the meatball ingredients except the egg white. Don't overwork the mixture or it will become too compact and the meatballs will be heavy. Gently work in the egg white. Shape into 36 1-inch balls (about 1 tablespoon each). Place on a large baking sheet so they don't touch. Refrigerate for 15 to 30 minutes, or until chilled.

2. Meanwhile, in a small bowl, whisk together the sauce ingredients. Set aside.

3. When the meatballs have chilled, heat 1 teaspoon oil in a large nonstick skillet over medium heat, swirling to coat the bottom. Cook half the meatballs for 3 to 4 minutes, or until browned on all sides, adjusting the heat as necessary. Transfer to the slow cooker. Repeat with the remaining 1 teaspoon oil and remaining meatballs.

4. Pour the tomato sauce mixture into the skillet. Bring to a boil on high, scraping to dislodge any browned bits. Pour over the meatballs. Cook, covered, on low for 4 to 6 hours or on high for 2 to 3 hours, or until the meatballs are no longer pink in the center.

COOK'S TIP

To save time and keep meatballs uniform in size, use a spring-loaded ice cream scoop to form them. For this recipe, try a #60 scoop; it holds about 1 tablespoon.

SERVES 12; 3 meatballs per serving

SLOW COOKER SIZE | SHAPE
1½- to 2½-quart | round or oval

SLOW COOKING TIME
4 to 6 hours ON LOW, **OR**
2 to 3 hours ON HIGH

MEATBALLS

1 pound ground skinless turkey breast

½ cup shredded carrot

½ cup shredded zucchini

2 large shallots or ½ medium onion, minced

¼ cup plain panko (Japanese-style bread crumbs)

1 tablespoon smoked paprika

2 large garlic cloves, minced

¼ teaspoon salt

¼ teaspoon pepper

1 large egg white, lightly beaten with a fork

SAUCE

1 8-ounce can no-salt-added tomato sauce

1½ tablespoons pure maple syrup

1 tablespoon smoked paprika

—————

1 teaspoon canola or corn oil and 1 teaspoon canola or corn oil, divided use

PER SERVING
Calories **78**
Total Fat **1.0 g**
  Saturated Fat **0.0 g**
  Trans Fat **0.0 g**
  Polyunsaturated Fat **0.5 g**
  Monounsaturated Fat **0.5 g**

Cholesterol **23 mg**
Sodium **81 mg**
Carbohydrates **6 g**
  Fiber **1 g**
  Sugars **3 g**
Protein **10 g**

Dietary Exchanges:
  ½ other carbohydrate,
  1½ lean meat

SERVES 8; 2 "wings" and
1 tablespoon sauce per
serving

SLOW COOKER SIZE | SHAPE
3- to 4½-quart | round
or oval

SLOW COOKING TIME
3 to 4 hours ON LOW, **OR**
1½ to 2 hours ON HIGH

CHERRY BARBECUE SAUCE

¼ cup barbecue sauce
(lowest sodium
available)

¼ cup all-fruit cherry
spread

OR

RED RANCH SAUCE

¼ cup low-fat buttermilk

¼ cup fat-free plain yogurt

1 teaspoon smoked paprika
(sweet or hot)

½ teaspoon chili powder

½ teaspoon garlic powder

½ teaspoon onion powder

½ teaspoon ground cumin

⅛ teaspoon cayenne

½ teaspoon chili powder

½ teaspoon garlic powder

½ teaspoon onion powder

½ teaspoon ground cumin

2 tablespoons all-purpose
flour

1 pound boneless, skinless
chicken breast halves, all
visible fat discarded, cut
into 3 x ½-inch strips (16
strips total)

¼ cup fat-free, low-sodium
chicken broth, such
as on page 48 (omit if
cooking the chicken with
Cherry Barbecue Sauce)

Saucy Boneless Chicken "Wings"

This healthier-for-you version of the popular appetizer is perfect for game day and potluck meals. Choose either a sweet-tart or kicked-up smoky sauce to elevate these wings to new heights.

1. If making the Cherry Barbecue Sauce, in a small bowl, stir together the Cherry Barbecue Sauce ingredients. Set aside.

2. If making the Red Ranch Sauce, in a small bowl, stir together the Red Ranch Sauce ingredients. Cover and refrigerate until serving time.

3. In a second small bowl, stir together ½ teaspoon chili powder, ½ teaspoon garlic powder, ½ teaspoon onion powder, and ½ teaspoon cumin. Stir in the flour.

4. Dip the chicken strips in the chili powder mixture, turning to coat and gently shaking off any excess. Using your fingertips, gently press the coating so it adheres to the chicken. Place the strips in the slow cooker. If using the Cherry Barbecue Sauce, stir the sauce together with the chicken; omit the broth. If using the Red Ranch Sauce, pour in the broth around the chicken. Cook, covered, on low for 3 to 4 hours or on high for 1½ to 2 hours.

PER SERVING (with Cherry Barbecue Sauce)
Calories **109**
Total Fat **1.5 g**
 Saturated Fat **0.5 g**
 Trans Fat **0.0 g**
 Polyunsaturated Fat **0.0 g**
 Monounsaturated Fat **0.5 g**

Cholesterol **36 mg**
Sodium **122 mg**
Carbohydrates **10 g**
 Fiber **0 g**
 Sugars **7 g**
 Protein **12 g**

Dietary Exchanges:
2 lean meat, 1 other carbohydrate

PER SERVING (with Red Ranch Sauce)
Calories **85**
Total Fat **1.5 g**
 Saturated Fat **0.5 g**
 Trans Fat **0.0 g**
 Polyunsaturated Fat **0.5 g**
 Monounsaturated Fat **0.5 g**

Cholesterol **37 mg**
Sodium **87 mg**
Carbohydrates **3 g**
 Fiber **0 g**
 Sugars **1 g**
 Protein **13 g**

Dietary Exchanges:
2 lean meat

SERVES 15; 3 mini tarts per serving

SLOW COOKER SIZE | SHAPE
3- to 4½-quart | round or oval

SLOW COOKING TIME
3 hours ON LOW plus 1 minute ON LOW, **OR**
1½ hours ON HIGH plus 1 minute ON HIGH

Cooking spray

1 teaspoon canola or corn oil

8 ounces lean ground pork

1 small onion (yellow preferred), finely chopped

+

4 cups finely shredded cabbage

4 ounces canned water chestnuts, drained and diced

½ cup matchstick-size carrot strips, chopped

½ cup snipped fresh cilantro (optional)

2 tablespoons sugar

2 tablespoons soy sauce (lowest sodium available)

1½ to 2 tablespoons grated peeled gingerroot

¼ teaspoon crushed red pepper flakes, or to taste

45 frozen mini phyllo shells (3 1.90-ounce boxes), thawed

Pork and Water Chestnut Mini Phyllo Tarts

Do you sometimes wonder what you could do with those petite phyllo shells in the frozen food section of your supermarket? Put an Asian spin on them with this sweet-and-spicy filling of ground pork, cabbage, and fresh ginger.

1. Lightly spray the slow cooker and a 2-cup heatproof glass measuring cup with cooking spray. Set aside.

2. In a large nonstick skillet, heat the oil over medium-high heat, swirling to coat the bottom. Cook the pork and onion for 3 minutes, or until the pork is browned on the outside and no longer pink in the center, stirring frequently to turn and break up the pork. Transfer to the measuring cup. Place in the slow cooker. Cook, covered, on low for 3 hours or on high for 1½ hours, or until the onion is very soft.

3. Carefully remove the cup. Quickly pour the pork mixture into the slow cooker. Stir in the remaining ingredients except the phyllo shells. Cook for 1 minute, or until the cabbage is slightly wilted, stirring frequently. If serving immediately, spoon the filling into the phyllo shells. To serve while the filling is still hot but not immediately, spoon the hot filling into a serving bowl, surround the bowl with the shells, and let your guests fill the shells. (If you fill the shells too soon, they will become soggy.)

COOK'S TIP

To save prep time, purchase packages of already cut matchstick-size carrots and shredded cabbage.

PER SERVING		Cholesterol **10 mg**	Dietary Exchanges:
Calories **110**		Sodium **107 mg**	½ **starch, 1 vegetable, 1 fat**
Total Fat **5.5 g**		Carbohydrates **11 g**	
Saturated Fat **1.0 g**		Fiber **1 g**	
Trans Fat **0.0 g**		Sugars **3 g**	
Polyunsaturated Fat **1.5 g**		Protein **3 g**	
Monounsaturated Fat **2.5 g**			

Open-Face Empanadas

Like traditional empanadas, these are filled with ground beef seasoned with cumin and cinnamon and accented with raisins and almonds. Instead of fatty pastry dough, though, healthy lettuce leaves keep all the goodness inside. For a fun, do-it-yourself appetizer, serve the empanada filling in a festive bowl surrounded by the lettuce leaves, and let everyone fill and wrap their own empanadas.

1. Heat a large nonstick skillet over medium-high heat. Cook the beef for 3 minutes, or until no longer pink on the outside, stirring occasionally to turn and break up the beef. Drain if necessary.

2. Stir in the onion, bell pepper, and garlic. Cook for 2 minutes, or until the beef is browned and the onion and bell pepper are beginning to soften, stirring occasionally. Transfer to the slow cooker.

3. Stir in the tomatoes with liquid, raisins, tomato paste, cumin, cinnamon, salt, and pepper. Cook, covered, on low for 6 to 8 hours or on high for 2½ to 4 hours, or until the beef is no longer pink in the center and the mixture is bubbling.

4. Stir in the almonds. Spoon about 3 tablespoons empanada mixture down the center of each lettuce leaf half and roll up jelly-roll style.

SERVES 12; 2 wraps per serving

SLOW COOKER SIZE | SHAPE
1½- to 2½-quart | round or oval

SLOW COOKING TIME
6 to 8 hours ON LOW, **OR**
2½ to 4 hours ON HIGH

1 pound extra-lean ground beef

1 large onion, chopped

1 medium green bell pepper, chopped

3 large garlic cloves, minced

1 14.5-ounce can no-salt-added diced tomatoes, undrained

⅓ cup dark raisins

1 tablespoon no-salt-added tomato paste

2 teaspoons ground cumin

½ teaspoon ground cinnamon

¼ teaspoon salt

⅛ teaspoon pepper

+

⅓ cup slivered almonds

12 leaves of leaf lettuce, halved lengthwise

PER SERVING
Calories **103**
Total Fat **3.5 g**
  Saturated Fat **1.0 g**
  Trans Fat **0.0 g**
  Polyunsaturated Fat **0.5 g**
  Monounsaturated Fat **1.5 g**

Cholesterol **21 mg**
Sodium **91 mg**
Carbohydrates **9 g**
  Fiber **2 g**
  Sugars **5 g**
Protein **10 g**

Dietary Exchanges:
  ½ **other carbohydrate,**
  1 lean meat

SERVES 10; 5 mini wraps per serving

SLOW COOKER SIZE | SHAPE
3- to 4½-quart | round or oval

SLOW COOKING TIME

3½ to 4 hours ON LOW plus 5 minutes ON HIGH, **OR**

1 hour 45 minutes to 2 hours ON HIGH plus 5 minutes ON HIGH

Cooking spray

1 teaspoon olive oil

1 medium onion, chopped

2 medium garlic cloves, minced

1 14-ounce can artichoke hearts, drained and chopped

1 teaspoon dried oregano, crumbled

———— ✛ ————

4 ounces spinach (about 4 cups), coarsely chopped

2 tablespoons light mayonnaise

1 tablespoon plus 2 teaspoons olive oil (extra virgin preferred)

½ cup shredded or grated Parmesan cheese

50 medium to large spinach leaves, stems discarded

Artichoke-Spinach "Mini Wraps"

Whether you're having guests over or simply feel like making a little something special, try these creamy mini wraps. Slow cook the artichoke-spinach mixture, spoon a small amount onto spinach leaves, fold the sides over, and enjoy.

1. Lightly spray the slow cooker and a 2-cup heatproof glass measuring cup with cooking spray. Set aside.

2. In a medium nonstick skillet, heat 1 teaspoon oil over medium-high heat, swirling to coat the bottom. Cook the onion for 3 minutes, or until soft, stirring frequently. Stir in the garlic and cook for 15 seconds, stirring constantly. Remove from the heat.

3. Stir in the artichokes and oregano. Spoon into the measuring cup. Place in the slow cooker. Cook, covered, on low for 3½ to 4 hours or on high for 1 hour 45 minutes to 2 hours, or until the onion is very soft.

4. Quickly and carefully spoon the artichoke mixture into the center of the slow cooker. Stir in the spinach and mayonnaise and re-cover the slow cooker. If using the low setting, change it to high. Cook for 5 minutes. Stir in the remaining 1 tablespoon plus 2 teaspoons oil. Transfer the mixture to a shallow serving dish. Sprinkle with the Parmesan.

5. Spoon 1 teaspoon of the artichoke mixture onto each spinach leaf. Fold the sides toward the center so they overlap slightly and form mini wraps.

PER SERVING
Calories **68**
Total Fat **4.0 g**
  Saturated Fat **1.0 g**
  Trans Fat **0.0 g**
  Polyunsaturated Fat **1.0 g**
  Monounsaturated Fat **2.5 g**

Cholesterol **2 mg**
Sodium **180 mg**
Carbohydrates **6 g**
  Fiber **2 g**
  Sugars **2 g**
  Protein **3 g**

Dietary Exchanges:
  1 vegetable, 1 fat

Crunchy Barbecue-Flavored Chickpeas

These smoky, spicy chickpeas are a healthy alternative to potato chips. For your next holiday gathering, mix these chickpeas together with Cajun-Spiced Pecans (page 38) and Cinnamon-Honey Peanuts (page 39) for the perfect party mix.

1. Put the chickpeas in the slow cooker. Add the oil, stirring to coat. Prop open the lid of the slow cooker with a chopstick or spoon. Cook on low for 8 to 10 hours or on high for $3\frac{1}{2}$ to 4 hours. You may stir the chickpeas once halfway through the cooking time, but this step isn't absolutely necessary.
2. About 10 minutes before the chickpeas have finished cooking, in a small bowl, stir together the remaining ingredients except the lemon juice. Set aside.
3. When the chickpeas are golden-brown and crunchy, sprinkle the lemon juice and paprika mixture over them, stirring to coat. Refrigerate any leftover chickpeas in an airtight container for up to three days.

FAST PREP!

SERVES 8; generous ¼ cup per serving

SLOW COOKER SIZE | SHAPE
3- to 4½-quart | oval or round

SLOW COOKING TIME
8 to 10 hours ON LOW, **OR**
3½ to 4 hours ON HIGH

2 15.5-ounce cans no-salt-added chickpeas, rinsed and drained

2 teaspoons olive oil

———— + ————

1 teaspoon smoked paprika (sweet or hot)

1 teaspoon chili powder

1 teaspoon garlic powder

1 teaspoon onion powder

¼ teaspoon cayenne

1 tablespoon fresh lemon juice

PER SERVING

Calories **125**	Cholesterol **0 mg**	Dietary Exchanges:
Total Fat **2.0 g**	Sodium **32 mg**	**1½ starch, ½ lean meat**
Saturated Fat **0.0 g**	Carbohydrates **20 g**	
Trans Fat **0.0 g**	Fiber **5 g**	
Polyunsaturated Fat **0.0 g**	Sugars **1 g**	
Monounsaturated Fat **1.0 g**	Protein **6 g**	

FAST PREP! ⏱

SERVES 8; ¼ cup per
serving

SLOW COOKER SIZE | SHAPE
3- to 4½-quart | oval or
round

SLOW COOKING TIME

1 to 1½ hours ON LOW, **OR**

30 to 45 minutes ON HIGH

2 cups unsalted, whole
pecans

2 teaspoons olive oil

+

1 teaspoon chili powder

1 teaspoon garlic powder

1 teaspoon onion powder

¼ teaspoon cayenne

1 tablespoon fresh lemon
juice

Cajun-Spiced Pecans

These jazzed up nuts are a powerhouse full of vitamins, minerals,
and healthy fats. For your next Super Bowl party, mix these pecans
together with Crunchy Barbecue-Flavored Chickpeas (page 37) and
Cinnamon-Honey Peanuts (page 39) for the ultimate game day snack
mix.

1. Put the pecans in the slow cooker. Add the oil, stirring to coat.
   Prop open the lid of the slow cooker with a chopstick or spoon.
   Cook on low for 1½ hours or on high for 30 to 45 minutes. You
   may stir the pecans once halfway through the cooking time, but
   this step isn't absolutely necessary.
2. About 10 minutes before the pecans have finished cooking, in a
   small bowl, stir together the remaining ingredients except the
   lemon juice. Set aside.
3. When the pecans are finished cooking, sprinkle the lemon juice
   and chili powder mixture over them, stirring to coat. Refrigerate
   any leftover pecans in an airtight container for up to three days.

PER SERVING
Calories **185**
Total Fat **19.0 g**
 Saturated Fat **1.5 g**
 Trans Fat **0.0 g**
 Polyunsaturated Fat **5.5 g**
 Monounsaturated Fat **11.0 g**

Cholesterol **0 mg**
Sodium **6 mg**
Carbohydrates **4 g**
 Fiber **3 g**
 Sugars **1 g**
Protein **2 g**

Dietary Exchanges:
 4 fat

Cinnamon-Honey Peanuts

These cinnamon-dusted nuts are a perfect-sized handful of sweet crunchy goodness to boost protein between meals.

1. Put the peanuts in the slow cooker. Add the oil, stirring to coat. Prop open the lid of the slow cooker with a chopstick or spoon. Cook on low for 1½ hours or on high for 30 to 45 minutes. Remove the lid and quickly stir in the fresh lemon or orange juice, honey, and cinnamon. Replace the lid. Cook for 20 minutes on low or 10 minutes on high.

2. About 10 minutes before the peanuts have finished cooking, place sheets of wax paper on a work surface or lightly spray a large baking sheet with cooking spray. Transfer the cooked peanuts to the wax paper or baking sheet. Let cool for 10 minutes before eating. Refrigerate any leftover peanuts in an airtight container for up to three days.

FAST PREP! ⏱

SERVES 16; 2 tablespoons per serving

SLOW COOKER SIZE | SHAPE
3- to 4½-quart | oval or round

SLOW COOKING TIME

1½ hours ON LOW, **OR**

30 to 45 minutes ON HIGH plus 20 minutes ON LOW, **OR**

10 minutes ON HIGH

2 cups unsalted peanuts
2 teaspoons olive oil

✦

1 tablespoon fresh lemon or orange juice
1 tablespoon honey
1 teaspoon ground cinnamon
Cooking spray (optional)

PER SERVING
Calories **111**
Total Fat **9.0 g**
  Saturated Fat **1.5 g**
  Trans Fat **0.0 g**
  Polyunsaturated Fat **3.0 g**
  Monounsaturated Fat **4.5 g**

Cholesterol **0 mg**
Sodium **1 mg**
Carbohydrates **5 g**
  Fiber **2 g**
  Sugars **2 g**
Protein **4 g**

Dietary Exchanges:
  ½ **other carbohydrate,**
  ½ **lean meat, 1½ fat**

SERVES 8; 1 cup per serving

SLOW COOKER SIZE | SHAPE
3- to 4½-quart | round or oval

SLOW COOKING TIME
4 hours 45 minutes to 5 hours 45 minutes ON LOW plus 15 minutes ON LOW, **OR**

2 hours 15 minutes to 2 hours 45 minutes ON HIGH plus 15 minutes ON HIGH

6 cups unsweetened apple cider or apple juice

2 cups 100% pomegranate-cherry juice or 100% pomegranate juice

2 tablespoons sugar (optional)

3 cinnamon sticks (each about 3 inches long)

8 whole cloves

⅛ to ¼ teaspoon anise seed

— + —

1 medium lemon, cut crosswise into ⅛-inch slices

Hot Pomegranate-Cherry Cider

Serve this delicious autumn treat in clear glass mugs so the light ruby color will shine through.

1. In the slow cooker, stir together the cider, pomegranate-cherry juice, sugar, and cinnamon sticks.
2. Put the cloves and anise seed in the center of a 4-inch-square piece of cheesecloth. Bring the ends together to make a bag. Tie it securely with kitchen twine. Add to the slow cooker. Cook, covered, on low for 4 hours 45 minutes to 5 hours 45 minutes or on high for 2 hours 15 minutes to 2 hours 45 minutes.
3. Quickly stir in the lemon slices and re-cover the slow cooker. Cook for 15 minutes. Discard the cinnamon sticks and cheesecloth bag before serving the cider.

COOK'S TIP
No cheesecloth? You can use the "bag" part of a teabag to hold the spices for this recipe. Simply open the teabag and discard the tea leaves. Fill the bag with the cloves and anise seed and tie securely with the teabag string.

PER SERVING
Calories **121**
Total Fat **0.0 g**
  Saturated Fat **0.0 g**
  Trans Fat **0.0 g**
  Polyunsaturated Fat **0.0 g**
  Monounsaturated Fat **0.0 g**

Cholesterol **0 mg**
Sodium **16 mg**
Carbohydrates **29 g**
  Fiber **0 g**
  Sugars **25 g**
Protein **0 g**

Dietary Exchanges:
  2 fruit

PER SERVING (with optional ingredient)
Calories **133**
Total Fat **0.0 g**
  Saturated Fat **0.0 g**
  Trans Fat **0.0 g**
  Polyunsaturated Fat **0.0 g**
  Monounsaturated Fat **0.0 g**

Cholesterol **0 mg**
Sodium **16 mg**
Carbohydrates **32 g**
  Fiber **0 g**
  Sugars **28 g**
Protein **0 g**

Dietary Exchanges:
  2 fruit

Mulled Pineapple-Citrus Punch

There's nothing complex about this four-ingredient punch except its flavor. The slow-simmered orange and lemon slices create a pleasantly potent undercurrent of citrus.

FAST PREP!

SERVES 8; ¾ cup per serving

SLOW COOKER SIZE | SHAPE
3- to 4½-quart | round or oval

SLOW COOKING TIME
4 to 5 hours ON LOW, **OR**
2 to 2½ hours ON HIGH

1. In the slow cooker, stir together the pineapple juice, orange and lemon slices, and brown sugar. Cook, covered, on low for 4 to 5 hours or on high for 2 to 2½ hours. Discard the orange and lemon slices (they may have lost their bright color).
2. Ladle the punch into cups. Garnish each cup with a half slice of the remaining orange or lemon.

46 ounces 100% pineapple juice

2 medium oranges, cut crosswise into ⅛-inch slices

1 medium lemon, cut crosswise into ⅛-inch slices

¼ cup firmly packed dark brown sugar

+

½ medium orange or ½ medium lemon, cut crosswise into 4 slices, then halved (optional)

COOK'S TIP
Stir 1 tablespoon of rum or bourbon into each punch cup just before serving, if desired.

PER SERVING
Calories **120**
Total Fat **0.0 g**
  Saturated Fat **0.0 g**
  Trans Fat **0.0 g**
  Polyunsaturated Fat **0.0 g**
  Monounsaturated Fat **0.0 g**

Cholesterol **0 mg**
Sodium **9 mg**
Carbohydrates **28 g**
  Fiber **0 g**
  Sugars **24 g**
Protein **0 g**

Dietary Exchanges:
  2 fruit

SLOW COOKER SIZE | SHAPE
3- or 3½-quart | round
or oval

SLOW COOKING TIME
6 to 8 hours ON LOW, **OR**
3 to 4 hours ON HIGH

3 14.5-ounce cans no-salt-
added diced tomatoes,
undrained

1 cup fresh orange juice

2 tablespoons chopped
onion

½ to 1 medium fresh
jalapeño, seeds and ribs
discarded, chopped

1 teaspoon sugar

1 teaspoon Worcestershire
sauce (lowest sodium
available)

¼ teaspoon salt

¼ to ¾ teaspoon red hot-
pepper sauce, or to taste

+

2 tablespoons fresh lime
juice

1 medium lime, thinly sliced
(optional)

Warm and Spicy Tomato Punch

This warm punch, with kicks of jalapeño and hot-pepper sauce, will
add spice to a winter gathering.

1. In a food processor or blender, process the tomatoes with liquid,
   orange juice, onion, jalapeño, sugar, Worcestershire sauce, salt,
   and hot-pepper sauce until smooth except for the tomato seeds.
   If you wish, strain the ingredients as you pour them into the
   slow cooker. Cook, covered, on low for 6 to 8 hours or on high for
   3 to 4 hours.
2. Just before serving, stir the lime juice into the punch. Float the
   lime slices on top.

COOK'S TIP

To make this punch for a larger crowd, double the amounts and use a
4- or 4½-quart round or oval slow cooker; the cooking time remains the
same. If you wish, add some vodka, tequila, or lemon rum to the punch
before serving.

Hot Chiles Hot chile peppers such as jalapeño, poblano, Anaheim, and
serrano contain oils that can burn your skin, lips, and eyes. Remember
to wear plastic gloves or wash your hands thoroughly with warm, soapy
water immediately after handling hot chiles.

PER SERVING
Calories **36**
Total Fat **0.0 g**
  Saturated Fat **0.0 g**
  Trans Fat **0.0 g**
  Polyunsaturated Fat **0.0 g**
  Monounsaturated Fat **0.0 g**

Cholesterol **0 mg**
Sodium **63 mg**
Carbohydrates **8 g**
  Fiber **1 g**
  Sugars **5 g**
Protein **1 g**

Dietary Exchanges:
  1 vegetable

Chai Tea

There's no need to run to the local coffee shop for a cup of chai tea when you can easily brew it at home in the slow cooker—and enjoy the enticing aroma of the Indian spices as they fill the air. The tea is equally good served hot or cold.

FAST PREP!

SERVES 8; 1 cup per serving

SLOW COOKER SIZE | SHAPE
3- to 4½-quart | round or oval

SLOW COOKING TIME
3 to 3½ hours ON HIGH

In the slow cooker, stir together all the ingredients except the tea bags. Add the tea bags, letting the tags hang over the side of the slow cooker. Cook, covered, on high for 3 to 3½ hours. Discard the tea bags. For hot tea, serve immediately. For cold tea, ladle the tea into a pitcher and refrigerate, covered, for up to three days. Serve the tea over ice.

COOK'S TIP

If the tiny grains of spice in the tea bother you, you can strain the tea through a fine-mesh sieve to remove most of them or through a coffee filter to remove all of them.

4 cups water

2 cups fat-free milk

2 cups fat-free half-and-half

¼ cup sugar (optional)

1½ teaspoons ground cinnamon

¾ teaspoon ground cardamom

½ teaspoon ground ginger

½ teaspoon ground nutmeg

¼ teaspoon ground cloves

8 single-serving bags of black tea (with tags preferred)

PER SERVING
Calories **64**
Total Fat **0.0 g**
  Saturated Fat **0.0 g**
  Trans Fat **0.0 g**
  Polyunsaturated Fat **0.0 g**
  Monounsaturated Fat **0.0 g**

Cholesterol **1 mg**
Sodium **90 mg**
Carbohydrates **12 g**
  Fiber **0 g**
  Sugars **7 g**
Protein **6 g**

Dietary Exchanges:
  1 fat-free mlik

PER SERVING (with optional ingredient)
Calories **88**
Total Fat **0.0 g**
  Saturated Fat **0.0 g**
  Trans Fat **0.0 g**
  Polyunsaturated Fat **0.0 g**
  Monounsaturated Fat **0.0 g**

Cholesterol **1 mg**
Sodium **90 mg**
Carbohydrates **18 g**
  Fiber **0 g**
  Sugars **13 g**
Protein **6 g**

Dietary Exchanges:
  1 fat-free mlik, ½ other carbohydrate

Soups

45 French Onion Soup

46 Sweet and Spicy Pumpkin Soup

48 Chicken Broth

49 Dark-Roasted Beef Broth

50 Harvest Vegetable Broth

51 Butternut Squash Bisque

52 Cream of Cauliflower Soup

53 Fresh Tomato Soup with Goat Cheese and Basil

54 Creamy Potato-Broccoli Soup

55 Double-Mushroom and Barley Soup

56 Corn and Wild Rice Soup

58 Italian Vegetable and Pasta Soup

59 Ribollita

60 Crab and Red Bell Pepper Soup

61 Cod and Clam Chowder

62 Chicken and Brown Rice Soup with Blue Cheese Crumbles

63 Thai Coconut-Chicken Soup

64 Herbed Chicken Soup with Arugula

65 Chicken and Bean Soup with Lemon and Basil

66 Spicy Chicken and Corn Soup

67 Country Chicken Noodle Soup

68 Chicken Pho

69 Chicken Tortilla Soup

70 Turkey Sausage and Lentil Soup

71 Smoked Turkey and Rice Soup with Fresh Sage

72 Jamaican Bean and Vegetable Soup

74 Bean Florentine Soup

75 Smoky Split Pea Soup

78 Persian Red Lentil Soup

79 Moroccan Lentil Soup

80 Curried Lentil and Vegetable Soup

81 Black Bean and Jalapeño Soup

82 Kale and Red Quinoa Soup

84 Black-Eyed Pea Soup with Meatless Crumbles

85 Beef Barley Soup with Vegetables

86 Countryside Beef and Garden Vegetable Soup

87 Balsamic Beef Borscht

88 Korean Beef Soup

89 Sherried Steak-and-Mushroom Soup

French Onion Soup

The slow cooker is perfect for making this classic soup because its deep, rich flavor depends on slowly caramelized onions. Instead of standing at the stove and cooking and stirring the onions for nearly an hour, you can just toss them in the slow cooker and let it do the work.

SERVES 4; 1 cup soup and 1 toast per serving

SLOW COOKER SIZE | SHAPE
3- to 4½-quart | round or oval

SLOW COOKING TIME
8 to 10 hours ON LOW plus 4 hours ON HIGH, **OR**

4 to 5 hours ON HIGH plus 4 hours ON HIGH

1. In the slow cooker, stir together the onions, oil, thyme, and pepper. Add the bay leaf. (There won't be any liquid right away, but the onions will soften and begin to release their juices.) Cook, covered, on low for 8 to 10 hours or on high for 4 to 5 hours, or until the onions are lightly browned and softened.
2. If using the low setting, change it to high. Quickly stir in the broth. Re-cover the slow cooker. Cook for 4 hours, or until the onions are very soft. Stir in the vinegar. Discard the bay leaf.
3. About 10 minutes before serving time, preheat the broiler. Cut out the toasts from the bread slices (ideally, the toasts should fit inside the soup bowls to soak up the soup). Arrange on a large baking sheet. Broil at least 4 inches from the heat for about 1 minute, or until toasted. Turn over the toasts. Broil for about 1 minute, or until lightly toasted. Remove from the broiler. Sprinkle one side of each toast with about 1½ teaspoons Parmesan. Return to the broiler. Broil for about 1 minute, or until the Parmesan has melted.
4. Ladle the soup into bowls. Top each serving with a toast.

3 large onions (about 1 pound total), thinly sliced lengthwise

1 tablespoon olive oil

¼ teaspoon dried thyme, crumbled

¼ teaspoon pepper

1 medium dried bay leaf

3½ cups fat-free, low-sodium beef broth, such as on page 49

1½ teaspoons balsamic vinegar

4 slices whole-grain bread (lowest sodium available)

2 tablespoons shredded or grated Parmesan cheese

COOK'S TIP
To cut out the toasts, use a round cookie cutter or the top of a water glass to create the perfect shape.

PER SERVING
Calories **134**
Total Fat **5.0 g**
  Saturated Fat **1.0 g**
  Trans Fat **0.0 g**
  Polyunsaturated Fat **0.5 g**
  Monounsaturated Fat **3.0 g**

Cholesterol **2 mg**
Sodium **128 mg**
Carbohydrates **18 g**
  Fiber **3 g**
  Sugars **6 g**
Protein **6 g**

Dietary Exchanges:
½ **starch, 2 vegetable, 1 fat**

SERVES 4; 1 cup per serving

SLOW COOKER SIZE | SHAPE
3- to 4½-quart | round
or oval

SLOW COOKING TIME
5 to 7 hours ON LOW, **OR**
2 to 2½ hours ON HIGH

2½ cups fat-free, low-
sodium vegetable broth,
such as on page 50

1 15-ounce can solid-pack
pumpkin (not pie filling)

1 medium potato, peeled
and chopped

½ medium onion, chopped

2 teaspoons dried minced
garlic

1 teaspoon light or dark
brown sugar

1 teaspoon minced chipotle
pepper canned in adobo
sauce

½ teaspoon ground
cinnamon

½ teaspoon ground ginger

━━━━ + ━━━━

¼ cup raw unsalted
pumpkin seeds with
shells

Cooking spray

½ teaspoon salt-free all-
purpose seasoning blend

⅛ teaspoon salt

½ teaspoon chopped fresh
rosemary (optional)

Sweet and Spicy Pumpkin Soup

Pumpkin scores high in nutrition, and this soup—with its flair from chipotle pepper and seasoned roasted pumpkin seeds—scores high in flavor, too!

1. In the slow cooker, stir together the vegetable broth, pumpkin, potato, onion, garlic, brown sugar, chipotle pepper, cinnamon, and ginger. Cook, covered, on low for 5 to 7 hours or on high for 2 to 2½ hours.
2. While the soup is cooking, preheat the oven to 350°F.
3. Spread the pumpkin seeds in a single layer on a baking sheet. Lightly spray the seeds with cooking spray. Roast for 8 to 10 minutes, or until golden, stirring once halfway through. Transfer the baking sheet to a cooling rack. Immediately sprinkle the seeds with the seasoning blend and salt, stirring to coat. Let cool for 15 to 20 minutes. Set aside.
4. In a food processor or blender (vent the blender lid), process the soup in batches until smooth. Serve the soup sprinkled with the pumpkin seeds and rosemary.

COOK'S TIP

Look in the Mexican food section of grocery stores for chipotle peppers (dried jalapeños that have a smoky flavor) canned in adobo sauce, also known as adobo paste, a moderately spicy mixture of chiles, vinegar, garlic, and herbs. You probably won't use an entire can for any single recipe, but the leftovers freeze nicely. Spread the peppers with sauce in a thin layer on a medium plate covered with cooking parchment or wax paper, then freeze them, uncovered, for about 2 hours, or just until firm. (This step will keep the peppers from sticking together later.) Transfer the peppers to an airtight freezer bag and freeze. Remove just the amount you need for your next recipe.

PER SERVING
Calories **140**
Total Fat **4.0 g**
  Saturated Fat **0.5 g**
  Trans Fat **0.0 g**
  Polyunsaturated Fat **1.5 g**
  Monounsaturated Fat **1.0 g**

Cholesterol **0 mg**
Sodium **124 mg**
Carbohydrates **23 g**
  Fiber **6 g**
  Sugars **6 g**
Protein **6 g**

Dietary Exchanges:
1½ starch, ½ fat

FAST PREP! ⏱

MAKES 10 CUPS; 1 cup per serving

SLOW COOKER SIZE | SHAPE
5- to 7-quart | round or oval

SLOW COOKING TIME
10 to 12 hours ON LOW (preferred), **OR**
5 to 6 hours ON HIGH

1½ pounds chicken wings or legs with skin or 1 chicken carcass, broken to fit cooker

1 large leek (white and light green parts) or onion, coarsely chopped

1 medium rib of celery, coarsely chopped

1 medium carrot, coarsely chopped

1 small parsnip or turnip, peeled and coarsely chopped (optional)

½ cup fresh parsley leaves, stems discarded

1 medium garlic clove, crushed

½ teaspoon whole peppercorns

1 medium dried bay leaf

1 sprig of fresh thyme or 1 teaspoon dried, crumbled (fresh preferred)

⅛ teaspoon salt

12 cups water (plus more as needed)

Chicken Broth

Making so-low-sodium chicken broth is so easy with a slow cooker. Just load the cooker and let the ingredients simmer. In addition to the cooking time, be sure to allow for at least six hours of chilling time so you can easily remove the fat, which rises to the top. Keep a regular supply in the freezer so you'll have plenty on hand whenever you make a dish that calls for broth, such as Cream of Cauliflower Soup (page 52), Chicken and Dumplings (page 126), and Tuscan Pork and Beans (page 188).

1. In the slow cooker, stir together all the ingredients except the water. Pour in the water, adding more if needed to cover all. Cook, covered, on low for 10 to 12 hours or on high for 5 to 6 hours.
2. Using a colander, strain the broth into a large bowl, being careful to avoid steam burns. Discard the solids. Cover and refrigerate the broth for at least 8 hours so the flavors blend and the fat rises to the surface. Discard the fat before reheating the broth.

COOK'S TIP

If you are not using the broth right away, store it in an airtight container in the refrigerator for up to two days. For storage up to three months, we suggest separating the desired amounts into resealable plastic freezer bags and laying them flat to freeze; they take up very little space that way. If you would rather use airtight freezer containers, those, of course, work well, too.

PER SERVING
Calories **10**
Total Fat **0.0 g**
  Saturated Fat **0.0 g**
  Trans Fat **0.0 g**
  Polyunsaturated Fat **0.0 g**
  Monounsaturated Fat **0.0 g**

Cholesterol **0 mg**
Sodium **54 mg**
Carbohydrates **1 g**
  Fiber **0 g**
  Sugars **0 g**
Protein **2 g**

Dietary Exchanges:
  Free

Dark-Roasted Beef Broth

This basic broth gets maximum flavor intensity by including instant coffee granules and roasted bones and veggies. After the broth slow cooks, you'll need to chill it for at least eight hours so the flavors can continue to mingle and the fat will solidify and be easy to remove. (See Cook's Tip on page 48 for storing broth.)

(See Cook's Tip on page 48 for storing broth.)

MAKES 8 CUPS; 1 cup per serving

SLOW COOKER SIZE | SHAPE
5- to 7-quart | round or oval

SLOW COOKING TIME
8 to 10 hours ON LOW, **OR**
4 to 6 hours ON HIGH

1. Preheat the oven to 475°F. Lightly spray the slow cooker and a broiler pan with cooking spray. Set the slow cooker aside.
2. Put the bones, onions, carrots, celery, and garlic in the pan. Lightly spray all with cooking spray. Roast for 40 minutes, or until richly browned, turning once halfway through. Transfer the bones, vegetables, garlic, and pan drippings to the slow cooker.
3. Stir in the remaining ingredients. Cook, covered, on low for 8 to 10 hours or on high for 4 to 6 hours.
4. Using a colander, strain the broth into a large bowl, being careful to avoid steam burns. Discard the solids. Cover and refrigerate the broth for at least 8 hours so the flavors blend and the fat rises to the surface. Discard the fat before reheating the broth.

Cooking spray

3 pounds beef bones

2 medium onions, each cut into 8 wedges

2 medium carrots, each cut into 4 pieces

1 medium rib of celery, cut into 4 pieces

8 whole garlic cloves

2½ quarts water

1½ tablespoons instant coffee granules

2 medium dried bay leaves

1 teaspoon pepper (coarsely ground preferred)

1 teaspoon dried thyme, crumbled

2 whole cloves

⅛ teaspoon salt

PER SERVING
Calories **10**
Total Fat **0.0 g**
  Saturated Fat **0.0 g**
  Trans Fat **0.0 g**
  Polyunsaturated Fat **0.0 g**
  Monounsaturated Fat **0.0 g**

Cholesterol **0 mg**
Sodium **66 mg**
Carbohydrates **1 g**
  Fiber **0 g**
  Sugars **0 g**
  Protein **2 g**

Dietary Exchanges:
  Free

SLOW COOKER SIZE | SHAPE
3- to 4½-quart | round
or oval

SLOW COOKING TIME
8 to 9 hours ON LOW, **OR**
4 to 5 hours ON HIGH

Cooking spray

1 teaspoon canola or corn
oil

1 medium green bell
pepper, coarsely
chopped

4 medium garlic cloves,
minced

2 quarts water

3 medium carrots, halved
crosswise

2 medium leeks (white part
only), halved

2 medium parsnips or
turnips, halved crosswise

1 large tomato, halved

1 cup tightly packed fresh
parsley leaves, stems
discarded

1 tablespoon dried thyme,
crumbled

4 medium dried bay leaves

1 teaspoon pepper
(coarsely ground
preferred)

3 whole cloves

⅛ teaspoon salt

Harvest Vegetable Broth

Just three cloves provide the subtle zing that makes this vegetable
broth so good. Like the chicken and beef broths on the preceding
pages, it is very handy to keep on hand for use in recipes in this
cookbook, to replace water when you are cooking vegetables and
grains for dinner, and to drop into other soups, stews, and casseroles
to intensify their flavor. (See Cook's Tip on page 48 for storing broth.)

1. Lightly spray the slow cooker with cooking spray. Set aside.
2. In a large nonstick skillet, heat the oil over medium-high heat,
   swirling to coat the bottom. Cook the bell pepper for 7 minutes,
   or until the edges are richly browned, stirring occasionally.
3. Stir in the garlic. Cook for 30 seconds, stirring constantly.
   Transfer to the slow cooker.
4. Stir in the remaining ingredients. Cook, covered, on low for 8 to
   9 hours or on high for 4 to 5 hours.
5. Using a colander, strain the broth into an airtight container,
   being careful to avoid steam burns. Discard the solids. Serve or
   cover and refrigerate the broth.

PER SERVING		
Calories 5	Cholesterol **0 mg**	Dietary Exchanges:
Total Fat **0.0 g**	Sodium **52 mg**	**Free**
Saturated Fat **0.0 g**	Carbohydrates **1 g**	
Trans Fat **0.0 g**	Fiber **0 g**	
Polyunsaturated Fat **0.0 g**	Sugars **0 g**	
Monounsaturated Fat **0.0 g**	Protein **0 g**	

Butternut Squash Bisque

You can enjoy this creamy soup alone or topped with a dollop of fat-free sour cream, chopped fresh pineapple, and chopped cilantro. It's a winner either way!

SERVES 8; scant 1 cup per serving

SLOW COOKER SIZE | SHAPE
3- to 4½-quart | round or oval

SLOW COOKING TIME
7½ to 8 hours ON LOW plus 15 minutes ON LOW, **OR**

3 hours 45 minutes to 4 hours ON HIGH plus 15 minutes ON LOW

1. Lightly spray the slow cooker with cooking spray. Put the squash, broth, carrots, onion, sugar, coriander, cumin, and ⅛ teaspoon salt in the slow cooker, stirring to combine. Cook, covered, on low for 7½ to 8 hours or on high for 3 hours 45 minutes to 4 hours, or until the squash is very tender.

2. In a food processor or blender (vent the blender lid), process the soup in batches until smooth. Return the soup to the slow cooker.

3. If using the high setting, change it to low. Stir the half-and-half and remaining ⅛ teaspoon salt into the soup. Cook, covered, for 15 minutes, or until heated through.

Cooking spray

36 ounces frozen butternut squash, thawed

3 cups fat-free, low-sodium chicken broth, such as on page 48

3 medium carrots, chopped into ½-inch pieces

1 medium red onion, chopped

¼ cup sugar

1 teaspoon ground coriander

½ teaspoon ground cumin

⅛ teaspoon salt

+

½ cup fat-free half-and-half

⅛ teaspoon salt

COOK'S TIP

If you want to use fresh butternut squash and convenience is important, look in the refrigerated section of the produce area for packages of already peeled chunks of squash. You'll need about 4 cups for this recipe. If you're more interested in saving money, prepare the squash yourself. For this recipe, buy a squash of about 2 pounds and pierce it with a fork in several places. Put the squash in a microwaveable pie pan or on a large rimmed plate, and microwave on 100 percent power (high) for 2 minutes, turning over halfway through. Using a vegetable peeler, remove the skin. Discard the seeds and strings. Cut the flesh into 1-inch cubes, transfer them to the slow cooker, and proceed as directed.

PER SERVING
Calories **129**
Total Fat **0.5 g**
  Saturated Fat **0.0 g**
  Trans Fat **0.0 g**
  Polyunsaturated Fat **0.0 g**
  Monounsaturated Fat **0.0 g**

Cholesterol **0 mg**
Sodium **132 mg**
Carbohydrates **31 g**
  Fiber **3 g**
  Sugars **13 g**
Protein **4 g**

Dietary Exchanges:
  2 starch

SERVES 6; scant 1 cup per serving

SLOW COOKER SIZE | SHAPE
3- to 4½-quart | round or oval

SLOW COOKING TIME
5 to 7 hours ON LOW, **OR**
3 to 5 hours ON HIGH

3 cups fat-free, low-sodium chicken broth, such as on page 48

1 medium head of cauliflower (about 1¾ pounds), florets cut into 1-inch pieces (about 4 cups)

1 medium baking potato (about 9 ounces), peeled and chopped

1 small onion, chopped

2 medium garlic cloves, chopped

⅛ teaspoon salt

+

2 teaspoons fresh lemon juice

Pinch of pepper (white preferred)

¼ cup plus 2 tablespoons shredded low-fat Cheddar cheese (sharp preferred)

Cream of Cauliflower Soup

Forget the high-fat, high-calorie cream! Puréed vegetables give this soup its luxurious, velvety texture.

1. In the slow cooker, stir together the broth, cauliflower, potato, onion, garlic, and salt. Cook, covered, on low for 5 to 7 hours or on high for 3 to 5 hours, or until the vegetables are tender.
2. In a food processor or blender (vent the blender lid), process the soup in batches until smooth. For piping hot soup, return the soup to the slow cooker. If using the low setting, change it to high. Reheat, covered, for 10 minutes.
3. Stir in the lemon juice and pepper. Ladle the soup into bowls. Sprinkle with the Cheddar.

COOK'S TIP

Any time you use a blender to purée a hot liquid, be sure to vent the cover so the steam can safely escape. If the blender you are using doesn't have a vented cover, allow the liquid to cool slightly, then blend and reheat.

PER SERVING
Calories 85
Total Fat **1.0 g**
  Saturated Fat **0.5 g**
  Trans Fat **0.0 g**
  Polyunsaturated Fat **0.0 g**
  Monounsaturated Fat **0.0 g**

Cholesterol **2 mg**
Sodium **151 mg**
Carbohydrates **15 g**
  Fiber **3 g**
  Sugars **3 g**
  Protein **6 g**

Dietary Exchanges:
  ½ **starch, 2 vegetable**

Fresh Tomato Soup with Goat Cheese and Basil

This soup brings the flavors of southern Italy to your table. It is especially delicious when tomatoes are at the height of their season, but you might need to substitute canned no-salt-added tomatoes when fresh are not available.

1. In the slow cooker, stir together the tomatoes, water, onion, garlic, salt, and pepper. Cook, covered, on low for 3 to 4 hours or on high for 2 hours.
2. In a food processor or blender (vent the blender lid), process the soup in batches until smooth. Serve sprinkled with the basil and goat cheese.

COOK'S TIPS

Toast whole-wheat bread (lowest sodium available) cubes and sprinkle just a few on the soup right before serving.

Cutting Fresh Basil To make thin strips of fresh basil (or chiffonade) for an attractive garnish, stack several leaves with the stem end pointing toward you. Roll tightly from bottom to top, making a cylinder. Cut it widthwise into thin ribbons.

SERVES 6; 1 heaping cup per serving

SLOW COOKER SIZE | SHAPE
5- to 7-quart | round or oval

SLOW COOKING TIME

3 to 4 hours ON LOW, **OR**

2 hours ON HIGH

3 pounds very ripe tomatoes, each tomato cut into 8 wedges

1 cup water

1 medium onion, minced

1 teaspoon dried minced garlic

¼ teaspoon salt

¼ teaspoon pepper

——————— + ———————

⅓ cup fresh basil, rolled and cut into thin strips

3 tablespoons goat cheese crumbles

PER SERVING
Calories **71**
Total Fat **2.0 g**
　Saturated Fat **1.0 g**
　Trans Fat **0.0 g**
　Polyunsaturated Fat **0.0 g**
　Monounsaturated Fat **0.5 g**

Cholesterol **5 mg**
Sodium **127 mg**
Carbohydrates **11 g**
　Fiber **3 g**
　Sugars **8 g**
Protein **4 g**

Dietary Exchanges:
　2 vegetable, ½ fat

SERVES 6; ⅔ cup per serving

SLOW COOKER SIZE | SHAPE
3- to 4-quart | round or oval

SLOW COOKING TIME

5 to 6 hours ON LOW plus 10 minutes ON HIGH, **OR**

3 to 4 hours ON HIGH plus 10 minutes ON HIGH

1 teaspoon olive oil

1 cup coarsely chopped onion

½ cup sliced leek (white and light green parts) or chopped onion

2 large garlic cloves, minced

2 cups fat-free, low-sodium chicken broth, such as on page 48

14 ounces russet potatoes, peeled and chopped (about 2 cups)

¼ teaspoon dried thyme, crumbled

¼ teaspoon salt

⅛ teaspoon pepper

— + —

9 ounces frozen broccoli florets, thawed

¼ cup fat-free half-and-half

Creamy Potato-Broccoli Soup

Using russet potatoes, also known as baking potatoes, is key to getting the best results with this soup. Along with the half-and-half, they make it lusciously creamy. The leek adds a sweet, mild onion flavor.

1. In a large nonstick skillet, heat the oil over medium heat, swirling to coat the bottom. Cook the onion and leek for 3 minutes, or until beginning to soften, stirring frequently.
2. Stir in the garlic. Cook for 30 seconds, stirring constantly. Transfer to the slow cooker.
3. Stir in the broth, potatoes, thyme, salt, and pepper. Cook, covered, on low for 5 to 6 hours or on high for 3 to 4 hours, or until the vegetables are tender.
4. If using the low setting, change it to high. Quickly add the broccoli and re-cover the slow cooker. Cook for 10 minutes, or until the broccoli is tender. For the best results, let the soup cool for about 15 minutes.
5. In a food processor or blender (vent the blender lid), process the soup in small batches until slightly smooth but with some texture, or to the desired consistency.
6. Just before serving, stir in the half-and-half.

PER SERVING
Calories **96**
Total Fat **1.0 g**
  Saturated Fat **0.0 g**
  Trans Fat **0.0 g**
  Polyunsaturated Fat **0.0 g**
  Monounsaturated Fat **0.5 g**

Cholesterol **0 mg**
Sodium **142 mg**
Carbohydrates **19 g**
  Fiber **3 g**
  Sugars **3 g**
Protein **4 g**

Dietary Exchanges:
1 starch, 1 vegetable

Double-Mushroom and Barley Soup

Dried mushrooms add an earthiness and depth to this soup and are a delightful contrast to the fresh, bright flavor of the dill.

In the slow cooker, stir together all the ingredients except the fresh dillweed. Cook, covered, on low for 5 to 7 hours or on high for 2 to 3 hours. Just before serving, sprinkle the soup with the fresh dillweed.

COOK'S TIP

Pearl barley has had the outer bran layer removed and has been steamed and polished. Even after processing, however, barley is rich in fiber and other nutrients.

PER SERVING
Calories **69**
Total Fat **0.5 g**
Saturated Fat **0.0 g**
Trans Fat **0.0 g**
Polyunsaturated Fat **0.0 g**
Monounsaturated Fat **0.0 g**

Cholesterol **0 mg**
Sodium **131 mg**
Carbohydrates **14 g**
  Fiber **3 g**
  Sugars **3 g**
Protein **4 g**

Dietary Exchanges:
½ **starch, 1 vegetable**

SERVES 4; 1¼ cups per serving

SLOW COOKER SIZE | SHAPE
3- to 4½-quart | round or oval

SLOW COOKING TIME
5 to 7 hours ON LOW, **OR**
2 to 3 hours ON HIGH

2¼ cups water

1¾ cups fat-free, low-sodium beef broth, such as on page 49

½ large Vidalia, Maui, Oso Sweet, or other sweet onion, chopped

4 ounces button mushrooms, sliced

1 medium carrot, chopped

1 medium rib of celery, chopped

¼ cup dried mushrooms, such as chanterelle or a mixture, chopped or broken up if large

3 tablespoons uncooked pearl barley (not quick-cooking or instant)

1 tablespoon dried minced garlic

¼ teaspoon pepper

⅛ teaspoon salt

1 teaspoon dried dillweed, crumbled

———— **+** ————

1 tablespoon snipped fresh dillweed

SERVES 10; ¾ cup per serving

SLOW COOKER SIZE | SHAPE
3- to 4½-quart | round or oval

SLOW COOKING TIME
5 to 7 hours ON LOW plus
    1 hour ON HIGH, **OR**
2½ to 3 hours ON HIGH plus
    1 hour ON HIGH

4 cups fat-free, low-sodium vegetable broth, such as on page 50
3 medium carrots, chopped
1 cup water
1 medium rib of celery, chopped
½ medium onion, chopped
¼ medium red bell pepper, chopped
2 teaspoons dried minced garlic
2 teaspoons dried sage
¼ teaspoon salt
¼ teaspoon pepper
1 cup frozen whole-kernel corn, thawed
½ cup uncooked wild rice, rinsed and drained

——— ✚ ———

1 tablespoon plus
    2 teaspoons coarsely chopped fresh basil (optional)

Corn and Wild Rice Soup

All it takes is a small amount of wild rice to elevate this soup, full of brightly colored vegetables, to special status.

1. In the slow cooker, stir together the broth, carrots, water, celery, onion, bell pepper, garlic, sage, salt, and pepper. Cook, covered, on low for 5 to 7 hours or on high for 2½ to 3 hours.
2. If using the low setting, change it to high. Quickly stir in the corn and rice and re-cover the slow cooker. Cook on high for 1 hour. Just before serving, sprinkle with the basil.

PER SERVING
Calories **62**
Total Fat **0.5 g**
    Saturated Fat **0.0 g**
    Trans Fat **0.0 g**
    Polyunsaturated Fat **0.0 g**
    Monounsaturated Fat **0.0 g**

Cholesterol **0 mg**
Sodium **100 mg**
Carbohydrates **14 g**
    Fiber **2 g**
    Sugars **2 g**
Protein **2 g**

Dietary Exchanges:
    1 starch

SERVES 8; ¾ cup per serving

SLOW COOKER SIZE | SHAPE
3- to 4½-quart | round or oval

SLOW COOKING TIME

8 to 10 hours ON LOW plus 20 minutes ON HIGH, **OR**

5 to 6 hours ON HIGH plus 20 minutes ON HIGH

---

4 cups fat-free, low-sodium vegetable broth, such as on page 50

1 14.5-ounce can no-salt-added diced tomatoes, undrained

2 medium carrots, chopped

2 medium ribs of celery, chopped

1 medium onion, chopped

2 medium garlic cloves, minced

½ teaspoon dried oregano, crumbled

½ teaspoon dried basil, crumbled

¼ teaspoon salt

⅛ teaspoon pepper

————— ✚ —————

1 cup dried whole-grain macaroni

3 tablespoons shredded or grated Parmesan cheese

Italian Vegetable and Pasta Soup

Pasta in a slow cooker? It works perfectly in this veggie-packed soup. Any leftovers will make a satisfying lunch later in the week.

1. In the slow cooker, stir together the broth, tomatoes with liquid, carrots, celery, onion, garlic, oregano, basil, salt, and pepper. Cook, covered, on low for 8 to 10 hours or on high for 5 to 6 hours.

2. If using the low setting, change it to high. Quickly stir in the macaroni and re-cover the slow cooker. Cook for 20 minutes, or until the macaroni is tender. Serve sprinkled with the Parmesan.

PER SERVING
Calories **85**
Total Fat **1.0 g**
  Saturated Fat **0.5 g**
  Trans Fat **0.0 g**
  Polyunsaturated Fat **0.0 g**
  Monounsaturated Fat **0.5 g**

Cholesterol **1 mg**
Sodium **157 mg**
Carbohydrates **16 g**
  Fiber **3 g**
  Sugars **4 g**
  Protein **3 g**

Dietary Exchanges:
  ½ **starch, 1 vegetable**

Ribollita

Ribollita means "twice cooked"; traditionally this Italian soup was made with leftover minestrone or other vegetable soup. Usually, the soup is thickened with chunks of bread, but we substitute toasted bread cubes sprinkled on top.

SERVES 8; 1¼ cups per serving

SLOW COOKER SIZE | SHAPE
5- to 7-quart | round or oval

SLOW COOKING TIME
8 to 10 hours ON LOW, **OR**
4 to 5 hours ON HIGH

1. Heat a medium nonstick skillet over medium heat. Cook the bacon for 5 minutes, or until browned, stirring frequently.
2. Stir in the onions. Cook for 3 minutes, or until soft, stirring frequently.
3. Stir in the garlic. Cook for 30 seconds, stirring constantly. Transfer to the slow cooker.
4. Stir in the broth, tomatoes with liquid, beans, cabbage, carrots, bell pepper, basil, and oregano. Cook, covered, on low for 8 to 10 hours or on high for 4 to 5 hours, or until the vegetables are tender.
5. Meanwhile, preheat the oven to 400°F. Arrange the bread cubes in a single layer on a small rimmed baking sheet. Lightly spray the tops with olive oil spray.
6. Bake the bread cubes for 5 to 8 minutes, or until lightly browned. If baked more than 2 hours in advance, transfer the bread cubes to an airtight container until needed.
7. Serve the soup topped with the bread cubes and sprinkled with the Parmesan.

2 slices turkey bacon, chopped

2 cups chopped onions

3 large garlic cloves, minced

4 cups fat-free, low-sodium chicken broth, such as on page 48

1 28-ounce can or 2 14.5-ounce cans no-salt-added diced tomatoes, undrained

1 15.5-ounce can no-salt-added cannellini beans, rinsed and drained

8 ounces cabbage, cut into 1-inch chunks (about 3 cups)

2 large carrots, cut crosswise into ½-inch pieces

1 medium green bell pepper, cut into 1½-inch squares

1 tablespoon dried basil, crumbled

2 teaspoons dried oregano, crumbled

———— + ————

2 slices whole-wheat bread (lowest sodium available), cut into ½-inch cubes

Olive oil spray

¼ cup shredded or grated Parmesan cheese

PER SERVING
Calories **141**
Total Fat **2.0 g**
 Saturated Fat **0.5 g**
 Trans Fat **0.0 g**
 Polyunsaturated Fat **0.0 g**
 Monounsaturated Fat **0.5 g**

Cholesterol **4 mg**
Sodium **185 mg**
Carbohydrates **24 g**
 Fiber **6 g**
 Sugars **8 g**
 Protein **8 g**

Dietary Exchanges:
½ **starch, 3 vegetable,**
½ **lean meat**

SERVES 4; 1 cup per serving

SLOW COOKER SIZE | SHAPE
3- to 4½-quart | round
or oval

SLOW COOKING TIME

3 to 3½ hours ON LOW plus
15 minutes ON HIGH, **OR**

1½ hours to 1 hour
45 minutes ON HIGH plus
15 minutes ON HIGH

Cooking spray

1 large red bell pepper,
diced

2 medium carrots, halved
lengthwise, then thinly
sliced crosswise

2 medium green onions,
chopped

2 tablespoons water

1 medium garlic clove,
minced

⅛ teaspoon cayenne

⅛ teaspoon salt

——————— + ———————

1 13.5- to 13.75-ounce can
lite coconut milk

1 cup fat-free half-and-half

6 ounces canned crabmeat,
drained, cartilage
discarded

½ cup snipped fresh
cilantro

2 medium green onions,
chopped

1 tablespoon fresh lime
juice

2 teaspoons sugar

1 teaspoon grated peeled
gingerroot, or to taste

1 medium lime, cut into
4 wedges

Crab and Red Bell Pepper Soup

Fresh ginger is the key ingredient in this slightly spicy, slightly sweet, creamy soup. For a higher level of heat and more pronounced kick, add extra fresh gingerroot instead of more dried cayenne.

1. Lightly spray the slow cooker with cooking spray. Put the bell pepper, carrots, 2 green onions, water, garlic, cayenne, and salt in the slow cooker, stirring to combine. Cook, covered, on low for 3 to 3½ hours or on high for 1½ hours to 1 hour 45 minutes, or until the carrots are tender.

2. If using the low setting, change it to high. Quickly stir in the remaining ingredients except the lime and re-cover the slow cooker. Cook for 15 minutes, or until heated through. Serve with the lime wedges to squeeze over the soup.

COOK'S TIP

Be sure to use only lite coconut milk; it has about 60 percent less fat than the regular version. Refrigerate leftover coconut milk in an airtight container for up to three days. You can use it in a smoothie by blending it with pineapple, banana, fat-free yogurt, and ice. Another use is drizzled over fresh mango and banana chunks for a light dessert.

PER SERVING
Calories **217**
Total Fat **5.5 g**
  Saturated Fat **3.5 g**
  Trans Fat **0.0 g**
  Polyunsaturated Fat **1.0 g**
  Monounsaturated Fat **1.0 g**

Cholesterol **83 mg**
Sodium **537 mg**
Carbohydrates **22 g**
  Fiber **3 g**
  Sugars **12 g**
Protein **20 g**

Dietary Exchanges:
  **2 vegetable, 1 other
  carbohydrate, 2½ lean
  meat**

Cod and Clam Chowder

During the last 10 or 20 minutes of cooking the chowder, stir in the mild, flaky fish. That's all the cooking it needs.

1. Drain the clams, pouring the juice into the slow cooker. Put the clams in an airtight container and refrigerate until needed. Add the potatoes, bell pepper, bottled clam juice, broth, celery, bay leaf, thyme, and pepper to the slow cooker, stirring to combine. Set aside.

2. In a medium nonstick skillet, heat the oil over medium-high heat, swirling to coat the bottom. Cook the carrots and onion for 5 minutes, or until the onion is soft, stirring frequently. Stir in the garlic. Cook for 30 seconds, stirring constantly. Stir into the potato mixture. Cook, covered, on low for 7 hours 40 to 45 minutes or on high for 3 hours 45 to 50 minutes.

3. About 20 minutes before the end of the cooking time if using the low setting, or 10 minutes if using the high setting, quickly stir in the fish and reserved clams and re-cover the slow cooker. Cook on low for 20 minutes or on high for 10 minutes, or until the fish flakes easily when tested with a fork.

4. Pour in the half-and-half, gently stirring for 2 to 3 minutes, or until heated through. Discard the bay leaf.

COOK'S TIP
The starch in potatoes is a natural thickening agent for long-cooking soups. Raw potatoes can be used to thicken slow cooker soups, but potatoes used to thicken soups cooked on the stovetop need to be cooked first.

SERVES 4; 1½ cups per serving

SLOW COOKER SIZE | SHAPE
3- to 4½-quart | round or oval

SLOW COOKING TIME
7 hours 40 to 45 minutes ON LOW plus 20 minutes ON LOW, **OR**

3 hours 45 to 50 minutes ON HIGH plus 10 minutes ON HIGH

1 6.5-ounce can chopped clams in clam juice (lowest sodium available)

2 medium russet potatoes (about 10 ounces total), peeled and shredded

1 medium red bell pepper, diced

1 8-ounce bottle clam juice (lowest sodium available)

1 cup fat-free, low-sodium chicken broth, such as on page 48

1½ medium ribs of celery, cut crosswise into ¼-inch slices

1 medium dried bay leaf

1 tablespoon snipped fresh thyme or 1 teaspoon dried thyme, crumbled

⅛ teaspoon pepper

2 teaspoons olive oil

3 medium carrots, cut crosswise into ¼-inch slices

1 cup chopped onion

1 medium garlic clove, minced

✦

12 ounces cod or other mild white fish fillets, about 1 inch thick, rinsed and patted dry, cut into 1-inch cubes

½ cup fat-free half-and-half

PER SERVING
Calories **236**
Total Fat **3.0 g**
  Saturated Fat **0.5 g**
  Trans Fat **0.0 g**
  Polyunsaturated Fat **0.5 g**
  Monounsaturated Fat **1.5 g**

Cholesterol **50 mg**
Sodium **487 mg**
Carbohydrates **31 g**
  Fiber **5 g**
  Sugars **8 g**
Protein **23 g**

Dietary Exchanges:
1½ starch, 2 vegetable, 2½ lean meat

SERVES 6; 1 cup soup, ⅓ cup rice, and 1 tablespoon cheese per serving

SLOW COOKER SIZE | SHAPE
3- to 4½-quart | round or oval

SLOW COOKING TIME
5½ to 6 hours ON LOW, **OR**

2 hours 45 minutes to 3 hours ON HIGH

Cooking spray

1 pound boneless, skinless chicken breasts, all visible fat discarded, cut into bite-size pieces

1 14.5-ounce can no-salt-added diced tomatoes, undrained

1¾ cups fat-free, low-sodium chicken broth, such as on page 48

1 large onion, diced

2 teaspoons sugar

2 teaspoons dried oregano, crumbled

1 teaspoon dried thyme, crumbled

½ teaspoon garlic powder

———— + ————

10 ounces frozen brown rice

2 tablespoons mild Louisiana-style hot-pepper sauce

1 tablespoon olive oil (extra virgin preferred)

¼ cup plus 2 tablespoons crumbled reduced-fat blue cheese

¼ cup snipped fresh parsley

Chicken and Brown Rice Soup with Blue Cheese Crumbles

No ordinary soup here! This unusual bowl of comfort features a good-size splash of mild Louisiana-style hot-pepper sauce and enough blue cheese to give it that wow factor. The flavorful chicken-vegetable soup tops microwaved brown rice.

1. Lightly spray the slow cooker with cooking spray. Put the chicken, tomatoes with liquid, broth, onion, sugar, oregano, thyme, and garlic powder in the slow cooker, stirring to combine. Cook, covered, on low for 5½ to 6 hours or on high for 2 hours 45 minutes to 3 hours, or until the onion is very soft.
2. About 10 minutes before serving the soup, prepare the rice using the package directions. Spoon into soup bowls.
3. Stir the hot sauce and oil into the soup. Ladle over the rice. Top with the blue cheese and parsley.

COOK'S TIP
Louisiana-style hot-pepper sauce is mild rather than wild, and it puts more flavor than heat in your dishes.

PER SERVING
Calories **217**
Total Fat **6.0 g**
  Saturated Fat **1.5 g**
  Trans Fat **0.0 g**
  Polyunsaturated Fat **0.0 g**
  Monounsaturated Fat **2.5 g**

Cholesterol **52 mg**
Sodium **242 mg**
Carbohydrates **19 g**
  Fiber **2 g**
  Sugars **5 g**
Protein **21 g**

Dietary Exchanges:
  1 starch, 1 vegetable, 2½ lean meat

Thai Coconut-Chicken Soup

This soup is a feast for the eyes as well as the palate. Adding bright red bell pepper strips, dark brown mushrooms, and deep green cilantro for only a few minutes at the end of the cooking time maintains their color and texture.

1. In the slow cooker, stir together the chicken, broth, carrot, gingerroot, serrano pepper, garlic, and lime zest. Cook, covered, on low for 5 to 6 hours or on high for $2\frac{1}{2}$ to 3 hours.

2. Using a slotted spoon, quickly skim off any solids and discard. Stir in the coconut milk, bell pepper, and mushrooms. Re-cover the slow cooker. If using the low setting, change to high. Cook for 15 to 20 minutes, or until the vegetables are tender-crisp. Serve the soup sprinkled with the cilantro and green onions.

PER SERVING
Calories **194**
Total Fat **6.0 g**
  Saturated Fat **2.5 g**
  Trans Fat **0.0 g**
  Polyunsaturated Fat **0.5 g**
  Monounsaturated Fat **1.0 g**

Cholesterol **73 mg**
Sodium **198 mg**
Carbohydrates **7 g**
  Fiber **2 g**
  Sugars **3 g**
Protein **26 g**

Dietary Exchanges:
  1 vegetable, 3 lean meat

FAST PREP!

SERVES 4; 1½ cups per serving

SLOW COOKER SIZE | SHAPE
  3- to 4½-quart | round or oval

SLOW COOKING TIME
5 to 6 hours ON LOW plus 15 to 20 minutes ON HIGH, **OR**

2½ to 3 hours ON HIGH plus 15 to 20 minutes ON HIGH

1 pound boneless, skinless chicken breasts, all visible fat discarded, cut into ½-inch cubes

2 cups fat-free, no-salt-added chicken broth, such as on page 48

1 medium carrot, cut into matchstick-size strips

1 tablespoon minced peeled gingerroot

½ to 1 medium fresh serrano pepper, seeds and ribs discarded, chopped

2 medium garlic cloves, minced

½ teaspoon grated lime zest

───── + ─────

1 cup lite coconut milk

½ medium red bell pepper, cut into matchstick-size strips

3 ounces shiitake mushrooms, stems discarded, sliced

¼ cup snipped fresh cilantro

¼ cup sliced green onions (green and white parts)

SLOW COOKER SIZE | SHAPE
3- to 4½-quart | round
or oval

SLOW COOKING TIME
3½ to 4 hours ON LOW, **OR**

1 hour 45 minutes to
2 hours ON HIGH

Cooking spray

1 8-ounce boneless, skinless
chicken breast, all visible
fat discarded

3 cups fat-free, low-sodium
chicken broth, such as
on page 48

½ teaspoon dried rosemary,
crushed

½ teaspoon dried oregano,
crumbled

½ teaspoon garlic powder

— + —

2 ounces dried whole-grain
vermicelli or spaghetti,
broken into thirds

1 ounce arugula or mixed
spring greens, coarsely
chopped (about 1 cup)

1 cup grape tomatoes,
quartered

4 medium green onions,
finely chopped

1 tablespoon olive oil (extra
virgin preferred)

¼ teaspoon salt

¼ teaspoon pepper, or to
taste (coarsely ground
preferred)

¼ cup shredded Asiago or
Parmesan cheese

Herbed Chicken Soup with Arugula

When it's almost serving time, turn off the slow cooker and let this herb soup barely "cook" the arugula, baby tomatoes, and green onions. You'll have soup and salad all in one bowl!

1. Lightly spray the slow cooker with cooking spray. Put the chicken, broth, rosemary, oregano, and garlic powder in the slow cooker, stirring to combine. Cook, covered, on low for 3½ to 4 hours or on high for 1 hour 45 minutes to 2 hours, or until the chicken is no longer pink in the center.

2. About 30 minutes before serving, prepare the pasta using the package directions, omitting the salt. Drain well in a colander. Set aside.

3. Using a slotted spoon, quickly transfer the chicken to a cutting board, leaving the liquid in the slow cooker. Re-cover the slow cooker. Cut the chicken into bite-size pieces.

4. Stir the chicken and remaining ingredients except the Asiago into the broth mixture. Turn off the slow cooker. Let stand, covered, for 5 minutes. Serve the soup sprinkled with the Asiago.

PER SERVING
Calories **207**
Total Fat **7.5 g**
  Saturated Fat **2.0 g**
  Trans Fat **0.0 g**
  Polyunsaturated Fat **1.5 g**
  Monounsaturated Fat **3.5 g**

Cholesterol **43 mg**
Sodium **332 mg**
Carbohydrates **17 g**
  Fiber **4 g**
  Sugars **3 g**
  Protein **18 g**

Dietary Exchanges:
  ½ **starch, 1 vegetable,
  2 lean meat**

Chicken and Bean Soup with Lemon and Basil

It's the last-minute addition of lemon zest and a heap of fresh basil that make this soup stand out.

1. Fill a small saucepan three-fourths full of water. Bring to a boil over high heat. Stir in the beans. Return to a boil. Reduce the heat and simmer for 15 minutes. Pour the beans into a colander and rinse. Pour into the slow cooker.
2. Stir in the broth, carrot, celery, onion, garlic, $\frac{1}{4}$ teaspoon salt, and $\frac{1}{8}$ teaspoon pepper. Cook, covered, on low for 8 to 10 hours or on high for 5 to 6 hours, or until the beans are tender.
3. Sprinkle the chicken with the remaining $\frac{1}{4}$ teaspoon salt and remaining $\frac{1}{8}$ teaspoon pepper.
4. In a large nonstick skillet, heat the oil over medium-high heat, swirling to coat the bottom. Cook the chicken for 5 to 6 minutes, or until lightly browned on the outside and no longer pink in the center, stirring occasionally.
5. Quickly stir the chicken, tomato, and lemon zest into the soup and re-cover the slow cooker. Cook for 5 minutes, or until the tomato is heated through. Just before serving, stir in the basil.

SERVES 4; generous 1½ cups per serving

SLOW COOKER SIZE | SHAPE
4- to 6-quart | round or oval

SLOW COOKING TIME
8 to 10 hours ON LOW plus 5 minutes ON LOW, **OR**
5 to 6 hours ON HIGH plus 5 minutes ON HIGH

1 cup dried cannellini beans, sorted for stones and shriveled beans, rinsed, and drained

5 cups fat-free, low-sodium chicken broth, such as on page 48

1 medium carrot, chopped

1 medium rib of celery, chopped

1 small onion, chopped

2 medium garlic cloves, minced

¼ teaspoon salt

⅛ teaspoon pepper

————— + —————

1 pound boneless, skinless chicken breasts, all visible fat discarded, cut into ½-inch cubes

¼ teaspoon salt

⅛ teaspoon pepper

2 teaspoons olive oil

1 large tomato, chopped

2 teaspoons grated lemon zest

¼ cup chopped fresh basil

PER SERVING
Calories **364**
Total Fat **5.5 g**
  Saturated Fat **1.0 g**
  Trans Fat **0.0 g**
  Polyunsaturated Fat **1.0 g**
  Monounsaturated Fat **2.5 g**

Cholesterol **73 mg**
Sodium **524 mg**
Carbohydrates **38 g**
  Fiber **10 g**
  Sugars **5 g**
Protein **40 g**

Dietary Exchanges:
  2 starch, 2 vegetable, 4½ lean meat

SERVES 4; 1½ cups per serving

SLOW COOKER SIZE | SHAPE
3- to 4-quart | round or oval

SLOW COOKING TIME
6 to 8 hours ON LOW, **OR**
3 to 4 hours ON HIGH

1 pound boneless, skinless chicken breasts, all visible fat discarded, cut into ½-inch cubes

¼ teaspoon salt and ¼ teaspoon salt, divided use

⅛ teaspoon pepper

2 teaspoons olive oil

3½ cups fat-free, low-sodium chicken broth, such as on page 48

1 14.5-ounce can no-salt-added diced tomatoes, undrained

10 ounces frozen whole-kernel corn, thawed

1 medium onion, diced

2 tablespoons no-salt-added tomato paste

½ medium fresh jalapeño, seeds and ribs discarded, minced

2 medium garlic cloves, minced

1 tablespoon chili powder

2 teaspoons ground cumin

+

2 tablespoons fresh lime juice

¼ cup snipped fresh cilantro

¼ cup shredded low-fat Cheddar cheese (sharp preferred)

Spicy Chicken and Corn Soup

This light one-dish meal gets a colorful and flavorful boost from tomatoes and corn, a hint of heat from the jalapeño, and a touch of freshness from lime juice and cilantro added just before serving.

1. Sprinkle both sides of the chicken with ¼ teaspoon salt and the pepper. Using your fingertips, gently press the seasonings so they adhere to the chicken.

2. In a large nonstick skillet, heat the oil over medium-high heat, swirling to coat the bottom. Cook the chicken for 5 to 6 minutes, or until lightly browned, stirring occasionally. Transfer to the slow cooker.

3. Stir in the broth, tomatoes with liquid, corn, onion, tomato paste, jalapeño, garlic, chili powder, cumin, and remaining ¼ teaspoon salt. Cook, covered, on low for 6 to 8 hours or on high for 3 to 4 hours, or until the vegetables are tender.

4. Stir in the lime juice. Ladle into bowls. Sprinkle each serving with the cilantro and Cheddar.

COOK'S TIP

To serve a crowd or just enjoy the soup for several meals, double the recipe and use a 4- or 5-quart slow cooker. Cover and refrigerate any leftover soup (without the lime juice, cilantro, and Cheddar) for up to four days, or freeze it for longer storage.

PER SERVING		Dietary Exchanges:
Calories **296**	Cholesterol **74 mg**	1½ **starch, 2 vegetable,**
Total Fat **7.0 g**	Sodium **573 mg**	**3 lean meat**
Saturated Fat **1.5 g**	Carbohydrates **29 g**	
Trans Fat **0.0 g**	Fiber **5 g**	
Polyunsaturated Fat **1.0 g**	Sugars **10 g**	
Monounsaturated Fat **3.0 g**	Protein **32 g**	

Country Chicken Noodle Soup

A bowl of chicken noodle soup is always welcome, and with a few unexpected ingredients—green peas, pimientos, and Cheddar—our version will surely satisfy the soup lover in you.

1. In a large nonstick skillet, heat the oil over medium-high heat, swirling to coat the bottom. Cook the chicken for 3 to 5 minutes on each side, or until lightly browned. Transfer to the slow cooker.
2. In the same skillet, cook the onion for 3 minutes, or until beginning to lightly brown, stirring frequently. Transfer to the slow cooker.
3. Stir in the broth, bay leaves, thyme, garlic powder, and pepper. Cook, covered, on low for $3\frac{1}{2}$ to 4 hours or on high for 1 hour 45 minutes to 2 hours, or until the chicken is no longer pink in the center.
4. Quickly transfer the chicken to a cutting board, stir the pasta into the broth mixture, and re-cover the slow cooker. If using the low setting, change it to high. Cook, covered, for 20 minutes, or until the pasta is tender.
5. Meanwhile, using one or two forks, shred the chicken. When the pasta is tender, stir the chicken and remaining ingredients except the Cheddar into the broth mixture. Let stand, covered, for 5 minutes.
6. Just before serving, discard the bay leaves. Sprinkle the soup with the Cheddar.

SERVES 4; 1¼ cups per serving

SLOW COOKER SIZE | SHAPE
3- to 4½-quart | round or oval

SLOW COOKING TIME
3½ to 4 hours ON LOW (preferred) plus 20 minutes ON HIGH, **OR**

1 hour 45 minutes to 2 hours ON HIGH plus 20 minutes ON HIGH

1 teaspoon canola or corn oil

1 8-ounce boneless, skinless chicken breast, all visible fat discarded

1 large onion, diced

3 cups fat-free, low-sodium chicken broth, such as on page 48

3 medium dried bay leaves

1 teaspoon dried thyme, crumbled

½ teaspoon garlic powder

½ teaspoon pepper (coarsely ground preferred)

——— + ———

2 ounces dried whole-grain no-yolk noodles

½ cup frozen green peas, thawed

1 4-ounce jar diced pimientos, undrained

¼ cup snipped fresh parsley

2 tablespoons light tub margarine

¼ teaspoon salt

¼ cup plus 2 tablespoons grated low-fat sharp Cheddar cheese

PER SERVING
Calories **210**
Total Fat **6.0 g**
  Saturated Fat **1.0 g**
  Trans Fat **0.0 g**
  Polyunsaturated Fat **1.5 g**
  Monounsaturated Fat **3.0 g**

Cholesterol **39 mg**
Sodium **388 mg**
Carbohydrates **19 g**
  Fiber **4 g**
  Sugars **4 g**
  Protein **20 g**

Dietary Exchanges:
1 starch, 1 vegetable, 2 lean meat

SLOW COOKER SIZE | SHAPE
3- to 4½-quart | round
or oval

SLOW COOKING TIME

3 to 4 hours ON LOW, **OR**

1½ to 2 hours ON HIGH

1 teaspoon ground
coriander

1 pound boneless, skinless
chicken breasts, all
visible fat discarded

4 cups fat-free, low-sodium
chicken broth, such as
on page 48

2 medium garlic cloves,
minced

1 tablespoon minced
peeled gingerroot

———— **+** ————

2 teaspoons fish sauce
(lowest sodium
available)

3 ounces dried medium
Asian rice stick noodles,
broken in half

2 medium green onions,
thinly sliced

1 medium fresh jalapeño,
seeds and ribs
discarded, thinly sliced
(optional)

¼ cup chopped fresh
cilantro

1 medium lime, cut into
4 wedges

Chicken Pho

A ginger-and-garlic–infused broth is the foundation for this aromatic and nourishing meal in a bowl. The rice noodles—a key ingredient in this Vietnamese soup—soak up the bold flavors of onions, chile peppers, and cilantro.

1. Sprinkle the coriander over both sides of the chicken. Transfer to the slow cooker. Add the broth, garlic, and gingerroot.

2. Cook, covered, on low for 3 to 4 hours or on high for 1½ to 2 hours, or until the chicken is no longer pink in the center. Quickly transfer the chicken to a large plate and using 2 forks, shred the chicken. Return to the slow cooker. Quickly stir in the fish sauce and re-cover the slow cooker.

3. About 15 minutes before serving time, prepare the noodles using the package directions. Transfer the noodles to bowls. Pour the soup over the noodles. Sprinkle with the green onions, jalapeño, and cilantro. Serve with the lime wedges.

COOK'S TIP

These delicate noodles taste best when they're not overcooked, so be sure to follow the package directions (most brands instruct you to soak them in boiling water for 10 to 15 minutes). Drain them as soon as they're tender to prevent them from absorbing too much water.

PER SERVING
Calories **229**
Total Fat **3.0 g**
  Saturated Fat **0.5 g**
  Trans Fat **0.0 g**
  Polyunsaturated Fat **0.5 g**
  Monounsaturated Fat **1.0 g**

Cholesterol **73 mg**
Sodium **353 mg**
Carbohydrates **20 g**
  Fiber **1 g**
  Sugars **1 g**
  Protein **27 g**

Dietary Exchanges:
  1½ **starch, 3 lean meat**

Chicken Tortilla Soup

A garnish of avocado bits, thinly sliced red bell pepper, and crisp tortilla strips adds texture and color to this popular soup.

1. In the slow cooker, stir together the chicken, corn, broth, tomatoes with liquid, onion, sugar, ancho powder, garlic, and salt. Cook, covered, on low for 6 to 8 hours or on high for 3 to 4 hours.
2. Meanwhile, preheat the oven to 350°F.
3. Arrange the tortilla strips in a single layer on a baking sheet. Bake for 8 to 10 minutes, or until crisp. Transfer the baking sheet to a cooling rack. Let the strips sit for about 15 minutes, or until cool. Transfer to an airtight container and set aside.
4. When the soup is ready, transfer 1 cup to a food processor or blender. Stir in the tortilla pieces. Let the mixture stand for 1 minute so the tortilla pieces soften. Process until smooth. Stir the mixture into the soup. Stir in the cilantro.
5. Ladle the soup into bowls. Sprinkle with the avocado, bell pepper, and reserved baked tortilla strips.

COOK'S TIP

Adding the processed soup and tortilla mixture to the rest of the soup gives the finished product more body and distributes the tortilla flavor.

SERVES 4; 1½ cups per serving

SLOW COOKER SIZE | SHAPE
3- to 4½-quart | round or oval

SLOW COOKING TIME
6 to 8 hours ON LOW, **OR**
3 to 4 hours ON HIGH

1 pound boneless, skinless chicken breasts, all visible fat discarded, cut into ½-inch cubes

2 cups frozen whole-kernel corn, thawed

2 cups fat-free, no-salt-added chicken broth, such as on page 48

1 14.5-ounce can no-salt-added diced tomatoes, undrained

¼ cup finely chopped onion

1 teaspoon sugar

1 teaspoon ancho powder

2 medium garlic cloves, minced

¼ teaspoon salt

+

2 6-inch corn tortillas, cut into ¼-inch-wide strips, and 1 6-inch corn tortilla, torn into pieces, divided use

2 to 4 tablespoons snipped fresh cilantro

¼ cup finely chopped avocado

¼ medium red bell pepper, cut into matchstick-size strips

PER SERVING
Calories **292**
Total Fat **5.5 g**
  Saturated Fat **1.0 g**
  Trans Fat **0.0 g**
  Polyunsaturated Fat **1.0 g**
  Monounsaturated Fat **2.0 g**
Cholesterol **73 mg**
Sodium **350 mg**
Carbohydrates **33 g**
  Fiber **5 g**
  Sugars **8 g**
Protein **30 g**
Dietary Exchanges:
  1½ starch, 2 vegetable, 3 lean meat

SERVES 8; 1½ cups per serving

SLOW COOKER SIZE | SHAPE
4- to 6-quart | round or oval

SLOW COOKING TIME
8 to 10 hours ON LOW, **OR**
5 to 6 hours ON HIGH

2 teaspoons olive oil

8 ounces mild or spicy Italian turkey sausage, casings discarded and sausage crumbled

1 medium onion, chopped

4 cups fat-free, low-sodium chicken broth, such as on page 48

4 cups water

1 pound dried brown lentils (about 2¼ cups), sorted for stones and shriveled lentils, rinsed, and drained

1 14.5-ounce can no-salt-added diced tomatoes, undrained

2 medium carrots, chopped

1 medium rib of celery, chopped

¼ cup no-salt-added tomato paste

2 teaspoons dried oregano, crumbled

1 teaspoon dried basil, crumbled

2 medium garlic cloves, minced

½ teaspoon salt

¼ teaspoon pepper

Turkey Sausage and Lentil Soup

This hearty soup is comforting to come home to on a winter evening. Serve it with warm crusty whole-grain bread and finish the meal with pear wedges for dessert.

1. In a large nonstick skillet, heat the oil over medium-high heat, swirling to coat the bottom. Cook the sausage and onion for 5 minutes, or until both are lightly browned, stirring occasionally. Transfer to the slow cooker.
2. Stir in the remaining ingredients. Cook, covered, on low for 8 to 10 hours or on high for 5 to 6 hours.

PER SERVING
Calories **284**
Total Fat **4.0 g**
  Saturated Fat **1.0 g**
  Trans Fat **0.0 g**
  Polyunsaturated Fat **1.0 g**
  Monounsaturated Fat **1.5 g**

Cholesterol **21 mg**
Sodium **379 mg**
Carbohydrates **41 g**
  Fiber **15 g**
  Sugars **8 g**
Protein **22 g**

Dietary Exchanges:
  2 starch, 2 vegetable, 2 very lean meat

Smoked Turkey and Rice Soup with Fresh Sage

Fresh sage sets this soup apart. Adding it at both the start and the end of the cooking time suffuses the soup with flavor.

1. Lightly spray the slow cooker with cooking spray. Place the turkey in the slow cooker. Stir in the broth, zucchini, bell pepper, onion, celery, carrot, 2 tablespoons sage, and the thyme. Cook, covered, on low for 5½ to 6 hours or on high for 2 hours 45 minutes to 3 hours, or until the onion is very soft.

2. Quickly transfer the turkey to a cutting board, leaving the broth mixture in the slow cooker. Set the turkey aside. Quickly stir the rice into the broth mixture and re-cover the slow cooker. If using the low setting, change it to high. Cook, covered, for 15 minutes, or until the rice is tender.

3. Meanwhile, bone the turkey leg. Cut the turkey into bite-size pieces. When the rice is cooked, stir the turkey, oil, salt, and remaining 2 tablespoons sage into the soup.

FAST PREP!

SERVES 4; 1½ cups per serving

SLOW COOKER SIZE | SHAPE
3- to 4½-quart | round or oval

SLOW COOKING TIME
5½ to 6 hours ON LOW plus 15 minutes ON HIGH, **OR**

2 hours 45 minutes to 3 hours ON HIGH plus 15 minutes ON HIGH

Cooking spray

1 8-ounce smoked turkey leg, skin discarded

3 cups fat-free, low-sodium chicken broth, such as on page 48

1 medium zucchini, chopped

1 medium red bell pepper, diced

1 medium onion, diced

1 medium rib of celery, thinly sliced

1 medium carrot, thinly sliced

2 tablespoons chopped fresh sage

1 teaspoon dried thyme, crumbled

—————— ✚ ——————

1 cup uncooked instant brown rice

1 tablespoon olive oil (extra virgin preferred)

¼ teaspoon salt

2 tablespoons chopped fresh sage

PER SERVING
Calories **215**
Total Fat **7.0 g**
 Saturated Fat **1.5 g**
 Trans Fat **0.0 g**
 Polyunsaturated Fat **1.5 g**
 Monounsaturated Fat **3.5 g**

Cholesterol **27 mg**
Sodium **454 mg**
Carbohydrates **27 g**
 Fiber **4 g**
 Sugars **6 g**
Protein **13 g**

Dietary Exchanges:
 2 vegetable, 1 starch, 1 lean meat, 1 fat

SERVES 4; 1¾ cups per serving

SLOW COOKER SIZE | SHAPE
3- to 4½-quart | round or oval

SLOW COOKING TIME
5 to 6 hours ON LOW, **OR**
2½ to 3 hours ON HIGH

2½ cups fat-free, low-sodium vegetable broth, such as on page 50

1 15.5-ounce can no-salt-added red kidney or black beans, rinsed and drained

1 14.5-ounce can no-salt-added diced tomatoes, undrained

1 medium sweet potato, peeled and cut into 1-inch cubes

2 medium carrots, cut crosswise into ¼- to ½-inch pieces

½ medium red bell pepper, chopped

½ medium onion, chopped

2 medium garlic cloves, minced

1 teaspoon ground cumin

⅛ teaspoon salt

⅛ teaspoon crushed red pepper flakes

———— + ————

Sprigs of fresh cilantro (optional)

Jamaican Bean and Vegetable Soup

Experience the flavor of a different culture right in your own kitchen with this soup, which was inspired by a traditional Jamaican dish, red pea soup (red peas are kidney beans). The hot pepper, tomatoes, and sweet potato also are common in Jamaican cooking.

In the slow cooker, stir together all the ingredients. Cook, covered, on low for 5 to 6 hours or on high for 2½ to 3 hours. Just before serving, garnish with the sprigs of cilantro.

PER SERVING
Calories **184**
Total Fat **0.5 g**
  Saturated Fat **0.0 g**
  Trans Fat **0.0 g**
  Polyunsaturated Fat **0.0 g**
  Monounsaturated Fat **0.0 g**

Cholesterol **0 mg**
Sodium **187 mg**
Carbohydrates **37 g**
  Fiber **13 g**
  Sugars **11 g**
Protein **10 g**

Dietary Exchanges:
  2 starch, 2 vegetable

SERVES 8; 1 cup per serving

SLOW COOKER SIZE | SHAPE
5- to 7-quart | round or oval

SLOW COOKING TIME
7 to 9 hours ON LOW, **OR**
4 to 5 hours ON HIGH

1 pound dried navy or Great Northern beans, sorted for stones and shriveled beans, rinsed, and drained

8 cups fat-free, low-sodium vegetable broth, such as on page 50, or water

1 large onion, diced

1 teaspoon dried minced garlic

1 teaspoon dried basil, crumbled

½ teaspoon salt

¼ teaspoon pepper

——————— ✛ ———————

6 ounces spinach (about 6 cups)

Bean Florentine Soup

Fresh spinach added at the end of the cooking time gives this side soup a nutritional boost and a pop of color.

1. Fill a large saucepan three-fourths full of water. Bring to a boil over high heat. Stir in the beans. Return to a boil. Reduce the heat and simmer for 15 minutes. Pour the beans into a colander and rinse.

2. Pour the beans into the slow cooker. Stir in the remaining ingredients except the spinach. Cook, covered, on low for 7 to 9 hours or on high for 4 to 5 hours. Just before serving, stir the spinach into the soup.

PER SERVING
Calories **203**
Total Fat **1.0 g**
  Saturated Fat **0.0 g**
  Trans Fat **0.0 g**
  Polyunsaturated Fat **0.5 g**
  Monounsaturated Fat **0.0 g**

Cholesterol **0 mg**
Sodium **215 mg**
Carbohydrates **38 g**
  Fiber **15 g**
  Sugars **2 g**
Protein **12 g**

Dietary Exchanges:
  2½ starch, 1 very lean meat

Smoky Split Pea Soup

Canned chipotle pepper adds a smoky hint to this soup, which is not only delicious but also high in fiber and low cost.

In the slow cooker, stir together all the ingredients except the vinegar and parsley. Cook, covered, on low for 8 to 10 hours or on high for 5 to 6 hours, or until the peas are tender. Stir in the vinegar. Serve sprinkled with the parsley.

COOK'S TIP

The amount of chipotle in this recipe adds a mild smokiness and a bit of spice. If you're tempted to add more, wait until the soup is done and taste it first; although some seasonings lose their strength with the long cooking time, the chile flavor can intensify.

PER SERVING
Calories **343**
Total Fat **1.5 g**
  Saturated Fat **0.0 g**
  Trans Fat **0.0 g**
  Polyunsaturated Fat **0.5 g**
  Monounsaturated Fat **0.0 g**

Cholesterol **0 mg**
Sodium **326 mg**
Carbohydrates **62 g**
  Fiber **25 g**
  Sugars **11 g**
Protein **23 g**

Dietary Exchanges:
  4 starch, 2 very lean meat

FAST PREP!

SERVES 5; 1½ cups per serving

SLOW COOKER SIZE | SHAPE
4- to 6-quart | round or oval

SLOW COOKING TIME
8 to 10 hours ON LOW, **OR**
5 to 6 hours ON HIGH

4 cups fat-free, low-sodium vegetable broth, such as on page 50

1 pound dried green split peas (about 2¼ cups), sorted for stones and shriveled peas, rinsed, and drained

2 cups water

2 medium carrots, chopped

2 medium ribs of celery, chopped

1 medium onion, diced

2 teaspoons ground cumin

2 teaspoons minced chipotle pepper canned in adobo sauce

2 medium garlic cloves, minced

½ teaspoon salt

¼ teaspoon pepper

+

1 tablespoon plus 1 teaspoon white wine vinegar

¼ cup plus 1 tablespoon coarsely chopped fresh Italian (flat-leaf) parsley

Smoky Split Pea Soup, page 75

SLOW COOKER SIZE | SHAPE
4- to 6-quart | round or oval

SLOW COOKING TIME
6 to 8 hours ON LOW, **OR**
3 to 4 hours ON HIGH

1 tablespoon olive oil

1½ cups chopped onions

4 large garlic cloves, minced

1 cup sliced carrots (1-inch pieces)

1 cup sliced celery (1-inch pieces)

4 cups fat-free, low-sodium vegetable broth, such as on page 50

1 pound dried red lentils (about 2 cups), sorted for stones and shriveled lentils, rinsed and drained

2 cups cauliflower florets (about 1½-inch pieces) (about 1¼-pound head)

1 teaspoon ground allspice

1 teaspoon paprika

½ teaspoon ground cinnamon

¼ teaspoon salt

¼ teaspoon pepper

¼ teaspoon ground cardamom

_____ + _____

¼ cup plus 2 tablespoons fat-free plain yogurt

Persian Red Lentil Soup

The spice mix in this soup is based on *baharat*, a Persian spice blend now used in many North African countries and from Turkey to Syria and Iran. Its slightly sweet flavor hides a kick of spice.

1. In a large nonstick skillet, heat the oil over medium-high heat, swirling to coat the bottom. Cook the onions for 3 minutes, or until soft, stirring frequently.
2. Stir in the garlic. Cook for 30 seconds, stirring constantly.
3. Stir in the carrots and celery. Cook for 2 minutes, or until beginning to soften, stirring frequently. Transfer to the slow cooker.
4. Stir the remaining ingredients except the yogurt into the onion mixture. Cook, covered, on low for 6 to 8 hours or on high for 3 to 4 hours, or until the lentils and vegetables are very tender.
5. Serve with a dollop of yogurt spooned onto each serving.

COOK'S TIPS

Red Lentils Smaller and rounder than the more common brown lentils, the red will cook to a softer, creamier consistency because they are skinless. If you can't find red lentils, you can use brown in this recipe.

Baharat Like many other traditional blends, *baharat* varies from cook to cook, but it often contains about nine spices. Black pepper, cinnamon, and allspice are quite common in *baharat,* which often includes cumin as well. Try using it to season meats, vegetables, and rice dishes.

PER SERVING
Calories **330**
Total Fat **3.5 g**
  Saturated Fat **0.5 g**
  Trans Fat **0.0 g**
  Polyunsaturated Fat **0.5 g**
  Monounsaturated Fat **2.0 g**

Cholesterol **0 mg**
Sodium **190 mg**
Carbohydrates **55 g**
  Fiber **20 g**
  Sugars **9 g**
  Protein **24 g**

Dietary Exchanges:
  3 starch, 2 vegetable, 2 lean meat

Moroccan Lentil Soup

Filled with spices popular in Moroccan cuisine, this budget-minded stew has international flavor befitting a gourmet meal.

SERVES 8; 1½ cups per serving

SLOW COOKER SIZE | SHAPE
5- to 7-quart | round or oval

SLOW COOKING TIME
8 to 10 hours ON LOW, **OR**
5 to 6 hours ON HIGH

1. In the slow cooker, stir together the broth, water, lentils, tomatoes with liquid, onion, bell pepper, tomato paste, garlic, gingerroot, cumin, turmeric, salt, and cinnamon. Cook, covered, on low for 8 to 10 hours or on high for 5 to 6 hours.
2. Just before serving, stir in the lime juice. Sprinkle each serving with the mint.

4 cups fat-free, low-sodium vegetable broth, such as on page 50

4 cups water

1 pound dried brown lentils (about 2¼ cups), sorted for stones and shriveled lentils, rinsed and drained

1 14.5-ounce can no-salt-added diced tomatoes, undrained

1 medium onion, chopped

1 medium red bell pepper, chopped

½ cup no-salt-added tomato paste

2 medium garlic cloves, minced

2 teaspoons grated peeled gingerroot

1 teaspoon ground cumin

1 teaspoon ground turmeric

½ teaspoon salt

⅛ teaspoon ground cinnamon

———— + ————

1 tablespoon fresh lime juice

½ cup snipped fresh mint, parsley, or cilantro or finely chopped green onions

PER SERVING
Calories **233**
Total Fat **1.0 g**
  Saturated Fat **0.0 g**
  Trans Fat **0.0 g**
  Polyunsaturated Fat **0.5 g**
  Monounsaturated Fat **0.0 g**
Cholesterol **0 mg**
Sodium **204 mg**
Carbohydrates **42 g**
  Fiber **15 g**
  Sugars **9 g**
Protein **17 g**

Dietary Exchanges:
2 starch, 2 vegetable, 1 lean meat

SERVES 4; generous
1⅔ cups per serving

SLOW COOKER SIZE | SHAPE
3- to 4½-quart | round
or oval

SLOW COOKING TIME
7 to 8 hours ON LOW, **OR**
3 to 4 hours ON HIGH

2 cups water

1 14.5-ounce can no-salt-
added diced tomatoes,
undrained

1¾ cups fat-free, low-
sodium vegetable broth,
such as on page 50

⅔ cup dried lentils, sorted
for stones and shriveled
lentils, rinsed, and
drained

2 medium carrots, chopped

1 medium potato, chopped

1 medium rib of celery,
chopped

½ medium onion, chopped

1 tablespoon plus 1
teaspoon curry powder

1 tablespoon dried minced
garlic

1½ teaspoons ground
cumin

½ teaspoon salt

½ teaspoon pepper

⅛ teaspoon crushed red
pepper flakes

Curried Lentil and Vegetable Soup

A hefty dose of curry powder flavors the lentils and vegetables in this soup and transforms it from ordinary to exotic.

In the slow cooker, stir together all the ingredients. Cook, covered, on low for 7 to 8 hours or on high for 3 to 4 hours.

COOK'S TIP

Whenever you cook with dried herbs and spices, you want them to still be aromatic and not "over the hill." This is especially so in slow cooking because seasonings that are past their prime not only won't add full flavor but may even give your dish a bitter or stale taste. It's recommended that you use dried herbs and spices within six months of purchase or freeze them for longer storage.

PER SERVING
Calories **211**
Total Fat **0.5 g**
  Saturated Fat **0.0 g**
  Trans Fat **0.0 g**
  Polyunsaturated Fat **0.0 g**
  Monounsaturated Fat **0.0 g**

Cholesterol **0 mg**
Sodium **75 mg**
Carbohydrates **42 g**
  Fiber **8 g**
  Sugars **9 g**
Protein **13 g**

Dietary Exchanges:
  **2 starch, 2 vegetable,
1 lean meat**

Black Bean and Jalapeño Soup

You might think that three jalapeños would make this soup too hot to handle, but they don't. Cooking them over a long period of time lessens the heat, but not the flavor. Still concerned? Discard the seeds and ribs before dicing the peppers.

1. In a large saucepan, stir together the water and beans. Bring to a boil over high heat. Reduce the heat and simmer for 2 minutes. Remove from the heat. Let stand, covered, for 1 hour.
2. Lightly spray the slow cooker with cooking spray. Rinse and drain the beans in a colander. Transfer to the slow cooker. Stir in the broth, onion, green chiles, jalapeños, bay leaves, thyme, and cumin. Cook, covered, on low for 9½ to 10 hours or on high for 4 hours 45 minutes to 5 hours, or until the beans are soft.
3. Stir in the oil and salt. Discard the bay leaves. Just before serving, sprinkle with the cilantro. Serve with the lime wedges to squeeze over the soup.

COOK'S TIP

If you have leftovers or make the soup in advance for more intense flavor, leave the bay leaves in until after you reheat the soup. Don't sprinkle with the cilantro or squeeze the lime wedges over the soup until serving time.

SERVES 4; 1 cup per serving

SLOW COOKER SIZE | SHAPE
3- to 4½-quart | round or oval

SLOW COOKING TIME
9½ to 10 hours ON LOW, **OR**
4 hours 45 minutes to 5 hours ON HIGH

1 quart water
8 ounces dried black beans (about 1 cup), sorted for stones and shriveled beans, rinsed, and drained

Cooking spray

3 cups fat-free, low-sodium vegetable broth, such as on page 50

1 medium onion, diced

1 4-ounce can chopped mild green chiles, undrained

3 medium fresh jalapeños, seeds and ribs discarded if desired, diced

2 medium dried bay leaves

½ teaspoon dried thyme, crumbled

½ teaspoon ground cumin

───── + ─────

2 tablespoons olive oil (extra virgin preferred)

¼ teaspoon salt

¼ cup snipped fresh cilantro

1 medium lime, cut into 4 wedges

PER SERVING
Calories **262**
Total Fat **7.5 g**
  Saturated Fat **1.0 g**
  Trans Fat **0.0 g**
  Polyunsaturated Fat **1.0 g**
  Monounsaturated Fat **5.0 g**

Cholesterol **0 mg**
Sodium **437 mg**
Carbohydrates **37 g**
  Fiber **13 g**
  Sugars **3 g**
  Protein **13 g**

Dietary Exchanges:
2 starch, 1 vegetable, 1 lean meat, 1 fat

FAST PREP! ⏱

SERVES 4; 1½ cups per
serving

SLOW COOKER SIZE | SHAPE
3- to 4½-quart | round
or oval

SLOW COOKING TIME
6 to 8 hours ON LOW, **OR**
2 to 3 hours ON HIGH

1 14.5-ounce can no-salt-
added whole tomatoes,
undrained

1 14.5-ounce can no-salt-
added Great Northern
beans, rinsed and
drained

4 cups coarsely chopped
kale (½ of a 5-ounce
bunch), any large stems
discarded

2 cups fat-free, low-sodium
vegetable broth, such as
on page 50

½ cup red quinoa, rinsed
and drained in a fine-
mesh sieve

1 medium carrot, cut into
½-inch slices (about
½ cup)

1 medium rib of celery, cut
into ½-inch slices (about
½ cup)

½ cup chopped red onion

1 tablespoon olive oil

2 medium garlic cloves,
minced

¾ teaspoon dried herbes
de Provence or dried
thyme, crumbled

½ teaspoon crushed red
pepper flakes

½ teaspoon smoked
paprika (sweet or hot)

¼ teaspoon salt

¼ teaspoon pepper

Kale and Red Quinoa Soup

This protein-packed soup is an ideal dinner for busy days. Herbes de
Provence lend a flavor of the French Riviera and the smoked paprika
harmonizes nicely with the pepperiness of the kale.

Put all the ingredients in the slow cooker. Cook, covered, on low
for 6 to 8 hours or on high for 2 to 3 hours, or until the vegetables
and quinoa are tender.

PER SERVING
Calories **245**
Total Fat **6.0 g**
  Saturated Fat **0.5 g**
  Trans Fat **0.0 g**
  Polyunsaturated Fat **1.0 g**
  Monounsaturated Fat **3.0 g**

Cholesterol **0 mg**
Sodium **294 mg**
Carbohydrates **40 g**
  Fiber **10 g**
  Sugars **6 g**
  Protein **10 g**

Dietary Exchanges:
  **2 starch, 2 vegetable,
  ½ lean meat**

SERVES 6; 1 cup per serving

SLOW COOKER SIZE | SHAPE
3- to 4½-quart | round
or oval

SLOW COOKING TIME
8 hours ON LOW, **OR**
4 hours ON HIGH

Cooking spray

3 cups fat-free, low-sodium vegetable broth, such as on page 50

16 ounces frozen black-eyed peas, thawed

1 medium red bell pepper, chopped

1 medium poblano pepper, seeds and ribs discarded, chopped

2 medium green onions, chopped

2 medium dried bay leaves

½ teaspoon dried thyme, crumbled

⅛ teaspoon ground cloves or allspice

———— + ————

1 tablespoon olive oil and 1 tablespoon olive oil (extra virgin preferred), divided use

6 ounces frozen meatless crumbles

2 teaspoons mild Louisiana-style hot-pepper sauce

½ teaspoon salt

2 medium green onions, chopped

Black-Eyed Pea Soup with Meatless Crumbles

Here's a "Meatless Monday" soup sure to please vegetarians and meat lovers alike. The meatless crumbles hold their ground-beef-like texture and take on the flavors of the other ingredients.

1. Lightly spray the slow cooker with cooking spray. Put the broth, peas, bell pepper, poblano, 2 green onions, bay leaves, thyme, and cloves in the slow cooker, stirring to combine. Cook, covered, on low for 8 hours or on high for 4 hours, or until the peas are tender.

2. About 5 minutes before the soup is ready, in a large nonstick skillet, heat 1 tablespoon oil over medium heat, swirling to coat the bottom. Cook the meatless crumbles for 3 minutes, or until browned, stirring frequently.

3. Stir the crumbles, hot-pepper sauce, salt, remaining 1 tablespoon oil, and remaining 2 chopped green onions into the soup. Discard the bay leaves before serving the soup.

PER SERVING
Calories **237**
Total Fat **5.5 g**
  Saturated Fat **0.5 g**
  Trans Fat **0.0 g**
  Polyunsaturated Fat **0.5 g**
  Monounsaturated Fat **3.5 g**

Cholesterol **0 mg**
Sodium **358 mg**
Carbohydrates **31 g**
  Fiber **8 g**
  Sugars **2 g**
Protein **16 g**

Dietary Exchanges:
  2 starch, 2 lean meat

Beef Barley Soup with Vegetables

Classic beef barley soup gets a tasty makeover courtesy of a wide array of colorful, healthy vegetables.

1. In the slow cooker, stir together all the ingredients except the barley. Cook, covered, on low for 5 hours 45 minutes to 7 hours 45 minutes or on high for 2½ to 3½ hours.

2. Quickly stir in the barley and re-cover the slow cooker. If using the high setting, change it to low. Cook for 15 minutes, or until the barley is tender.

PER SERVING
Calories **271**
Total Fat **8.5 g**
  Saturated Fat **3.0 g**
  Trans Fat **0.0 g**
  Polyunsaturated Fat **0.5 g**
  Monounsaturated Fat **3.5 g**

Cholesterol **71 mg**
Sodium **269 mg**
Carbohydrates **23 g**
  Fiber **4 g**
  Sugars **4 g**
Protein **27 g**

Dietary Exchanges:
  1 starch, 1 vegetable, 3 lean meat

FAST PREP!

SERVES 4; 1¾ cups per serving

SLOW COOKER SIZE | SHAPE
4- to 6-quart | round or oval

SLOW COOKING TIME
5 hours 45 minutes to 7 hours 45 minutes ON LOW plus 15 minutes ON LOW, **OR**

2½ to 3½ hours ON HIGH plus 15 minutes ON LOW

1 pound lean stew meat, all visible fat discarded

3½ cups fat-free, low-sodium beef broth, such as on page 49

½ cup water

1 medium green bell pepper, diced

⅔ cup chopped onion

⅔ cup frozen whole-kernel corn, thawed

⅔ cup frozen cut (not chopped) broccoli

½ cup sliced carrot

1 packet (1 teaspoon) salt-free beef bouillon

1 teaspoon dried thyme, crumbled

1 teaspoon extra-spicy salt-free all-purpose seasoning blend (optional)

½ teaspoon pepper

¼ teaspoon salt

+

⅓ cup uncooked quick-cooking barley

SLOW COOKER SIZE | SHAPE
3- to 4½-quart | round
or oval

SLOW COOKING TIME

7½ to 8 hours ON LOW plus
30 minutes ON HIGH, **OR**

3 hours 45 minutes to
4 hours ON HIGH plus
30 minutes ON HIGH

1 teaspoon canola or corn
oil

12 ounces boneless chuck
shoulder pot roast, all
visible fat discarded

1 cup water and 1 cup
water, divided use

4 medium tomatoes,
chopped

1 large red or yellow bell
pepper, chopped

1 cup fresh cauliflower
florets (about 1-inch
pieces)

1 medium red potato
(about 6 ounces),
chopped

4 ounces fresh or frozen
cut green beans, cut into
1½-inch pieces if fresh,
thawed if frozen

1 medium rib of celery,
thinly sliced crosswise

2 tablespoons no-salt-
added tomato paste

1½ tablespoons sugar

1 tablespoon
Worcestershire sauce
(lowest sodium
available)

1 tablespoon cider vinegar

2 teaspoons dried oregano,
crumbled

1 packet (1 teaspoon) salt-
free beef bouillon

¼ teaspoon salt

✛

1½ cups coarsely chopped
cabbage

Countryside Beef and Garden Vegetable Soup

The pot roast in this soup cooks to such sublime tenderness that you can easily shred it with a fork.

1. In a medium nonstick skillet, heat the oil over medium heat, swirling to coat the bottom. Cook the beef on one side for 3 minutes, or until browned. Transfer with the browned side up to the slow cooker.

2. Pour 1 cup water into the skillet, scraping the bottom and side to dislodge any browned bits. Pour into the slow cooker. Stir in the remaining ingredients including the additional 1 cup water but not the cabbage. Cook, covered, on low for 7½ to 8 hours or on high for 3 hours 45 minutes to 4 hours, or until the beef is very tender.

3. Quickly transfer the beef to a cutting board, leaving the liquid in the slow cooker. Quickly stir in the cabbage and re-cover the slow cooker. If using the low setting, change it to high. Cook for 30 minutes, or until the cabbage is tender.

4. Meanwhile, using one or two forks, shred the beef. Set aside until the cabbage is ready. Stir the beef into the soup.

COOK'S TIP
Using precut veggies from the wide range in the produce area or salad bar of your grocery store will save you time. In addition, when you need only a small amount, you can actually save money with precut produce because you buy only what you need—no wasted veggies.

PER SERVING
Calories **173**
Total Fat **5.0 g**
  Saturated Fat **1.5 g**
  Trans Fat **0.0 g**
  Polyunsaturated Fat **0.5 g**
  Monounsaturated Fat **2.5 g**

Cholesterol **30 mg**
Sodium **252 mg**
Carbohydrates **19 g**
  Fiber **4 g**
  Sugars **10 g**
Protein **14 g**

Dietary Exchanges:
  ½ **starch, 2 vegetable,**
  1½ **lean meat**

Balsamic Beef Borscht

Often made primarily of beets and served hot or cold as a side dish, borscht can also be a hearty meal when you add beef and lots of other vegetables to the mix. The sweetness of the balsamic vinegar brings out the flavor of the vegetables, and the bit of sour cream provides a nice color contrast to the soup.

SERVES 8; 1½ cups per serving

SLOW COOKER SIZE | SHAPE
3- to 4½-quart | round or oval

SLOW COOKING TIME
8 to 10 hours ON LOW, **OR**
4 to 5 hours ON HIGH

1. In a large nonstick skillet, heat 1 teaspoon oil over medium-high heat, swirling to coat the bottom. Cook the beef for 5 minutes, or until browned on all sides, stirring occasionally. Transfer to the slow cooker. Set aside.

2. In the same skillet, heat the remaining 1 teaspoon oil, still over medium-high heat, swirling to coat the bottom. Cook the celery, onion, and garlic for 5 minutes, or until softened, stirring occasionally and reducing the heat to medium if necessary. Spread over the beef.

3. Making a layer of each, add the cabbage, beets, carrots, and bell pepper. Don't stir. Put the bay leaf on top. Set aside.

4. In a large bowl, whisk together the broth and tomato paste. Whisk in the water, salt, and pepper. Pour into the slow cooker. Don't stir. Cook, covered, on low for 8 to 10 hours or on high for 4 to 5 hours, or until the beef is tender. Discard the bay leaf.

5. Just before serving, stir in the vinegar. Top each serving with a teaspoon of sour cream.

1 teaspoon olive oil and 1 teaspoon olive oil, divided use

1½ pounds boneless top round steak, all visible fat discarded, diced and patted dry

2 medium ribs of celery, sliced crosswise into ¼-inch pieces

1 medium onion, chopped

4 medium garlic cloves, minced

4 cups finely sliced green or red cabbage (about 1 pound)

3 medium beets (about 1 pound total), peeled and diced

1 cup thinly sliced carrots

1 medium red, yellow, or green bell pepper, diced

1 medium dried bay leaf

2 cups fat-free, low-sodium beef broth, such as on page 49, or water

1 6-ounce can no-salt-added tomato paste

4 cups water

½ teaspoon salt

½ teaspoon pepper

---

2 tablespoons balsamic vinegar

2 tablespoons plus 2 teaspoons fat-free sour cream (optional)

PER SERVING
Calories **178**
Total Fat **3.5 g**
  Saturated Fat **1.0 g**
  Trans Fat **0.0 g**
  Polyunsaturated Fat **0.5 g**
  Monounsaturated Fat **2.0 g**

Cholesterol **43 mg**
Sodium **261 mg**
Carbohydrates **15 g**
  Fiber **4 g**
  Sugars **9 g**
Protein **22 g**

Dietary Exchanges:
  3 vegetable, 2½ lean meat

SERVES 6; 1½ cups per
serving

SLOW COOKER SIZE | SHAPE
3- to 4½-quart | round
or oval

SLOW COOKING TIME
8 to 10 hours ON LOW plus
5 to 8 minutes ON LOW, **OR**
4 to 5 hours ON HIGH plus
5 to 8 minutes ON LOW

5 cups fat-free, low-sodium
beef broth, such as on
page 49

2 cups chopped onions

1 large red bell pepper, cut
into 1-inch squares

1 cup sliced carrots (¼-inch
pieces)

2 tablespoons soy
sauce (lowest sodium
available)

1 tablespoon toasted
sesame oil

3 large garlic cloves,
minced

¼ to ½ teaspoon chili garlic
sauce or paste

+

2 cups fresh bean sprouts

6 ounces dried linguine-
style rice noodles

1 teaspoon canola or corn
oil

1 pound boneless top
sirloin steak, all visible
fat discarded, cut into
thin strips

¼ cup thinly sliced green
onions

1 tablespoon sesame seeds,
dry-roasted

Korean Beef Soup

A slow-cooked, veggie-rich beef broth makes the flavorful base for
this soup, which is a simplified version of a Korean soup that usually
calls for marrow bones and knuckle bones to be simmered in the
stock.

1. In the slow cooker, stir together the broth, onions, bell pepper,
   carrots, soy sauce, sesame oil, garlic, and chili garlic sauce. Cook,
   covered, on low for 8 to 10 hours or on high for 4 to 5 hours, or
   until the vegetables are tender.
2. Quickly stir in the bean sprouts and rice noodles and re-cover
   the slow cooker. If using the high setting, change it to low. Cook
   for 5 to 8 minutes, or until the bean sprouts are steaming hot
   (this is very important for food safety) and the rice noodles are
   tender but with a slight bite.
3. Meanwhile, in a large nonstick skillet, heat the canola oil over
   medium-high heat, swirling to coat the bottom. Cook the beef
   for 3 to 5 minutes, or until browned on the outside but still pink
   in the center, stirring constantly. Don't overcook or the beef
   will become tough. Stir the beef into the soup. Ladle into bowls.
   Sprinkle with the green onions and sesame seeds.

COOK'S TIP

If you can't find linguine-style rice noodles, you can substitute whole-
grain linguine. Prepare the pasta using the package directions, omitting
the salt, before adding it to the slow cooker.

PER SERVING
Calories **306**
Total Fat **7.5 g**
  Saturated Fat **2.0 g**
  Trans Fat **0.0 g**
  Polyunsaturated Fat **2.0 g**
  Monounsaturated Fat **3.5 g**

Cholesterol **40 mg**
Sodium **261 mg**
Carbohydrates **34 g**
  Fiber **4 g**
  Sugars **7 g**
Protein **25 g**

Dietary Exchanges:
  1½ **starch, 2 vegetable,
2½ lean meat**

Sherried Steak-and-Mushroom Soup

Sherry adds an elegant touch to this soup, elevating an otherwise simple meal to one that brightens a cold evening.

SERVES 4; 1½ cups per serving

SLOW COOKER SIZE | SHAPE
3- to 4½-quart | round or oval

SLOW COOKING TIME
7½ to 8 hours ON LOW, **OR**

3 hours 45 minutes to 4 hours ON HIGH

1. Lightly spray the slow cooker with cooking spray. Set aside.
2. In a large nonstick skillet, heat the oil over medium heat, swirling to coat the bottom. Cook the beef for 3 minutes, or until browned, stirring occasionally. Transfer to the slow cooker.
3. In the same skillet, cook the shallots for 3 minutes, or until beginning to lightly brown, stirring occasionally. Transfer to the slow cooker.
4. Stir in the water, ½ cup sherry, the mushrooms, leeks, and bouillon. Cook, covered, on low for 7½ to 8 hours or on high for 3 hours 45 minutes to 4 hours, or until the beef is very tender.
5. Stir in the remaining ingredients.

Cooking spray

2 teaspoons canola or corn oil

1 pound boneless sirloin steak, all visible fat discarded, cut into ½-inch cubes

4 medium shallots, chopped

2 cups water

½ cup dry sherry

8 ounces sliced button mushrooms

2 medium leeks (white part only), thinly sliced

3 packets (1 tablespoon) salt-free beef bouillon

——————— + ———————

½ cup fat-free half-and-half

¼ cup dry sherry

2 tablespoons light tub margarine

1 tablespoon sugar

½ teaspoon pepper (coarsely ground preferred)

½ teaspoon salt

PER SERVING
Calories **295**
Total Fat **7.5 g**
  Saturated Fat **1.5 g**
  Trans Fat **0.0 g**
  Polyunsaturated Fat **1.5 g**
  Monounsaturated Fat **4.0 g**

Cholesterol **56 mg**
Sodium **426 mg**
Carbohydrates **20 g**
  Fiber **2 g**
  Sugars **9 g**
Protein **29 g**

Dietary Exchanges:
  2 vegetable, ½ other carbohydrate, 3 lean meat

Seafood

91 Lemony Fish and Vegetable Stew ⏱

92 Mahi Mahi Tacos ⏱

94 Fish Amandine in Foil ⏱

95 Creole Catfish

96 Citrus Cod ⏱

97 Asparagus-and-Sole Rolls ⏱

98 Coconut Curry Halibut with Green Beans and Roasted Red Bell Peppers

100 Salmon Fillets with Pineapple-Melon Relish ⏱

101 Mojito Salmon ⏱

102 Jerk Salmon with Orange-Brown Sugar Glaze ⏱

103 Salmon with Cucumber-Dill Aïoli ⏱

105 Lime-Infused Tilapia

106 Tilapia with Lemon Potatoes ⏱

107 Whole Rosemary Trout ⏱

108 Super-Simple Asian Tuna ⏱

109 Spanish-Style Tuna

110 Sicilian Tuna Farfalle

111 Cioppino with White Wine ⏱

112 Mediterranean Fish Stew with Rouille

114 Shrimp Jambalaya ⏱

115 Shrimp and Chicken Paella

116 Low-Country Boil with Shrimp and Smoked Turkey Sausage

118 Shrimp-and-Fish Bayou Gumbo

119 Shrimp and Grits

Lemony Fish and Vegetable Stew

This easy Italian recipe turns simple ingredients into a satisfying fish stew. Stir in fresh parsley and lemon just before serving the stew for a bit of panache.

FAST PREP!

SERVES 5; 1½ cups per serving

SLOW COOKER SIZE | SHAPE
4- to 6-quart | round or oval

SLOW COOKING TIME
8 to 10 hours ON LOW plus 20 minutes ON HIGH, **OR**
5 to 6 hours ON HIGH plus 20 minutes ON HIGH

1. In the slow cooker, stir together the tomatoes with liquid, broth, carrots, celery, onion, tomato paste, garlic, basil, oregano, and pepper. Cook, covered, on low for 8 to 10 hours or on high for 5 to 6 hours, or until the vegetables are tender.
2. If using the low setting, change it to high. Quickly stir in the fish and re-cover the slow cooker. Cook for 20 minutes, or until the fish flakes easily when tested with a fork. Just before serving, stir in the parsley, lemon zest, and lemon juice.

2 14.5-ounce cans no-salt-added diced tomatoes, undrained

2 cups fat-free, low-sodium chicken broth, such as on page 48

2 medium carrots, chopped

2 medium ribs of celery, chopped

1 medium onion, chopped

¼ cup no-salt-added tomato paste

2 medium garlic cloves, minced

½ teaspoon dried basil, crumbled

½ teaspoon dried oregano, crumbled

⅛ teaspoon pepper

———————— + ————————

1 pound thin mild white fish fillets, such as tilapia or cod, rinsed and patted dry, cut into ½-inch squares

2 tablespoons snipped fresh parsley

2 teaspoons grated lemon zest

1 tablespoon fresh lemon juice

COOK'S TIP

When you check the fish for doneness, work as quickly as you can and re-cover the slow cooker quickly as well so you don't lose a lot of heat (in case you need to continue cooking the fish).

PER SERVING
Calories **168**
Total Fat **1.5 g**
 Saturated Fat **0.5 g**
 Trans Fat **0.0 g**
 Polyunsaturated Fat **0.5 g**
 Monounsaturated Fat **0.5 g**

Cholesterol **45 mg**
Sodium **136 mg**
Carbohydrates **17 g**
 Fiber **4 g**
 Sugars **10 g**
Protein **22 g**

Dietary Exchanges:
 3 vegetable, 2½ lean meat

SERVES 4; 2 tacos per
serving

SLOW COOKER SIZE | SHAPE
3- to 4½-quart | round
or oval
SLOW COOKING TIME
1½ to 2 hours ON LOW, **OR**
30 minutes to 1 hour ON
HIGH

½ teaspoon ground cumin

½ teaspoon dried oregano,
crumbled

½ teaspoon paprika

½ teaspoon chili powder

½ teaspoon onion powder

½ teaspoon garlic powder

¼ teaspoon salt

¼ teaspoon pepper

1 pound mahi mahi fillets,
rinsed and patted dry

½ cup 100% pineapple juice

1 14.5-ounce can no-salt-
added black beans,
rinsed and drained

————— + —————

½ cup thinly sliced red
cabbage

½ cup diced tomato

¼ cup sliced black olives,
drained

2 medium green onions,
thinly sliced

8 6-inch corn tortillas

Mahi Mahi Tacos

A delight for the eyes as well as the taste buds, these tacos are just
what you've been craving. Mahi mahi has a slightly stronger flavor
than most types of white fish, so it teams well with the sweet-
tartness of pineapple juice. Jet-black beans and a multicolored fresh
vegetable topping add visual appeal.

1. In a small bowl, stir together the cumin, oregano, paprika, chili
   powder, onion powder, garlic powder, salt, and pepper.
2. Sprinkle the cumin mixture over both sides of the fish. Using
   your fingertips, gently press the mixture so it adheres to the
   fish. Place in the slow cooker. Pour the pineapple juice around
   the fish. Spoon the beans over the fish. Cook, covered, on low for
   1½ to 2 hours or on high for 30 minutes to 1 hour.
3. When the fish has almost finished cooking, in a medium bowl,
   stir together the cabbage, tomato, black olives, and green onions.
   Cover and refrigerate until serving time.
4. When the fish is cooked, transfer it to a cutting board. Using two
   forks, shred the fish. Return to the slow cooker.
5. Warm the tortillas using the package directions. Place on plates.
   Using a slotted spoon, transfer about ¼ cup of the fish and bean
   mixture to the center of each tortilla. Top each serving with
   2 tablespoons of the cabbage mixture.

COOK'S TIP
You can make the cabbage topping in advance—up to two or three days,
or the night before or morning of the day you plan to make the tacos.
Just cover and refrigerate it until serving time.

PER SERVING
Calories **289**
Total Fat **2.5 g**
  Saturated Fat **0.5 g**
  Trans Fat **0.0 g**
  Polyunsaturated Fat **0.5 g**
  Monounsaturated Fat **1.0 g**

Cholesterol **83 mg**
Sodium **365 mg**
Carbohydrates **37 g**
  Fiber **7 g**
  Sugars **8 g**
  Protein **29 g**

Dietary Exchanges:
  **2 starch, 1 vegetable,
  3 lean meat**

FAST PREP!

SERVES 4; 3 ounces fish per
serving

SLOW COOKER SIZE | SHAPE
3- to 4½-quart | oval

SLOW COOKING TIME
1½ to 2 hours ON HIGH

4 slices red onion

4 thin mild white fish fillets,
such as tilapia, sole, or
walleye (about 4 ounces
each), rinsed and patted
dry

¼ teaspoon pepper

¼ teaspoon paprika

⅛ teaspoon salt

1 tablespoon plus
1 teaspoon sliced
almonds

2 tablespoons sliced green
onions

1 medium lemon, cut into
4 wedges

Fish Amandine in Foil

This take on fish amandine, which calls for all the fillets to be
enclosed in one aluminum foil packet, would be delicious with a
crisp salad, steamed carrots seasoned with your favorite herb, and a
whole-grain roll.

1. Cut an 18 x 12-inch sheet of aluminum foil. Put the foil on a flat
   surface so that a long end faces you. Place the onion slices in the
   middle of the foil, making two rows of two slices each. Space
   the slices somewhat apart—they will form a "rack" for the fish.
   Center a fillet on each onion slice so that the fillets are parallel
   to the short ends of the foil and the thin ends of the fish overlap
   in the middle. Sprinkle the fish with the pepper, paprika, and
   salt. Using your fingertips, gently press the seasonings so they
   adhere to the fish. Sprinkle with the almonds.

2. Bring the short ends of the foil together and crimp to seal.
   Leaving a small amount of airspace in the packet, crimp the long
   ends (don't bring them to the center). Place the packet in the
   slow cooker. Cook, covered, on high for 1½ to 2 hours, or until
   the fish flakes easily when tested with a fork. (Use the tines of a
   fork to carefully open the packet away from you so you don't get
   a steam burn.)

3. When the fish is done, carefully remove the packet from the slow
   cooker. Again using the tines of a fork, carefully open it away
   from you. Sprinkle the fish with the green onions. Serve the
   lemon wedges on the side to squeeze over the fish.

COOK'S TIP

An oval slow cooker works best for this recipe because you want to lay
the foil packet as flat as possible in the cooker.

PER SERVING
Calories **126**
Total Fat **3.0 g**
  Saturated Fat **0.5 g**
  Trans Fat **0.0 g**
  Polyunsaturated Fat **0.5 g**
  Monounsaturated Fat **1.0 g**

Cholesterol **57 mg**
Sodium **133 mg**
Carbohydrates **2 g**
  Fiber **1 g**
  Sugars **1 g**
Protein **23 g**

Dietary Exchanges:
  3 lean meat

Creole Catfish

Creole cooking reflects the best of French, Spanish, and African cuisines and is a popular style of cooking in New Orleans. Its signature "holy trinity" of chopped green bell peppers, onions, and celery is included in this dish—along with tomatoes, another key Creole ingredient.

SERVES 4; 3 ounces fish and ½ cup vegetables per serving

SLOW COOKER SIZE | SHAPE
3- to 4½-quart | round or oval

SLOW COOKING TIME
2½ hours ON LOW plus 1 hour ON LOW, **OR**

1 hour ON HIGH plus 30 minutes ON HIGH

1 14.5-ounce can no-salt-added diced tomatoes, undrained

1 cup thinly sliced red or green bell peppers, or a combination

1 medium rib of celery, thinly sliced

½ cup thinly sliced red onion

2 medium garlic cloves, minced

1 teaspoon coarsely chopped fresh thyme

½ teaspoon salt-free Creole seasoning blend and 1 teaspoon salt-free Creole seasoning blend, divided use

½ teaspoon salt

1 medium dried bay leaf

✦

1 pound catfish fillets, rinsed and patted dry

1. Pour the tomatoes with liquid into the slow cooker. Arrange the bell peppers, celery, and onion on top of the tomatoes. Sprinkle the garlic, thyme, ½ teaspoon Creole seasoning, and salt over the vegetables. Place the bay leaf on top. Cook, covered, on low for 2½ hours or on high for 1 hour.

2. About 5 minutes before the tomato mixture has finished cooking, sprinkle the remaining 1 teaspoon Creole seasoning over both sides of the fish. Using your fingertips, gently press the mixture so it adheres to the fish. Quickly transfer the fish to the slow cooker and re-cover it. Cook on low for 1 hour or on high for 30 minutes, or until the fish flakes easily when tested with a fork. Discard the bay leaf before serving.

COOK'S TIP
You can make your own salt-free Creole seasoning blend. In a small bowl, stir together 1 teaspoon each of chili powder, garlic powder, onion powder, paprika, cumin, and dried oregano, crumbled. You'll have 2 tablespoons total (enough to make this recipe four times). Store it in a jar with a tight-fitting lid in a cool spot for up to two months.

PER SERVING
Calories **146**
Total Fat **3.5 g**
  Saturated Fat **1.0 g**
  Trans Fat **0.0 g**
  Polyunsaturated Fat **1.0 g**
  Monounsaturated Fat **1.0 g**

Cholesterol **66 mg**
Sodium **361 mg**
Carbohydrates **8 g**
  Fiber **2 g**
  Sugars **5 g**
Protein **20 g**

Dietary Exchanges:
1 vegetable, 3 lean meat

SERVES 4; 3 ounces fish per serving

SLOW COOKER SIZE | SHAPE
3- to 4½-quart | round or oval

SLOW COOKING TIME
1½ to 2 hours ON HIGH

4 cod or other mild white fish fillets (about 4 ounces each), about ½ inch thick, rinsed and patted dry

1 tablespoon grated orange zest

½ cup fresh orange juice

2 tablespoons snipped fresh parsley

1 teaspoon fresh lemon juice

1 medium garlic clove, minced

———— + ————

1 tablespoon plus 1 teaspoon chopped green onions (green part only)

Citrus Cod

Fresh orange juice and zest, with a bit of lemon juice added for good measure, are the major flavor components of this easy fish dish.

1. Place the fish in the slow cooker.
2. In a small bowl, stir together the remaining ingredients except the green onions. Pour over the fish, gently turning to coat. Cook, covered, on high for 1½ to 2 hours, or until the fish flakes easily when tested with a fork. Serve sprinkled with the green onions.

COOK'S TIP

Any number of factors may affect your choice of fish for this and other recipes that call for mild white fish. Let your taste preferences and the availability, freshness, price, and current recommendations for seafood sustainability guide your selections.

PER SERVING
Calories **101**
Total Fat **1.0 g**
　Saturated Fat **0.0 g**
　Trans Fat **0.0 g**
　Polyunsaturated Fat **0.0 g**
　Monounsaturated Fat **0.0 g**

Cholesterol **43 mg**
Sodium **63 mg**
Carbohydrates **4 g**
　Fiber **0 g**
　Sugars **3 g**
Protein **18 g**

Dietary Exchanges:
　3 lean meat

Asparagus-and-Sole Rolls

Spring has sprung and the really thin spears of asparagus have arrived. Wrap some in mild fish fillets, turn on the slow cooker, and in an hour or so, enjoy your dinner.

FAST PREP!

SERVES 4; 1 roll per serving

SLOW COOKER SIZE | SHAPE
3- to 4½-quart | round or oval

SLOW COOKING TIME
1 to 1½ hours ON HIGH

1. Put the shallot, lemon slices, and water in the slow cooker. Set aside.
2. Wrap a fish fillet around a bundle of 5 asparagus spears. Transfer the roll with the smooth side up to the slow cooker. Repeat with the remaining fish and asparagus. Sprinkle with the pepper and salt. Cook, covered, on high for 1 to 1½ hours, or until the fish flakes easily when tested with a fork. Transfer to plates.
3. Sprinkle the rolls with the parsley. Serve the lemon wedges on the side for squeezing over all.

1 medium shallot, sliced

½ medium lemon, cut crosswise into 4 slices

¼ cup water

4 sole or other thin mild fish fillets (about 4 ounces each), rinsed and patted dry

20 pencil-thin asparagus spears (each about 6 inches long), trimmed

¼ teaspoon pepper

⅛ teaspoon salt

———— + ————

1 tablespoon plus 1 teaspoon snipped fresh parsley

1 medium lemon, cut into 4 wedges

COOK'S TIP

If you can't find pencil-thin asparagus spears, cut thicker spears lengthwise to the proper thickness, or use 3 slightly larger spears instead of the 5 thin ones for each roll.

PER SERVING
Calories **100**
Total Fat **2.0 g**
  Saturated Fat **0.5 g**
  Trans Fat **0.0 g**
  Polyunsaturated Fat **0.5 g**
  Monounsaturated Fat **0.5 g**

Cholesterol **51 mg**
Sodium **409 mg**
Carbohydrates **4 g**
  Fiber **2 g**
  Sugars **2 g**
Protein **16 g**

Dietary Exchanges:
  1 vegetable, 3 lean meat

SERVES 4; 3 ounces fish, ½ cup vegetables, ½ cup broth, and ½ cup rice per serving

SLOW COOKER SIZE | SHAPE
3- to 4½-quart | round or oval

SLOW COOKING TIME
3 to 3½ hours ON LOW plus 30 minutes ON LOW, **OR**

1½ to 2 hours ON HIGH plus 15 minutes ON HIGH

1 cup fat-free, low-sodium chicken broth, such as on page 48

¼ cup lite coconut milk

1 tablespoon Thai red curry paste

1 teaspoon grated lime zest

1 tablespoon fresh lime juice

2 teaspoons fish sauce (lowest sodium available)

2 medium garlic cloves, minced

1 teaspoon minced peeled gingerroot

2 cups green beans, trimmed

1 8-ounce can sliced bamboo shoots, drained and slivered

½ cup roasted red bell peppers, drained if bottled, thinly sliced

2 medium green onions, sliced into 1-inch pieces

—————— + ——————

4 halibut fillets (about 4 ounces each), rinsed and patted dry

1 cup uncooked brown (or regular) jasmine rice

2 tablespoons coarsely chopped fresh basil

2 tablespoons coarsely chopped fresh cilantro

Coconut Curry Halibut with Green Beans and Roasted Red Bell Peppers

The harmony of sweet, sour, and spicy flavors in this Asian-inspired dish stimulates the appetite. The halibut, whose velvety texture will melt in your mouth, rests on a fluffy bed of jasmine rice.

1. In the slow cooker, whisk together the broth, coconut milk, curry paste, lime zest, lime juice, fish sauce, garlic, and gingerroot. Stir in the green beans, bamboo shoots, roasted peppers, and green onions. Cook, covered, on low for 3 to 3½ hours or on high for 1½ to 2 hours.

2. Quickly stir in the fish and re-cover the slow cooker. Cook for 30 minutes on low or 15 minutes on high, or until the fish flakes easily when tested with a fork.

3. About 15 minutes before serving time, prepare the rice using the package directions, omitting the salt and margarine.

4. To serve, spoon the rice into shallow bowls. Place a fish fillet on each serving of rice. Spoon the green bean mixture around the fish. Ladle the cooking liquid over all. Garnish with the basil and cilantro.

COOK'S TIP

You can prepare the rice up to two to three days in advance. It will keep, covered, in the refrigerator. Microwave it with 1 to 2 tablespoons of water in a covered microwaveable bowl on 100 percent power (high) for 2 to 3 minutes to reheat it.

PER SERVING
Calories 313
Total Fat **3.5 g**
  Saturated Fat **1.0 g**
  Trans Fat **0.0 g**
  Polyunsaturated Fat **0.5 g**
  Monounsaturated Fat **0.5 g**

Cholesterol **56 mg**
Sodium **370 mg**
Carbohydrates **43 g**
  Fiber **5 g**
  Sugars **3 g**
Protein **26 g**

Dietary Exchanges:
  2½ starch, 1 vegetable, 3 lean meat

SERVES 4; 3 ounces fish and ⅓ cup relish per serving

SLOW COOKER SIZE | SHAPE
3- to 4½-quart | round or oval

SLOW COOKING TIME
3 hours ON LOW, **OR**
1½ hours ON HIGH

Cooking spray

1 large lemon, cut crosswise into 6 slices

4 salmon fillets with skin (about 5 ounces each), rinsed and patted dry

¼ cup water

1 teaspoon salt-free steak seasoning blend

½ teaspoon dried thyme, crumbled

¼ teaspoon garlic powder

¼ teaspoon salt

———— + ————

½ cup diced fresh pineapple

½ cup diced cantaloupe

3 tablespoons to ¼ cup chopped fresh mint

1 medium fresh jalapeño, seeds and ribs discarded, minced

2 tablespoons finely chopped red onion

1 teaspoon grated lemon zest

1 tablespoon fresh lemon juice

2 teaspoons sugar

Salmon Fillets with Pineapple-Melon Relish

Steak seasoning blend is an unexpected but surprisingly effective flavoring for moist salmon fillets, made even more delicious with a minty, zesty fruit relish.

1. Lightly spray the slow cooker with cooking spray. Arrange the lemon slices in a single layer in the slow cooker. Place the fish with the skin side down on the lemon. Pour the water over the fish.

2. In a small bowl, stir together the seasoning blend, thyme, garlic powder, and salt. Sprinkle over the fish. Using your fingertips, gently press the seasonings so they adhere to the fish. Cook, covered, on low for 3 hours or on high for 1½ hours, or to the desired doneness.

3. About 15 minutes before serving time, in a small bowl, stir together the remaining ingredients. Set the relish aside.

4. Using a slotted spatula, transfer the fish to a serving platter, discarding the cooking liquid and lemon. Serve the fish with the relish spooned on top or at the side.

PER SERVING
Calories **183**
Total Fat **5.0 g**
  Saturated Fat **1.0 g**
  Trans Fat **0.0 g**
  Polyunsaturated Fat **1.0 g**
  Monounsaturated Fat **1.5 g**

Cholesterol **53 mg**
Sodium **241 mg**
Carbohydrates **9 g**
  Fiber **1 g**
  Sugars **6 g**
Protein **25 g**

Dietary Exchanges:
  ½ **fruit, 3 lean meat**

Mojito Salmon

A topping with fresh mint and lime mimics a refreshing mojito and pairs perfectly with the silky consistency of slow-cooked salmon.

1. Put the onion in the slow cooker. Pour in the water and wine. Add the lime slices. Place the fish on top. Cook, covered, on low for 1½ to 2 hours or on high for 1 hour to 1 hour 15 minutes, or until the desired doneness. Check the fish at the minimum cooking time to make sure it doesn't overcook.

2. Just before serving, in a small bowl, stir together the remaining ingredients except the lime wedges.

3. When the fish is ready, using a slotted spatula, carefully transfer it to a platter. Discard the cooking liquid, onion, and lime. Sprinkle the fish with the parsley mixture. Serve with the lime wedges to squeeze on top.

FAST PREP!

SERVES 6; 3 ounces fish per serving

SLOW COOKER SIZE | SHAPE
3-quart | round or oval (preferred)

SLOW COOKING TIME
1½ to 2½ hours ON LOW, **OR**
1 hour to 1 hour 15 minutes ON HIGH

1½ large onions, coarsely chopped

2¼ cups water

¾ cup dry white wine (regular or nonalcoholic) or water

½ medium lime, cut into 3 slices

1½ pounds salmon fillet, about 1 inch thick, skin discarded, rinsed and patted dry

＋

3 tablespoons snipped fresh Italian (flat-leaf) parsley

3 tablespoons thinly sliced green onions

1½ tablespoons chopped fresh mint

1 tablespoon grated lime zest

1½ medium limes, cut into wedges

PER SERVING
Calories **151**
Total Fat **5.0 g**
  Saturated Fat **1.0 g**
  Trans Fat **0.0 g**
  Polyunsaturated Fat **1.0 g**
  Monounsaturated Fat **1.5 g**

Cholesterol **53 mg**
Sodium **90 mg**
Carbohydrates **1 g**
  Fiber **0 g**
  Sugars **0 g**
Protein **24 g**

Dietary Exchanges:
  3 lean meat

SERVES 4; 3 ounces fish and 2 tablespoons sauce per serving

SLOW COOKER SIZE | SHAPE
3- to 4½-quart | round or oval

SLOW COOKING TIME
1½ to 2 hours ON LOW, **OR**
30 minutes to 1 hour
ON HIGH

2 teaspoons salt-free jerk seasoning blend

4 salmon fillets (about 4 ounces each), rinsed and patted dry

1 teaspoon grated orange zest

½ cup fresh orange juice

1 tablespoon fresh lime juice

1 tablespoon light brown sugar

Jerk Salmon with Orange–Brown Sugar Glaze

Jerk seasoning contains a range of spices that creates its one-of-a-kind flavor. Cumin and garlic and onion powders add savoriness and cinnamon, allspice, and ginger add sweetness. In this seafood dish reminiscent of the islands, jerk flavoring is teamed with citrus and brown sugar. Serve with roasted carrots or brussels sprouts.

1. Sprinkle the jerk seasoning over both sides of the fish. Using your fingertips, gently press the mixture so it adheres to the fish. Transfer to the slow cooker. Sprinkle the orange zest over the fish. Pour the orange and lime juices around it. Sprinkle the brown sugar over the fish. Cook, covered, on low for 1½ to 2 hours or on high for 30 minutes to 1 hour.

2. At serving time, transfer the fish to plates. Spoon the cooking liquid over the fish.

COOK'S TIP

You can make your own salt-free jerk seasoning blend. In a small bowl, stir together 1 teaspoon each of allspice, cinnamon, cumin, garlic powder, onion powder, ginger, paprika, and thyme. You'll have 2 tablespoons plus 2 teaspoons total (enough to make this recipe four times). Store it in a jar with a tight-fitting lid in a cool spot for up to two months.

PER SERVING
Calories **176**
Total Fat **5.0 g**
  Saturated Fat **1.0 g**
  Trans Fat **0.0 g**
  Polyunsaturated Fat **1.0 g**
  Monounsaturated Fat **1.5 g**

Cholesterol **53 mg**
Sodium **88 mg**
Carbohydrates **7 g**
  Fiber **0 g**
  Sugars **6 g**
Protein **24 g**

Dietary Exchanges:
  ½ **other carbohydrate,**
  3 lean meat

Salmon with Cucumber-Dill Aïoli

Using a slow cooker is the ultimate way to poach salmon because the fish will cook slowly and evenly. This poached salmon is served with a garlicky mayonnaise known as aïoli (ay-OH-lee or i-OH-lee), given a twist here with the addition of cucumber and fresh dillweed.

FAST PREP!

SERVES 6; 3 ounces fish and 1 heaping tablespoon aïoli per serving

SLOW COOKER SIZE | SHAPE 3-quart | round or oval (preferred)

SLOW COOKING TIME 1½ to 2½ hours ON LOW, **OR** 1 hour to 1 hour 15 minutes ON HIGH

1. Put the onions and garlic in the slow cooker. Pour in the water. Add the lemon slices. Place the fish on top. Cook, covered, on low for 1½ to 2½ hours or on high for 1 hour to 1 hour 15 minutes, or until the fish is the desired doneness. Watch the fish carefully to make sure it doesn't overcook.
2. Just before serving, place the chopped cucumber on a cutting board. Using the side of a chef's knife or the tines of a fork, crush the cucumber. Transfer it and any liquid to a small bowl. Stir in the remaining ingredients to make the aïoli.
3. When the fish is ready, using a slotted spatula, carefully transfer it to a platter. Discard the cooking liquid, onion, garlic, and lemon. Serve with the aïoli to spoon on top or use as a dipping sauce.

1½ large onions, coarsely chopped

4 to 5 large garlic cloves, coarsely chopped

3 cups water

3 slices lemon

1½ pounds salmon fillet, about 1 inch thick, skin discarded, rinsed and patted dry

+

3 tablespoons finely chopped peeled and seeded cucumber

¼ cup plus 2 tablespoons light mayonnaise

1½ teaspoons snipped fresh dillweed

¾ teaspoon fresh lemon juice

¾ to 1½ medium garlic cloves, minced

Dash of pepper

COOK'S TIP

Using crushed cucumber will yield a smoother sauce that still has some texture.

PER SERVING
Calories **135**
Total Fat **7.0 g**
  Saturated Fat **1.0 g**
  Trans Fat **0.0 g**
  Polyunsaturated Fat **3.0 g**
  Monounsaturated Fat **2.0 g**

Cholesterol **40 mg**
Sodium **188 mg**
Carbohydrates **1 g**
  Fiber **0 g**
  Sugars **0 g**
Protein **16 g**

Dietary Exchanges:
  2½ lean meat

Lime-Infused Tilapia

Here, tilapia is seasoned with fresh lime zest, cooked in a broth infused with lime, and served with tomatillo salsa with a hint of lime.

1. Zest the limes, reserving 1½ teaspoons for the fish and ¾ teaspoon for the salsa. Cut 3 thin slices from one of the limes. Set aside the 1½ teaspoons zest and the lime slices. Save the remaining limes and zest for another use.

2. In a medium nonstick skillet, heat the oil over medium heat, swirling to coat the bottom. Cook 1 cup onion for 3 minutes, or until beginning to soften, stirring occasionally. Stir in the garlic. Cook for 30 seconds, stirring constantly. Transfer to the slow cooker. Top with the lime slices.

3. Sprinkle both sides of the fish with the salt, pepper, and 1½ teaspoons of the reserved lime zest. Using your fingertips, gently press the seasonings so they adhere to the fish. Place the fish in the slow cooker; you may need to make two layers. Pour in the water, adding more if needed to barely cover the fish. Cook, covered, on low for 2 to 2½ hours or on high for 1 hour to 1 hour 15 minutes, or until the fish just begins to flake when tested with a fork.

4. Using a slotted spatula, carefully transfer the fish to plates. Discard the cooking liquid, onion, and lime.

5. Meanwhile, in a food processor or blender, process the tomatillos, serrano pepper, remaining ⅓ cup onion, and remaining ¾ teaspoon reserved lime zest until almost smooth. Stir in the cilantro. At serving time, spoon the salsa over the fish. Garnish with the lime wedges.

SERVES 4; 3 ounces fish and ¼ cup salsa per serving

SLOW COOKER SIZE | SHAPE
1½- to 2½-quart | round or oval (preferred)

SLOW COOKING TIME
2 to 2½ hours ON LOW, **OR**
1 hour to 1 hour 15 minutes ON HIGH

1 medium and 1 large lime
1 teaspoon olive oil
1 cup chopped onion
2 medium garlic cloves, minced
1 pound tilapia or other thin mild white fish fillets, such as catfish, sole, striped bass, or red snapper, rinsed and patted dry
¼ teaspoon salt
⅛ teaspoon pepper
2 cups water (plus more as needed)

———— + ————

8 ounces tomatillos, papery husks discarded, rinsed well and coarsely chopped (about 1¾ cups)
½ small serrano pepper, seeds and ribs discarded, minced (about 1 teaspoon)
⅓ cup coarsely chopped onion
3 tablespoons snipped fresh cilantro or several whole cilantro leaves
1 medium lime, cut into 4 wedges

PER SERVING
Calories **145**
Total Fat **3.5 g**
  Saturated Fat **1.0 g**
  Trans Fat **0.0 g**
  Polyunsaturated Fat **1.0 g**
  Monounsaturated Fat **1.5 g**

Cholesterol **57 mg**
Sodium **206 mg**
Carbohydrates **5 g**
  Fiber **2 g**
  Sugars **3 g**
  Protein **24 g**

Dietary Exchanges:
  1 vegetable, 3 lean meat

SERVES 4; 3 ounces fish,
¾ cup potatoes, and
⅓ cup broth per serving

SLOW COOKER SIZE | SHAPE
5- to 7-quart | oval

SLOW COOKING TIME
5 hours ON HIGH plus
30 minutes ON HIGH

2½ cups fat-free, low-
sodium chicken broth,
such as on page 48

1 pound medium red
potatoes (about 3),
halved and thinly sliced

1 small onion, thinly sliced

1 medium garlic clove

2 teaspoons grated lemon
zest

1 tablespoon fresh lemon
juice

⅛ teaspoon salt

⅛ teaspoon pepper

+

4 tilapia or other thin
mild fish fillets (about
4 ounces each), rinsed
and patted dry

2 teaspoons grated lemon
zest

⅛ teaspoon salt

⅛ teaspoon pepper

2 tablespoons snipped
fresh parsley

Tilapia with Lemon Potatoes

The slow cooker makes this elegant dish easy enough for a
weeknight. Let the potatoes simmer in the cooker while you go
about your day, then add the fish and cook for 30 minutes. All that's
left to do is cook your favorite green vegetable to serve alongside.

1. In the slow cooker, stir together the broth, potatoes, onion,
    garlic, 2 teaspoons lemon zest, the lemon juice, ⅛ teaspoon salt,
    and ⅛ teaspoon pepper. If the potatoes aren't submerged in the
    broth, add enough water to cover. Cook, covered, on high for
    5 hours.

2. Sprinkle the fish on both sides with the remaining 2 teaspoons
    lemon zest, remaining ⅛ teaspoon salt, and remaining
    ⅛ teaspoon pepper. Using your fingertips, gently press the
    seasonings so they adhere to the fish. Transfer to the slow
    cooker, quickly arranging the fish in a single layer on the
    potatoes. Re-cover the slow cooker. Cook for 30 minutes, or until
    the fish flakes easily when tested with a fork.

3. At serving time, transfer the fish to soup bowls (large shallow
    bowls preferred). Stir the parsley into the potato mixture. Spoon
    the potatoes around the fish. Spoon the broth over all.

COOK'S TIP
Although you can cook this dish on low (for 8 hours, plus 30 minutes on
high after the fish is added), the potatoes turn an unappealing shade of
brown.

PER SERVING		
Calories **210**	Cholesterol **57 mg**	Dietary Exchanges:
Total Fat **2.0 g**	Sodium **261 mg**	**1½ starch, 3 lean meat**
Saturated Fat **0.5 g**	Carbohydrates **22 g**	
Trans Fat **0.0 g**	Fiber **3 g**	
Polyunsaturated Fat **0.5 g**	Sugars **3 g**	
Monounsaturated Fat **0.5 g**	Protein **27 g**	

Whole Rosemary Trout

The slow cooker produces an extremely moist trout, this one suffused with savory rosemary. Add mixed-fruit salad and sautéed spinach for colorful, nutritious sides.

1. Lightly spray the slow cooker with cooking spray.
2. Spread the shallot slices in the slow cooker.
3. Sprinkle the cavity of each trout with pepper. Place a sprig of rosemary in each trout. Place the trout in the slow cooker (there may be some overlap). Cook, covered, on high for 1½ to 2 hours, or until the fish flakes easily when tested with a fork.

FAST PREP!

SERVES 4; 3 ounces fish per serving

SLOW COOKER SIZE | SHAPE
5- to 7-quart | oval

SLOW COOKING TIME
1½ to 2 hours ON HIGH

Cooking spray

1 medium shallot, sliced

4 whole trout (about 8 ounces each), rinsed and patted dry, heads discarded if desired

¼ teaspoon pepper

4 sprigs of fresh rosemary

¼ cup water

PER SERVING
Calories **124**
Total Fat **4.5 g**
  Saturated Fat **1.0 g**
  Trans Fat **0.0 g**
  Polyunsaturated Fat **1.0 g**
  Monounsaturated Fat **1.0 g**

Cholesterol **98 mg**
Sodium **69 mg**
Carbohydrates **0 g**
  Fiber **0 g**
  Sugars **0 g**
Protein **20 g**

Dietary Exchanges:
  3 lean meat

SERVES 4; 3 ounces fish per serving

SLOW COOKER SIZE | SHAPE
3- to 4½-quart | round or oval

SLOW COOKING TIME
1 to 1½ hours ON HIGH

4 medium green onions

1 1-pound tuna steak, about 1 inch thick, rinsed and patted dry, cut into 4 pieces

2 teaspoons soy sauce (lowest sodium available)

1 teaspoon minced peeled gingerroot

1 medium garlic clove, minced

¼ to ½ teaspoon chili sauce, such as sriracha

Super-Simple Asian Tuna

Stir-fry or steam a colorful combination of vegetables to serve with this spicy tuna steak, which cooks on a "rack" of green onions. Adjust the amount of chili sauce to suit your love of spice.

1. Arrange the green onions in a single row in the slow cooker. Place the steaks crosswise on the green onions.
2. In a small bowl, whisk together the remaining ingredients. Spread over the fish. Cook, covered, on high for 1 to 1½ hours, or until the fish is the desired doneness. Serve with the cooking liquid spooned on top.

COOK'S TIP

When shopping for chili sauce for this recipe, be sure to buy the kind made primarily of hot peppers and garlic, not the mild tomato-based product that is often used as the sauce for shrimp cocktail.

PER SERVING
Calories **137**
Total Fat **0.5 g**
  Saturated Fat **0.0 g**
  Trans Fat **0.0 g**
  Polyunsaturated Fat **0.0 g**
  Monounsaturated Fat **0.0 g**

Cholesterol **44 mg**
Sodium **131 mg**
Carbohydrates **3 g**
  Fiber **1 g**
  Sugars **1 g**
  Protein **28 g**

Dietary Exchanges:
  3 lean meat

Spanish-Style Tuna

Fishermen in northern Spain are said to make a similar stew using ingredients they commonly carry aboard ship, such as the potatoes, bell peppers, onion, olive oil, garlic, and paprika used here, to complement their tuna catch.

1. Lightly spray the slow cooker with cooking spray. Put the potatoes and bell peppers in the slow cooker. Set aside.

2. In a large skillet, heat the oil over medium-high heat, swirling to coat the bottom. Cook the onion for 3 minutes, or until tender, stirring frequently. Stir in the garlic. Cook for 30 seconds, stirring constantly. Stir in the flour. Cook for 2 to 3 minutes, stirring constantly.

3. Pour in the broth, stirring to combine. Bring to a boil, still over medium-high heat. Boil for 1 minute, or until thickened, stirring constantly. Stir in the remaining ingredients except the fish. Pour into the slow cooker. Cook, covered, on low for 4 to 6 hours or on high for 2 to 3 hours, or until the potatoes are tender when pierced with a fork.

4. Quickly stir in the fish and re-cover the slow cooker. If using the low setting, change it to high. Cook for 5 to 20 minutes, or until the fish reaches the desired doneness. Discard the bay leaf before serving the fish.

SERVES 4; 3 ounces fish and ¾ cup vegetables per serving

SLOW COOKER SIZE | SHAPE
3- to 4½-quart | round or oval

SLOW COOKING TIME
4 to 6 hours ON LOW plus 5 to 20 minutes ON HIGH, **OR**
2 to 3 hours ON HIGH plus 5 to 20 minutes ON HIGH

Cooking spray
1 pound small red potatoes, 1½- to 2 inch-diameter, quartered
1 medium green bell pepper, diced
1 medium red bell pepper, diced
2 teaspoons olive oil
1 cup finely chopped onion
2 medium garlic cloves, minced
2 tablespoons all-purpose flour
1 cup fat-free, low-sodium chicken broth, such as on page 48
8 ounces Italian plum (Roma) tomatoes, seeded and chopped (about 1 cup)
1 small fresh jalapeño, seeds and ribs discarded, minced
1 medium dried bay leaf
½ teaspoon smoked paprika
¼ teaspoon salt
⅛ teaspoon pepper

——— + ———

1 pound tuna steaks, about 1 inch thick, rinsed and patted dry, cut into 1-inch cubes

PER SERVING
Calories **281**
Total Fat **3.5 g**
  Saturated Fat **0.5 g**
  Trans Fat **0.0 g**
  Polyunsaturated Fat **0.5 g**
  Monounsaturated Fat **2.0 g**

Cholesterol **44 mg**
Sodium **237 mg**
Carbohydrates **30 g**
  Fiber **5 g**
  Sugars **7 g**
Protein **32 g**

Dietary Exchanges:
1½ starch, 2 vegetable, 3 lean meat

SLOW COOKER SIZE | SHAPE
2- to 3-quart | round or
oval

SLOW COOKING TIME
8 to 10 hours ON LOW plus
15 minutes ON LOW, **OR**

3½ to 4½ hours ON HIGH plus
15 minutes ON LOW

1 tablespoon olive oil

1½ cups chopped onions

2 medium ribs of celery,
including leaves, cut
crosswise into ½-inch
pieces

3 large garlic cloves,
minced

2 pounds 4 ounces Italian
plum (Roma) tomatoes,
chopped (about 6 cups)

1 tablespoon no-salt-added
tomato paste

¼ teaspoon salt

¼ teaspoon pepper

————— ✚ —————

5 ounces canned very low
sodium white albacore
tuna, packed in water,
drained and flaked

¼ cup halved kalamata
olives

8 ounces dried whole-grain
bow-tie pasta (farfalle)

2 tablespoons snipped
fresh basil

Sicilian Tuna Farfalle

Slow cooking intensifies the sweetness of tomatoes, the staple
ingredient for the simple, chunky sauce in this dish. Once the sauce
is ready, add tuna and kalamata olives to warm up while you boil the
pasta. A perfect weeknight entrée, this dish needs only a salad of
mixed greens garnished with sweet onion and cucumber to round
out the menu.

1. In a medium skillet, heat the oil over medium-high heat,
    swirling to coat the bottom. Cook the onions for 3 minutes or
    until soft, stirring frequently.
2. Stir in the celery and garlic. Cook for 30 seconds, stirring
    constantly. Transfer to the slow cooker.
3. Stir in the tomatoes, tomato paste, salt, and pepper. Cook,
    covered, on low for 8 to 10 hours or on high for 3½ to 4½ hours,
    or until the tomatoes are tender.
4. If using the high setting, change it to low. Quickly stir the tuna
    and olives into the sauce and re-cover the slow cooker. Cook for
    15 minutes.
5. Meanwhile, prepare the pasta using the package directions,
    omitting the salt. Drain well in a colander. Serve the pasta
    topped with the sauce. Sprinkle with the basil.

COOK'S TIP
Italian plum (Roma) tomatoes are the best tomatoes to use for
this sauce because they have lots of thick pulp and less juice than
other tomatoes.

PER SERVING
Calories **383**
Total Fat **9.0 g**
  Saturated Fat **1.0 g**
  Trans Fat **0.0 g**
  Polyunsaturated Fat **1.5 g**
  Monounsaturated Fat **5.0 g**

Cholesterol **15 mg**
Sodium **367 mg**
Carbohydrates **61 g**
  Fiber **11 g**
  Sugars **13 g**
  Protein **20 g**

Dietary Exchanges:
  **3 starch, 3 vegetable,
  1½ lean meat**

Cioppino with White Wine

Let this fish stew's saucy tomato base simmer on its own until almost mealtime, then add scallops, mussels, and finally bite-size pieces of mild fish. The result is perfection, since the slow cooker assures the gentle handling that seafood needs.

1. Lightly spray the slow cooker with cooking spray. Put the tomatoes with liquid, onion, wine, garlic, and red pepper flakes in the slow cooker, stirring to combine. Cook, covered, on low for 5 hours or on high for 2½ hours, or until the onion is very soft.

2. If using the low setting, change it to high. Quickly stir in the scallops and mussels (don't add the fish here) and re-cover the slow cooker. Cook for 20 minutes.

3. Quickly and gently stir in the fish and the remaining ingredients. Re-cover the slow cooker. Cook for 15 minutes, or until the fish flakes easily when tested with a fork. Discard any unopened mussels. Ladle the cioppino into bowls.

COOK'S TIP

Don't be tempted to add the fish with the scallops and mussels. It will overcook and break down, giving the dish an unappealing texture.

PER SERVING
Calories **229**
Total Fat **9.0 g**
  Saturated Fat **1.5 g**
  Trans Fat **0.0 g**
  Polyunsaturated Fat **1.0 g**
  Monounsaturated Fat **5.5 g**

Cholesterol **45 mg**
Sodium **414 mg**
Carbohydrates **12 g**
  Fiber **2 g**
  Sugars **5 g**
Protein **21 g**

Dietary Exchanges:
2 vegetable, 3 lean meat

FAST PREP!

SERVES 4; 1¼ cups per serving

SLOW COOKER SIZE | SHAPE
4- to 6-quart | round or oval

SLOW COOKING TIME

5 hours ON LOW plus
  20 minutes ON HIGH plus
  15 minutes ON HIGH, **OR**

2½ hours ON HIGH plus
  20 minutes ON HIGH plus
  15 minutes ON HIGH

Cooking spray

1 14.5-ounce can no-salt-added diced tomatoes, undrained

1 medium onion, diced

½ cup dry white wine (regular or nonalcoholic)

2 medium garlic cloves, minced

⅛ to ¼ teaspoon crushed red pepper flakes

— + —

6 ounces bay or sea scallops, rinsed and patted dry, sea scallops quartered if large

12 fresh debearded and rinsed mussels in the shell

6 ounces tilapia fillets, rinsed and patted dry, cut into 1-inch pieces

¼ cup chopped fresh basil

2 tablespoons olive oil

⅛ teaspoon salt

SLOW COOKER SIZE | SHAPE
3- to 4½-quart | round
or oval

SLOW COOKING TIME
4 hours ON LOW plus 10 to 15
minutes ON HIGH, **OR**

2 hours ON HIGH plus 10 to 15
minutes ON HIGH

2 teaspoons olive oil

1¼ cups chopped onions

1 medium fennel bulb,
chopped (about 1½
cups), stems discarded,
fronds reserved

4 medium garlic cloves,
minced

1 32-ounce can no-salt-
added diced tomatoes,
undrained

¾ cup water

⅛ teaspoon pepper

——————— + ———————

8 ounces fresh debearded
and rinsed mussels in the
shell

5 ounces cod, rinsed and
patted dry, cut into
1-inch pieces

5 ounces shucked clams

¼ cup chopped fresh Italian
(flat-leaf) parsley

3 tablespoons light
mayonnaise

1 tablespoon minced
roasted red bell pepper

½ medium garlic clove,
minced

1 or 2 dashes of cayenne, or
to taste

Mediterranean Fish Stew with Rouille

Similar to bouillabaisse, this hearty stew features an assortment of seafood in a tomato base with the addition of a rouille (ROO–ee), a spicy reddish sauce (*rouille* is the French word for "rust").

1. In a medium nonstick skillet, heat the oil over medium heat, swirling to coat the bottom. Cook the onions for 3 minutes, or until beginning to soften, stirring occasionally. Stir in the fennel. Cook for 3 minutes, or until slightly softened, stirring occasionally. Stir in the 4 minced garlic cloves. Cook for 30 seconds, stirring constantly. Transfer to the slow cooker.

2. Stir in the tomatoes with liquid, water, and pepper. Cook, covered, on low for 4 hours or on high for 2 hours, or until the onions and fennel are tender.

3. If using the low setting, change it to high. Quickly stir in the mussels and re-cover the slow cooker. Cook for 3 minutes. Quickly stir in the fish and clams and re-cover the slow cooker. Cook for 5 to 8 minutes, or until the mussels have opened. Discard any unopened mussels. Stir in the parsley.

4. While the seafood cooks, in a small bowl, stir together the mayonnaise, bell pepper, remaining ½ minced garlic clove, and the cayenne for the rouille. Just before serving, stir 2 tablespoons of the rouille into the stew. Garnish each serving with 1½ teaspoons of the remaining rouille and the fennel fronds.

PER SERVING
Calories **233**
Total Fat **6.5 g**
  Saturated Fat **1.0 g**
  Trans Fat **0.0 g**
  Polyunsaturated Fat **2.5 g**
  Monounsaturated Fat **2.5 g**

Cholesterol **40 mg**
Sodium **496 mg**
Carbohydrates **24 g**
  Fiber **5 g**
  Sugars **9 g**
Protein **19 g**

Dietary Exchanges:
  **5 vegetable, 2 lean
  meat**

SERVES 4; 1½ cups per serving

SLOW COOKER SIZE | SHAPE
3- to 4½-quart | round or oval

SLOW COOKING TIME

5 to 6 hours ON LOW plus 30 minutes ON HIGH, **OR**

2½ to 3 hours ON HIGH plus 30 minutes ON HIGH

1 14.5-ounce can no-salt-added tomatoes, undrained

1 cup water (if cooking on low) or 1½ cups water (if cooking on high)

½ cup finely chopped onion

1 medium rib of celery, sliced crosswise

1 small green bell pepper, chopped

2 ounces lower-sodium, low-fat smoked ham, all visible fat discarded, finely chopped

2 teaspoons dried parsley, crumbled

1 teaspoon dried oregano, crumbled

2 medium garlic cloves, minced

½ teaspoon dried thyme, crumbled

⅛ to ¼ teaspoon cayenne

1 medium dried bay leaf

━━━━━ ✛ ━━━━━

8 ounces raw medium shrimp, thawed if frozen, peeled, rinsed, and patted dry

1 cup frozen cut okra, thawed

1 cup uncooked instant brown rice

¼ cup snipped fresh parsley

Shrimp Jambalaya

The word "jambalaya" is thought to come from *jambon*, the French word for "ham." It's a given, then, that ham is one of the primary ingredients of jambalaya; however, you don't need much when you use smoked ham and chop it finely to distribute its distinct flavor throughout the dish.

1. In the slow cooker, stir together the tomatoes with liquid, water, onion, celery, bell pepper, ham, parsley, oregano, garlic, thyme, cayenne, and bay leaf. Cook, covered, on low for 5 to 6 hours or on high for 2½ to 3 hours, or until the vegetables are tender.
2. If using the low setting, change it to high. Quickly stir in the shrimp, okra, and rice and re-cover the slow cooker. Cook for 30 minutes, or until the rice is tender. Discard the bay leaf. Serve the jambalaya sprinkled with the parsley.

PER SERVING
Calories **196**
Total Fat **2.0 g**
  Saturated Fat **0.5 g**
  Trans Fat **0.0 g**
  Polyunsaturated Fat **0.5 g**
  Monounsaturated Fat **0.5 g**

Cholesterol **78 mg**
Sodium **472 mg**
Carbohydrates **30 g**
  Fiber **4 g**
  Sugars **7 g**
Protein **14 g**

Dietary Exchanges:
  1½ **starch, 2 vegetable,**
  1½ **lean meat**

Shrimp and Chicken Paella

To preserve their bright colors and avoid overcooking, wait until the end before adding the shrimp and peas to the chicken, rice, and tomato foundation of this traditional dish from Spain.

SERVES 4; 1½ cups per serving

SLOW COOKER SIZE | SHAPE
2½- to 3½-quart | round or oval

SLOW COOKING TIME
2 hours 15 minutes to 2½ hours ON LOW plus 10 to 15 minutes ON HIGH (preferred), **OR**

1 hour 15 minutes to 1½ hours ON HIGH plus 10 to 15 minutes ON HIGH

1. In a medium bowl, stir together the paprika, oregano, garlic powder, salt, and pepper. Sprinkle all over the chicken. Using your fingertips, gently press the seasonings so they adhere to the chicken.

2. In a medium nonstick skillet, heat 1 teaspoon oil over medium-high heat, swirling to coat the bottom. Cook the chicken for 3 to 5 minutes on each side, or until lightly browned on both sides. Transfer to a medium plate.

3. Reduce the heat to medium. Add the remaining ½ teaspoon oil, swirling to coat the bottom. Cook the onions for 1½ minutes, stirring frequently.

4. Stir in the rice. Cook for 1 minute, stirring constantly. Transfer to the slow cooker.

5. Place the chicken on the onion mixture. Top with the tomato. Pour the broth over all. Don't stir. Cook, covered, on low for 2 hours 15 minutes to 2½ hours or on high for 1 hour 15 minutes to 1½ hours, or until the rice is tender, almost all the liquid is absorbed, and the chicken is no longer pink in the center.

6. If using the low setting, change it to high. Quickly stir in the shrimp and peas and re-cover the slow cooker. Cook for 10 to 15 minutes, or until the shrimp are pink on the outside and the peas are tender.

1 tablespoon paprika

1 teaspoon dried oregano, crumbled

½ teaspoon garlic powder

¼ teaspoon salt

¼ teaspoon pepper

2 boneless, skinless chicken breasts (about 4 ounces each), each cut crosswise into 4 pieces

1 teaspoon olive oil and ½ teaspoon olive oil, divided use

1½ cups chopped onions

1 cup uncooked converted rice

1 large tomato, chopped

2 cups fat-free, low-sodium chicken broth, such as on page 48

———————— + ————————

8 ounces raw large shrimp, peeled, rinsed, and patted dry

½ cup frozen green peas, thawed

PER SERVING
Calories **348**
Total Fat **4.0 g**
  Saturated Fat **0.5 g**
  Trans Fat **0.0 g**
  Polyunsaturated Fat **0.5 g**
  Monounsaturated Fat **2.0 g**

Cholesterol **108 mg**
Sodium **583 mg**
Carbohydrates **49 g**
  Fiber **3 g**
  Sugars **5 g**
  Protein **27 g**

Dietary Exchanges:
3 starch, 1 vegetable, 3 lean meat

SERVES 4; 1 cup boil
(2 ounces shrimp, 1 piece
sausage, 2 pieces corn,
and 2 potato halves) per
serving

SLOW COOKER SIZE | SHAPE
3- to 4½-quart | round
or oval

SLOW COOKING TIME
4 to 6 hours ON LOW plus
1 hour ON LOW, **OR**

2½ to 3 hours ON HIGH plus
30 minutes ON HIGH

1 pound medium red
potatoes, halved

4 ounces low-fat smoked
turkey sausage (casings
discarded if desired), cut
diagonally into 4 1-inch
pieces

1 cup fat-free, low-sodium
chicken broth, such as
on page 48

½ cup dry vermouth or
dry white wine (regular
or nonalcoholic), or
2 tablespoons white
balsamic vinegar

½ cup water

1 medium lemon, thinly
sliced

2 teaspoons reduced-
sodium seafood boil
seasoning

1 medium dried bay leaf

¼ teaspoon pepper

¼ to ½ teaspoon red hot-
pepper sauce

⅛ teaspoon salt

—————— + ——————

10 ounces peeled and
deveined raw medium
shrimp or 12 ounces
shrimp in the shell (21/25
count per pound)

2 whole ears of corn, husks
and silk discarded, each
ear cut into 4 pieces

Low-Country Boil
with Shrimp and Smoked
Turkey Sausage

This is a meal worthy of spreading newspapers on the table for an
authentic rustic dining experience. You can opt to peel and eat your
shrimp, or go with peeled and deveined. Serve with a crusty whole-
wheat roll and a big, dark green, leafy salad.

1. Place the potatoes and sausage in the slow cooker. Pour in the
   broth, vermouth, and water. Stir in the lemon, seafood boil
   seasoning, bay leaf, pepper, hot-pepper sauce, and salt. Cook,
   covered, on low for 4 to 6 hours or on high for 2½ to 3 hours.

2. Quickly add the shrimp and corn and re-cover the slow cooker.
   Cook for 1 hour on low or 30 minutes on high, or until the shrimp
   are pink on the outside and the corn is tender. Using a slotted
   spoon, transfer the shrimp, sausage, and vegetables to shallow
   serving bowls. (You can spoon the cooking liquid over each
   serving if desired.) Discard the bay leaf before serving.

PER SERVING
Calories **266**
Total Fat **5.0 g**
  Saturated Fat **1.5 g**
  Trans Fat **0.0 g**
  Polyunsaturated Fat **1.5 g**
  Monounsaturated Fat **1.5 g**

Cholesterol **143 mg**
Sodium **580 mg**
Carbohydrates **30 g**
  Fiber **3 g**
  Sugars **5 g**
  Protein **24 g**

Dietary Exchanges:
  2 starch, 3 lean meat

SLOW COOKER SIZE | SHAPE
3- to 4½-quart | round or oval

SLOW COOKING TIME

5½ to 6 hours ON LOW plus 15 minutes ON HIGH, **OR**

2 hours 45 minutes to 3 hours ON HIGH plus 15 minutes ON HIGH

2 tablespoons canola or corn oil

2 tablespoons all-purpose flour

1 large green bell pepper, chopped

1 cup fresh or frozen chopped okra, thawed if frozen

1 medium onion, chopped

1 medium rib of celery, sliced

1 14.5-ounce can no-salt-added tomatoes, undrained

2 medium dried bay leaves

2 teaspoons salt-free seafood seasoning blend

¾ teaspoon dried thyme, crumbled

———————— + ————————

8 ounces raw or frozen medium shrimp, thawed if frozen, peeled, rinsed, and patted dry

8 ounces tilapia or other thin mild white fish fillets, rinsed and patted dry, cut into 1-inch pieces

2 tablespoons mild Louisiana-style hot-pepper sauce

2 teaspoons olive oil (extra virgin preferred)

⅛ teaspoon salt

Shrimp-and-Fish Bayou Gumbo

Making gumbo can require a lot of attention, and if you include crabmeat, the dish can be expensive. This recipe takes care of both! The slow cooker does much of the work for you, and after cooking briefly, the tilapia breaks down and acquires a crablike texture—but for a fraction of the cost. While the fish is cooking, prepare some instant brown rice on the stovetop to create the perfect bed for this delicious gumbo.

1. In a large nonstick skillet, heat the oil over medium heat, swirling to coat the bottom. Cook the flour for 5 minutes, or until caramel color, stirring constantly. Cook the bell pepper, okra, onion, and celery for 4 minutes, or until the onion is soft, stirring frequently. Transfer to the slow cooker.

2. Stir in the tomatoes with liquid, bay leaves, seasoning blend, and thyme. Cook, covered, on low for 5½ to 6 hours or on high for 2 hours 45 minutes to 3 hours.

3. If using the low setting, change it to high. Quickly stir in the remaining ingredients and re-cover the slow cooker. Cook for 15 minutes, or until the shrimp is pink on the outside. Discard the bay leaves before serving the gumbo.

COOK'S TIP

If possible, refrigerate the gumbo overnight in an airtight container so the flavors blend.

PER SERVING
Calories **214**
Total Fat **7.5 g**
    Saturated Fat **1.0 g**
    Trans Fat **0.0 g**
    Polyunsaturated Fat **1.5 g**
    Monounsaturated Fat **4.5 g**

Cholesterol **100 mg**
Sodium **494 mg**
Carbohydrates **16 g**
    Fiber **3 g**
    Sugars **7 g**
    Protein **22 g**

Dietary Exchanges:
    3 vegetable, 3 lean meat

Shrimp and Grits

Shrimp and grits is a southern specialty that has become a favorite in restaurants around the country. You can easily replicate the dish at home using a slow cooker. It generates the steady heat needed to yield perfect grits.

SERVES 5; ½ cup shrimp mixture and heaping ½ cup grits per serving

SLOW COOKER SIZE | SHAPE
1½- to 2½-quart | round or oval

SLOW COOKING TIME
3 to 4 hours ON LOW plus 10 minutes ON HIGH, **OR**
1½ to 2 hours ON HIGH plus 10 minutes ON HIGH

3 cups water
¼ teaspoon pepper
⅛ teaspoon salt
1 cup yellow or white grits (stone-ground preferred)

———— + ————

9 ounces frozen whole-kernel corn, thawed
1 teaspoon olive oil
¾ cup chopped onion
½ cup chopped green bell pepper
2 large garlic cloves, minced
1 pound raw medium shrimp, peeled, rinsed, and patted dry
1½ cups chopped tomatoes
¼ teaspoon red hot-pepper sauce, or to taste

1. In the slow cooker, stir together the water, pepper, and salt. Slowly stir in the grits. Cook, covered, on low for 3 to 4 hours or on high for 1½ to 2 hours, or until the water is absorbed and the grits are tender.
2. If using the low setting, change it to high. Quickly stir in the corn and re-cover the slow cooker. Cook for 10 minutes, or until the corn is tender.
3. While the corn is cooking, in a large nonstick skillet, heat the oil over medium heat, swirling to coat the bottom. Cook the onion and bell pepper for 3 minutes, or until beginning to soften, stirring frequently.
4. Stir in the garlic. Cook for 30 seconds, stirring constantly.
5. Stir the shrimp, tomatoes, and hot-pepper sauce into the onion mixture. Cook for 2 to 3 minutes, or until the shrimp are pink on the outside and the tomatoes are hot. Serve over the grits.

PER SERVING
Calories **250**
Total Fat **2.5 g**
  Saturated Fat **0.5 g**
  Trans Fat **0.0 g**
  Polyunsaturated Fat **0.5 g**
  Monounsaturated Fat **1.5 g**

Cholesterol **114 mg**
Sodium **569 mg**
Carbohydrates **42 g**
  Fiber **4 g**
  Sugars **5 g**
Protein **17 g**

Dietary Exchanges:
  2½ starch, 1 vegetable, 2 lean meat

Poultry

121 Chicken and Fresh Fennel Cassoulet ⏱

122 Chicken with Autumn Vegetables ⏱

124 Slow-Roasted Tarragon Chicken ⏱

126 Chicken and Dumplings

128 Athens Chicken Pinwheels on Pasta

130 Mediterranean Chicken ⏱

131 Artichoke-Lemon Chicken

133 Moroccan Chicken Thighs with Raisin-and-Carrot Couscous

134 Garlic Chicken with Honey-Lemon Sauce

135 White Chicken Chili

136 Pepper-Pineapple Chicken

137 Curry-Rubbed Chicken

138 Rosemary Chicken with Bell Peppers

139 Chicken, Mushrooms, and Pearl Onions in Red Wine

140 Chicken with Black Beans and Sweet Potatoes ⏱

141 Chicken and Tomato Stew with Kalamata Olives

142 Pad Thai with Chicken

144 Cajun-Sauced Drumsticks

145 Chicken Cacciatore

146 Mole Chicken Tacos

147 Chicken Sofrito

148 Turkey Breast with Gravy

149 Barbecue-Spiced Turkey Breast ⏱

150 Turkey Meat Loaf with Creamy Chicken Gravy

151 Turkey and Sweet Potato Stew ⏱

153 Pulled Turkey Tostadas with Cucumber Guacamole

155 Turkey Cassoulet with Gremolata

156 Southwestern Turkey Meatballs

157 Beer Barrel Turkey Chili

158 Hot Stuffed Peppers ⏱

159 Peach-Glazed Cornish Hen for Two

Chicken and Fresh Fennel Cassoulet

A combination of fennel, sun-dried tomatoes, and herbs richly flavors the beans and chicken in this casserole.

1. In the slow cooker, make one layer each of the fennel, onion, and tomatoes. Sprinkle with the garlic. Place the chicken on top. Sprinkle the mixture with the oregano, pepper, and salt. Pour the broth over all. Don't stir. Cook, covered, on low for 4 to 5 hours or on high for 2½ to 3 hours.
2. Pour the beans over the chicken. Sprinkle with the parsley. Don't stir. Cook, covered, on low for 30 minutes to 1 hour or on high for 15 to 30 minutes, or until the chicken is no longer pink in the center.

COOK'S TIPS

Although most recipes calling for fennel use only the bulb, there are uses for all parts of the plant. First, cut the fernlike fronds, or leaves, from the stems and the stems from the bulb. After discarding the tips of any fronds that seem coarse, use the fronds as a garnish or snip them to use as a seasoning (add just before serving the dish). The stems can be thinly sliced to use in salads, but many people find them too tough and use them primarily to season broths.

To prepare the bulb, which is used as a vegetable, trim the bottom, halve and core the bulb, then thinly slice it. Use sliced fennel raw in a tossed salad or slaw or with fruits, such as oranges and apples. Fennel also is tasty when you simmer or braise it, such as in soups, stews, pot roasts, or vegetable dishes. The aniselike, but milder and sweeter, flavor of fennel becomes more delicate with cooking.

FAST PREP! ⏱

SERVES 4; 3 ounces chicken and 1 cup vegetables per serving

SLOW COOKER SIZE | SHAPE
3- to 4½-quart | round or oval

SLOW COOKING TIME
4 to 5 hours ON LOW plus 30 minutes to 1 hour ON LOW (preferred), **OR**

2½ to 3 hours ON HIGH plus 15 to 30 minutes ON HIGH

1 medium fennel bulb, trimmed, thinly sliced, and quartered

1 medium Vidalia, Maui, Oso Sweet, or other sweet onion, thinly sliced and quartered

¼ cup matchstick-size dry-packed sun-dried tomatoes

2 medium garlic cloves, minced

4 boneless, skinless chicken breast halves (about 4 ounces each), all visible fat discarded

½ teaspoon dried oregano, crumbled

¼ teaspoon pepper

⅛ teaspoon salt

½ cup fat-free, low-sodium chicken broth, such as on page 48

—— + ——

1 15.5-ounce can no-salt-added Great Northern beans, rinsed and drained

2 tablespoons snipped fresh Italian (flat-leaf) parsley

PER SERVING
Calories **268**
Total Fat **4.0 g**
  Saturated Fat **0.5 g**
  Trans Fat **0.0 g**
  Polyunsaturated Fat **0.5 g**
  Monounsaturated Fat **1.0 g**

Cholesterol **73 mg**
Sodium **283 mg**
Carbohydrates **27 g**
  Fiber **10 g**
  Sugars **4 g**
Protein **30 g**

Dietary Exchanges:
1 starch, 2 vegetable, 3 very lean meat

FAST PREP! ⏱️

SERVES 6; 3 ounces chicken, ¾ cup vegetables, and ½ cup broth per serving

SLOW COOKER SIZE | SHAPE
5- to 7-quart | oval

SLOW COOKING TIME
8 to 10 hours ON LOW, **OR**
5 to 6 hours ON HIGH

1 teaspoon ground cumin

½ teaspoon pepper

½ teaspoon salt

¾ pound butternut squash, peeled, seeds and strings discarded, cut into 1-inch pieces (about 2 cups)

1 medium red potato, halved, then each half quartered

1 medium carrot, halved lengthwise and cut crosswise into 1-inch pieces

1 small onion, cut into thin wedges

½ medium fresh jalapeño, seeds and ribs discarded, minced

2 medium garlic cloves, chopped

2 cups fat-free, low-sodium chicken broth, such as on page 48

1 medium lime, quartered

6 sprigs of fresh cilantro

1 3-pound chicken, skin, all visible fat, and giblets discarded

✦

¼ cup snipped fresh cilantro and ¼ cup chopped fresh cilantro, divided use

2 tablespoons fresh lime juice

Chicken with Autumn Vegetables

Based on sancocho, a spicy stew native to the Canary Islands, Puerto Rico, and some Central and South American countries, our version features a whole chicken and hearty vegetables simmered in a jalapeño-spiked broth. It's just soupy enough to require a bowl rather than a plate.

1. In a small dish, stir together the cumin, pepper, and salt. Set aside.

2. In a large bowl, stir together the squash, potato, carrot, onion, jalapeño, and garlic. Add ¾ teaspoon of the cumin mixture, stirring to coat. Set the remaining cumin mixture aside. Transfer the squash mixture to the slow cooker. Pour in the broth.

3. Place the lime quarters and sprigs of cilantro in the cavity of the chicken. Sprinkle the remaining cumin mixture all over the chicken. Using your fingertips, gently press the mixture so it adheres to the chicken. Place the chicken on the squash mixture. Cook, covered, on low for 8 to 10 hours or on high for 5 to 6 hours, or until the thickest part of a breast registers 165°F on an instant-read thermometer.

4. Transfer the chicken to a cutting board, leaving the squash mixture and liquid in the crock. Let the chicken stand for 15 minutes so the juices can redistribute. (The chicken will cook a little more during the standing time.)

5. Add the snipped cilantro and lime juice to the slow cooker, stirring to combine.

6. Carve the chicken into slices. Transfer to soup bowls. Spoon the squash mixture and broth around the chicken. Garnish with the chopped cilantro.

PER SERVING
Calories **196**
Total Fat **3.5 g**
  Saturated Fat **1.0 g**
  Trans Fat **0.0 g**
  Polyunsaturated Fat **1.0 g**
  Monounsaturated Fat **1.0 g**

Cholesterol **76 mg**
Sodium **314 mg**
Carbohydrates **15 g**
  Fiber **2 g**
  Sugars **3 g**
  Protein **26 g**

Dietary Exchanges:
  1 starch, 3 lean meat

COOK'S TIP

Use the vegetables listed here as a guideline when you make this stew. You can use about 4 cups of almost any hearty vegetables you have on hand, such as sweet potatoes, bell peppers, turnips, rutabagas, or leeks.

FAST PREP!

SERVES 6; 3½ ounces
chicken per serving

SLOW COOKER SIZE | SHAPE
3- to 4½-quart | round
or oval

SLOW COOKING TIME
1 hour ON HIGH plus 3½ to
4 hours ON LOW

Cooking spray

¼ cup snipped fresh
parsley

2 tablespoons olive oil

1 tablespoon grated lemon
zest

2 teaspoons dried tarragon,
crumbled

1½ teaspoons smoked
paprika

1 teaspoon dried thyme,
crumbled

½ teaspoon garlic powder

1 4-pound roasting chicken
(with skin), all visible fat
and giblets discarded

1 medium lemon, cut into
4 wedges

Slow-Roasted Tarragon Chicken

For succulent, savory, and rich-tasting "roasted" chicken, stuff the seasonings under the skin so their flavors permeate the chicken as it slow cooks. Side dishes such as sweet potatoes and asparagus go well with this chicken.

1. Lightly spray the slow cooker with cooking spray. Set aside.
2. In a small bowl, stir together the parsley, oil, lemon zest, tarragon, paprika, thyme, and garlic powder.
3. Carefully loosen the skin from the breast and drumsticks by gently inserting your fingers between the skin and the meat, making a pocket for the parsley mixture. Don't break the skin. Discard any fat beneath the skin. Still working carefully, spread the parsley mixture under the loosened skin as well as possible.
4. Put the lemon wedges in the cavity. Place the chicken with the breast side up in the slow cooker. Cook, covered, on high for 1 hour. Change the setting to low. Cook for 3½ to 4 hours, or until the internal temperature at the thickest part of the breast reaches 165°F.
5. Transfer the chicken to a cutting board, leaving the pan drippings in the slow cooker. Let stand for 15 minutes so the juices can redistribute. (The chicken will cook a little more during the standing time.) Before carving the chicken, carefully remove the skin so the seasonings remain in place.

6. Meanwhile, pour the drippings into a 2-cup glass measuring cup. Place in the freezer for 15 minutes to cool slightly.

7. Pour the drippings into a quart-size resealable plastic bag. Hold the bag so that one of the bottom ends points down over a medium bowl (forming a "pastry bag"). This will let the fat rise to the top. Snip the pointed end. Let the drippings flow into the bowl, stopping just before the layer of fat gets to the point. Discard the fat. If the juices are too cool, transfer them to a small saucepan. Bring to a boil over medium-high heat. Serve the juices with the chicken.

COOK'S TIP

Made from ground smoked sweet peppers, smoked paprika adds a wonderful wood-smoked flavor to food. Try sprinkling some on soups, salads, or fish, or use it to enhance salsa, dips, rice dishes, marinades, and many other foods that would work well with a smoky flavor.

PER SERVING
Calories **218**
Total Fat **9.0 g**
  Saturated Fat **1.5 g**
  Trans Fat **0.0 g**
  Polyunsaturated Fat **1.5 g**
  Monounsaturated Fat **4.5 g**

Cholesterol **100 mg**
Sodium **118 mg**
Carbohydrates **1 g**
  Fiber **1 g**
  Sugars **0 g**
Protein **32 g**

Dietary Exchanges:
  3½ **lean meat**

SERVES 4; 3 ounces chicken, 1 cup vegetables, and 1 dumpling per serving

SLOW COOKER SIZE | SHAPE
3- to 4½-quart | round or oval (preferred)

SLOW COOKING TIME
4 to 5 hours ON HIGH plus 25 to 30 minutes ON HIGH

Cooking spray

3 medium carrots, sliced

2 medium ribs of celery, sliced

8 ounces frozen shelled edamame, thawed

1 4-ounce jar sliced pimiento, drained

1 teaspoon canola or corn oil and 1 teaspoon canola or corn oil, divided use

4 boneless, skinless chicken breast halves (about 4 ounces each), all visible fat discarded

1 cup finely chopped onion

2 cups fat-free, low-sodium chicken broth and ⅔ cup fat-free, low-sodium chicken broth, such as on page 48, divided use

2 tablespoons no-salt-added tomato paste

¼ cup all-purpose flour

1 tablespoon finely chopped fresh rosemary

⅛ teaspoon salt

¼ teaspoon pepper

Chicken and Dumplings

Homemade chicken and dumplings is pure comfort food that's worth a little extra hands-on time. (You'll need to prepare the dumpling batter 35 to 40 minutes before serving.) Adding edamame gives this popular dish a contemporary twist and a nutritional boost.

1. Lightly spray the slow cooker with cooking spray. Put the carrots, celery, edamame, and pimiento in the slow cooker, stirring to combine. Set aside.

2. In a large nonstick skillet, heat 1 teaspoon oil over medium-high heat, swirling to coat the bottom. Cook the chicken for 3 to 5 minutes on each side, or until lightly browned. Transfer to the slow cooker.

3. Put the remaining 1 teaspoon oil in the skillet, swirling to coat the bottom. Cook the onion for 3 minutes, or until soft, stirring frequently. Stir in 2 cups broth and the tomato paste. Set aside.

4. Put ¼ cup flour in a small bowl. Whisk in the rosemary, ¼ teaspoon salt, the pepper, and the remaining ⅔ cup broth. Stir into the onion mixture. Bring to a boil, still over medium high, stirring frequently. Boil for 2 to 3 minutes, or until thickened and bubbly, stirring frequently and adjusting the heat if necessary. Pour over the chicken. Don't stir. Cook, covered, on high for 4 to 5 hours, or until the chicken is no longer pink in the center.

5. About 10 minutes before the chicken is cooked, prepare the dumpling dough. In a medium bowl, stir together the cornmeal, remaining ⅓ cup flour, the baking powder, onion powder, and remaining ¼ teaspoon salt. Stir in the parsley.

6. In a small bowl, whisk together the half-and-half and remaining 2 tablespoons oil. Stir into the flour mixture until the batter is just moistened but no flour is visible.

7. When the chicken is ready, quickly transfer it to a large plate, leaving the onion mixture in the slow cooker. Stir the onion mixture and re-cover the slow cooker (leave it set on high). Cover the chicken to keep warm until serving time. Set aside. Using a serving spoon, quickly drop four equal portions of the dumpling dough on top of the onion mixture in the slow cooker. Re-cover the slow cooker. Cook on high for 25 to 30 minutes, or until a wooden toothpick inserted in the center of one of the dumplings comes out clean. (Don't remove the lid while cooking the dumplings.) Serve the dumplings and vegetables alongside the chicken.

COOK'S TIP

Don't prepare the dumpling mixture ahead of time; it will lose its leavening ability.

DUMPLINGS

⅓ cup yellow cornmeal

⅓ cup all-purpose flour

1 teaspoon baking powder

¼ teaspoon onion powder

¼ teaspoon salt

2 tablespoons finely snipped fresh parsley

¼ cup plus 2 tablespoons fat-free half-and-half

2 tablespoons canola or corn oil

PER SERVING

Calories **466**
Total Fat **15.5 g**
  Saturated Fat **1.5 g**
  Trans Fat **0.0 g**
  Polyunsaturated Fat **4.5 g**
  Monounsaturated Fat **8.0 g**

Cholesterol **73 mg**
Sodium **580 mg**
Carbohydrates **45 g**
  Fiber **7 g**
  Sugars **10 g**
Protein **38 g**

Dietary Exchanges:
  2 starch, 3 vegetable, 4 lean meat

SERVES 4; 3 ounces chicken, ½ cup pasta, and 2 tablespoons sauce per serving

SLOW COOKER SIZE | SHAPE
3- to 4½-quart | round or oval

SLOW COOKING TIME
3½ to 4½ hours ON LOW (preferred), **OR**
2 to 2½ hours ON HIGH

2 large boneless, skinless chicken breasts (about 8 ounces each), all visible fat discarded, pounded to ¼-inch thickness

1 teaspoon olive oil

¼ cup finely chopped red bell pepper

¼ cup finely chopped onion

¼ cup chopped button mushrooms

2 medium garlic cloves, minced

½ teaspoon dried oregano, crumbled

⅛ teaspoon salt

1 tablespoon balsamic vinegar

½ cup fat-free, low-sodium chicken broth, such as on page 48

Athens Chicken Pinwheels on Pasta

A light sauce flecked with red bell pepper and parsley tops Greek-inspired chicken pinwheels and whole-grain pasta. Serve this Mediterranean-flavored meal with a dark green leafy salad lightly dressed with a lemon vinaigrette.

1. Put the chicken on a large plate. Lightly brush both sides of the chicken with the oil.
2. In a small bowl, stir together ¼ cup bell pepper, the onion, mushrooms, garlic, oregano, and salt. Spread over each piece of chicken, leaving about a ½-inch border uncovered. Roll up from one of the long ends, jelly-roll style, tucking the ends under. Tie each roll in several places with kitchen twine. Transfer to the slow cooker.
3. Brush the tops of the rolls with the vinegar. Pour ½ cup broth around, not over, the chicken. Cook, covered, on low for 3½ to 4½ hours or on high for 2 to 2½ hours.
4. About 20 minutes before serving time, prepare the pasta using the package directions, omitting the salt. Drain well in a colander.
5. Meanwhile, transfer the rolls to a cutting board. Let stand, covered, for 10 minutes for easier slicing. Cut the rolls crosswise into slices about ¾ inch thick.

6. While the pasta boils and the rolls stand, in a small saucepan, stir together the remaining ³/₄ cup broth, remaining 2 tablespoons bell pepper, and the pepper. Cook over medium-high heat for 6 to 8 minutes, or until reduced to about ¹/₂ cup. Remove the sauce from the heat. Stir in the parsley and lemon juice.

7. Toss the pasta with about ¹/₄ cup of the sauce. Spoon the pasta onto a serving platter. Arrange the pinwheels over the pasta. Drizzle with the remaining sauce.

COOK'S TIPS

Larger chicken breasts are better than small for slow cooker chicken rolls since there is more area to accommodate the filling. Because you'll cut the cooked rolls before arranging the slices on the pasta, everyone will get the same amount, even though you use two breasts for four servings.

Replace the pasta with whole-wheat couscous or brown rice for a change.

——————— + ———————

4 ounces dried whole-grain spaghetti

³/₄ cup fat-free, low-sodium chicken broth, such as on page 48

2 tablespoons finely chopped red bell pepper

¹/₄ teaspoon pepper

1 tablespoon snipped fresh Italian (flat-leaf) parsley

¹/₂ teaspoon fresh lemon juice

PER SERVING
Calories **260**
Total Fat **5.0 g**
  Saturated Fat **1.0 g**
  Trans Fat **0.0 g**
  Polyunsaturated Fat **1.0 g**
  Monounsaturated Fat **2.0 g**

Cholesterol **73 mg**
Sodium **224 mg**
Carbohydrates **25 g**
  Fiber **4 g**
  Sugars **3 g**
Protein **29 g**

Dietary Exchanges:
  1½ **starch, 3 very lean meat**

SERVES 4; 3 ounces chicken and 1½ cups vegetables per serving

SLOW COOKER SIZE | SHAPE
3- to 4½-quart | round or oval

SLOW COOKING TIME
4 to 6 hours ON LOW

Cooking spray

1½ pounds red potatoes, peeled and cut into ¾-inch cubes

3 medium green onions, white and green parts thinly sliced on the diagonal and kept separated, divided use

1 medium garlic clove, minced

¼ teaspoon dried oregano, crumbled; ¼ teaspoon dried oregano, crumbled; and ½ teaspoon dried oregano, crumbled, divided use

¼ teaspoon salt

¼ teaspoon pepper

1 medium lemon, peel cut into strips, juice reserved; and 1 medium lemon, cut crosswise into 8 slices, divided use

4 boneless, skinless chicken breast halves (about 4 ounces each), all visible fat discarded

＋

2 medium tomatoes, chopped

¼ cup crumbled low-fat feta cheese

Mediterranean Chicken

Ingredients commonly used in cooking throughout the Mediterranean area—lemon, garlic, and oregano—permeate the chicken breasts and vegetables in this aromatic dish. Fresh tomatoes, green onions, and feta cheese add the finishing touch.

1. Lightly spray the slow cooker with cooking spray. Make a layer of half the potatoes. Sprinkle with half the white parts of the green onions (reserve the green parts), half the garlic, ¼ teaspoon oregano, half the salt, and half the pepper. Top with half the lemon peel strips and 2 lemon slices. Repeat with another layer of the same ingredients. Don't stir.
2. Place the chicken on the vegetables. Sprinkle with the final ½ teaspoon oregano. Top each piece of chicken with 1 of the remaining 4 lemon slices.
3. Pour the reserved lemon juice around, not over, the chicken, so the seasonings stay in place. Cook, covered, on low for 4 to 6 hours, or until the chicken is no longer pink in the center.
4. Serve the chicken with the potato mixture and cooking liquid. Garnish with the tomatoes, feta, and reserved green parts of the green onions.

COOK'S TIP
Use a potato peeler or sharp knife to remove strips of lemon peel. Don't cut deep enough to get the white pith—it's bitter. Cut the strips to the desired size.

PER SERVING
Calories **290**
Total Fat **4.5 g**
  Saturated Fat **1.5 g**
  Trans Fat **0.0 g**
  Polyunsaturated Fat **0.5 g**
  Monounsaturated Fat **1.5 g**

Cholesterol **76 mg**
Sodium **439 mg**
Carbohydrates **33 g**
  Fiber **5 g**
  Sugars **5 g**
Protein **30 g**

Dietary Exchanges:
  2 starch, 1 vegetable, 3 lean meat

Artichoke-Lemon Chicken

Tart fresh lemon pairs perfectly with chicken and artichokes in this dish. Serve it with brown rice, whole-grain pasta, or whole-wheat couscous to soak up all the delicious broth.

SERVES 4; 3 ounces chicken and ¾ cup vegetable mixture per serving

SLOW COOKER SIZE | SHAPE
4- to 6-quart | round or oval (preferred)

SLOW COOKING TIME
5 to 6 hours ON LOW (preferred), **OR**
4 to 5 hours ON HIGH

1. Put the artichokes, lemon, garlic, 1 teaspoon rosemary, ⅛ teaspoon salt, and ⅛ teaspoon pepper in the slow cooker, tossing to combine. Pour in the broth. Set aside.
2. In a small bowl, stir together the remaining 2 teaspoons rosemary, remaining ⅛ teaspoon salt, and remaining ⅛ teaspoon pepper. Sprinkle over both sides of the chicken. Using your fingertips, gently press the seasonings so they adhere to the chicken.
3. In a large nonstick skillet, heat the oil over medium heat, swirling to coat the bottom. Cook the chicken for 3 to 5 minutes on each side, or until lightly browned. Place the chicken on the artichoke mixture. Don't stir. Cook, covered, on low for 5 to 6 hours or on high for 4 to 5 hours, or until the chicken is no longer pink in the center and the artichokes and lemon are tender.

16 ounces frozen artichoke hearts, thawed

1 small lemon, thinly sliced

1 medium garlic clove, minced

1 teaspoon chopped fresh rosemary and 2 teaspoons chopped fresh rosemary, divided use

⅛ teaspoon salt and ⅛ teaspoon salt, divided use

⅛ teaspoon pepper and ⅛ teaspoon pepper, divided use

¾ cup fat-free, low-sodium chicken broth, such as on page 48

4 boneless, skinless chicken breast halves (about 4 ounces each), all visible fat discarded

2 teaspoons olive oil

COOK'S TIPS

You can use a round slow cooker, but you'll need to stack the chicken breasts.

Frozen Artichoke Hearts Make artichoke hearts a staple in your freezer. No salt is added during packaging, so they contain less sodium than the canned variety.

PER SERVING
Calories **211**
Total Fat **5.0 g**
  Saturated Fat **1.0 g**
  Trans Fat **0.0 g**
  Polyunsaturated Fat **0.5 g**
  Monounsaturated Fat **2.5 g**

Cholesterol **73 mg**
Sodium **348 mg**
Carbohydrates **13 g**
  Fiber **9 g**
  Sugars **1 g**
Protein **27 g**

Dietary Exchanges:
  2 vegetable, 3 lean meat

Moroccan Chicken Thighs with Raisin-and-Carrot Couscous

Cinnamon and a touch of allspice add a background hint of sweetness, giving the chicken a rich, complex flavor. Couscous is the perfect side dish.

SERVES 4; 1 thigh and ½ cup couscous per serving

SLOW COOKER SIZE | SHAPE
1½- to 2½-quart | round or oval

SLOW COOKING TIME
4 to 6 hours ON LOW, **OR**
2 to 3 hours ON HIGH

2 teaspoons smoked paprika

1 teaspoon ground cumin

1 teaspoon ground cinnamon

¼ teaspoon pepper

¼ teaspoon ground turmeric

Dash of ground allspice

4 bone-in, skinless chicken thighs (about 5 ounces each)

1 teaspoon olive oil

¼ cup water

——————— + ———————

1 cup water

¾ cup uncooked whole-wheat couscous

¼ cup dark raisins

¼ cup shredded carrot

3 tablespoons chopped fresh cilantro or several whole cilantro leaves

1. In a small bowl, stir together the paprika, cumin, cinnamon, pepper, turmeric, and allspice. Sprinkle over both sides of the chicken. Using your fingertips, gently press the seasonings so they adhere to the chicken.

2. In a medium nonstick skillet, heat the oil over medium-high heat, swirling to coat the bottom. Cook the chicken for 3 to 5 minutes on each side, or until browned, turning once halfway through. Transfer to the slow cooker.

3. Pour ¼ cup water into the skillet. Bring to a boil, scraping to dislodge any browned bits. Pour over the chicken. Cook, covered, on low for 4 to 6 hours or on high for 2 to 3 hours, or until the chicken is no longer pink in the center.

4. About 10 minutes before serving time, in a small saucepan, bring the remaining 1 cup water to a boil over high heat. Stir in the couscous, raisins, and carrot. Remove the pan from the heat. Let stand, covered, for 5 minutes, or until the water is absorbed and the couscous is tender. Fluff with a fork.

5. Spoon the couscous onto plates. Place the chicken on the couscous. Spoon the cooking liquid over the couscous if desired. Garnish with the cilantro.

PER SERVING
Calories **364**
Total Fat **10.0 g**
    Saturated Fat **2.5 g**
    Trans Fat **0.0 g**
    Polyunsaturated Fat **2.5 g**
    Monounsaturated Fat **4.0 g**

Cholesterol **72 mg**
Sodium **70 mg**
Carbohydrates **44 g**
    Fiber **7 g**
    Sugars **7 g**
Protein **27 g**

Dietary Exchanges:
    2½ starch, ½ fruit, 3 lean meat

SERVES 4; 3 ounces chicken and 2 tablespoons sauce

SLOW COOKER SIZE | SHAPE
3- to 4½-quart | round or oval

SLOW COOKING TIME
2 to 2½ hours ON LOW, **OR**
1 hour 30 minutes to 2 hours ON HIGH

4 boneless, skinless chicken breast halves (about 4 ounces each), all visible fat discarded

¼ teaspoon salt

¼ teaspoon pepper and pinch of pepper, divided use

1 tablespoon all-purpose flour and 2 teaspoons all-purpose flour, divided use

2 teaspoons olive oil and 1 teaspoon olive oil, divided use

1 large garlic clove, minced

⅓ cup fat-free, low-sodium chicken broth, such as on page 48

———— **+** ————

¼ teaspoon grated lemon zest

2 teaspoons fresh lemon juice

2 teaspoons honey

½ teaspoon minced fresh thyme or rosemary

Garlic Chicken with Honey-Lemon Sauce

Serve the chicken and sweet citrus sauce over a whole grain, such as quinoa, brown rice, or barley, and with steamed green beans or broccoli for a meal that's as satisfying as it is simple.

1. Sprinkle both sides of the chicken with the salt and ¼ teaspoon pepper, then with 1 tablespoon flour.
2. In a large skillet, heat 2 teaspoons oil over medium-high heat, swirling to coat the bottom. Cook the chicken for 2 minutes on each side, or just until lightly browned. Transfer to the slow cooker.
3. Reduce the heat to medium. In the same skillet, heat the remaining 1 teaspoon oil, swirling to coat the bottom. Cook the garlic and the remaining 2 teaspoons flour for 1 minute, or until the garlic is fragrant, whisking constantly. Pour in the broth. Cook for 30 seconds, or until the mixture comes to a boil and thickens slightly, whisking constantly. Pour the mixture into the slow cooker.
4. Cook, covered, on low for 2 to 2½ hours or on high for 1 hour 30 minutes to 2 hours, or until the chicken is no longer pink in the center. Transfer to a serving platter.
5. Stir the lemon zest, lemon juice, honey, thyme, and the remaining pinch of pepper into the cooking liquid in the slow cooker. Spoon the sauce over the chicken.

COOK'S TIP
Stirring the sauce together after the chicken has cooked ensures that the flavors of the lemon, honey, and thyme really shine through.

PER SERVING
Calories **185**
Total Fat **6.5 g**
  Saturated Fat **1.0 g**
  Trans Fat **0.0 g**
  Polyunsaturated Fat **1.0 g**
  Monounsaturated Fat **3.5 g**

Cholesterol **73 mg**
Sodium **280 mg**
Carbohydrates **6 g**
  Fiber **0 g**
  Sugars **3 g**
  Protein **25 g**

Dietary Exchanges:
  ½ **other carbohydrate,**
  3 lean meat

White Chicken Chili

Score big by serving this chili after the game. It will provide a change of pace from the more common ground beef, red beans, and tomato.

1. In a large nonstick skillet, heat the oil over medium-high heat, swirling to coat the bottom. Cook the chicken for 4 to 5 minutes, or just until very lightly browned, stirring frequently. Drain if necessary. Transfer to the slow cooker.

2. Add the beans, broth, onion, green chiles, garlic, cumin, oregano, and cayenne, stirring to combine. Cook, covered, on low for 5 to 6 hours or on high for 2½ to 3 hours.

3. If using the low setting, change it to high. Quickly stir in the corn and re-cover the slow cooker. Cook for 30 minutes. Serve the chili topped with the sour cream, Monterey Jack cheese, and cilantro.

COOK'S TIP

In addition to the garnishes called for, you may want to offer chopped white or green onions and sliced fresh jalapeños for those craving more heat.

PER SERVING
Calories **326**
Total Fat **7.0 g**
   Saturated Fat **2.0 g**
   Trans Fat **0.0 g**
   Polyunsaturated Fat **0.5 g**
   Monounsaturated Fat **2.0 g**

Cholesterol **80 mg**
Sodium **354 mg**
Carbohydrates **32 g**
   Fiber **9 g**
   Sugars **5 g**
Protein **34 g**

Dietary Exchanges:
1½ starch, 1 vegetable, 4 lean meat

SERVES 4; 1⅓ cups chili plus 1 tablespoon sour cream and 1 tablespoon cheese per serving

SLOW COOKER SIZE | SHAPE
3- to 4½-quart | round or oval

SLOW COOKING TIME
5 to 6 hours ON LOW plus 30 minutes ON HIGH, **OR**

2½ to 3 hours ON HIGH plus 30 minutes ON HIGH

1 teaspoon olive oil

1 pound boneless, skinless chicken breasts, all visible fat discarded, cut into 1-inch cubes

1 15.5-ounce can no-salt-added Great Northern beans, rinsed and drained

1¾ cups fat-free, low-sodium chicken broth, such as on page 48

1 large sweet onion, chopped

1 4-ounce can diced green chiles, drained

1 tablespoon dried minced garlic

1 teaspoon ground cumin

½ teaspoon dried oregano, crumbled

⅛ teaspoon cayenne

——— ✦ ———

⅔ cup frozen whole-kernel corn, thawed

¼ cup fat-free sour cream

¼ cup shredded low-fat Monterey Jack cheese

1 tablespoon plus 1 teaspoon snipped fresh cilantro

SERVES 4; 3 ounces chicken, ½ cup fruit and vegetable mixture, and ½ cup rice per serving

SLOW COOKER SIZE | SHAPE
3- to 4½-quart | round or oval

SLOW COOKING TIME
4 to 5 hours ON LOW plus 10 to 15 minutes ON HIGH

2 boneless, skinless chicken breasts (about 8 ounces each), all visible fat discarded, halved

1 8-ounce can pineapple chunks in their own juice, drained and juice reserved

1 8-ounce can sliced water chestnuts, rinsed and drained

1 medium red bell pepper, cut into 1-inch cubes

½ cup fat-free, no-salt-added chicken broth, such as on page 48

1 teaspoon minced peeled gingerroot

1 medium garlic clove, minced

＋

2 tablespoons cornstarch

2 tablespoons plain rice vinegar

1 tablespoon soy sauce (lowest sodium available)

1 cup uncooked instant brown rice

¼ cup thinly sliced green onions (green and white parts), cut on the diagonal

Pepper-Pineapple Chicken

Sliced water chestnuts provide extra crunch for this leisurely, low-fat take on classic sweet-and-sour chicken.

1. Place the chicken in the slow cooker. Top with the pineapple, water chestnuts, and bell pepper. Don't stir.
2. In a small bowl, whisk together the broth, gingerroot, garlic, and reserved pineapple juice. Pour into the slow cooker. Don't stir. Cook, covered, on low for 4 to 5 hours, or until the chicken is no longer pink in the center.
3. Using a slotted spoon, quickly transfer the chicken to a large plate, leaving the pineapple mixture in the slow cooker. Re-cover the slow cooker. Cover the plate to keep warm. Set aside.
4. Change the slow cooker setting to high. Put the cornstarch in a small bowl. Add the vinegar and soy sauce, whisking to dissolve. Quickly stir into the pineapple mixture in the slow cooker. Re-cover the slow cooker. Cook for 10 to 15 minutes, or until the sauce has thickened. Return the chicken to the slow cooker, turning to coat with the sauce.
5. Meanwhile, prepare the rice using the package directions, omitting the salt and margarine. Spoon onto plates. Top with the chicken mixture. Sprinkle with the green onions.

PER SERVING
Calories **298**
Total Fat **4.0 g**
  Saturated Fat **0.5 g**
  Trans Fat **0.0 g**
  Polyunsaturated Fat **1.0 g**
  Monounsaturated Fat **1.0 g**

Cholesterol **73 mg**
Sodium **250 mg**
Carbohydrates **37 g**
  Fiber **4 g**
  Sugars **10 g**
Protein **28 g**

Dietary Exchanges:
  1½ starch, ½ fruit, 1 vegetable, 3 very lean meat

Curry-Rubbed Chicken

A medley of spices gives this dish so much over-the-top flavor that you'll never miss the salt shaker.

1. Put the apricots and onion in the slow cooker. Set aside.
2. In a small bowl, stir together the curry powder, ginger, cinnamon, cumin, and cayenne. Sprinkle over both sides of the chicken. Using your fingertips, gently press the seasonings so they adhere to the chicken. Place the chicken on the apricot mixture. Don't stir.
3. In the same small bowl, whisk together the tomato sauce, orange juice, and honey. Pour over the chicken. Don't stir. Cook, covered, on low for 4 to 5 hours or on high for 2½ to 3 hours, or until the chicken is no longer pink in the center.
4. About 10 minutes before serving time, prepare the couscous using the package directions, omitting the salt. Spoon the chicken and sauce over the couscous. Sprinkle with the parsley.

COOK'S TIPS

To serve eight, double all the ingredients and add 1 hour to the cooking time if you're using the high setting or 2 hours for the low setting.

Cutting sticky foods To cut dried apricots or other sticky foods easily, use kitchen shears lightly sprayed with cooking spray.

SERVES 4; 3 ounces chicken, ⅓ cup sauce, and ½ cup couscous per serving

SLOW COOKER SIZE | SHAPE
3- to 4½-quart | round or oval

SLOW COOKING TIME
4 to 5 hours ON LOW (preferred), **OR**
2½ to 3 hours ON HIGH

¼ cup chopped dried apricots

¼ cup finely chopped onion

½ teaspoon curry powder

½ teaspoon ground ginger

¼ teaspoon ground cinnamon

¼ teaspoon ground cumin

⅛ teaspoon cayenne

2 boneless, skinless chicken breasts (about 8 ounces each), all visible fat discarded, halved

1 8-ounce can no-salt-added tomato sauce

¼ cup fresh orange juice

1 tablespoon honey

——— + ———

1 cup uncooked whole-wheat couscous

¼ cup snipped fresh parsley

PER SERVING
Calories **362**
Total Fat **4.0 g**
  Saturated Fat **0.5 g**
  Trans Fat **0.0 g**
  Polyunsaturated Fat **0.5 g**
  Monounsaturated Fat **1.0 g**
Cholesterol **73 mg**
Sodium **147 mg**
Carbohydrates **53 g**
  Fiber **6 g**
  Sugars **14 g**
Protein **31 g**

Dietary Exchanges:
2½ starch, ½ fruit, 1 vegetable, 3 very lean meat

SERVES 6; 3 ounces chicken and ½ cup bell pepper mixture per serving

SLOW COOKER SIZE | SHAPE
3- to 4½-quart | round or oval

SLOW COOKING TIME
3 to 5 hours ON LOW (preferred), **OR**
1½ to 2½ hours ON HIGH

¼ teaspoon salt

¼ teaspoon pepper

6 boneless, skinless chicken breast halves (about 4 ounces each), all visible fat discarded

2 teaspoons olive oil

1 large onion, halved, then sliced

3 large garlic cloves, minced

3 medium bell peppers, each a different color, cut lengthwise into ½-inch strips

1 tablespoon finely chopped fresh rosemary

Rosemary Chicken with Bell Peppers

Chicken breasts cook in a colorful mélange of bell peppers seasoned with fresh rosemary. Steam some fresh broccoli and toss a salad to serve alongside.

1. Sprinkle the salt and pepper over both sides of the chicken. Using your fingertips, gently press the seasonings so they adhere to the chicken.
2. In a large nonstick skillet, heat the oil over medium-high heat, swirling to coat the bottom. Cook the chicken for 3 to 5 minutes on each side, or until browned. Transfer the chicken to a large plate. Set aside.
3. In the same skillet, cook the onion for 3 minutes, or until beginning to soften, stirring frequently. Stir in the garlic. Cook for 30 seconds, stirring constantly. Transfer to the slow cooker. Stir in the bell peppers.
4. Arrange the chicken on the onion mixture. Don't stir. Sprinkle with the rosemary. Cook, covered, on low for 3 to 5 hours or on high for 1½ to 2½ hours, or until the chicken is no longer pink in the center. Serve the chicken topped with the bell pepper mixture. Spoon the cooking liquid over all.

PER SERVING
Calories **167**
Total Fat **4.5 g**
    Saturated Fat **1.0 g**
    Trans Fat **0.0 g**
    Polyunsaturated Fat **0.5 g**
    Monounsaturated Fat **2.0 g**

Cholesterol **73 mg**
Sodium **232 mg**
Carbohydrates **6 g**
    Fiber **2 g**
    Sugars **3 g**
Protein **25 g**

Dietary Exchanges:
    1 vegetable, 3 lean meat

Chicken, Mushrooms, and Pearl Onions in Red Wine

Impressive enough to serve for the holidays but easy to prepare, this dish is inspired by the French classic *coq au vin*. Add *haricots verts* (or even regular green beans) and fingerling potatoes as side dishes.

SERVES 6; 3 ounces chicken and ¾ cup vegetables per serving

SLOW COOKER SIZE | SHAPE
3- to 4½-quart | round or oval

SLOW COOKING TIME
4 to 6 hours ON LOW

1. In a large nonstick skillet, heat 1 teaspoon oil over medium-high heat, swirling to coat the bottom. Cook the mushrooms for 4 minutes, or until browned, stirring frequently. Stir in the garlic. Cook for 30 seconds, stirring constantly. Transfer to the slow cooker.

2. Stir in the onions and tomatoes. Sprinkle the tapioca over all. Add the bay leaf. Set aside.

3. In the same skillet, heat the remaining 1 teaspoon oil, still over medium-high heat, swirling to coat the bottom. Cook the chicken for 3 to 5 minutes on each side, or until browned. Place the chicken on the mushroom mixture. Don't stir.

4. In a small bowl, whisk together the remaining ingredients. Pour over the chicken. Don't stir. Cook, covered, on low for 4 to 6 hours, or until the chicken is no longer pink in the center. Discard the bay leaf. Transfer the chicken to plates. Spoon the mushroom mixture and sauce on top.

1 teaspoon olive oil and 1 teaspoon olive oil, divided use

12 ounces medium button mushrooms, quartered

3 medium garlic cloves, minced

16 ounces frozen pearl onions, thawed

4 medium Italian plum (Roma) tomatoes, seeded and chopped

2 tablespoons uncooked instant, or quick-cooking, tapioca

1 medium dried bay leaf

6 boneless, skinless chicken breast halves (about 4 ounces each), all visible fat discarded

½ cup fat-free, low-sodium chicken broth, such as on page 48

½ cup dry red wine (regular or nonalcoholic)

¼ cup no-salt-added tomato paste

2 tablespoons snipped fresh parsley

1½ teaspoons dried thyme, crumbled

¼ teaspoon salt

¼ teaspoon pepper

PER SERVING
Calories **255**
Total Fat **5.0 g**
  Saturated Fat **1.0 g**
  Trans Fat **0.0 g**
  Polyunsaturated Fat **1.0 g**
  Monounsaturated Fat **2.0 g**

Cholesterol **73 mg**
Sodium **258 mg**
Carbohydrates **21 g**
  Fiber **2 g**
  Sugars **7 g**
Protein **28 g**

Dietary Exchanges:
  4 vegetable, 3 lean meat

SERVES 4; 3 ounces chicken
and 1 cup vegetable
mixture per serving

SLOW COOKER SIZE | SHAPE
4- to 6-quart | round or
oval

SLOW COOKING TIME

7 to 8 hours ON LOW
(preferred), **OR**

3½ to 4 hours ON HIGH

2 small sweet potatoes
(about 1 pound total),
cut into 1-inch cubes

1 cup chopped onion

1 15.5-ounce can no-salt-
added black beans,
rinsed and drained

4 boneless, skinless
chicken breast halves
(about 4 ounces each),
all visible fat discarded

1 cup fat-free, low-sodium
chicken broth, such as
on page 48

½ cup mild salsa (lowest
sodium available)

3 tablespoons chopped
chipotle peppers canned
in adobo sauce

1 tablespoon uncooked
instant, or quick-
cooking, tapioca

1 teaspoon smoked paprika

1 teaspoon garlic powder

½ teaspoon pepper

½ teaspoon ground allspice

⅛ teaspoon salt

———— + ————

¼ cup snipped fresh
cilantro

1 medium lime, cut into
4 wedges

Chicken with Black Beans and Sweet Potatoes

The rich depth of flavor in this stewlike chicken dish comes largely from chipotle peppers in adobo sauce and from smoked paprika. The result is south-of-the-border comfort food at its best.

1. In the slow cooker, make one layer each, in order, of the sweet potatoes, onion, and beans. Place the chicken on top.
2. In a small bowl, whisk together the broth, salsa, chipotle peppers, tapioca, paprika, garlic powder, pepper, allspice, and salt. Pour over the chicken. Don't stir. Cook, covered, on low for 7 to 8 hours or on high for 3½ to 4 hours, or until the chicken is no longer pink in the center. Ladle onto plates. Sprinkle with the cilantro. Serve with the lime wedges to squeeze over all.

PER SERVING
Calories **375**
Total Fat **3.5 g**
  Saturated Fat **0.5 g**
  Trans Fat **0.0 g**
  Polyunsaturated Fat **0.5 g**
  Monounsaturated Fat **1.0 g**

Cholesterol **73 mg**
Sodium **548 mg**
Carbohydrates **50 g**
  Fiber **9 g**
  Sugars **11 g**
  Protein **33 g**

Dietary Exchanges:
  **3 starch, 1 vegetable,
  3½ lean meat**

Chicken and Tomato Stew with Kalamata Olives

Ingredients popular all around the Mediterranean Sea shine in this vibrant stew. Serve it in bowls so you can scrape up every drop of the wonderful sauce.

1. Lightly spray the slow cooker with cooking spray. Put the chicken and tomatoes in the slow cooker.
2. In a small bowl, whisk together the wine, tomato paste, garlic powder, and red pepper flakes until smooth. Pour over the chicken mixture. Don't stir. Cook, covered, on low for $3\frac{1}{2}$ to 4 hours or on high for 1 hour 45 minutes to 2 hours, or until the chicken is no longer pink in the center.
3. About 20 minutes before serving time, prepare the pasta using the package directions, omitting the salt. Drain well in a colander.
4. When the chicken is ready, leave it in the slow cooker and coarsely shred using one or two forks.
5. Stir the spinach, olives, oregano, oil, and salt into the shredded chicken. Ladle over the pasta.

SERVES 4; 1 slightly heaping cup per serving

SLOW COOKER SIZE | SHAPE
3- to $4\frac{1}{2}$-quart | round or oval

SLOW COOKING TIME
$3\frac{1}{2}$ to 4 hours ON LOW (preferred), **OR**
1 hour 45 minutes to 2 hours ON HIGH

Cooking spray

1 pound boneless, skinless chicken breasts, all visible fat discarded

4 medium tomatoes, chopped

$\frac{1}{2}$ cup dry white wine (regular or nonalcoholic)

$\frac{1}{4}$ cup no-salt-added tomato paste

$\frac{1}{2}$ teaspoon garlic powder

$\frac{1}{4}$ teaspoon crushed red pepper flakes

———— + ————

3 ounces whole-grain egg noodles or whole-grain linguine, broken into thirds if using linguine

2 ounces (about 2 cups) fresh spinach, coarsely chopped

16 kalamata olives, coarsely chopped

3 tablespoons chopped fresh oregano

$1\frac{1}{2}$ tablespoons olive oil (extra virgin preferred)

$\frac{1}{8}$ teaspoon salt

PER SERVING
Calories **356**
Total Fat **13.0 g**
  Saturated Fat **2.0 g**
  Trans Fat **0.0 g**
  Polyunsaturated Fat **2.0 g**
  Monounsaturated Fat **8.0 g**

Cholesterol **73 mg**
Sodium **478 mg**
Carbohydrates **26 g**
  Fiber **5 g**
  Sugars **6 g**
Protein **29 g**

Dietary Exchanges:
1 starch, 2 vegetable, 3 lean meat, $\frac{1}{2}$ **fat**

SERVES 4; 1½ cups per serving

SLOW COOKER SIZE | SHAPE
3- to 4½-quart | round or oval

SLOW COOKING TIME
4 to 6 hours ON LOW plus 45 minutes ON LOW, **OR**

2½ to 3 hours ON HIGH plus 30 minutes ON HIGH

1 cup thinly sliced onion

1 cup thinly sliced red bell pepper

1 cup thinly sliced yellow bell pepper

1 pound boneless, skinless chicken breasts, all visible fat discarded

1 cup fat-free, low-sodium chicken broth, such as on page 48

½ cup lite coconut milk

4 medium green onions, sliced into 1-inch pieces

2 tablespoons soy sauce (lowest sodium available)

1 tablespoon dark brown sugar

1 teaspoon grated lime zest

1 tablespoon lime juice

2 teaspoons crushed red pepper flakes

2 teaspoons fish sauce (lowest sodium available)

2 medium garlic cloves, minced

1 teaspoon minced peeled gingerroot

— + —

4 ounces dried medium Asian rice stick noodles

¼ cup unsalted chopped peanuts, dry-roasted

¼ cup chopped cilantro

1 lime, cut into 4 wedges

Pad Thai with Chicken

With its contrasting sweet and sour flavors, pad thai is Thailand's most popular noodle dish. It began as a stir-fried street food. Slow cooking makes the chicken tender and easy to shred and allows the rice noodles to soak up the citrusy broth.

1. In the slow cooker, make one layer each, in order, of the onion and bell peppers. Place the chicken on the bell peppers. In a medium bowl, stir together the broth, coconut milk, green onions, soy sauce, brown sugar, lime zest, lime juice, red pepper flakes, fish sauce, garlic, and gingerroot. Pour the broth mixture into the slow cooker. Cook, covered, on low for 4 to 6 hours or on high for 2½ to 3 hours.

2. Quickly transfer the chicken to a cutting board. Re-cover the slow cooker. Using two forks, shred the chicken. Or thinly slice it if desired. Return the chicken to the slow cooker, quickly stir in the noodles, and re-cover the slow cooker.

3. Cook for 45 minutes on low or 30 minutes on high, or until the noodles are tender.

4. To serve, spoon the pad thai into shallow bowls. Sprinkle the peanuts and cilantro over each serving. Garnish with the lime wedges.

PER SERVING
Calories **375**
Total Fat **9.5 g**
  Saturated Fat **2.5 g**
  Trans Fat **0.0 g**
  Polyunsaturated Fat **2.0 g**
  Monounsaturated Fat **3.0 g**

Cholesterol **73 mg**
Sodium **550 mg**
Carbohydrates **41 g**
  Fiber **4 g**
  Sugars **10 g**
Protein **30 g**

Dietary Exchanges:
  2 starch, 2 vegetable, 3 lean meat

SERVES 4; 2 drumsticks,
⅓ cup sauce, and ½ cup
rice per serving

SLOW COOKER SIZE | SHAPE
3- to 4½-quart | round
or oval

SLOW COOKING TIME
6 hours ON LOW, **OR**
3 hours ON HIGH

Cooking spray

8 chicken drumsticks
(about 5 ounces each),
skin and all visible fat
discarded

1 8-ounce can no-salt-
added tomato sauce

1 tablespoon mild
Louisiana-style hot-
pepper sauce (lowest
sodium available)

2 teaspoons Worcestershire
sauce (lowest sodium
available)

1½ teaspoons dried
oregano, crumbled

1 teaspoon dried thyme,
crumbled

½ teaspoon garlic powder

¼ teaspoon salt

—————— + ——————

10 ounces frozen brown
rice

Cajun-Sauced Drumsticks

Take a break from chicken breasts and serve up some "Cajun comfort" with these drumsticks and their slightly spicy tomato sauce. This dish uses one of the milder versions of hot-pepper sauce, providing flavor rather than heat.

1. Lightly spray the slow cooker with cooking spray. Put the chicken in the slow cooker.
2. In a small bowl, stir together the remaining ingredients except the rice. Pour over the chicken. Cook, covered, on low for 6 hours or on high for 3 hours, or until the chicken is no longer pink in the center. Be careful not to overcook.
3. About 5 minutes before serving time, prepare the rice using the package directions. Serve the chicken and sauce over the rice.

COOK'S TIP

To remove the skin from the poultry easily, use paper towels. The towels let you get a firmer grip on the skin and keep your fingers from slipping.

PER SERVING
Calories **308**
Total Fat **7.5 g**
  Saturated Fat **1.5 g**
  Trans Fat **0.0 g**
  Polyunsaturated Fat **1.5 g**
  Monounsaturated Fat **2.0 g**

Cholesterol **108 mg**
Sodium **292 mg**
Carbohydrates **22 g**
  Fiber **2 g**
  Sugars **3 g**
Protein **36 g**

Dietary Exchanges:
  **1 starch, 1 vegetable,
4 lean meat**

Chicken Cacciatore

Although you can use any whole-grain pasta you prefer in this Italian classic, we recommend ribbons of fettuccine to support the thick, chunky sauce.

1. In the slow cooker, stir together the mushrooms, tomatoes with liquid, onion, celery, carrot, broth, garlic, Italian seasoning, salt, pepper, and bay leaf. Add the chicken thighs, spooning the sauce over them. Cook, covered, on low for 6 to 7 hours or on high for 3 to 3½ hours, or until the chicken is no longer pink in the center and the vegetables are tender.

2. If using the low setting, change it to high. Quickly stir in the tomato paste and vinegar and re-cover the slow cooker. Cook for 15 minutes. Discard the bay leaf.

3. Meanwhile, prepare the pasta using the package directions, omitting the salt. Drain well in a colander. Serve the chicken mixture over the pasta. Sprinkle with the basil.

SERVES 6; 3 ounces chicken, ½ cup sauce, and ⅔ cup pasta per serving

SLOW COOKER SIZE | SHAPE
3- to 4½-quart | round or oval

SLOW COOKING TIME
6 to 7 hours ON LOW plus 15 minutes ON HIGH, **OR**
3 to 3½ hours ON HIGH plus 15 minutes ON HIGH

6 ounces medium button mushrooms, quartered (about 2 cups)

1 14.5-ounce can no-salt-added diced tomatoes, undrained

1 medium onion, chopped

1 medium rib of celery, sliced

1 medium carrot, chopped

½ cup fat-free, low-sodium chicken broth, such as on page 48, or water

2 medium garlic cloves, minced

1 teaspoon dried Italian seasoning, crumbled

¼ teaspoon salt

¼ teaspoon pepper

1 medium dried bay leaf

6 boneless, skinless chicken thighs (about 4 ounces each), all visible fat discarded

———— + ————

1 6-ounce can no-salt-added tomato paste

1 tablespoon balsamic vinegar

6 ounces dried whole-grain fettuccine

¼ cup shredded fresh basil

PER SERVING
Calories **338**
Total Fat **9.5 g**
  Saturated Fat **2.5 g**
  Trans Fat **0.0 g**
  Polyunsaturated Fat **2.5 g**
  Monounsaturated Fat **3.5 g**

Cholesterol **74 mg**
Sodium **225 mg**
Carbohydrates **36 g**
  Fiber **6 g**
  Sugars **11 g**
Protein **28 g**

Dietary Exchanges:
  1½ starch, 3 vegetable, 3 lean meat

SERVES 4; 2 tacos per serving

SLOW COOKER SIZE | SHAPE
3- to 4½-quart | round or oval

SLOW COOKING TIME
4 to 6 hours ON LOW, **OR**
2 to 3 hours ON HIGH

1 tablespoon chili powder

1 tablespoon ground cumin

½ teaspoon salt

⅛ teaspoon cayenne, or more to taste

1 pound boneless, skinless chicken thighs, all visible fat discarded, cut into 1-inch cubes

2 teaspoons canola or corn oil

1 medium onion, chopped

2 medium garlic cloves, minced

½ cup strong brewed coffee

1 14.5-ounce can no-salt-added diced tomatoes, drained

1 large red bell pepper, chopped

2 tablespoons no-salt-added tomato paste

1 tablespoon unsweetened cocoa powder

1 teaspoon dried oregano, crumbled

+

2 tablespoons fresh lime juice

½ teaspoon honey

8 6-inch corn tortillas

2 medium radishes, thinly sliced

2 medium green onions, thinly sliced

¼ cup chopped fresh cilantro

2 medium limes, cut into 4 wedges each

Mole Chicken Tacos

When making mole sauce from scratch, the cook often spends hours toasting and grinding spices and chiles. Mole sauce, which comes in a variety of colors and flavors, most often contains onions and garlic, chiles, nuts or seeds, spices, dried fruit, and some Mexican chocolate. These tacos offer authentic mole flavor, but with minimal work.

1. In a small bowl, stir together the chili powder, cumin, salt, and cayenne.
2. Place the chicken in a medium bowl. Sprinkle half the chili powder mixture over the chicken. Stir to coat. Set the remaining chili powder mixture aside.
3. In a large skillet, heat the oil over medium-high heat, swirling to coat the bottom. Cook the chicken for 5 minutes, or until browned on all sides, stirring frequently. Transfer to the slow cooker.
4. Reduce the heat to medium. In the same skillet, cook the onion for 3 minutes, or until almost soft, stirring frequently. Stir in the garlic. Cook for 1 minute, or until fragrant, stirring constantly. Stir in the coffee. Cook for 2 minutes, or until the mixture comes to a boil, scraping to dislodge any browned bits. Transfer the onion mixture to the slow cooker. Stir in the tomatoes, bell pepper, tomato paste, cocoa powder, and oregano.
5. Cook, covered, on low for 4 to 6 hours or on high for 2 to 3 hours, or until the chicken is no longer pink in the center. Stir in the lime juice, honey, and the remaining chili powder mixture.
6. About 10 minutes before the chicken mixture has finished cooking, warm the tortillas using the package directions. Transfer to plates. Using a slotted spoon, transfer the chicken mixture to the centers of the tortillas. Top with the radishes, green onions, and cilantro. Serve with the lime wedges.

PER SERVING
Calories **307**
Total Fat **10.5 g**
　Saturated Fat **2.0 g**
　Trans Fat **0.0 g**
　Polyunsaturated Fat **2.5 g**
　Monounsaturated Fat **4.5 g**

Cholesterol **106 mg**
Sodium **464 mg**
Carbohydrates **31 g**
　Fiber **6 g**
　Sugars **10 g**
Protein **23 g**

Dietary Exchanges:
　1 starch, 3 vegetable, 3 lean meat

Chicken Sofrito

Sofrito has its origins in Latin America and always includes the "holy trinity" of tomatoes, bell peppers, and garlic that are slowly simmered to create a hearty sauce.

SERVES 4; 1 chicken thigh, ½ cup rice, and generous ½ cup vegetables and sauce per serving

SLOW COOKER SIZE | SHAPE
3- to 4½-quart | round or oval

SLOW COOKING TIME
4 to 6 hours ON LOW, OR
2 to 3 hours ON HIGH

1. In a small bowl, stir together the paprika, salt, pepper, and cayenne. Place the chicken on a large plate. Sprinkle half the paprika mixture over both sides of the chicken. Using your fingertips, gently press the mixture so it adheres to the chicken. Set the remaining paprika mixture aside.

2. In a large skillet, heat the oil over medium-high heat, swirling to coat the bottom. Cook the chicken for 5 minutes, or until browned on all sides, stirring frequently. Transfer to the slow cooker.

3. Reduce the heat to medium. In the same skillet, cook the onion and bell pepper for 3 minutes, or until the onion is soft and the bell pepper is tender, stirring frequently. Stir in the garlic. Cook for 1 minute, or until fragrant, stirring constantly. Transfer the onion mixture to the slow cooker. Stir in the tomatoes and tomato paste.

4. Cook, covered, on low for 4 to 6 hours or on high for 2 to 3 hours, or until the chicken is no longer pink in the center.

5. About 5 minutes before serving time, prepare the rice using package directions, omitting the salt and margarine. Transfer the rice to plates. Place the chicken on the rice.

6. Stir the lemon juice and the remaining paprika mixture into the cooking liquid in the slow cooker. Spoon the sauce over the chicken and rice. Sprinkle with the cilantro.

1 teaspoon paprika

½ teaspoon salt

¼ teaspoon pepper

⅛ teaspoon cayenne

1 pound boneless, skinless chicken thighs, all visible fat discarded

2 teaspoons canola or corn oil

1 medium onion, chopped

1 medium red bell pepper, chopped

2 medium garlic cloves, minced

1 14.5-ounce can no-salt-added diced tomatoes, drained

2 tablespoons no-salt-added tomato paste

———— + ————

10 ounces frozen brown rice

1 tablespoon fresh lemon juice

¼ cup chopped fresh cilantro

COOK'S TIP

Spoon leftover tomato paste into the sections of an ice cube tray and freeze. Transfer the frozen cubes to a resealable plastic bag and return to the freezer.

PER SERVING
Calories **294**
Total Fat **9.5 g**
  Saturated Fat **2.0 g**
  Trans Fat **0.0 g**
  Polyunsaturated Fat **2.0 g**
  Monounsaturated Fat **4.0 g**

Cholesterol **106 mg**
Sodium **382 mg**
Carbohydrates **29 g**
  Fiber **4 g**
  Sugars **8 g**
Protein **23 g**

Dietary Exchanges:
  1 starch, 2 vegetable, 2½ lean meat

SERVES 15; 3 ounces turkey and 2 tablespoons gravy per serving

SLOW COOKER SIZE | SHAPE
5- to 7-quart | oval

SLOW COOKING TIME
8 to 10 hours ON LOW, **OR**
5 to 6 hours ON HIGH

1 teaspoon dried sage

½ teaspoon salt

¼ teaspoon pepper

1 5½-pound whole bone-in turkey breast, skin and all visible fat discarded

¼ cup fat-free, low-sodium chicken broth, such as on page 48

———— + ————

¾ to 1 cup fat-free, low-sodium chicken broth, such as on page 48

¼ cup all-purpose flour

¼ cup cold water

¼ teaspoon dried sage

¼ teaspoon salt

¼ teaspoon pepper

Turkey Breast with Gravy

If you're intimidated by the prospect of roasting a whole turkey, this recipe offers a delicious and easy option: slow cook a whole breast.

1. In a small bowl, stir together 1 teaspoon sage, ½ teaspoon salt, and ¼ teaspoon pepper. Sprinkle all over the turkey. Using your fingertips, gently press the seasonings so they adhere to the turkey.

2. Pour ¼ cup broth into the slow cooker. Add the turkey. Cook, covered, on low for 8 to 10 hours or on high for 5 to 6 hours, or until the thickest part of the breast registers 160°F on an instant-read thermometer. Transfer the turkey to a cutting board. Cover loosely. Let stand for 10 to 15 minutes to finish cooking (it should reach a minimum of 165°F) before slicing.

3. Pour the cooking liquid through a strainer into a 2-cup glass measuring cup, discarding any solids. Pour in enough of the remaining ¾ to 1 cup broth to make 2 cups of liquid. Pour into a medium saucepan. Set aside.

4. Put the flour in a small bowl. Pour in the water, whisking to dissolve. Whisk the flour mixture, remaining ¼ teaspoon sage, remaining ¼ teaspoon salt, and remaining ¼ teaspoon pepper into the broth mixture. Cook over medium-high heat for 3 minutes, or until the gravy comes to a boil and thickens, whisking frequently. Serve with the turkey.

PER SERVING
Calories **155**
Total Fat **1.0 g**
　Saturated Fat **0.5 g**
　Trans Fat **0.0 g**
　Polyunsaturated Fat **0.0 g**
　Monounsaturated Fat **0.0 g**

Cholesterol **82 mg**
Sodium **185 mg**
Carbohydrates **2 g**
　Fiber **0 g**
　Sugars **0 g**
　Protein **33 g**

Dietary Exchanges:
3 lean meat

Barbecue-Spiced Turkey Breast

There's no need to fire up the barbecue grill when you can turn to this recipe instead. Smoky paprika and chili, garlic, and onion powders add the taste of the grill without the fuss. Serve with corn on the cob or a refreshing salad of cucumber and tomatoes.

FAST PREP!

SERVES 6; 3 ounces turkey per serving

SLOW COOKER SIZE | SHAPE
3- to 3½-quart | round or oval (preferred)

SLOW COOKING TIME
6 to 8 hours ON LOW, **OR**
3 to 4 hours ON HIGH

1. In a small bowl, stir together all the ingredients except the turkey. Sprinkle all over the turkey. Using your fingertips, gently press the seasonings so they adhere to the turkey. Transfer with the meaty side up to the slow cooker.

2. Cook, covered, on low for 6 to 8 hours or on high for 3 to 4 hours, or until the thickest part of the breast registers 160°F on an instant-read thermometer.

3. Transfer the turkey to a cutting board. Cover loosely. Let stand for 10 to 15 minutes to finish cooking (it should reach a minimum of 165°F) before slicing. Serve with the cooking juices if desired.

2 teaspoons smoked paprika

1 teaspoon paprika

1 teaspoon dried sage

1 teaspoon firmly packed light or dark brown sugar

½ teaspoon chili powder

½ teaspoon garlic powder

½ teaspoon onion powder

½ teaspoon pepper

1 bone-in turkey breast half (about 2 pounds), skin and all visible fat discarded

COOK'S TIP

The USDA recommends cooking turkey (whole, pieces, or ground) to a minimum of 165°F (at the end of any standing time). If you prefer to cook your turkey a bit more, up to about 175°F, adjust the time and temperature accordingly.

PER SERVING
Calories **142**
Total Fat **1.0 g**
　Saturated Fat **0.5 g**
　Trans Fat **0.0 g**
　Polyunsaturated Fat **0.5 g**
　Monounsaturated Fat **0.0 g**

Cholesterol **74 mg**
Sodium **64 mg**
Carbohydrates **2 g**
　Fiber **1 g**
　Sugars **1 g**
Protein **30 g**

Dietary Exchanges:
　4 lean meat

SLOW COOKER SIZE | SHAPE
3- to 4½-quart | round or oval (preferred)

SLOW COOKING TIME
4 hours ON LOW, **OR**
2 hours ON HIGH

Cooking spray

12 ounces ground skinless turkey breast

1 3.5-ounce sweet Italian turkey breakfast sausage link, casing discarded

½ medium red or orange bell pepper, chopped

½ cup snipped fresh parsley

2 large egg whites

⅓ cup uncooked quick-cooking oatmeal

¾ teaspoon dried sage

½ teaspoon dried thyme, crumbled

¼ teaspoon dried fennel seeds, crushed

Paprika to taste

———— + ————

1 tablespoon olive oil

1 tablespoon all-purpose flour

¾ cup fat-free milk

1 packet (1 teaspoon) salt-free chicken bouillon

⅛ teaspoon salt

Turkey Meat Loaf with Creamy Chicken Gravy

Seasoned with a bit of turkey sausage and fresh sage, this loaf is comfort food at its best.

1. Lightly spray the slow cooker with cooking spray.
2. In a large bowl, using your hands or a spoon, combine the turkey, sausage, bell pepper, parsley, egg whites, oatmeal, sage, thyme, and fennel seeds. Transfer the mixture to the slow cooker. Depending on the shape of your slow cooker, shape into an oval or round loaf that is 2 inches thick, leaving a ½-inch border between it and the side of the crock. Sprinkle with the paprika. Cook, covered, on low for 4 hours or on high for 2 hours, or until the meat loaf registers 160°F on an instant-read thermometer and is no longer pink in the center.
3. Using a flat spatula, transfer the meat loaf to a cutting board. Let stand for 5 minutes to finish cooking (it should reach a minimum of 165°F) before slicing or cutting into wedges.
4. While the meat loaf stands, in a medium nonstick skillet, heat the oil over medium heat, swirling to coat the bottom. Whisk in the flour. Cook for 1 minute, whisking constantly. Gradually whisk in the milk, bouillon, and salt. Cook for 4 minutes, or until thickened and reduced to ½ cup. Serve over the meat loaf.

COOK'S TIP

Leaving space between the meat loaf and the side of the crock helps the meat loaf retain its shape and makes it easier to remove the loaf from the slow cooker.

PER SERVING
Calories **252**
Total Fat **9.0 g**
  Saturated Fat **1.5 g**
  Trans Fat **0.0 g**
  Polyunsaturated Fat **2.0 g**
  Monounsaturated Fat **4.0 g**
Cholesterol **93 mg**
Sodium **312 mg**
Carbohydrates **11 g**
  Fiber **2 g**
  Sugars **3 g**
  Protein **30 g**
Dietary Exchanges:
  ½ **starch, 4 lean meat**

Turkey and Sweet Potato Stew

Classic fall ingredients—sweet potatoes and turkey—are highlighted in this stew. The seasonings add a hint of heat to help chase away the chill of a cool evening.

1. In the slow cooker, stir together the turkey, broth, carrots, onion, sweet potatoes, garlic, cumin, curry powder, ginger, and pepper. Cook, covered, on low for 5 to 6 hours or on high for 2½ to 3 hours.

2. Put the flour in a small bowl. Pour in the water, whisking to dissolve. Quickly whisk into the stew and re-cover the slow cooker. If using the low setting, change it to high. Cook for 30 minutes.

COOK'S TIP

Sweet potatoes cook a little more quickly in the slow cooker than carrots do, so this recipe calls for cutting the sweet potatoes into larger cubes and slicing the carrots more thinly to even out the cooking times.

PER SERVING
Calories **314**
Total Fat **1.0 g**
  Saturated Fat **0.5 g**
  Trans Fat **0.0 g**
  Polyunsaturated Fat **0.5 g**
  Monounsaturated Fat **0.0 g**
Cholesterol **70 mg**
Sodium **210 mg**
Carbohydrates **42 g**
  Fiber **8 g**
  Sugars **14 g**
Protein **33 g**

Dietary Exchanges:
2 starch, 3 vegetable, 3 lean meat

FAST PREP!

SERVES 4; 1½ cups per serving

SLOW COOKER SIZE | SHAPE
3- to 4½-quart | round or oval

SLOW COOKING TIME
5 to 6 hours ON LOW plus 30 minutes ON HIGH, **OR**
2½ to 3 hours ON HIGH plus 30 minutes ON HIGH

1 1-pound turkey tenderloin, all visible fat discarded, cut into 1-inch cubes

1¾ cups fat-free, low-sodium chicken broth, such as on page 48

4 medium carrots, cut crosswise into medium slices

1 large Vidalia, Maui, Oso Sweet, or other sweet onion, coarsely chopped

2 medium sweet potatoes (10 to 11 ounces each), peeled and cut into 1-inch cubes

1 tablespoon dried minced garlic

1 teaspoon ground cumin

½ teaspoon curry powder

¼ teaspoon ground ginger

¼ teaspoon pepper

———— + ————

2 tablespoons all-purpose flour

2 tablespoons cold water

Pulled Turkey Tostadas with Cucumber Guacamole

Turkey breast slow cooked in salsa and then shredded partners with more salsa and guacamole to top crisp tortillas. Cucumber adds a pleasing crunch to traditional guacamole.

SERVES 6; 1 tostada per serving

SLOW COOKER SIZE | SHAPE
3- to 3½-quart | round or oval (preferred)

SLOW COOKING TIME
5 to 8 hours ON LOW, **OR**
2½ to 4 hours ON HIGH

1. In a medium or large nonstick skillet, heat the oil over medium-high heat, swirling to coat the bottom. Cook the turkey for 5 to 7 minutes, or until browned, turning once halfway through. Transfer with the meaty side up to the slow cooker. Set aside.

2. Meanwhile, for the salsa, in a small bowl, stir together the tomatoes, bell pepper, ½ cup onion, 1 teaspoon serrano pepper, and garlic. Stir in 1 tablespoon cilantro. Spoon 1 cup salsa into a small airtight container. Refrigerate until needed. Pour the remaining salsa over the turkey.

3. Cook the turkey, covered, on low for 5 to 8 hours or on high for 2½ to 4 hours, or until the thickest part of the breast registers about 155°F on an instant-read thermometer. Transfer the turkey to a cutting board, leaving the salsa in the slow cooker. Let stand for 15 minutes to continue cooking. The breast should reach a minimum of 165°F. Cut the turkey into ½-inch slices. Using your hands or two forks, pull the meat apart into long shreds. Transfer to a medium bowl.

4. Using a slotted spoon, transfer the solid salsa ingredients from the slow cooker to the bowl with the turkey, stirring to combine. Discard the liquid remaining in the slow cooker.

5. Meanwhile, preheat the oven to 425°F.

6. Arrange the tortillas in a single layer on a baking sheet. Lightly spray both sides of the tortillas with cooking spray. Bake the tortillas for 7 to 10 minutes, or until crisp and lightly browned on the edges. Transfer to a large plate to keep from overcooking. Set aside.

(recipe continues)

1 teaspoon olive oil

1 bone-in turkey breast half (about 2 pounds), skin and all visible fat discarded

2 cups chopped tomatoes

½ cup chopped green bell pepper

½ cup chopped onion

1 teaspoon chopped serrano pepper, seeds and ribs discarded

1 medium garlic clove, minced

1 tablespoon snipped fresh cilantro

— + —

6 6-inch corn tortillas

Cooking spray

½ medium avocado, chopped and mashed

⅓ cup finely chopped peeled cucumber

1 tablespoon chopped onion

1 tablespoon snipped fresh cilantro

½ teaspoon chopped serrano pepper, seeds and ribs discarded if desired

¼ cup plus 2 tablespoons fat-free sour cream (optional)

1 large lime, cut into 6 wedges (optional)

7. For the guacamole, in a medium bowl, stir together the avocado, cucumber, remaining 1 tablespoon onion, remaining 1 tablespoon cilantro, and remaining ½ teaspoon serrano pepper.
8. At serving time, spoon the turkey mixture over the tortillas. Top with the reserved 1 cup salsa and the guacamole. Spoon a dollop of sour cream on each tostada and serve with the lime wedges to squeeze over all.

COOK'S TIP

For crispier tortillas, arrange the tortillas on the baking sheet and let them stand for 30 minutes before baking. The edges of the tortillas will curl slightly as they begin to dry.

PER SERVING
Calories **219**
Total Fat **4.5 g**
 Saturated Fat **1.0 g**
 Trans Fat **0.0 g**
 Polyunsaturated Fat **1.0 g**
 Monounsaturated Fat **2.5 g**

Cholesterol **74 mg**
Sodium **87 mg**
Carbohydrates **13 g**
 Fiber **3 g**
 Sugars **3 g**
 Protein **31 g**

Dietary Exchanges:
 ½ **starch, 1 vegetable, 4 lean meat**

PER SERVING (with optional toppings)
Calories **234**
Total Fat **4.5 g**
 Saturated Fat **1.0 g**
 Trans Fat **0.0 g**
 Polyunsaturated Fat **1.0 g**
 Monounsaturated Fat **2.5 g**

Cholesterol **77 mg**
Sodium **99 mg**
Carbohydrates **15 g**
 Fiber **3 g**
 Sugars **4 g**
 Protein **32 g**

Dietary Exchanges:
 ½ **starch, 1 vegetable, 4 lean meat**

Turkey Cassoulet with Gremolata

Gremolata is a fresh seasoning mixture of parsley, garlic, and lemon zest. It adds color and brings a bright flavor to this hearty one-dish meal.

1. In the slow cooker, stir together the beans, bell pepper, leek, and broth. Set aside.
2. Sprinkle the thyme, salt, and pepper all over the turkey. Using your fingertips, gently press the seasonings so they adhere to the turkey.
3. In a large nonstick skillet, heat the oil over medium-high heat, swirling to coat the bottom. Cook the turkey for 2 minutes on each side, or until browned. Place on the bean mixture. Don't stir. Cook, covered, on low for 4 to 5 hours or on high for 2 to 2½ hours, or until the turkey is no longer pink in the center.
4. Just before serving time, in a small bowl, stir together the parsley, lemon zest, and garlic. Set the gremolata aside.
5. Using a slotted spoon, transfer the turkey and the bean mixture to plates. Discard the cooking liquid. Sprinkle the turkey and the bean mixture with the gremolata.

COOK'S TIP

If turkey breast "steaks" are available at your supermarket, you can substitute them for the tenderloin. You'll need four 4-ounce pieces.

SERVES 4; 3 ounces turkey and 1 cup beans and vegetables per serving

SLOW COOKER SIZE | SHAPE
3- to 4½-quart | round or oval

SLOW COOKING TIME
4 to 5 hours ON LOW, **OR**
2 to 2½ hours ON HIGH

1 15.5-ounce can no-salt-added cannellini beans, rinsed and drained

1 large red bell pepper, chopped

1 large leek (white and light green parts), sliced (about 1½ cups)

1 cup fat-free, low-sodium chicken broth, such as on page 48

1 teaspoon dried thyme, crumbled

¼ teaspoon salt

¼ teaspoon pepper

1 pound turkey tenderloin, all visible fat discarded, cut crosswise into 4 pieces

1 teaspoon olive oil

———— + ————

⅓ cup snipped fresh parsley

1 tablespoon grated lemon zest

2 or 3 medium garlic cloves, minced

PER SERVING
Calories **255**
Total Fat **3.0 g**
  Saturated Fat **0.5 g**
  Trans Fat **0.0 g**
  Polyunsaturated Fat **0.5 g**
  Monounsaturated Fat **1.0 g**

Cholesterol **70 mg**
Sodium **258 mg**
Carbohydrates **21 g**
  Fiber **6 g**
  Sugars **4 g**
  Protein **35 g**

Dietary Exchanges:
  1 starch, 1 vegetable, 4 lean meat

SERVES 4; 4 meatballs and ½ cup sauce per serving

SLOW COOKER SIZE | SHAPE
3- to 4½-quart | round or oval

SLOW COOKING TIME
8 to 10 hours ON LOW, **OR**
5 to 6 hours ON HIGH

1 pound ground skinless turkey breast

1 large egg white

¼ cup whole-wheat bread crumbs (lowest sodium available)

¼ cup minced onion and ¼ cup minced onion, divided use

½ medium fresh jalapeño, seeds and ribs discarded, minced

1 teaspoon chili powder and 1 teaspoon chili powder, divided use

½ teaspoon ground cumin and ½ teaspoon ground cumin, divided use

1 medium garlic clove, minced, and 1 medium garlic clove, minced, divided use

⅛ teaspoon salt and ⅛ teaspoon salt, divided use

2 teaspoons olive oil

1 14.5-ounce can no-salt-added diced tomatoes, undrained

1 8-ounce can no-salt-added tomato sauce

+

¼ cup snipped fresh cilantro

Southwestern Turkey Meatballs

These jalapeño-spiked meatballs are delicious on their own and over whole-grain spaghetti, brown rice, or whole-wheat couscous as well. Steamed broccoli or green beans make a colorful accompaniment.

1. In a medium bowl, using your hands or a spoon, combine the turkey, egg white, bread crumbs, ¼ cup onion, the jalapeño, 1 teaspoon chili powder, ½ teaspoon cumin, 1 garlic clove, and ⅛ teaspoon salt. Shape into 16 balls.

2. In a large nonstick skillet, heat the oil over medium-high heat, swirling to coat the bottom. Cook the meatballs for 6 minutes, or until lightly browned, turning frequently.

3. Meanwhile, in the slow cooker, stir together the tomatoes with liquid, tomato sauce, remaining ¼ cup onion, remaining 1 teaspoon chili powder, remaining ½ teaspoon cumin, remaining 1 garlic clove, and remaining ⅛ teaspoon salt. Set aside.

4. When the meatballs are ready, add to the sauce. Cook, covered, on low for 8 to 10 hours or on high for 5 to 6 hours. Just before serving, stir in the cilantro.

COOK'S TIP

When you have heels or leftover slices of bread, make bread crumbs. Put coarsely torn pieces of bread in the food processor and process until they reach the desired size and texture. Use right away for soft crumbs, or spread the pieces in a single layer on a plate and let stand overnight for dried crumbs. Freeze in airtight plastic freezer bags for up to two months.

PER SERVING
Calories **237**
Total Fat **3.5 g**
  Saturated Fat **0.5 g**
  Trans Fat **0.0 g**
  Polyunsaturated Fat **0.5 g**
  Monounsaturated Fat **2.0 g**

Cholesterol **70 mg**
Sodium **285 mg**
Carbohydrates **17 g**
  Fiber **3 g**
  Sugars **8 g**
  Protein **32 g**

Dietary Exchanges:
  ½ **starch, 2 vegetable, 3 lean meat**

Beer Barrel Turkey Chili

Heavily seasoned with chili powder, smoked paprika, cumin, and beer, this chili will satisfy poultry lovers—and even people who think chili has to be beefy. Use the leftover chili as a topping for baked potatoes or serve it over whole-grain no-yolk egg noodles or brown rice for an easy weeknight meal.

SERVES 4; 1¾ cups per serving

SLOW COOKER SIZE | SHAPE
3- to 4½-quart | round or oval

SLOW COOKING TIME
7½ to 8 hours ON LOW, **OR**
3 hours 45 minutes to 4 hours ON HIGH

1. Lightly spray the slow cooker with cooking spray. Set aside.
2. In a large skillet, heat 1 teaspoon oil over medium-high heat, swirling to coat the bottom. Cook the ground turkey and sausage for 3 minutes, or until no longer pink on the outside, stirring frequently. Transfer to the slow cooker.
3. Stir in the tomatoes with liquid, beer, onion, ketchup, chili powder, sugar, paprika, 2 teaspoons cumin, the oregano, garlic, and salt. Cook, covered, on low for 7½ to 8 hours or on high for 3 hours 45 minutes to 4 hours, or until the onion is very soft.
4. Stir in the remaining 1 tablespoon oil and 1 teaspoon cumin. Serve topped with the sour cream, cilantro, and green onions.

COOK'S TIP

Beer adds a richer flavor to chili and enhances the spices. The hops add bitterness, while the malt adds sweetness. The alcohol will evaporate during the cooking process. The darker the brew, the more flavor it will impart.

Cooking spray

1 teaspoon olive oil

8 ounces ground skinless turkey breast

4 ounces low-fat turkey breakfast sausage

1 14.5-ounce can no-salt-added diced tomatoes, undrained

12 ounces light beer (regular or nonalcoholic)

1 medium onion, chopped

3 tablespoons no-salt-added ketchup

3 tablespoons chili powder

1 tablespoon sugar

1 tablespoon smoked paprika

2 teaspoons ground cumin

1 teaspoon dried oregano, crumbled

2 medium garlic cloves, minced

½ teaspoon salt

——— + ———

1 tablespoon olive oil

1 teaspoon ground cumin

1 cup fat-free sour cream

½ cup snipped fresh cilantro

4 medium green onions, finely chopped

PER SERVING
Calories **350**
Total Fat **8.0 g**
  Saturated Fat **1.5 g**
  Trans Fat **0.0 g**
  Polyunsaturated Fat **1.5 g**
  Monounsaturated Fat **4.0 g**

Cholesterol **66 mg**
Sodium **565 mg**
Carbohydrates **38 g**
  Fiber **4 g**
  Sugars **16 g**
Protein **25 g**

Dietary Exchanges:
2 vegetable, 2 other carbohydrate, 3 lean meat

SERVES 4; 1 stuffed pepper
per serving

SLOW COOKER SIZE | SHAPE
3½- to 5-quart | round
or oval

SLOW COOKING TIME

5½ to 6 hours ON LOW, **OR**

2 hours 45 minutes to
3 hours ON HIGH

Cooking spray

1 8-ounce can no-salt-
added tomato sauce

1½ teaspoons minced
chipotle pepper canned
in adobo sauce

1 teaspoon sugar

½ teaspoon dry mustard

¼ teaspoon salt

8 ounces extra-lean ground
beef

1 small onion, diced

2 large egg whites

⅓ cup yellow cornmeal

1 3.5-ounce sweet Italian
turkey breakfast sausage
link, casing discarded

1 medium fresh jalapeño,
seeds and ribs
discarded, finely
chopped

1 teaspoon ground cumin

4 medium bell peppers, any
color or combination,
tops, seeds, and ribs
discarded

Hot Stuffed Peppers

Stuffed peppers became really popular in the 1950s, and variations
of the original have remained family favorites ever since. This version
uses a mixture of sweet Italian turkey breakfast sausage and ground
beef, flavored with jalapeño and chipotle peppers, cornmeal, and
cumin for a little taste of Mexico in every bite. Try a variety of bell
peppers for a more colorful dish.

1. Lightly spray the slow cooker with cooking spray. Set aside.
2. In a small bowl, stir together the tomato sauce, chipotle pepper,
   sugar, mustard, and salt.
3. In a large bowl, using your hands or a spoon, combine half the
   tomato sauce mixture with the remaining ingredients except the
   bell peppers. Stuff the peppers with the mixture.
4. Arrange the peppers in the slow cooker. Spoon the remaining
   tomato sauce mixture on top of the peppers. Cook, covered, on
   low for 5½ to 6 hours or on high for 2 hours 45 minutes to 3
   hours, or until the stuffing registers 160°F on an instant-read
   thermometer.
5. Turn off the slow cooker. Let the peppers stand, uncovered, for
   15 minutes so the stuffing continues to cook to the minimum
   safe temperature of 165°F. The cornmeal will thicken during
   the standing time, firming up the stuffing, and the flavors will
   blend more.

PER SERVING
Calories **253**
Total Fat **8.0 g**
  Saturated Fat **2.0 g**
  Trans Fat **0.0 g**
  Polyunsaturated Fat **1.5 g**
  Monounsaturated Fat **2.5 g**

Cholesterol **71 mg**
Sodium **398 mg**
Carbohydrates **25 g**
  Fiber **4 g**
  Sugars **9 g**
  Protein **21 g**

Dietary Exchanges:
  ½ **starch, 3 vegetable,
  2½ lean meat**

Peach-Glazed Cornish Hen for Two

A Cornish hen is an elegant entrée for two, and the slow cooker makes an easy job of cooking it to tender perfection. Seasoned with soy sauce, mustard, garlic, and ginger, this hen is finished with a quick peach glaze that has a hint of ginger. Serve it with fingerling potatoes and sautéed broccolini.

SERVES 2; ½ hen per serving

SLOW COOKER SIZE | SHAPE
1½- to 2½-quart | round or oval (preferred)

SLOW COOKING TIME
4 to 6 hours ON LOW, **OR**
2 to 3 hours ON HIGH

Cooking spray

2 teaspoons soy sauce (lowest sodium available)

1 teaspoon Dijon mustard

½ teaspoon garlic powder

¼ teaspoon ground ginger

1 24-ounce Cornish hen, halved lengthwise, all visible fat, tail, and giblets discarded

———— **+** ————

¼ cup all-fruit peach spread

¼ teaspoon plain rice vinegar

Dash of ground ginger

1. Lightly spray the slow cooker with cooking spray. Set aside.
2. In a small bowl, stir together the soy sauce, mustard, garlic powder, and ¼ teaspoon ginger. Spoon over both sides of the hen halves. Using your fingertips, gently rub the soy sauce mixture into the hen. Transfer with the breast side up to the slow cooker. Cook, covered, on low for 4 to 6 hours or on high for 2 to 3 hours, or until the thickest part of the breast registers 165°F on an instant-read thermometer. Discard the skin. Transfer the hen halves to plates, reserving the cooking liquid.
3. Pour the liquid into a medium saucepan. Bring to a boil over high heat. Boil for 1 to 2 minutes, or until reduced by half. Transfer to a small bowl.
4. Meanwhile, in a small microwaveable bowl, stir together the fruit spread, vinegar, and the remaining dash of ginger. Microwave on high for 30 to 50 seconds, or until the fruit spread is melted. Spoon the glaze over the hen halves. Serve with the cooking liquid.

COOK'S TIP

Ask the butcher to halve the Cornish hen lengthwise for you. Or you can cut it yourself. Place the hen with the breast side down on a cutting board. Using kitchen shears, start at the bottom near the thigh and cut on either side of the backbone up to the neck. Discard the backbone. Cut through the breastbone in the center of the hen to separate it into halves.

PER SERVING
Calories **260**
Total Fat **5.0 g**
  Saturated Fat **1.5 g**
  Trans Fat **0.0 g**
  Polyunsaturated Fat **1.0 g**
  Monounsaturated Fat **1.5 g**

Cholesterol **133 mg**
Sodium **281 mg**
Carbohydrates **22 g**
  Fiber **0 g**
  Sugars **16 g**
Protein **30 g**

Dietary Exchanges:
1½ other carbohydrate, 4 lean meat

Meats

161 Swiss Steak with Melting Tomatoes and Onions

163 Beef and Bell Pepper Gyros with Tzatziki Sauce

164 Brisket with Exotic-Mushroom and Onion Gravy

166 Cabernet-Simmered Beef Roast with Rosemary

168 Indonesian Beef with Couscous

169 Coffee Kettle Pot Roast

170 Beef Vindaloo

172 Sauerbraten

173 Flank Steak Fajitas

174 Asian Lettuce Wraps 🕑

175 Flank Steak with Artichoke Ratatouille 🕑

176 Chunky Chili con Carne

177 Beef and Brew Stew

178 Five-Way Cincinnati-Style Chili

179 Beef Stew with Fresh Mango

182 Beef Goulash with Lemon 🕑

183 Country Cassoulet

184 Molasses-Glazed Beef and Veggie Meat Loaf 🕑

185 Picadillo Beef

186 Cuban-Style Pork with Orange

187 Alsatian Pork-and-Potato Casserole

188 Tuscan Pork and Beans

189 Jerk Pork Loin with Mango Salsa 🕑

191 Pork Tenderloin with Cherry and Peach Salsa

192 Pork and Butternut Stew

193 Four-Seed Pork Loin 🕑

194 Pork Carnitas

195 Salad Greens with Lime and Herb Pulled Pork 🕑

196 Pork-and-Beans Chili 🕑

197 Pork Chops with Grape Tomatoes and Fresh Basil

200 German Schnitzel

201 Garlicky Lamb Steaks with Green Olive and Tomato Relish

Swiss Steak with Melting Tomatoes and Onions

The long slow cooking process is perfect not only for making round steak fork-tender but also for blending fresh tomato and onion wedges into a savory "melted" topping for the steak.

1. Sprinkle 1 tablespoon thyme, the garlic, salt, and pepper over both sides of the beef. Using your fingertips, gently press the seasonings so they adhere to the beef. Put the flour on a large plate. Add the beef, turning to coat. Using your fingertips, gently press the flour so as much as possible adheres to the beef.

2. In a large nonstick skillet, heat 1 teaspoon oil over medium-high heat, swirling to coat the bottom. Cook the beef for 3 to 5 minutes, or until browned, turning once halfway through. Transfer to a separate large plate.

3. Reduce the heat to medium low. Pour the remaining ½ teaspoon oil into the skillet, swirling to coat the bottom. Cook the onions for 2 minutes, stirring frequently. Transfer to the slow cooker. Top with the beef. Pile the tomatoes on the beef. Sprinkle with the remaining 2 teaspoons thyme. Don't stir. Cook, covered, on low for 6 to 8 hours or on high for 3 to 4 hours, or until the beef is fork-tender.

4. Transfer the beef to a large plate. Let stand, loosely covered, for 10 minutes before slicing. Pour the onion mixture into a colander held over a medium skillet. Set the onion mixture and the liquid aside separately.

5. After slicing the beef, bring the strained liquid to a boil over medium-high heat. Put the cornstarch in a small bowl. Pour in the water, whisking to dissolve. Whisk into the sauce. Boil for 1 minute, stirring frequently. Spoon the onion mixture over the beef. Serve with the sauce.

SERVES 6; 3 ounces beef and ½ cup sauce per serving

SLOW COOKER SIZE | SHAPE
3- to 4½-quart | oval (oval is necessary)

SLOW COOKING TIME
6 to 8 hours ON LOW, **OR**
3 to 4 hours ON HIGH

1 tablespoon chopped fresh thyme and 2 teaspoons chopped fresh thyme, divided use

3 medium garlic cloves, minced

½ teaspoon salt

¼ teaspoon pepper

1½ pounds boneless top round steak, all visible fat discarded

2 tablespoons all-purpose flour

1 teaspoon olive oil and ½ teaspoon olive oil, divided use

2 large onions, cut into 1-inch wedges

3 large tomatoes, cut into ½-inch wedges (about 3 cups)

+

2 tablespoons cornstarch
2 tablespoons water

PER SERVING
Calories 211
Total Fat **4.5 g**
  Saturated Fat **1.5 g**
  Trans Fat **0.0 g**
  Polyunsaturated Fat **0.5 g**
  Monounsaturated Fat **2.5 g**
Cholesterol **57 mg**
Sodium **233 mg**
Carbohydrates **15 g**
  Fiber **3 g**
  Sugars **7 g**
Protein **27 g**

Dietary Exchanges:
  3 vegetable, 3 lean meat

Beef and Bell Pepper Gyros with Tzatziki Sauce

These beefy sandwiches are easy to put together and the recipe makes use of pantry basics that you probably already have on hand. The beef is spiked with Greek flavors. Topped with fresh veggies and a refreshing cucumber-yogurt sauce, these sandwiches are not your typical slow-cooker meal.

1. Spread the beef on a large plate. Sprinkle the pepper and salt over the beef. Stir to coat.

2. In a large skillet, heat 2 teaspoons oil over medium-high heat, swirling to coat the bottom. Cook the beef for 5 minutes, or until browned on all sides, stirring frequently. Transfer to the slow cooker.

3. Reduce the heat to medium. Heat the remaining 1 teaspoon oil in the skillet, swirling to coat the bottom. Cook the onion for 3 minutes, or until almost soft, stirring frequently. Stir in the garlic. Cook for 1 minute, or until fragrant, stirring constantly. Stir in the water and oregano. Cook for 2 minutes, or until the mixture comes to a boil, scraping to dislodge any browned bits. Transfer the mixture to the slow cooker.

4. Stir in the bell pepper. Cook, covered, on low for 8 to 9 hours or on high for 4 to 5 hours, or until the beef is tender.

5. About 10 minutes before serving time, in a small bowl, stir together the sauce ingredients.

6. At serving time, warm the pitas using the package directions. Using a slotted spoon, transfer the beef mixture to the centers of the pitas. Top with the romaine, tomato, and red onion. Spoon the sauce over all. Serve with the lemon wedges.

SERVES 4; 1 gyro per serving

SLOW COOKER SIZE | SHAPE
3- to 4½-quart | round or oval

SLOW COOKING TIME
8 to 9 hours ON LOW, **OR**
4 to 5 hours ON HIGH

1 1-pound boneless sirloin steak, all visible fat discarded, cut into ¼-inch strips
½ teaspoon pepper
¼ teaspoon salt
2 teaspoons olive oil and 1 teaspoon olive oil, divided use
1 medium onion, thinly sliced lengthwise
3 medium garlic cloves, minced
¼ cup water
1 teaspoon dried oregano
1 large red bell pepper, thinly sliced

—————— + ——————

TZATZIKI SAUCE

¼ cup fat-free plain Greek yogurt
¼ of a large seedless cucumber or 1 mini cucumber, peeled and coarsely shredded
1 tablespoon chopped fresh parsley
½ teaspoon minced garlic
Pinch of ground cumin
Pinch of cayenne

—————— + ——————

4 whole-wheat pita breads (lowest sodium available)
1 cup shredded romaine
1 medium tomato, diced
½ small red onion, thinly sliced
1 lemon, cut into 4 wedges

PER SERVING
Calories **379**
Total Fat **8.5 g**
  Saturated Fat **2.0 g**
  Trans Fat **0.0 g**
  Polyunsaturated Fat **1.5 g**
  Monounsaturated Fat **4.5 g**

Cholesterol **58 mg**
Sodium **545 mg**
Carbohydrates **43 g**
  Fiber **7 g**
  Sugars **7 g**
Protein **34 g**

Dietary Exchanges:
2 starch, 2 vegetable, 3 lean meat

SERVES 8; 3 ounces beef
and ¼ cup gravy per
serving

SLOW COOKER SIZE | SHAPE
3- to 4½-quart | round or
oval (preferred)

SLOW COOKING TIME
8 to 10 hours ON LOW

1 ounce dried sliced
mushrooms, such
as shiitake, porcini,
or chanterelle, or a
combination (about
1 cup)

1 cup warm water

2 tablespoons chopped
fresh thyme or
2 teaspoons dried
thyme, crumbled

¼ teaspoon salt

¼ teaspoon pepper

1 2-pound flat-end brisket,
all visible fat discarded

1 teaspoon olive oil and
½ teaspoon olive oil,
divided use

2 cups cubed onions
(1-inch pieces) (about
2 large)

3 large garlic cloves,
minced

½ cup fat-free, low-sodium
beef broth, such as on
page 49

———— + ————

2 tablespoons all-purpose
flour

2 tablespoons water

Brisket with Exotic-Mushroom and Onion Gravy

Brisket is a flavorful cut of beef that lends itself to long and slow moist cooking. In this recipe, it's topped with a pile of onions and dried mushrooms that season the cooking broth, which in turn becomes the gravy base.

1. In a small bowl, soak the dried mushrooms in 1 cup warm water for 20 to 30 minutes, or until they are soft. In a small sieve, drain the mushrooms, reserving the soaking water. Strain the soaking water through a fine sieve or coffee filter to remove any dirt. Set the mushrooms and soaking water aside.

2. Sprinkle the thyme, salt, and pepper over both sides of the beef. Using your fingertips, gently press the seasonings so they adhere to the beef.

3. In a large nonstick skillet, heat 1 teaspoon oil over medium-high heat, swirling to coat the bottom. Cook the beef for 4 to 6 minutes, or until browned, turning once halfway through. Transfer to a large plate. Set aside.

4. Reduce the heat to medium. Add the remaining ½ teaspoon oil, swirling to coat the bottom. Cook the onions and garlic for 1 minute, stirring frequently. Transfer to the slow cooker. Stir in the mushrooms.

5. Place the brisket on top of the onion mixture. Don't stir. Set aside.

6. Pour the broth and reserved soaking water into the skillet. Increase the heat to high and bring to a boil, scraping to dislodge any browned bits. Pour over the brisket.

7. Cook, covered, on low for 8 to 10 hours, or until very tender. Transfer the beef to a separate large plate, reserving the onion mixture. Cover the beef loosely. Let stand for 10 minutes before slicing.

8. During the standing time, put the flour in a small bowl. Add the remaining 2 tablespoons water, whisking to dissolve. Pour the onion mixture from the slow cooker into a large skillet. Bring to a boil over high heat.

9. Slowly whisk about half the flour mixture into the gravy. Bring to a boil, whisking constantly. Whisk in the remaining flour mixture 1 teaspoon at a time until the desired consistency. Boil for 1 minute, whisking constantly. Serve the gravy over the beef.

COOK'S TIP

Be sure to buy the flat end of the brisket. It is the leanest part and slices well.

PER SERVING
Calories **188**
Total Fat **5.5 g**
  Saturated Fat **2.0 g**
  Trans Fat **0.0 g**
  Polyunsaturated Fat **0.5 g**
  Monounsaturated Fat **2.5 g**

Cholesterol **74 mg**
Sodium **165 mg**
Carbohydrates **8 g**
  Fiber **1 g**
  Sugars **2 g**
Protein **26 g**

Dietary Exchanges:
  1 vegetable, 3 lean meat

SERVES 8; 3 ounces beef and 2 tablespoons sauce per serving

SLOW COOKER SIZE | SHAPE
3- to 4½-quart | round or oval (preferred)

SLOW COOKING TIME
7 to 9 hours ON LOW, **OR**
3½ to 4½ hours ON HIGH

2 tablespoons finely chopped fresh rosemary or 2 teaspoons dried rosemary, crushed

3 large garlic cloves, minced

¼ teaspoon salt

¼ teaspoon pepper

1 2-pound boneless sirloin tip roast, any netting or kitchen string and all visible fat discarded

1 teaspoon olive oil and ½ teaspoon olive oil, divided use

1 large onion, coarsely chopped

1 cup cabernet sauvignon or other hearty red wine (regular or nonalcoholic) or fat-free, low-sodium beef broth, such as on page 49

———— + ————

1½ teaspoons cornstarch

2 teaspoons water

Cabernet-Simmered Beef Roast with Rosemary

The hearty wine not only helps tenderize and flavor the roast but also creates a rich-tasting, intense sauce for this elegant entrée.

1. In a small bowl, stir together the rosemary, garlic, salt, and pepper. Sprinkle over both sides of the beef. Using your fingertips, gently press the seasonings so they adhere to the beef.

2. In a medium nonstick skillet, heat 1 teaspoon oil over medium-high heat, swirling to coat the bottom. Cook the beef for 6 to 8 minutes, turning to brown on all sides. Transfer to a large plate.

3. Reduce the heat to medium. Put the remaining ½ teaspoon oil in the skillet, swirling to coat the bottom. Cook the onion for 3 minutes, or until beginning to soften, stirring frequently. Transfer the onion to the slow cooker. Place the beef on top. Don't stir. Set aside.

4. Pour the wine into the skillet. Increase the heat to high and bring to a boil. Boil for 1 minute, scraping to dislodge any browned bits. Pour over the beef.

5. Cook, covered, on low for 7 to 9 hours or on high for 3½ to 4½ hours, or until the beef is tender when pierced with a knife and registers 155°F on an instant-read thermometer for medium doneness. Transfer the beef to a cutting board, leaving the cooking liquid in the slow cooker. Cover the beef loosely. Let stand for 10 minutes before slicing. The temperature will rise about 5 degrees.

6. During the standing time, using a fine-mesh strainer, strain the cooking liquid into a large skillet. Discard the solids. Bring the liquid to a boil over high heat. Boil for 3 to 5 minutes, or until reduced by one-third (to about 1 cup), stirring occasionally.

7. Meanwhile, put the cornstarch in a small bowl. Pour in the water, whisking to dissolve. Set aside.

8. When the sauce is reduced, slowly whisk about half the cornstarch mixture into the gravy. Bring to a boil, whisking constantly. Whisk in the remaining cornstarch mixture 1 teaspoon at a time until the desired consistency. Boil for 1 minute, whisking constantly. Serve the gravy over the beef.

PER SERVING
Calories **181**
Total Fat **5.0 g**
  Saturated Fat **2.0 g**
  Trans Fat **0.0 g**
  Polyunsaturated Fat **0.5 g**
  Monounsaturated Fat **3.0 g**

Cholesterol **56 mg**
Sodium **116 mg**
Carbohydrates **2 g**
  Fiber **0 g**
  Sugars **0 g**
  Protein **24 g**

Dietary Exchanges:
  3 lean meat

SERVES 8; ½ cup beef
  mixture and ½ cup
  couscous per serving

SLOW COOKER SIZE | SHAPE
3- to 4½-quart | round
or oval

SLOW COOKING TIME
8 to 8½ hours ON LOW, **OR**
4 hours to 4 hours
  15 minutes ON HIGH

Cooking spray

1 teaspoon canola or corn
  oil and 1 tablespoon
  canola or corn oil,
  divided use

2 pounds lean boneless
  chuck roast, all visible fat
  discarded, cut into 1-inch
  cubes

1 medium onion, cut into
  8 wedges

2 medium Italian plum
  (Roma) tomatoes

4 medium garlic cloves

1 tablespoon crushed red
  pepper flakes

1½ teaspoons grated
  peeled gingerroot

1 cup water and 1 cup
  water, divided use

2 packets (2 teaspoons)
  salt-free instant beef
  bouillon

1 tablespoon sugar

1 teaspoon salt

———— ✚ ————

1 cup uncooked whole-
  wheat couscous

½ cup finely chopped
  green onions

Indonesian Beef with Couscous

Cooking a paste of herbs, spices, and chiles in a bit of hot oil is the key to this international dish.

1. Lightly spray the slow cooker with cooking spray. Set aside.
2. In a large nonstick skillet, heat 1 teaspoon oil over medium-high heat, swirling to coat the bottom. Cook one-third of the beef for 2 to 3 minutes, or until browned on all sides, stirring frequently. Drain on paper towels. Brown the remaining beef in two batches. Transfer to the slow cooker.
3. Meanwhile, in a food processor or blender, process the onion, tomatoes, garlic, red pepper flakes, and gingerroot until smooth. Set aside.
4. In the same skillet, heat the remaining 1 tablespoon oil over medium-high heat, swirling to coat the bottom. Cook the onion mixture for 8 minutes, or until thickened to a pastelike consistency, stirring constantly. Transfer to the slow cooker. Pour 1 cup water into the skillet. Bring to a boil over medium-high heat. Boil for 1 minute, scraping to dislodge any browned bits. Pour into the slow cooker. Stir in the bouillon, sugar, salt, and the remaining 1 cup water. Cook, covered, on low for 8 to 8½ hours or on high for 4 hours to 4 hours 15 minutes, or until the beef is tender.
5. Just before serving time, prepare the couscous using the package directions, omitting the salt. Fluff with a fork. Stir in the green onions. Spoon onto plates. Top with the beef mixture.

PER SERVING
Calories **281**
Total Fat **7.5 g**
  Saturated Fat **2.0 g**
  Trans Fat **0.0 g**
  Polyunsaturated Fat **1.0 g**
  Monounsaturated Fat **3.5 g**

Cholesterol **44 mg**
Sodium **335 mg**
Carbohydrates **28 g**
  Fiber **4 g**
  Sugars **4 g**
Protein **26 g**

Dietary Exchanges:
  2 starch, 3 lean meat

Coffee Kettle Pot Roast

Molasses and instant coffee add deep flavor to this very tender roast, which will remind you of Sunday dinner at Grandma's house.

1. Lightly spray the slow cooker with cooking spray. Set aside.
2. In a medium bowl, stir together the tomato sauce, coffee granules, molasses, bouillon, onion and garlic powders, pepper, and salt. Set aside.
3. In a large nonstick skillet, heat the oil over medium-high heat, swirling to coat the bottom. Cook the beef on one side for 3 minutes, or until browned. Put the beef with the browned side up in the slow cooker.
4. Pour the water into the skillet, scraping the bottom and side to dislodge any browned bits. Pour over the beef.
5. Stir in the tomato sauce mixture. Cook, covered, on low for 8 hours or on high for 3 hours 45 minutes to 4 hours, or until the beef is tender. You won't need to cut the roast—it will fall apart.
6. About 20 minutes before serving time, prepare the pasta using the package directions, omitting the salt. Drain well in a colander. Serve the beef and sauce over the pasta.

COOK'S TIP

Although they are similar in texture, whole-grain no-yolk noodles contain more fiber than the traditional no-yolk noodles.

SERVES 8; 3 ounces beef, ½ cup noodles, and ¼ cup sauce per serving

SLOW COOKER SIZE | SHAPE
3- to 4½-quart | round or oval

SLOW COOKING TIME
8 hours ON LOW, **OR**
3 hours 45 minutes to 4 hours ON HIGH

Cooking spray

1 8-ounce can no-salt-added tomato sauce

1 tablespoon instant coffee granules

2 tablespoons dark molasses

3 packets (1 tablespoon) salt-free instant beef bouillon

1 teaspoon onion powder

1 teaspoon garlic powder

½ teaspoon pepper (coarsely ground preferred)

¼ teaspoon salt

1 teaspoon canola or corn oil

1 2-pound boneless chuck shoulder roast, all visible fat discarded, cut to fit in slow cooker if necessary

½ cup water

— + —

8 ounces dried whole-grain no-yolk noodles

PER SERVING
Calories **299**
Total Fat **8.0 g**
  Saturated Fat **2.5 g**
  Trans Fat **0.0 g**
  Polyunsaturated Fat **0.5 g**
  Monounsaturated Fat **3.0 g**

Cholesterol **65 mg**
Sodium **149 mg**
Carbohydrates **29 g**
  Fiber **4 g**
  Sugars **6 g**
Protein **28 g**

Dietary Exchanges:
  2 starch, 3 lean meat

SERVES 4; ¾ cup beef and
sauce and ½ cup rice per
serving

SLOW COOKER SIZE | SHAPE
3- to 4½-quart | round
or oval

SLOW COOKING TIME
8 to 9 hours ON LOW, **OR**
4 to 5 hours ON HIGH

½ teaspoon ground cumin

½ teaspoon ground
turmeric

½ teaspoon salt

¼ teaspoon pepper

¼ teaspoon ground
cinnamon

⅛ teaspoon cayenne

1 1-pound boneless sirloin
steak, all visible fat
discarded, cut into 1-inch
cubes

2 teaspoons canola or corn
oil and 1 teaspoon canola
or corn oil, divided use

1 medium onion, chopped

1 tablespoon minced
peeled gingerroot

4 medium garlic cloves,
minced

1 14.5-ounce can no-salt-
added diced tomatoes,
undrained

⅓ cup water

2 tablespoons cider
vinegar and ½ teaspoon
cider vinegar, divided
use

———— + ————

10 ounces frozen brown
rice

¼ cup chopped fresh
cilantro

Beef Vindaloo

This traditional Indian curry dish is perfect for the slow cooker. Its
enticing blend of fragrant Middle Eastern spices creates a welcoming
aroma to come home to. The tomatoes fall apart as the dish cooks,
creating a rich, full-bodied sauce that coats the beef.

1. In a small bowl, stir together the cumin, turmeric, salt, pepper,
   cinnamon, and cayenne.
2. Put the beef in a medium bowl. Sprinkle half the cumin mixture
   over the beef. Stir to coat. Set the remaining cumin mixture aside.
3. In a large skillet, heat 2 teaspoons oil over medium-high heat,
   swirling to coat the bottom. Cook the beef for 5 minutes, or until
   browned on all sides, stirring frequently. Transfer to the slow
   cooker.
4. Reduce the heat to medium. Heat the remaining 1 teaspoon oil
   in the skillet, swirling to coat the bottom. Cook the onion for
   3 minutes, or until almost soft, stirring frequently. Stir in the
   gingerroot and garlic. Cook for 1 minute, or until fragrant, stirring
   constantly. Stir in the tomatoes with liquid and water. Cook for 2
   minutes, or until the mixture comes to a boil, scraping to dislodge
   any browned bits. Transfer the mixture to the slow cooker.
5. Stir in 2 tablespoons vinegar. Cook, covered, on low for 8 to 9
   hours or on high for 4 to 5 hours, or until the beef is tender. Stir
   in the remaining ½ teaspoon vinegar and the reserved cumin
   mixture.
6. About 5 minutes before serving time, prepare the rice using the
   package directions, omitting any salt and margarine. Serve the
   beef and sauce over the rice. Sprinkle with the cilantro.

COOK'S TIP
Using ½ teaspoon cayenne makes this a mildly spicy dish. Taste it
before serving and add more cayenne if desired.

PER SERVING
Calories **292**
Total Fat **7.5 g**
  Saturated Fat **1.5 g**
  Trans Fat **0.0 g**
  Polyunsaturated Fat **1.5 g**
  Monounsaturated Fat **4.0 g**

Cholesterol **58 mg**
Sodium **377 mg**
Carbohydrates **26 g**
  Fiber **3 g**
  Sugars **6 g**
Protein **28 g**

Dietary Exchanges:
  **1 starch, 2 vegetable,
  3 lean meat**

SERVES 12; 3 ounces beef, ½ cup cabbage mixture, and 3 tablespoons gravy per serving

SLOW COOKER SIZE | SHAPE
5- to 7-quart | oval

SLOW COOKING TIME

4 to 5 hours ON LOW plus 4 to 5 hours ON LOW plus 15 minutes ON WARM or LOW (preferred), **OR**

2 to 2½ hours ON HIGH plus 2 to 2½ hours ON HIGH plus 15 minutes ON WARM or LOW

2 cups fat-free, low-sodium beef broth, such as on page 49

1 cup water

1 cup cider vinegar

½ cup firmly packed light brown sugar

1 teaspoon ground allspice

1 teaspoon ground ginger

½ teaspoon ground cloves

1 4-pound top round roast or eye-of-round roast, all visible fat discarded

———— **+** ————

2 teaspoons canola or corn oil

1 medium Vidalia, Maui, Oso Sweet, or other sweet onion, thinly sliced and quartered (about 2 cups)

———— **+** ————

5 cups shredded red cabbage (about 15 ounces)

2 large semitart apples, such as Gala or Jonathan, diced

2 tablespoons cornstarch

Water as needed plus ¼ cup cold water, divided use

⅓ cup crushed low-fat gingersnaps

Sauerbraten

Marinating the beef overnight tenderizes and flavors this famous German dish, so be sure to plan ahead when making it.

1. In a glass bowl, stir together the broth, 1 cup water, the vinegar, sugar, allspice, ginger, and cloves. Add the beef, turning to coat. Cover and refrigerate for 8 to 24 hours, turning occasionally. At cooking time, drain the beef and pat dry, reserving the marinade.

2. In a large nonstick skillet, heat the oil over medium-high heat. Cook the beef for 10 minutes, or until browned.

3. Spread the onion in the slow cooker. Place the beef on the onion. Pour 2 cups of the reserved marinade over the beef. Cover and refrigerate the remaining marinade. Cook, covered, on low for 4 to 5 hours or on high for 2 to 2½ hours.

4. Quickly arrange the cabbage and apples around the beef and re-cover the slow cooker. Cook on low for 4 to 5 hours or on high for 2 to 2½ hours, or until the beef registers 155°F to 160°F.

5. If using the high setting, change it to low. Quickly transfer the beef to a cutting board. Re-cover the slow cooker. Let the beef stand, covered, for about 15 minutes, or until it registers 160°F to 165°F. Slice the beef.

6. During the standing time, pour 2 cups of the remaining marinade into a medium saucepan. Bring to a rolling boil over high heat. Boil for 5 minutes. Pour into a liquid measuring cup. Add enough water to measure 1¾ cups. Pour into the pan. Reduce the heat to medium.

7. Put the cornstarch in a small bowl. Add the remaining ¼ cup cold water, whisking to dissolve. Gradually stir into the gravy. Cook for 1 minute, stirring constantly. Whisk in the gingersnaps.

8. Transfer the sliced beef and cabbage mixture to plates. Spoon the gravy over the beef.

PER SERVING
Calories **276**
Total Fat **5.0 g**
   Saturated Fat **1.5 g**
   Trans Fat **0.0 g**
   Polyunsaturated Fat **0.5 g**
   Monounsaturated Fat **2.5 g**

Cholesterol **77 mg**
Sodium **127 mg**
Carbohydrates **21 g**
   Fiber **2 g**
   Sugars **16 g**
Protein **35 g**

Dietary Exchanges:
   1 fruit, 1 vegetable, 5 lean meat

Flank Steak Fajitas

The mixture of spices is key to the success of these great-tasting fajitas. If you wish, dress them up with additional toppings, such as hot chiles, green onions, and lime wedges to squeeze over the filling.

SERVES 5; 3 ounces beef, ½ cup vegetable mixture, and 1 tortilla per serving

SLOW COOKER SIZE | SHAPE
2- to 3½-quart | oval

SLOW COOKING TIME
4 to 6 hours ON LOW, **OR**
2 to 3 hours ON HIGH

1. In a medium nonstick skillet, heat ½ teaspoon oil over medium heat, swirling to coat the bottom. Cook the onions for 1 to 2 minutes, or until barely beginning to soften, stirring frequently. Transfer to the slow cooker. Set aside.

2. In a small bowl, stir together the cumin, chili powder, garlic powder, salt, pepper, and chipotle powder. Sprinkle over both sides of the beef. Using your fingertips, gently press the seasonings so they adhere to the beef.

3. In the same skillet, heat 1 teaspoon oil over medium-high heat, swirling to coat the bottom. Cook the beef for 4 to 6 minutes, or until browned, turning once halfway through. Place the beef on the onions. Top with the tomatoes. Don't stir. Cook, covered, on low for 4 to 6 hours or on high for 2 to 3 hours, or until the beef is tender.

4. Transfer the beef to a cutting board, leaving the onion mixture in the slow cooker. Let the beef stand, loosely covered, for 10 minutes before thinly slicing. Meanwhile, using a slotted spoon, transfer the onions and tomatoes to a medium bowl, discarding any liquid remaining in the slow cooker. Stir in the cilantro and beef slices, discarding any juices that remain.

5. Meanwhile, in a medium skillet over medium heat, heat the remaining 2 teaspoons oil, swirling to coat the bottom. Cook the bell peppers over medium heat for 2 minutes, or until beginning to soften. Increase the heat to medium high. Cook for 1 to 3 minutes, or until the peppers are lightly browned and tender-crisp, stirring frequently.

6. Just before serving time, warm the tortillas using the package directions. Spoon the beef mixture onto the tortillas. Top with the bell pepper mixture. Roll up jelly-roll style.

½ teaspoon olive oil and 1 teaspoon olive oil, divided use

2 medium to large onions, sliced crosswise

1 teaspoon ground cumin

1 teaspoon chili powder

½ teaspoon garlic powder

¼ teaspoon salt

¼ teaspoon pepper

⅛ teaspoon chipotle powder

1¼ pounds flank steak, all visible fat discarded

2 large tomatoes, chopped

+

3 tablespoons snipped fresh cilantro

2 teaspoons olive oil

1 large green bell pepper, sliced lengthwise

1 large red bell pepper, sliced lengthwise

5 8-inch fat-free whole-wheat tortillas (lowest sodium available)

PER SERVING
Calories **371**
Total Fat **12.0 g**
  Saturated Fat **3.5 g**
  Trans Fat **0.0 g**
  Polyunsaturated Fat **1.5 g**
  Monounsaturated Fat **6.0 g**

Cholesterol **48 mg**
Sodium **516 mg**
Carbohydrates **37 g**
  Fiber **7 g**
  Sugars **11 g**
Protein **29 g**

Dietary Exchanges:
  1½ starch, 2 vegetable, 3 lean meat, ½ fat

SERVES 4; 2 wraps per serving

SLOW COOKER SIZE | SHAPE
3- to 4½-quart | round or oval

SLOW COOKING TIME
8 to 10 hours ON LOW, **OR**
4 to 5 hours ON HIGH

1 1-pound flank steak or flat-end brisket, all visible fat discarded, cut to fit if necessary

1 cup matchstick-size strips of peeled jícama (about 1 small)

2 tablespoons plain rice vinegar

1 tablespoon soy sauce (lowest sodium available)

1 teaspoon minced peeled gingerroot

¼ to ½ teaspoon crushed red pepper flakes

———— **+** ————

1 tablespoon cornstarch and (if needed) 1 tablespoon cornstarch, divided use

1 tablespoon plain rice vinegar

1 tablespoon water (if needed)

½ cup matchstick-size strips of red bell pepper

¼ cup sliced green onions

8 Bibb or Boston lettuce leaves

Asian Lettuce Wraps

Pick these wraps up to eat them, or shred the lettuce and serve the beef mixture on top.

1. Put the beef in the slow cooker. Top with the jícama.
2. In a small bowl, whisk together 2 tablespoons vinegar, the soy sauce, gingerroot, and red pepper flakes. Pour over the beef. Cook, covered, on low for 8 to 10 hours or on high for 4 to 5 hours, or until the beef is tender and the desired doneness. Transfer the beef to a cutting board, leaving the jícama mixture in the slow cooker. Set aside.
3. Put 1 tablespoon cornstarch in a small bowl. Add the remaining 1 tablespoon vinegar, whisking to dissolve. Stir into the jícama mixture. If the sauce still seems watery (more likely if cooking on low), put the remaining 1 tablespoon cornstarch in the same small bowl. Add 1 tablespoon water, whisking to dissolve. Stir into the jícama mixture. Stir in the bell pepper and green onions. Set aside.
4. Slice the beef diagonally across the grain if making wraps, or use one or two forks to shred it if serving on top of the lettuce. Return the beef to the slow cooker, stirring to coat.
5. To make wraps, spoon the filling down the center of each lettuce leaf. Fold the left and right sides of the lettuce toward the center. Starting from the unfolded end closest to you, roll the wrap toward the other end to enclose the filling. If you prefer, shred the lettuce and serve the beef and sauce on top.

PER SERVING
Calories **202**
Total Fat **6.5 g**
　Saturated Fat **3.0 g**
　Trans Fat **0.0 g**
　Polyunsaturated Fat **0.5 g**
　Monounsaturated Fat **3.0 g**

Cholesterol **48 mg**
Sodium **146 mg**
Carbohydrates **9 g**
　Fiber **2 g**
　Sugars **2 g**
Protein **24 g**

Dietary Exchanges:
　1 vegetable, 3 lean meat

Flank Steak with Artichoke Ratatouille

Frozen artichoke hearts stand in for the traditional eggplant in a ratatouille sauce that blankets slices of tender flank steak. For variety, use half a yellow summer squash and half a zucchini instead of choosing just one of them.

1. Sprinkle both sides of the beef with the Italian seasoning, salt, and pepper. Using your fingertips, gently press the seasonings so they adhere to the beef. Transfer to the slow cooker.
2. Sprinkle the onion and garlic over the beef. Pour in the tomatoes with liquid and vinegar. Cook, covered, on low for 8 to 10 hours or on high for 4 to 5 hours, or until the beef is tender. Transfer to a cutting board. Set aside.
3. If using the low setting, change it to high. Quickly stir in the artichoke hearts, squash, and bell pepper and re-cover the slow cooker. Cook for 30 minutes, or until tender.
4. Meanwhile, slice the beef diagonally across the grain or, using one or two forks, shred it. Cover to keep warm. Set aside until the ratatouille is ready.
5. Put the beef on plates. Using a slotted spoon, spoon the ratatouille over the beef. If you prefer, spoon the ratatouille alongside. Sprinkle with the parsley.

PER SERVING
Calories **237**
Total Fat **6.5 g**
  Saturated Fat **3.0 g**
  Trans Fat **0.0 g**
  Polyunsaturated Fat **0.5 g**
  Monounsaturated Fat **3.0 g**

Cholesterol **48 mg**
Sodium **234 mg**
Carbohydrates **16 g**
  Fiber **6 g**
  Sugars **6 g**
Protein **27 g**

Dietary Exchanges:
  3 vegetable, 3 lean meat

FAST PREP!

SERVES 4; 3 ounces beef and ¾ cup ratatouille per serving

SLOW COOKER SIZE | SHAPE
3- to 4½-quart | round or oval

SLOW COOKING TIME
8 to 10 hours ON LOW plus 30 minutes ON HIGH, **OR**

4 to 5 hours ON HIGH plus 30 minutes ON HIGH

1 1-pound flank steak, all visible fat discarded, cut to fit in your slow cooker if necessary

1 teaspoon dried Italian seasoning, crumbled

¼ teaspoon salt

¼ teaspoon pepper

½ cup finely chopped onion

2 medium garlic cloves, minced

1 14.5-ounce can no-salt-added diced tomatoes, undrained

2 tablespoons red wine vinegar

       +

8 ounces frozen artichoke hearts, thawed (about 2 cups)

1 small yellow summer squash or zucchini, halved lengthwise and thinly sliced crosswise (about 1½ cups)

1 medium red or green bell pepper, cut into matchstick-size strips (about 1 cup)

¼ cup snipped fresh parsley

SERVES 4; scant 1¾ cups per serving

SLOW COOKER SIZE | SHAPE
3- to 4½-quart | round or oval

SLOW COOKING TIME
6 to 8 hours ON LOW plus 30 minutes ON LOW, **OR**

4 to 5 hours ON HIGH plus 30 minutes ON HIGH

1 tablespoon chili powder

1 teaspoon ground cumin

½ teaspoon salt

¼ teaspoon dried oregano, crumbled

¼ teaspoon pepper

1 pound boneless top sirloin steak, all visible fat discarded, cut into ½-inch cubes

2 teaspoons olive oil

2 14.5-ounce cans no-salt-added diced tomatoes, undrained

1 medium onion, chopped

1 medium green bell pepper, chopped

¼ cup water

2 tablespoons no-salt-added tomato paste

2 medium garlic cloves, minced

✦

1 15.5-ounce can no-salt-added kidney beans, rinsed and drained

2 medium green onions, thinly sliced

Chunky Chili con Carne

Cubes of browned, spice–coated sirloin enhance this chili. All you need to serve on the side is a small wedge of jalapeño cornbread.

1. In a small bowl, stir together the chili powder, cumin, salt, oregano, and pepper. Sprinkle 1 teaspoon over both sides of the beef. Using your fingertips, gently press the seasonings so they adhere to the beef. Set the remaining mixture aside.

2. In a large nonstick skillet, heat the oil over medium-high heat, swirling to coat the bottom. Cook the beef for 5 minutes, or until browned on all sides, stirring frequently. Transfer to the slow cooker.

3. Stir in the tomatoes with liquid, onion, bell pepper, water, tomato paste, garlic, and reserved chili powder mixture. Cook, covered, on low for 6 to 8 hours or on high for 4 to 5 hours, or until the beef is tender.

4. Quickly stir in the beans and re-cover the slow cooker. Cook for 30 minutes. Serve sprinkled with the green onions.

PER SERVING
Calories **335**
Total Fat **7.0 g**
  Saturated Fat **2.0 g**
  Trans Fat **0.0 g**
  Polyunsaturated Fat **0.5 g**
  Monounsaturated Fat **4.0 g**

Cholesterol **60 mg**
Sodium **409 mg**
Carbohydrates **33 g**
  Fiber **12 g**
  Sugars **12 g**
Protein **35 g**

Dietary Exchanges:
  1 starch, 3 vegetable, 4 lean meat

Beef and Brew Stew

Dark beer gives this stew its complex flavor. You'll definitely want to soak up all the sauce, so serve the stew over whole-wheat no-yolk noodles, brown rice, or mashed potatoes made with heart-healthy ingredients.

1. Spread the beef on a large plate. Sprinkle the salt and pepper over the beef. Toss to coat.
2. In a large nonstick skillet, heat the oil over medium-high heat, swirling to coat the bottom. Cook the beef and onion for 5 minutes, or until the beef is browned on all sides, stirring frequently. Transfer to the slow cooker.
3. Stir in the broth, beer, turnips, carrots, celery, garlic, and thyme. Cook, covered, on low for 8 to 10 hours or on high for 5 to 6 hours, or until the beef and vegetables are tender.
4. Put the flour in a small bowl. Add the water, whisking to dissolve. Quickly pour into the beef mixture, stirring until well combined, and re-cover the slow cooker. If using the low setting, change it to high. Cook for 10 minutes, or until the sauce is slightly thickened. Stir in the parsley and vinegar.

COOK'S TIP

If you don't care for dark beer, you can use light beer instead, or for a nonalcoholic alternative, substitute an additional 1½ cups of fat-free, low-sodium beef broth, such as on page 49, for the beer.

SERVES 4; 1½ cups per serving

SLOW COOKER SIZE | SHAPE
3- to 4½-quart | round or oval

SLOW COOKING TIME
8 to 10 hours ON LOW plus 10 minutes ON HIGH, **OR**
5 to 6 hours ON HIGH plus 10 minutes ON HIGH

1 pound boneless sirloin steak, all visible fat discarded, cut into ½-inch cubes

¼ teaspoon salt

¼ teaspoon pepper

2 teaspoons olive oil

1 small onion, chopped

1¼ cups fat-free, low-sodium beef broth, such as on page 49

12 ounces dark beer (see Cook's Tip)

2 medium turnips or potatoes (about 1 pound total), peeled and cut into ½-inch cubes

2 medium carrots, halved lengthwise and cut crosswise into ½-inch slices

1 medium rib of celery, chopped

2 medium garlic cloves, minced

¼ teaspoon dried thyme, crumbled

_____ **+** _____

2 tablespoons all-purpose flour

2 tablespoons cold water

2 tablespoons snipped fresh parsley (optional)

1 tablespoon balsamic vinegar

PER SERVING
Calories **263**
Total Fat **5.5 g**
  Saturated Fat **1.5 g**
  Trans Fat **0.0 g**
  Polyunsaturated Fat **0.5 g**
  Monounsaturated Fat **3.0 g**

Cholesterol **58 mg**
Sodium **312 mg**
Carbohydrates **19 g**
  Fiber **3 g**
  Sugars **7 g**
Protein **28 g**

Dietary Exchanges:
  ½ **starch, 2 vegetable, 3 lean meat**

SERVES 6; 1 cup chili and
1 cup pasta per serving

SLOW COOKER SIZE | SHAPE
3- to 4½-quart | round
or oval

SLOW COOKING TIME
5 to 7 hours ON LOW, **OR**
3 to 3½ hours ON HIGH

1 pound extra-lean ground
beef

1 15.5-ounce can no-salt-
added kidney beans,
rinsed and drained

1 14.5-ounce can no-salt-
added diced tomatoes,
undrained

⅔ cup chopped onion

3 tablespoons cider vinegar

2 teaspoons chili powder

1 teaspoon ground
cinnamon

1 teaspoon dried minced
garlic

1 teaspoon ground cumin

½ teaspoon ground allspice

¼ teaspoon salt

¼ teaspoon pepper

— + —

12 ounces dried whole-
grain spaghetti

1 tablespoon unsweetened
cocoa powder

1 teaspoon sugar

¼ cup plus 2 tablespoons
diced onion

¾ cup low-fat shredded
sharp Cheddar cheese

Five-Way Cincinnati-Style Chili

You don't have to be from Ohio to enjoy the aroma and distinctive taste of Cincinnati chili, which features cinnamon, allspice, and chocolate or cocoa. The typical version is called "five-way" because the chili (1) is served over spaghetti (2) and garnished with beans (3), raw onion (4), and cheese (5), although we veered from tradition a bit by cooking the beans in the chili.

1. In a large nonstick skillet, cook the beef over medium-high heat for 3 to 5 minutes, or until browned on the outside and no longer pink in the center, stirring occasionally to turn and break up the beef. Drain if needed. Transfer to the slow cooker.
2. Stir in the beans, tomatoes with liquid, ⅔ cup onion, vinegar, chili powder, cinnamon, garlic, cumin, allspice, salt, and pepper. Cook, covered, on low for 5 to 7 hours or on high for 3 to 3½ hours.
3. About 15 minutes before serving time, prepare the pasta using the package directions, omitting the salt. Drain well in a colander.
4. Stir the cocoa powder and sugar into the chili until combined.
5. Spoon the pasta onto plates. Top with the chili, the remaining ¼ cup plus 2 tablespoons onion, and the Cheddar.

PER SERVING
Calories **447**
Total Fat **8.0 g**
  Saturated Fat **3.0 g**
  Trans Fat **0.0 g**
  Polyunsaturated Fat **1.0 g**
  Monounsaturated Fat **2.5 g**

Cholesterol **45 mg**
Sodium **269 mg**
Carbohydrates **64 g**
  Fiber **11 g**
  Sugars **9 g**
Protein **33 g**

Dietary Exchanges:
  **4 starch, 1 vegetable,
  3 lean meat**

Beef Stew with Fresh Mango

Fresh mango and cilantro add the perfect balance to this beef stew with its full-flavored complements of Worcestershire sauce, chili powder, and just a bit of cinnamon. Serving it over whole-wheat couscous is an easy way to boost your fiber intake.

SERVES 6; 1 cup stew and ½ cup couscous per serving

SLOW COOKER SIZE | SHAPE
5- to 7-quart | round or oval

SLOW COOKING TIME
8 to 9 hours ON LOW, **OR**
5 to 5½ hours ON HIGH

1. In the slow cooker, stir together the beef, tomatoes, onion, bell pepper, Worcestershire sauce, chili powder, garlic, cinnamon, salt, and pepper. Cook, covered, on low for 8 to 9 hours or on high for 5 to 5½ hours, or until the beef is tender.
2. About 10 minutes before serving time, prepare the couscous using the package directions, omitting the salt and substituting the broth for the water. Spoon into bowls. Ladle the stew onto the couscous. Top with the mango and cilantro.

COOK'S TIP

If you have any stew and couscous left over, make tacos! Combine the stew and couscous, warm the mixture in the microwave, spoon onto warmed corn tortillas, and top each with a dollop of fat-free sour cream and a little shredded low-fat Cheddar cheese. Roll up jelly-roll style or eat using a knife and fork.

1½ pounds lean stew meat (1-inch cubes), all visible fat discarded

2 14.5-ounce cans no-salt-added diced tomatoes, drained

1 medium onion, cut into 6 wedges

1 large red bell pepper, cut lengthwise into ½-inch strips

2 tablespoons Worcestershire sauce (lowest sodium available)

1 tablespoon chili powder

2 medium garlic cloves, minced

½ teaspoon ground cinnamon

¼ teaspoon salt

¼ teaspoon pepper

+

1 cup uncooked whole-wheat couscous

1½ cups fat-free, low-sodium beef broth, such as on page 49, or fat-free, low-sodium vegetable broth, such as on page 50

1 medium mango, cut into bite-size pieces

½ cup chopped fresh cilantro

PER SERVING
Calories **395**
Total Fat **9.0 g**
  Saturated Fat **3.0 g**
  Trans Fat **0.0 g**
  Polyunsaturated Fat **0.5 g**
  Monounsaturated Fat **3.5 g**

Cholesterol **71 mg**
Sodium **224 mg**
Carbohydrates **50 g**
  Fiber **8 g**
  Sugars **15 g**
Protein **30 g**

Dietary Exchanges:
  2 starch, 2 vegetable, ½ fruit, 3 lean meat

Beef Stew with Fresh
Mango, page 179

SERVES 6; 1½ cups per serving

SLOW COOKER SIZE | SHAPE
3- to 4½-quart | round or oval

SLOW COOKING TIME
8 to 10 hours ON LOW plus 30 minutes ON HIGH, **OR**

4 to 5 hours ON HIGH plus 30 minutes ON HIGH

2 cups baby carrots, halved crosswise

1 large onion, diced

1½ pounds boneless top round or eye-of-round roast, all visible fat discarded, cut into 1-inch cubes

1 pound unpeeled red potatoes, cut into 1-inch cubes

2 tablespoons uncooked instant tapioca

1 cup fat-free, low-sodium beef broth, such as on page 49

¼ cup no-salt-added tomato paste

1 tablespoon paprika

2 medium garlic cloves, minced

½ teaspoon caraway seeds, crushed

½ teaspoon dried marjoram, crumbled

¼ teaspoon dried thyme

¼ teaspoon salt

+

12 ounces green beans, trimmed, cut into bite-size pieces

2 tablespoons finely chopped lemon zest

2 tablespoons fat-free sour cream (optional)

Beef Goulash with Lemon

Caraway seeds, marjoram, thyme, and lots of paprika help season this one-dish meal, but it's the addition of lemon zest that sets it apart. Tapioca, better known as a dessert, is used in this entrée recipe to thicken the stew.

1. In the slow cooker, make one layer each, in order, of the carrots, onion, beef, and potatoes. Sprinkle with the tapioca. Don't stir.
2. In a small bowl, whisk together the broth, tomato paste, paprika, garlic, caraway seeds, marjoram, thyme, and salt. Pour over the vegetables and beef in the slow cooker. Don't stir. Cook, covered, on low for 8 to 10 hours or on high for 4 to 5 hours.
3. Quickly stir the beans and lemon zest into the goulash and re-cover the slow cooker. If using the low setting, change it to high. Cook for 30 minutes, or until the beans are tender. Ladle into bowls. Top each serving with a dollop of sour cream.

COOK'S TIPS

Caraway Seeds The fruit of an herb in the carrot family, caraway seeds are very popular in German, Austrian, and Hungarian foods. To release their flavor, crush them in a mortar and pestle.

Citrus Zest A microplane makes quick work of removing and grating the peel, or zest, of citrus fruit. Be careful to avoid cutting into any of the pith, the bitter white covering just beneath the peel. Measuring will be easy if you work over a sheet of wax paper, which you can fold to pour the zest into a measuring spoon. Any remaining zest can be frozen for later use.

PER SERVING
Calories **268**
Total Fat **3.5 g**
  Saturated Fat **1.5 g**
  Trans Fat **0.0 g**
  Polyunsaturated Fat **0.5 g**
  Monounsaturated Fat **1.5 g**

Cholesterol **58 mg**
Sodium **223 mg**
Carbohydrates **30 g**
  Fiber **6 g**
  Sugars **9 g**
  Protein **30 g**

Dietary Exchanges:
  1 starch, 3 vegetable, 3 very lean meat

Country Cassoulet

With its coarse textures and aromatic flavors, this beef and bean dish is evocative of the French countryside.

SERVES 4; 1½ cups per serving

SLOW COOKER SIZE | SHAPE
3- to 4½-quart | round or oval

SLOW COOKING TIME
8 to 10 hours ON LOW, **OR**
4 to 5 hours ON HIGH

1. Fill a large saucepan three-fourths full of water. Bring to a boil over high heat. Stir in the beans. Return to a boil. Reduce the heat and simmer for 15 minutes. Pour the beans into a colander and rinse. Pour into the slow cooker. Set aside.
2. In a large nonstick skillet, heat the oil over medium-high heat, swirling to coat the bottom. Cook the beef for 4 to 6 minutes, or until browned on all sides, stirring frequently. Transfer to the slow cooker.
3. Stir in the remaining ingredients except the parsley. Cook, covered, on low for 8 to 10 hours or on high for 4 to 5 hours, or until the beans are tender. Discard the bay leaf. Ladle into bowls. Sprinkle with the parsley.

1 cup dried navy beans (about 6 ounces), sorted for stones and shriveled beans, rinsed, and drained

1 teaspoon olive oil

1 pound lean stew meat (1-inch cubes), all visible fat discarded

4 cups fat-free, low-sodium beef broth, such as on page 49

2 medium carrots, sliced crosswise

1 medium onion, cut into 16 wedges

1 medium rib of celery, sliced crosswise

2 medium garlic cloves, minced

1 medium dried bay leaf

1 teaspoon dried herbes de Provence, crumbled

¼ teaspoon salt

¼ teaspoon pepper

—————— ✦ ——————

¼ cup snipped fresh parsley

COOK'S TIP

Herbes de Provence is a standout seasoning blend containing dried herbs commonly found in southern France, such as basil, lavender, marjoram, rosemary, sage, and thyme. Try this aromatic mixture for seasoning soups, stews, vinaigrettes, and roasted or grilled pork, poultry, and vegetables.

PER SERVING

Calories **382**
Total Fat **10.0 g**
  Saturated Fat **3.0 g**
  Trans Fat **0.0 g**
  Polyunsaturated Fat **1.0 g**
  Monounsaturated Fat **4.5 g**

Cholesterol **71 mg**
Sodium **295 mg**
Carbohydrates **39 g**
  Fiber **15 g**
  Sugars **5 g**
Protein **34 g**

Dietary Exchanges:
2 starch, 2 vegetable, 3½ lean meat

SERVES 4; 1 slice or wedge per serving

SLOW COOKER SIZE | SHAPE
3- to 4½-quart | round or oval (preferred)

SLOW COOKING TIME
3 hours 45 minutes to 5 hours 45 minutes ON LOW plus 5 to 10 minutes ON HIGH, **OR**

1 hour 45 minutes to 2 hours 45 minutes ON HIGH plus 5 to 10 minutes ON HIGH

Cooking spray
1 pound extra-lean ground beef
1 medium onion, finely chopped
⅔ cup shredded carrots
⅔ cup shredded cabbage
⅔ cup finely chopped broccoli florets
½ cup plain panko (Japanese-style bread crumbs)
2 large egg whites
½ teaspoon garlic powder
½ teaspoon dried thyme, crumbled
¼ teaspoon salt
¼ teaspoon pepper

———— + ————

2 tablespoons no-salt-added ketchup
1 tablespoon light molasses

Molasses-Glazed Beef and Veggie Meat Loaf

Shredded carrots, cabbage, and broccoli make this meat loaf lighter and healthier than most. The glaze adds color and a final layer of flavor.

1. Fold an 18-inch-long piece of aluminum foil lengthwise in thirds. Place the foil in the slow cooker so it runs the length of the cooker and hangs over the two short sides (assuming use of an oval cooker). The foil will help you remove the cooked meat loaf from the slow cooker later. Lightly spray the foil and the inside of the slow cooker with cooking spray. Set aside.
2. Crumble the beef into a large bowl. Add the onion, carrots, cabbage, and broccoli. Using your hands or a spoon, gently combine.
3. Work in the panko, egg whites, garlic powder, thyme, salt, and pepper. Depending on the shape of your slow cooker, shape into an oval or round loaf 2½ to 3 inches thick. Place in the slow cooker so the foil strip is under the middle of the meat loaf. Cook, covered, on low for 3 hours 45 minutes to 5 hours 45 minutes or on high for 1 hour 45 minutes to 2 hours 45 minutes, or until the internal temperature of the meat loaf reaches 160°F on an instant-read thermometer.
4. About 30 minutes before serving time, in a small bowl, stir together the ketchup and molasses. Set aside.
5. When the meat loaf is ready, quickly spread the glaze over the top and re-cover the slow cooker. If using the low setting, change it to high. Cook for 5 to 10 minutes, or until the glaze is hot. Grasping the ends of the foil, carefully lift the meat loaf from the slow cooker. Transfer to a cutting board. Cover loosely. Let stand for 10 minutes before slicing or cutting into wedges.

PER SERVING
Calories **213**
Total Fat **5.0 g**
  Saturated Fat **2.0 g**
  Trans Fat **0.0 g**
  Polyunsaturated Fat **0.5 g**
  Monounsaturated Fat **2.0 g**

Cholesterol **60 mg**
Sodium **275 mg**
Carbohydrates **18 g**
  Fiber **2 g**
  Sugars **9 g**
Protein **26 g**

Dietary Exchanges:
  1 vegetable, 1 starch, 3 lean meat

Picadillo Beef

A spicy favorite in Spanish-speaking countries and the Philippines (where it is known as giniling), picadillo (pee-kah-DEE-yoh) usually contains ground beef and tomatoes, with the other ingredients varying by region. Our version features raisins, almonds, and a number of spices and is served over brown rice. Keep the ribs and seeds in the pepper so you'll get the full effect of the heat.

1. Lightly spray the slow cooker with cooking spray. Set aside.
2. In a large nonstick skillet, cook the beef over medium-high heat for 3 to 5 minutes, or until browned on the outside and no longer pink in the center, stirring occasionally to turn and break up the beef. Remove the skillet from the heat.
3. Stir in the tomatoes with liquid, onion, raisins, bay leaves, serrano pepper, sugar, cinnamon, cumin, nutmeg, garlic powder, thyme, and allspice. Transfer to the slow cooker. Cook, covered, on low for 6 hours or on high for 3 hours, or until the onion is very soft.
4. About 5 minutes before serving time, prepare the rice using the package directions.
5. Discard the bay leaves from the picadillo. Stir in the almonds, salt, and pepper. Spoon over the rice.

PER SERVING
Calories **339**
Total Fat **9.0 g**
 Saturated Fat **2.5 g**
 Trans Fat **0.0 g**
 Polyunsaturated Fat **1.5 g**
 Monounsaturated Fat **4.0 g**

Cholesterol **60 mg**
Sodium **229 mg**
Carbohydrates **40 g**
 Fiber **5 g**
 Sugars **16 g**
Protein **27 g**

Dietary Exchanges:
 **1 fruit, 1 starch,
 2 vegetable,
 3 lean meat**

SERVES 4; scant 1 cup beef mixture per serving

SLOW COOKER SIZE | SHAPE
3- to 4½-quart | round or oval

SLOW COOKING TIME
6 hours ON LOW, **OR**
3 hours ON HIGH

Cooking spray
1 pound extra-lean ground beef
1 14.5-ounce can no-salt-added diced tomatoes, undrained
1 medium onion, diced
⅓ cup dark or golden raisins
2 medium dried bay leaves
1 medium fresh serrano pepper or jalapeño with ribs and seeds, finely chopped
2 teaspoons sugar
¾ teaspoon ground cinnamon
½ teaspoon ground cumin
½ teaspoon ground nutmeg
½ teaspoon garlic powder
½ teaspoon dried thyme, crumbled
¼ teaspoon ground allspice

———— + ————

10 ounces frozen brown rice
¼ cup slivered almonds, dry-roasted (about 1 ounce)
¼ teaspoon salt
¼ teaspoon pepper

SERVES 6; 3 ounces pork per serving

SLOW COOKER SIZE | SHAPE
3- to 4½-quart | round or oval

SLOW COOKING TIME
6 to 8 hours ON LOW, **OR**
3 to 4 hours ON HIGH

1 medium orange, cut into 8 wedges

½ teaspoon pepper

½ teaspoon salt

1 1½-pound boneless pork loin roast, any netting or kitchen twine and all visible fat discarded

1 teaspoon olive oil

2 tablespoons minced onion

1 tablespoon chopped fresh oregano

1½ teaspoons cumin seeds, crushed using a mortar and pestle

2 medium garlic cloves, minced

½ teaspoon grated orange zest

Cuban-Style Pork with Orange

Many of the seasonings found in a typical Cuban adobo—a piquant sauce including garlic, cumin, oregano, and orange—are used to flavor this pork roast. In this recipe, the pork cooks on orange wedges, which provide moisture and act as a cooking rack, allowing the fat to drain away from the roast.

1. Lightly squeeze the orange wedges to release only some of their juice into the slow cooker. Add the wedges, each with one flat side down.

2. Sprinkle the pepper and salt all over the pork. Using your fingertips, gently press the seasonings so they adhere to the pork. In a medium nonstick skillet, heat the oil over medium-high heat, swirling to coat the bottom. Cook the pork for 4 to 6 minutes, turning to brown on all sides. Transfer to a large plate.

3. Reduce the heat to medium. Add the remaining ingredients, stirring to combine. Cook for 2 minutes, or until the onion begins to soften and the ingredients are fragrant. Spread over the pork. Place the pork on the orange wedges. Cook, covered, on low for 6 to 8 hours or on high for 3 to 4 hours, or until the pork registers 145°F on an instant-read thermometer.

4. Transfer the pork to a cutting board. Discard the orange wedges. Let the pork stand, loosely covered, for 10 minutes before slicing.

PER SERVING
Calories **183**
Total Fat **7.5 g**
  Saturated Fat **3.0 g**
  Trans Fat **0.0 g**
  Polyunsaturated Fat **0.5 g**
  Monounsaturated Fat **4.0 g**

Cholesterol **65 mg**
Sodium **242 mg**
Carbohydrates **3 g**
  Fiber **0 g**
  Sugars **1 g**
Protein **25 g**

Dietary Exchanges:
  3 lean meat

Alsatian Pork-and-Potato Casserole

Reminiscent of a dish you might enjoy in Alsace, where the cuisine is more German than French, this casserole uses everyday ingredients to create a satisfying meal. The low heat is needed for tenderness.

1. Lightly spray the slow cooker with cooking spray. Set aside.
2. In a large skillet, heat 1 teaspoon oil over medium-high heat, swirling to coat the bottom. Cook the pork for 3 to 4 minutes on each side, or until browned. Transfer to a large plate. Set aside.
3. Add the remaining 1 teaspoon oil to the skillet, swirling to coat the bottom. Cook the onions for 8 to 10 minutes, or until softened and golden, stirring frequently and adjusting the heat.
4. In the slow cooker, make one layer each of half the potatoes and half the onions. Sprinkle with half the garlic and all the caraway seeds, thyme, salt, and pepper. Arrange the pork on the onions. Repeat with the remaining potatoes, onions, and garlic. Don't stir.
5. Pour 1 cup broth into the skillet. Cook over medium heat for 5 minutes, or until hot.
6. Put the cornstarch in a small bowl. Add the remaining ½ cup broth, whisking to dissolve. Whisk into the broth in the skillet. Cook for 1 minute, or until thickened, whisking constantly. Pour over the ingredients in the slow cooker. Cook, covered, on low for 6 to 7 hours, or until the pork is slightly pink in the center.
7. Quickly arrange the bell pepper on top of the casserole and re-cover the slow cooker. Cook for 20 to 30 minutes, or until the bell pepper is tender.

COOK'S TIP

Mandolines and inexpensive v-blade slicers make quick work of slicing potatoes and onions to uniform thickness.

SERVES 8; 3 ounces pork and 1 cup vegetables per serving

SLOW COOKER SIZE | SHAPE
5- to 7-quart | round or oval

SLOW COOKING TIME
6 to 7 hours ON LOW plus 20 to 30 minutes ON LOW

Cooking spray

1 teaspoon olive oil and 1 teaspoon olive oil, divided use

8 boneless center-cut pork chops (about 4 ounces each), all visible fat discarded, patted dry

2 medium onions, cut crosswise into ¼-inch slices

2 pounds red potatoes, peeled, cut crosswise into ¼-inch slices

2 medium garlic cloves, minced

1½ teaspoons caraway seeds

1½ teaspoons dried thyme, crumbled

½ teaspoon salt

¼ teaspoon pepper

1 cup fat-free, low-sodium chicken broth and ½ cup fat-free, low-sodium chicken broth, such as on page 48, divided use

2 tablespoons cornstarch

———— + ————

1 medium red bell pepper, cut into ¼-inch rings

PER SERVING
Calories **266**
Total Fat **7.0 g**
  Saturated Fat **2.0 g**
  Trans Fat **0.0 g**
  Polyunsaturated Fat **1.0 g**
  Monounsaturated Fat **3.0 g**

Cholesterol **60 mg**
Sodium **234 mg**
Carbohydrates **25 g**
  Fiber **3 g**
  Sugars **4 g**
Protein **25 g**

Dietary Exchanges:
  1½ starch, 3 lean meat

SLOW COOKER SIZE | SHAPE
2- to 3-quart | round or oval

SLOW COOKING TIME
8 to 12 hours ON LOW, **OR**
4 to 6 hours ON HIGH

½ cup dried Great Northern beans, sorted for stones and shriveled beans, rinsed, and drained

1 large red bell pepper, chopped

¾ cup fat-free, low-sodium chicken broth, such as on page 48

1 teaspoon olive oil

1 1½-pound boneless pork loin roast, any netting or kitchen twine and all visible fat discarded

½ teaspoon salt

¼ teaspoon pepper

2 tablespoons finely chopped fresh rosemary

4 medium garlic cloves, minced

1 teaspoon dried fennel seeds, crushed

Tuscan Pork and Beans

As the pork loin, with its crust of rosemary, garlic, and fennel, slowly cooks atop the beans, it infuses them with robust flavor.

1. Fill a small saucepan three-fourths full of water. Bring to a boil over high heat. Stir in the beans. Return to a boil. Reduce the heat and simmer for 15 minutes. Pour the beans into a colander and rinse. Pour into the slow cooker. Stir in the bell pepper and broth.

2. Meanwhile, in a medium nonstick skillet, heat the oil over medium-high heat, swirling to coat the bottom. Cook the pork for 4 to 6 minutes, turning to brown all sides. Transfer to a large plate. Sprinkle the salt and pepper over the top side of the pork. Using your fingertips, gently press the seasonings so they adhere to the pork.

3. In a small bowl, stir together the rosemary, garlic, and fennel seeds. Sprinkle over the top of the pork. Place the pork with the seasoned side up on the beans. Cook, covered, on low for 8 to 12 hours or on high for 4 to 6 hours, or until the pork is fork-tender and the beans are creamy and very tender.

4. Transfer the pork to a cutting board, leaving the bean mixture in the slow cooker. Let the pork stand, loosely covered, for 10 minutes before slicing. Serve over the beans or with the beans on the side.

COOK'S TIP
For this recipe, you don't need to test the pork for doneness with a thermometer. It will cook past the minimum internal temperature needed for food safety (145°F) to get to the fork-tender stage.

PER SERVING
Calories **230**
Total Fat **8.0 g**
  Saturated Fat **3.0 g**
  Trans Fat **0.0 g**
  Polyunsaturated Fat **1.0 g**
  Monounsaturated Fat **4.0 g**

Cholesterol **65 mg**
Sodium **250 mg**
Carbohydrates **10 g**
  Fiber **4 g**
  Sugars **1 g**
Protein **28 g**

Dietary Exchanges:
½ **starch**, 3½ **lean meat**

Jerk Pork Loin with Mango Salsa

Mango salsa makes a colorful pairing for this delectable, spicy pork dish. Once the pork roast is slow cooking, you can make and refrigerate the salsa, or toss it together just before serving the meal.

1. In the slow cooker, stir together the water, onion, and thyme. Set aside.
2. Sprinkle the seasoning blend all over the pork. Using your fingertips, gently press the seasoning so it adheres to the pork. Transfer to the slow cooker.
3. Drizzle 1 tablespoon lime juice over the pork. Cook, covered, on low for 6 to 7 hours or on high for 3 to 3½ hours, or until the pork registers 145°F on an instant-read thermometer.
4. Transfer the pork to a cutting board. Let stand for about 10 minutes. Cut the pork into thin slices or shred it using one or two forks.
5. Meanwhile, in a medium bowl, stir together the remaining ingredients. Cover and refrigerate until needed if made in advance, or prepare shortly before serving time and set aside.
6. When the pork is ready, spoon the salsa on top.

FAST PREP!

SERVES 8; 3 ounces pork and ¼ cup salsa per serving

SLOW COOKER SIZE | SHAPE
3- to 4½-quart | round or oval

SLOW COOKING TIME
6 to 7 hours ON LOW, **OR**
3 to 3½ hours ON HIGH

1 cup water
½ medium onion, sliced
1 sprig of fresh thyme
1 teaspoon salt-free Jamaican jerk seasoning blend
1 2-pound boneless pork loin roast, any netting or kitchen twine and all visible fat discarded
1 tablespoon fresh lime juice

—————— + ——————

2 medium mangoes, chopped
½ cup finely chopped red bell pepper
¼ cup chopped green onions (green and white parts)
¼ cup snipped fresh cilantro
2 tablespoons fresh lime juice
¼ teaspoon crushed red pepper flakes

PER SERVING
Calories **221**
Total Fat **7.0 g**
  Saturated Fat **2.5 g**
  Trans Fat **0.0 g**
  Polyunsaturated Fat **0.5 g**
  Monounsaturated Fat **3.5 g**

Cholesterol **65 mg**
Sodium **50 mg**
Carbohydrates **14 g**
  Fiber **2 g**
  Sugars **12 g**
Protein **25 g**

Dietary Exchanges:
  1 fruit, 3 lean meat

Pork Tenderloin with Cherry and Peach Salsa

The unusually flavored salsa, with its blend of fruity, spicy, and tangy notes, is a worthy accompaniment for the delicious, succulent pork.

1. Lightly spray the slow cooker with cooking spray. Set aside.
2. In a small bowl, stir together the chili powder, cinnamon, garlic powder, allspice, salt, and cayenne. Sprinkle over both sides of the pork. Using your fingertips, gently press the seasonings so they adhere to the pork.
3. In a large nonstick skillet, heat the oil over medium-high heat, swirling to coat the bottom. Cook the pork for 4 minutes, or until browned, turning once halfway through. Remove the skillet from the heat. Transfer the pork to the slow cooker.
4. Pour the water into the skillet, scraping the bottom and side to dislodge any browned bits. Pour around, not over, the pork. Cook, covered, on low for 2 hours to 2 hours 15 minutes or on high for 1 hour to 1 hour 10 minutes, or until the pork registers 145°F on an instant-read thermometer. Quickly transfer the pork to a cutting board. Discard the cooking liquid.
5. If using the low setting, change it to high. Put the remaining ingredients except the gingerroot in the slow cooker, stirring to combine. Cook, covered, for 15 minutes, or until heated through. Meanwhile, let the pork stand for about 10 minutes before slicing.
6. When the salsa is hot, stir in the gingerroot. Serve the salsa with the pork.

COOK'S TIP

It's important not to overcook pork tenderloin—or it won't be tender! Season it, brown it a bit, and cook it in the slow cooker just for a while.

SERVES 4; 3 ounces pork and ⅓ cup salsa per serving

SLOW COOKER SIZE | SHAPE
3- to 4½-quart | round or oval

SLOW COOKING TIME
2 hours to 2 hours 15 minutes ON LOW plus 15 minutes ON HIGH, **OR**

1 hour to 1 hour 10 minutes ON HIGH plus 15 minutes ON HIGH

Cooking spray
2 teaspoons chili powder
½ teaspoon ground cinnamon
½ teaspoon garlic powder
¼ teaspoon ground allspice
¼ teaspoon salt
⅛ teaspoon cayenne
1 1-pound pork tenderloin, all visible fat discarded
1 teaspoon canola or corn oil
¼ cup water

———— + ————

1 cup frozen dark sweet cherries, thawed, coarsely chopped
1 cup frozen unsweetened peach slices, thawed, diced
1 medium fresh jalapeño, seeds and ribs discarded, finely chopped
1 tablespoon sugar
1½ teaspoons balsamic vinegar
1 teaspoon grated peeled gingerroot

PER SERVING
Calories **198**
Total Fat **4.0 g**
　Saturated Fat **1.0 g**
　Trans Fat **0.0 g**
　Polyunsaturated Fat **1.0 g**
　Monounsaturated Fat **2.0 g**

Cholesterol **74 mg**
Sodium **229 mg**
Carbohydrates **15 g**
　Fiber **3 g**
　Sugars **10 g**
Protein **25 g**

Dietary Exchanges:
1 fruit, 3 lean meat

SERVES 4; 1¼ cups per serving

SLOW COOKER SIZE | SHAPE
3- to 4½-quart | round or oval

SLOW COOKING TIME
5 to 6 hours ON LOW

1½ pounds butternut squash, peeled, seeds and strings discarded, cut into 1-inch cubes, or 16 to 18 ounces refrigerated cubes

1 medium onion, chopped

1 1-pound pork tenderloin, all visible fat discarded, cut into 1-inch cubes

1 medium green or red bell pepper, diced

2 tablespoons uncooked instant, or quick-cooking, tapioca

½ cup fat-free, low-sodium chicken broth, such as on page 48

¼ cup no-salt-added tomato paste

2 tablespoons honey

2 tablespoons balsamic vinegar

1 teaspoon ground cumin

½ to 1 teaspoon chipotle powder

¼ teaspoon salt

¼ teaspoon pepper

—————— ✦ ——————

1½ cups uncooked instant brown rice

¼ cup snipped fresh cilantro (optional)

Pork and Butternut Stew

Ground chipotle pepper is a great ingredient to have on hand to add subtle smokiness and kick up the heat of an everyday dish. It and honey are the "secret" ingredients that make this stew special.

1. In the slow cooker, make one layer each, in order, of the squash, onion, pork, and bell pepper, sprinkling about 1½ teaspoons tapioca over each layer as you go.
2. In a small bowl, whisk together the broth, tomato paste, honey, vinegar, cumin, chipotle powder, salt, and pepper. Pour into the slow cooker. Don't stir. Cook, covered, on low for 5 to 6 hours.
3. About 20 minutes before serving time, prepare the rice using the package directions, omitting the salt and margarine.
4. Serve the stew over the rice. Garnish with the cilantro.

COOK'S TIP

To make any raw whole winter squash easier to cut, microwave it first. Pierce the squash in several places with the tip of a knife. Place the squash on a paper towel. For a 1½-pound squash, as in this recipe, microwave on 100 percent power (high) for about 3 minutes. Using a kitchen towel to keep from burning your fingers, transfer the squash to a cutting board. Still using the towel, hold the squash in place and carefully cut it in the desired number of pieces.

PER SERVING
Calories **380**
Total Fat **4.0 g**
 Saturated Fat **1.0 g**
 Trans Fat **0.0 g**
 Polyunsaturated Fat **1.0 g**
 Monounsaturated Fat **1.0 g**
Cholesterol **74 mg**
Sodium **243 mg**
Carbohydrates **60 g**
 Fiber **6 g**
 Sugars **18 g**
 Protein **29 g**
Dietary Exchanges:
 3½ starch,
 2 vegetable,
 3 very lean meat

Four-Seed Pork Loin

The slow cooker mellows a combination of spices to create an extremely flavorful pork roast.

1. In the slow cooker, stir together ⅔ cup cider and the onion. Set aside.

2. On a large piece of wax paper, combine the fennel, caraway, dill, and celery seeds. Spread them in a single layer. Set aside.

3. Brush the mustard all over the pork. Gently roll the pork in the seeds to coat. Place the pork in the slow cooker. Cook, covered, on low for 6 to 7 hours or on high for 3 to 3½ hours, or until the pork registers 145°F on an instant-read thermometer.

4. Leaving the cooking liquid in the slow cooker, transfer the pork to a cutting board. Let the pork stand for about 10 minutes. Slice the pork. Cover to keep warm.

5. While the pork is standing, strain the cooking liquid into a small saucepan.

6. Put the cornstarch in a small bowl. Add the remaining 1 tablespoon cider, whisking to dissolve. Whisk into the cooking liquid. Cook over medium heat for 2 minutes, or until the sauce is thickened and bubbly, whisking constantly. Serve spooned over the pork.

COOK'S TIP

You can crush seeds by using a mortar and pestle or spreading them in a single layer on a cutting board and either pressing them with the side of a chef's knife blade or rolling over them with a rolling pin.

FAST PREP!

SERVES 8; 3 ounces pork and 2 tablespoons sauce per serving

SLOW COOKER SIZE | SHAPE
3- to 4½-quart | round or oval

SLOW COOKING TIME
6 to 7 hours ON LOW, **OR**
3 to 3½ hours ON HIGH

⅔ cup unsweetened apple cider or apple juice

½ medium onion, sliced

1 teaspoon fennel seeds, crushed

1 teaspoon caraway seeds, crushed

1 teaspoon dill seeds, crushed

1 teaspoon celery seeds, crushed

1 tablespoon spicy brown mustard

1 2-pound boneless pork loin roast, any netting or kitchen twine and all visible fat discarded

————— ✛ —————

1 tablespoon cornstarch

1 tablespoon unsweetened apple cider or apple juice

PER SERVING
Calories **188**
Total Fat **7.0 g**
  Saturated Fat **2.5 g**
  Trans Fat **0.0 g**
  Polyunsaturated Fat **0.5 g**
  Monounsaturated Fat **3.5 g**

Cholesterol **65 mg**
Sodium **68 mg**
Carbohydrates **5 g**
  Fiber **1 g**
  Sugars **3 g**
  Protein **25 g**

Dietary Exchanges:
  ½ **other carbohydrate,**
  3 lean meat

SERVES 4; 2 tacos per serving

SLOW COOKER SIZE | SHAPE
3- to 4½-quart | round or oval

SLOW COOKING TIME
6 to 8 hours ON LOW, **OR**
3 to 4 hours ON HIGH

1 tablespoon ground cumin

½ teaspoon chipotle powder

½ teaspoon salt

¼ teaspoon pepper

1 1-pound pork tenderloin, all visible fat discarded, cut into 1-inch cubes

2 teaspoons canola or corn oil and 1 teaspoon canola or corn oil, divided use

1 medium onion, thinly sliced lengthwise

2 medium garlic cloves, minced

½ cup fresh orange juice

1 teaspoon dried oregano, crumbled

———— + ————

8 6-inch corn tortillas

1 medium tomato, chopped

2 medium green onions, thinly sliced

¼ cup chopped fresh cilantro

2 medium limes, each cut into 4 wedges

Pork Carnitas

Traditionally made using fattier cuts of pork that are often simmered in a generous amount of lard, carnitas aren't usually considered heart-healthy fare. However, this healthier version uses lean pork tenderloin that simmers in orange juice to make it succulent.

1. In a small bowl, stir together the cumin, chipotle powder, salt, and pepper.
2. Place the pork in a medium bowl. Sprinkle half the cumin mixture over the pork. Stir to coat. Set the remaining cumin mixture aside.
3. In a large skillet, heat 2 teaspoons oil over medium-high heat, swirling to coat the bottom. Cook the pork for 5 minutes, or until browned all over, stirring frequently. Transfer to the slow cooker.
4. Reduce the heat to medium. Heat the remaining 1 teaspoon oil in the skillet, swirling to coat the bottom. Cook the onion for 3 minutes, or until almost soft, stirring frequently. Stir in the garlic. Cook for 1 minute, or until fragrant, stirring constantly. Stir in the orange juice. Cook for 2 minutes, or until the mixture comes to a boil, scraping to dislodge any browned bits. Transfer the onion mixture to the slow cooker. Stir in the oregano.
5. Cook, covered, on low for 6 to 8 hours or on high for 3 to 4 hours, or until the pork is tender. Stir in the remaining cumin mixture.
6. Just before serving time, warm the tortillas using the package directions. Transfer to plates. Using a slotted spoon, transfer the pork mixture to the centers of the tortillas. Top with the tomato, green onions, and cilantro. Serve with the lime wedges.

COOK'S TIP

Spices can lose their punch when they've been slow cooked for hours. Using half the spice mixture at the start of the cooking time and then adding the remaining half at the end of the cooking time gives the finished dish the fullest flavor.

PER SERVING
Calories **256**
Total Fat **7.5 g**
  Saturated Fat **1.5 g**
  Trans Fat **0.0 g**
  Polyunsaturated Fat **2.0 g**
  Monounsaturated Fat **3.5 g**

Cholesterol **60 mg**
Sodium **397 mg**
Carbohydrates **23 g**
  Fiber **4 g**
  Sugars **7 g**
Protein **24 g**

Dietary Exchanges:
  1 starch, 1 vegetable, 3 lean meat

Salad Greens with Lime and Herb Pulled Pork

A mild version of pico de gallo dresses a bed of fresh salad greens topped with herb-rubbed pork. Squeeze fresh lime juice over the salad for some extra zing.

1. In the slow cooker, stir together the onion, water, jalapeño, and 3 garlic cloves. Set aside.
2. In a small bowl, stir together the cumin, oregano, pepper, and salt. Sprinkle all over the pork. Using your fingertips, gently press the seasonings so they adhere to the pork.
3. Place the pork in the slow cooker. Drizzle the lime juice over the pork. Cook, covered, on low for 7 to 8 hours or on high for 3½ to 4 hours, or until the pork is fork-tender. (The pork will be past the minimum internal temperature of 145°F at this point.)
4. Meanwhile, in a medium bowl, stir together the tomatoes, red onion, cilantro, and the remaining garlic clove. If you make the pico de gallo 1 hour or more in advance, cover and refrigerate until needed. If less than 1 hour, set the uncovered pico de gallo aside.
5. Transfer the pork to a cutting board, leaving the onion mixture in the slow cooker. Let the pork stand for 3 minutes. Using your hands or two forks, pull the meat apart into long shreds. Stir into the onion mixture to "wet" the pork.
6. Just before serving, arrange the lettuce on plates. Using a slotted spoon or tongs, put the pork on the lettuce, discarding the onion mixture. Top with the pico de gallo. Serve with the lime wedges for squeezing over all.

PER SERVING
Calories **170**
Total Fat **3.0 g**
  Saturated Fat **1.0 g**
  Trans Fat **0.0 g**
  Polyunsaturated Fat **0.5 g**
  Monounsaturated Fat **1.0 g**
Cholesterol **74 mg**
Sodium **223 mg**
Carbohydrates **11 g**
  Fiber **3 g**
  Sugars **6 g**
  Protein **26 g**
Dietary Exchanges:
2 vegetable, 3 lean meat

FAST PREP!

SERVES 4; 3 ounces pork, 1½ cups lettuce, and ¼ cup pico de gallo per serving

SLOW COOKER SIZE | SHAPE
3- to 4½-quart | round or oval

SLOW COOKING TIME
7 to 8 hours ON LOW, **OR**
3½ to 4 hours ON HIGH

1 medium onion, cut into 12 wedges
½ cup water
1 medium fresh jalapeño, seeds and ribs discarded, chopped
3 medium garlic cloves, minced
1 teaspoon ground cumin
1 teaspoon dried oregano, crumbled
¼ teaspoon pepper
¼ teaspoon salt
1 1-pound pork tenderloin, all visible fat discarded
1 tablespoon fresh lime juice

———— + ————

1 cup chopped seeded tomatoes (2 medium)
2 tablespoons finely chopped red onion
2 tablespoons snipped fresh cilantro
1 medium garlic clove, minced
6 cups torn fresh lettuces, spinach, or a combination
1 small lime, cut into 4 wedges

SERVES 4; 1½ cups per serving

SLOW COOKER SIZE | SHAPE
4- to 6-quart | round or oval

SLOW COOKING TIME

5 to 7 hours ON LOW, **OR**

2 to 3 hours ON HIGH

1 28-ounce can no-salt-added diced or whole peeled tomatoes, undrained, diced if whole

1 pound boneless lean pork loin roast or chops, any netting or kitchen twine and all visible fat discarded, cut into 1½-inch cubes

1 15.5-ounce can no-salt-added black beans or no-salt-added pinto beans, rinsed and drained

1 medium onion, chopped

1 medium fresh jalapeño, seeds and ribs discarded, chopped

3 tablespoons red wine vinegar

2 teaspoons dried minced garlic

2 teaspoons chili powder

1 teaspoon ground cumin

1 teaspoon dried oregano, crumbled

¼ teaspoon salt

¼ teaspoon pepper

———— + ————

¼ cup fat-free sour cream (optional)

¼ cup shredded or grated fat-free sharp Cheddar cheese (optional)

Snipped fresh cilantro (optional)

Pork-and-Beans Chili

If your idea of chili means ground beef and red beans, try this quick-to-fix pork-and-black bean version instead. It's guaranteed to change your way of thinking about your usual bowl of red.

In the slow cooker, stir together the tomatoes with liquid, pork, beans, onion, jalapeño, vinegar, garlic, chili powder, cumin, oregano, salt, and pepper. Cook, covered, on low for 5 to 7 hours or on high for 2 to 3 hours. Ladle into bowls. Top each serving with the sour cream, Cheddar, and cilantro.

PER SERVING
Calories **326**
Total Fat **8.0 g**
  Saturated Fat **3.0 g**
  Trans Fat **0.0 g**
  Polyunsaturated Fat **0.5 g**
  Monounsaturated Fat **3.5 g**

Cholesterol **64 mg**
Sodium **239 mg**
Carbohydrates **31 g**
  Fiber **7 g**
  Sugars **12 g**
  Protein **31 g**

Dietary Exchanges:
  1 starch, 3 vegetable, 3½ lean meat

PER SERVING (with optional garnishes)
Calories **352**
Total Fat **8.0 g**
  Saturated Fat **3.0 g**
  Trans Fat **0.0 g**
  Polyunsaturated Fat **0.5 g**
  Monounsaturated Fat **3.5 g**

Cholesterol **68 mg**
Sodium **321 mg**
Carbohydrates **34 g**
  Fiber **7 g**
  Sugars **13 g**
  Protein **34 g**

Dietary Exchanges:
  1½ starch, 3 vegetable, 3½ lean meat

Pork Chops with Grape Tomatoes and Fresh Basil

For an easy Italian meal, serve this dish, beautiful with its vibrant topping of red tomatoes and deep green basil, with whole-wheat orzo and broccoli rabe.

SERVES 4; 1 pork chop and ¼ cup sauce per serving

SLOW COOKER SIZE | SHAPE
2½- to 3½-quart | round or oval

SLOW COOKING TIME
2½ to 3½ hours ON LOW, **OR**
1½ to 2 hours ON HIGH

3 medium garlic cloves, minced

¼ teaspoon salt

¼ teaspoon pepper

4 lean bone-in pork rib chops (about 6 ounces each), all visible fat discarded

1 teaspoon olive oil

⅓ cup dry white wine (regular or nonalcoholic) or fat-free, low-sodium chicken broth, such as on page 48

1½ cups grape tomatoes, halved

———————— + ————————

2 tablespoons loosely packed chopped fresh basil

1. Sprinkle the garlic, salt, and pepper over both sides of the pork. Using your fingertips, gently press the seasonings so they adhere to the pork.
2. In a large nonstick skillet, heat the oil over medium-high heat, swirling to coat the bottom. Cook the pork for 4 to 6 minutes, or until browned, turning once halfway through. Arrange in a single layer in the slow cooker (the ends of the chops may slightly overlap).
3. Pour the wine into the skillet. Increase the heat to high and bring to a boil, scraping the bottom and side to dislodge any browned bits. Boil for 30 seconds to 1 minute, or until the mixture is reduced by about half. Pour over the pork.
4. Spread the tomatoes over the pork. Cook, covered, on low for 2½ to 3½ hours or on high for 1½ to 2 hours, or until the pork is tender and slightly pink in the very center.
5. Transfer the pork to plates. Using a slotted spoon, spoon the tomatoes over the pork. Set aside. Pour the cooking liquid into a medium skillet. Bring to a boil over high heat. Boil for 2 to 4 minutes, or until reduced by one-third (to about ¼ cup). Pour over the pork and tomatoes. Sprinkle with the basil.

PER SERVING
Calories **222**
Total Fat **9.5 g**
  Saturated Fat **2.5 g**
  Trans Fat **0.0 g**
  Polyunsaturated Fat **1.0 g**
  Monounsaturated Fat **3.5 g**

Cholesterol **68 mg**
Sodium **216 mg**
Carbohydrates **5 g**
  Fiber **1 g**
  Sugars **2 g**
  Protein **26 g**

Dietary Exchanges:
  1 vegetable, 3 lean meat

Pork Chops with Grape
Tomatoes and Fresh Basil,
page 197

Braised Broccoli
Rabe with Cherry
Tomatoes,
page 253

SLOW COOKER SIZE | SHAPE
   3- to 4½-quart | oval
SLOW COOKING TIME
5 to 6 hours ON LOW, **OR**
2½ to 3 hours ON HIGH

Cooking spray

2 large egg whites or
   ½ cup egg substitute,
   lightly beaten

¼ cup low-fat buttermilk

1 cup whole-wheat panko
   (Japanese-style bread
   crumbs) or plain dry
   bread crumbs (lowest
   sodium available)

1 teaspoon garlic powder

½ teaspoon dried thyme,
   crumbled

½ teaspoon paprika

¼ teaspoon salt

¼ teaspoon pepper

4 boneless pork loin chops
   (about 4 ounces each),
   all visible fat discarded,
   pounded to ½-inch
   thickness

German Schnitzel

Slow cooking produces tender, juicy schnitzel with a crisp crust; it's a healthier approach than the traditional fried version—plus you won't have the cleanup that goes with panfrying. Serve steamed green beans and roasted potatoes as sides.

1. Lightly spray the inside of the slow cooker with cooking spray. Place a metal rack with short legs, such as a pressure cooker rack, in the bottom of the slow cooker (no need to spray the rack). If you don't have a rack, take a sheet of aluminum foil that's 3 feet in length and fold it in half lengthwise. Fold in half lengthwise again. Twist the foil to create a "rope." Coil the rope at the bottom of the slow cooker. It will lift the pork so it won't get too soggy.

2. In a medium shallow dish, whisk together the egg whites and buttermilk. In a separate medium shallow dish, stir together the remaining ingredients except the pork. Dip the pork in the egg white mixture, then in the panko mixture, turning to coat at each step and gently shaking off any excess. Using your fingertips, gently press the coating so it adheres to the pork.

3. Transfer the pork to the rack in the slow cooker. Cook, covered, on low for 5 to 6 hours or on high for 2½ to 3 hours.

PER SERVING
Calories **206**
Total Fat **3.5 g**
   Saturated Fat **1.0 g**
   Trans Fat **0.0 g**
   Polyunsaturated Fat **0.5 g**
   Monounsaturated Fat **1.0 g**

Cholesterol **60 mg**
Sodium **259 mg**
Carbohydrates **16 g**
   Fiber **2 g**
   Sugars **1 g**
Protein **27 g**

Dietary Exchanges:
   1 starch, 3 lean meat

Garlicky Lamb Steaks with Green Olive and Tomato Relish

A lively relish of tangy green olives, sweet grape tomatoes, crunchy almonds, and fragrant basil and mint tops these rich-tasting lamb steaks.

SERVES 4; 3 ounces lamb and 2 tablespoons relish per serving

SLOW COOKER SIZE | SHAPE
2- to 3-quart | round or oval

SLOW COOKING TIME
3 to 5 hours ON LOW, **OR**
1½ to 2½ hours ON HIGH

1. Sprinkle the garlic, ¼ teaspoon pepper, and the salt over both sides of the lamb. Using your fingertips, gently press the seasonings so they adhere to the lamb.
2. In a large nonstick skillet, heat the oil over medium-high heat, swirling to coat the bottom. Cook the lamb for 3 to 5 minutes, or until browned, turning once halfway through. Transfer to a large plate. Set aside.
3. In the same skillet, still over medium-high heat, cook the onion for 3 minutes, or until soft, stirring frequently. Transfer the onion to the slow cooker. Place the lamb on the onion.
4. Pour the broth into the skillet. Increase the heat to high and bring to a boil, scraping the bottom and side to dislodge any browned bits. Pour over the lamb. Cook, covered, on low for 3 to 5 hours or on high for 1½ to 2½ hours, or until the lamb is tender.
5. Just before serving time, in a small bowl, stir together the remaining ingredients. Spoon the relish over the lamb.

3 medium garlic cloves, minced
¼ teaspoon pepper
⅛ teaspoon salt
4 boneless top round lamb steaks (about 4 ounces each), all visible fat discarded
1 teaspoon olive oil
1 large onion, cut into ½-inch wedges
½ cup fat-free, low-sodium chicken broth, such as on page 48

+

¼ cup pitted green olives or pimiento-stuffed olives, chopped
¼ cup chopped grape tomatoes
1 tablespoon slivered almonds, chopped
1 tablespoon chopped fresh basil
1½ teaspoons chopped fresh mint
⅛ teaspoon minced garlic
⅛ teaspoon pepper

PER SERVING
Calories **212**
Total Fat **11.0 g**
  Saturated Fat **3.0 g**
  Trans Fat **0.0 g**
  Polyunsaturated Fat **1.0 g**
  Monounsaturated Fat **5.5 g**
Cholesterol **68 mg**
Sodium **308 mg**
Carbohydrates **7 g**
  Fiber **2 g**
  Sugars **4 g**
Protein **22 g**
Dietary Exchanges:
  1 vegetable, 3 lean meat, ½ fat

Vegetarian Entrées

203 Cauliflower-Crust Pizza with Vegetable Topping and Balsamic Glaze

206 Mexican-Style Barley and Black Beans ⏱

207 "Baked" Potatoes Stuffed with Blue Cheese and Meatless Crumbles

208 Barley Risotto with Mushrooms and Spinach

209 White and Greens Lasagna

212 Zucchini and Tomato Risotto

213 Nutty Brown Rice and Arugula Toss ⏱

214 Rustic Two-Cheese Ratatouille

215 Veggies and Pasta with Blue Cheese

216 Beans and Greens Enchiladas ⏱

218 Layered Pasta Casserole

219 Italian Artichoke-Stuffed Bell Peppers

220 Gingered Lentils and Quinoa

221 Greek Lentils ⏱

223 Black and Red Bean Chili with Peppery Sour Cream

224 East Indian Spiced Beans with Apricot Rice

225 Mexican Stuffed Squash

226 Cuban-Style Black Beans and Rice

227 Red-Bean Spaghetti

228 Spaghetti Squash Noodle Bowl

230 Bean and Roasted Vegetable Stew

231 Louisiana Vegetable Stew ⏱

232 Cranberry Bean and Sweet Potato Chili

233 Thai Vegetable Curry

235 Parmesan Polenta with Roasted Vegetables

236 Chickpea and Vegetable Stew

238 Spicy Vegetable Curry

239 Chickpea, Cucumber, and Tomato Salad with Feta

240 Tofu Tikka Masala

241 Vegetable Stew with Cornmeal Dumplings ⏱

Cauliflower-Crust Pizza with Vegetable Topping and Balsamic Glaze

We've all heard of vegetables on our pizza, but what about under it? Cauliflower plays a supporting role in this recipe and takes the place of traditional flour to form a thin, crunchy crust. A small drizzle of a sweet, tart glaze makes a big splash over a rainbow topping of vegetables.

1. Lightly spray the slow cooker with cooking spray. In a medium bowl, stir together the cauliflower, Parmesan, egg whites, egg, and oregano. Using your hands, gently press the mixture to form a crust in the bottom of the slow cooker.

2. In the same medium bowl (rinsed and wiped clean), whisk together the tomato sauce, basil, and salt until combined. Spread over the cauliflower crust.

3. Place the meatless crumbles, mushrooms, and all the bell peppers on the tomato sauce. Sprinkle the sun-dried tomatoes over all. Cook, covered, on low for 4 to 5 hours or on high for 2 to 2½ hours, or until the mushrooms are soft and the bell peppers are tender.

4. Quickly sprinkle the mozzarella over the vegetable topping. Re-cover the slow cooker and cook for 30 minutes on low or 15 minutes on high, or until the mozzarella has melted.

5. While the mozzarella is melting, in a small saucepan, stir together the vinegar and honey. Bring to a simmer over medium-high heat. Reduce the heat to medium low and simmer for about 8 to 10 minutes, until the mixture is reduced by half (to about ¼ cup), swirling the pan and stirring occasionally.

6. Using a wide spatula, gently lift the pizza from the slow cooker and transfer to a work surface. Drizzle the glaze over the pizza. Cut into slices.

SERVES 4; 2 slices per serving

SLOW COOKER SIZE | SHAPE
3- to 4½-quart | round or oval

SLOW COOKING TIME
4 to 5 hours ON LOW plus 30 minutes ON LOW, **OR**

2 to 2½ hours ON HIGH plus 15 minutes ON HIGH

Cooking spray

2 cups finely chopped cauliflower florets and stems (about ¼ of a large head of cauliflower)

¼ cup shredded or grated Parmesan cheese

2 large egg whites

1 large egg or ¼ cup egg substitute

1 teaspoon dried oregano, crumbled

1 8-ounce can no-salt-added tomato sauce

¼ cup coarsely chopped fresh basil

¼ teaspoon salt

1¼ cups frozen meatless crumbles, thawed

½ cup sliced button mushrooms

½ cup sliced orange bell peppers

½ cup sliced yellow bell peppers

½ cup sliced green bell peppers

4 sun-dried tomatoes, snipped into ½-inch pieces

＋

½ cup shredded low-fat mozzarella cheese

GLAZE

½ cup balsamic vinegar

1 tablespoon honey or pure maple syrup

PER SERVING
Calories **206**
Total Fat **4.5 g**
  Saturated Fat **2.0 g**
  Trans Fat **0.0 g**
  Polyunsaturated Fat **0.5 g**
  Monounsaturated Fat **1.5 g**

Cholesterol **55 mg**
Sodium **536 mg**
Carbohydrates **24 g**
  Fiber **6 g**
  Sugars **14 g**
Protein **20 g**

Dietary Exchanges:
2 vegetable, 1 other carbohydrate, 2 lean meat

Cauliflower–Crust Pizza with Vegetable Topping and Balsamic Glaze, page 203

SERVES 4; 1¼ cups per serving

SLOW COOKER SIZE | SHAPE
3- to 4½-quart | round or oval

SLOW COOKING TIME

3 hours ON LOW, **OR**

1½ hours ON HIGH

Cooking spray

2 cups water

1 cup quick-cooking barley

1 medium red bell pepper, chopped

1 medium onion, chopped

＋

½ 15.5-ounce can no-salt-added black beans, rinsed and drained

1 medium poblano pepper, seeds and ribs discarded, thinly sliced lengthwise and cut crosswise into 2-inch strips

2 tablespoons fresh lime juice

2 tablespoons olive oil (extra virgin preferred)

2 medium garlic cloves, minced

½ teaspoon salt

¼ cup snipped fresh cilantro

Mexican-Style Barley and Black Beans

Take a break from the expected by making this barley dish instead of rice the next time you want to eat Mexican. It's a stick-to-your-ribs entrée, so come to the table hungry!

1. Lightly spray the slow cooker with cooking spray. Stir in the water, barley, bell pepper, and onion. Cook, covered, on low for 3 hours or on high for 1½ hours, or until the barley is tender. Transfer to a large bowl.
2. Stir in the remaining ingredients except the cilantro. Gently stir in the cilantro.

PER SERVING
Calories **261**
Total Fat **7.5 g**
  Saturated Fat **1.0 g**
  Trans Fat **0.0 g**
  Polyunsaturated Fat **1.0 g**
  Monounsaturated Fat **5.0 g**

Cholesterol **0 mg**
Sodium **301 mg**
Carbohydrates **43 g**
  Fiber **8 g**
  Sugars **6 g**
Protein **8 g**

Dietary Exchanges:
  2½ starch, 1 vegetable, 1 fat

"Baked" Potatoes Stuffed with Blue Cheese and Meatless Crumbles

Simply wrap potatoes in aluminum foil, pop them in the slow cooker, and know they'll be waiting for you at mealtime. You can make the filling in about 5 minutes.

SERVES 4; 1 potato, ¼ cup meatless crumble mixture, and 2 tablespoons cheese per serving

SLOW COOKER SIZE | SHAPE
3- to 4½-quart | round or oval

SLOW COOKING TIME
5½ to 6 hours ON LOW, **OR**
2 hours 45 minutes to 3 hours ON HIGH

1. Wrap each potato tightly in aluminum foil. Place in the slow cooker. Cook, covered, on low for 5½ to 6 hours or on high for 2 hours 45 minutes to 3 hours, or until the potatoes are tender when pierced with a fork. Remove the potatoes from the slow cooker. Set aside, still wrapped.

2. About 5 minutes before serving time, in a medium nonstick skillet, heat the oil over medium heat, swirling to coat the bottom. Cook the meatless crumbles, dillweed, and pepper for 3 minutes, or until heated through and beginning to brown, stirring frequently. Remove from the heat. Stir in the green onions, saving a small amount to sprinkle over the potatoes if desired.

3. Split the potatoes in half lengthwise. Fluff with a fork. Spoon the blue cheese onto each potato. Top with the meatless crumble mixture. Sprinkle with any remaining green onions.

4 6-ounce Yukon Gold or red potatoes, each pierced with a fork in several places

+

2 teaspoons canola or corn oil

6 ounces frozen meatless crumbles

1½ teaspoons dried dillweed, crumbled

¼ teaspoon pepper (coarsely ground preferred)

2 medium green onions, finely chopped

½ cup low-fat blue cheese

COOK'S TIP

Wrapping the potatoes in aluminum foil keeps the moisture in and prevents the skins from drying out. Using Yukon Gold or red potatoes will ensure that you'll have a moister potato after baking.

PER SERVING
Calories **254**
Total Fat **5.0 g**
  Saturated Fat **2.0 g**
  Trans Fat **0.0 g**
  Polyunsaturated Fat **1.0 g**
  Monounsaturated Fat **2.0 g**

Cholesterol **8 mg**
Sodium **353 mg**
Carbohydrates **36 g**
  Fiber **6 g**
  Sugars **2 g**
Protein **16 g**

Dietary Exchanges:
  2½ starch, 2 lean meat

SERVES 4; 1½ cups per serving

SLOW COOKER SIZE | SHAPE
3- to 4½-quart | round or oval

SLOW COOKING TIME
2 hours ON HIGH plus
15 minutes ON HIGH

2 teaspoons olive oil

8 ounces button mushrooms, sliced

1 small onion, diced

3½ cups fat-free, low-sodium vegetable broth, such as on page 50

1½ cups uncooked pearl barley (not quick-cooking or instant)

2 medium garlic cloves, minced

¼ teaspoon salt

¼ teaspoon pepper

— + —

2 ounces spinach (about 2 cups), chopped

¼ cup fat-free, low-sodium vegetable broth, such as on page 50

½ cup shredded or grated Parmesan cheese

2 tablespoons fresh lemon juice

Barley Risotto with Mushrooms and Spinach

Although most often used in soups, barley can be the main ingredient of a satisfying entrée, as it is here. You can also serve this risotto in half-cup portions as a healthy side to simply prepared seafood, poultry, or beef. Either way, wait until serving time to add the Parmesan and lemon juice so you'll get the maximum effect.

1. In a large nonstick skillet, heat the oil over medium-high heat, swirling to coat the bottom. Cook the mushrooms and onion for 6 to 8 minutes, or until the mushrooms are soft, stirring frequently. Transfer to the slow cooker.
2. Stir in 3½ cups broth, the barley, garlic, salt, and pepper. Cook, covered, on high for 2 hours, or until the barley is tender.
3. Stir in the spinach and the remaining ¼ cup broth. Cook, covered, on high for 15 minutes, or until the spinach is wilted.
4. Stir in the Parmesan and lemon juice.

COOK'S TIP
Instead of using spinach, try other quick-cooking greens, such as chopped Swiss chard, escarole, or arugula, for a change.

PER SERVING
Calories **361**
Total Fat **6.0 g**
  Saturated Fat **2.5 g**
  Trans Fat **0.0 g**
  Polyunsaturated Fat **1.0 g**
  Monounsaturated Fat **2.5 g**

Cholesterol **7 mg**
Sodium **385 mg**
Carbohydrates **65 g**
  Fiber **13 g**
  Sugars **5 g**
  Protein **14 g**

Dietary Exchanges:
  4 starch, 1 vegetable, ½ lean meat

White and Greens Lasagna

Full of the goodness of greens in the form of Swiss chard and spinach, this lasagna is cooked with a white sauce flavored with fresh tarragon and garlic. There's no need to pre-cook the whole-wheat lasagna noodles—just make sure they're well coated with the sauce as you layer the ingredients.

SERVES 8; 1½ cups per serving

SLOW COOKER SIZE | SHAPE
3- to 4½-quart | round or oval (preferred)

SLOW COOKING TIME
4 to 6 hours ON LOW plus 10 minutes ON LOW, **OR**

2 to 3 hours ON HIGH plus 10 minutes ON HIGH

1. Lightly spray the slow cooker and a large saucepan with cooking spray. Set the slow cooker aside.
2. In the pan, cook 3 minced garlic cloves over medium heat for 1 minute, stirring constantly. Pour the evaporated milk into the pan. Bring to a boil, still over medium heat, stirring frequently.
3. Put the cornstarch in a small bowl. Add 3 tablespoons water, whisking to dissolve. Whisk into the evaporated milk mixture. Return to a boil, still over medium heat. Boil for 1 minute, whisking constantly. Remove from the heat. Whisk in the tarragon, salt, and ⅛ teaspoon pepper. Set the sauce aside.
4. In a large nonstick skillet, heat the oil over medium heat, swirling to coat the bottom. Cook the onion for 3 minutes, or until slightly softened, stirring frequently. Stir in the chard. Cook for 2 minutes, or until almost wilted, stirring constantly. Stir in the spinach and the remaining 3 minced garlic cloves. Cook for 1 minute, or until the spinach is hot, the garlic is fragrant, and the chard is wilted, stirring constantly. Stir in the remaining ⅛ teaspoon pepper. Remove the skillet from the heat. Set aside.
5. In a small bowl, whisk together the ricotta and egg white until smooth. Whisk in ½ cup 4-cheese blend and the Parmesan.

(recipe continues)

Cooking spray

3 medium garlic cloves, minced, and 3 medium garlic cloves, minced, divided use

36 ounces fat-free evaporated milk

3 tablespoons cornstarch

⅓ cup chopped tarragon

¼ teaspoon salt

⅛ teaspoon pepper and ⅛ teaspoon pepper, divided use

1 tablespoon olive oil

1 large onion, chopped

4 cups sliced Swiss chard leaves (½-inch slices)

10 ounces frozen chopped spinach, thawed, drained, and squeezed until very dry

1 cup low-fat ricotta

1 large egg white

½ cup shredded low-fat 4-cheese Italian blend and ½ cup shredded low-fat 4-cheese Italian blend, divided use

¼ cup shredded or grated Parmesan cheese

9 dried oven-ready whole-wheat lasagna noodles

1½ cups grape tomatoes, halved

+

⅓ cup shredded low-fat 4-cheese Italian blend

6. Spread 1 cup sauce in the slow cooker. Arrange 3 noodles on the sauce, breaking them to fit as needed. (They won't fit perfectly. There may be some overlap or gaps.) Spoon one-third of the ricotta mixture over the noodles, spreading gently. Sprinkle one-third of the onion mixture over the ricotta. Top with one-third of the tomatoes. Pour in 1 cup sauce, spreading to cover. Repeat the layers twice, beginning with the noodles. Sprinkle with ½ cup 4-cheese blend.

7. Cook, covered, on low for 4 to 6 hours or on high for 2 to 3 hours, or until the noodles are tender. Quickly sprinkle the remaining ⅓ cup 4-cheese blend over the lasagna and re-cover the slow cooker. Cook for 10 minutes, or until the cheese has melted. Let stand, uncovered, for 15 to 20 minutes, or until set.

COOK'S TIP

To cut Swiss chard leaves easily, stack several leaves and tightly roll them lengthwise. Cut crosswise into the desired width (½ inch for this recipe). One bunch will give you more than enough chard for this recipe.

PER SERVING
Calories **337**
Total Fat **7.0 g**
 Saturated Fat **3.0 g**
 Trans Fat **0.0 g**
 Polyunsaturated Fat **0.5 g**
 Monounsaturated Fat **2.0 g**

Cholesterol **23 mg**
Sodium **495 mg**
Carbohydrates **44 g**
 Fiber **3 g**
 Sugars **21 g**
 Protein **24 g**

Dietary Exchanges:
2 vegetable, 1 fat-free milk, 1½ starch, 1 lean meat

SERVES 4; 1¾ cups per serving

SLOW COOKER SIZE | SHAPE
3- to 4½-quart | round or oval

SLOW COOKING TIME
1 hour plus 45 minutes
ON HIGH

2 teaspoons olive oil

1 small onion, chopped

1½ cups uncooked arborio rice

1 medium garlic clove, minced

3 cups fat-free, low-sodium vegetable broth, such as on page 50

½ teaspoon salt

¼ teaspoon pepper

———— + ————

1½ cups diced zucchini

1¼ cups fat-free, low-sodium vegetable broth, such as on page 50

———— + ————

1 large tomato, chopped

½ cup shredded or grated Parmesan cheese

¼ cup chopped fresh basil

Zucchini and Tomato Risotto

If you love the creaminess of risotto but not all the stirring it requires, try making it in your slow cooker. Our version adds fresh zucchini, tomato, and basil for color, flavor, and texture.

1. In a large nonstick skillet, heat the oil over medium-high heat, swirling to coat the bottom. Cook the onion, covered, for 6 minutes, or until tender, stirring occasionally. Stir in the rice and garlic. Cook, covered, for 1 minute. Transfer to the slow cooker.
2. Stir in 3 cups broth, the salt, and pepper. Cook, covered, on high for 1 hour.
3. Quickly stir in the zucchini and the remaining 1½ cups broth and re-cover the slow cooker. Cook on high for 45 minutes, or until the rice is tender. Turn off the slow cooker.
4. Stir in the tomato, Parmesan, and basil. Let stand, covered, for 5 minutes before serving.

PER SERVING
Calories **337**
Total Fat **5.5 g**
  Saturated Fat **2.0 g**
  Trans Fat **0.0 g**
  Polyunsaturated Fat **0.5 g**
  Monounsaturated Fat **2.5 g**

Cholesterol **7 mg**
Sodium **523 mg**
Carbohydrates **61 g**
  Fiber **3 g**
  Sugars **4 g**
Protein **10 g**

Dietary Exchanges:
  3½ starch, 1 vegetable, ½ lean meat

Nutty Brown Rice and Arugula Toss

Blue cheese, pine nuts, and fresh basil, rosemary, and lemon zest all play major roles in flavoring this chickpea and rice dish. A smart choice as a meatless entrée, the versatile recipe also makes a great side to serve 12 people. Not a blue cheese fan? Use low-fat feta cheese instead.

1. Lightly spray the slow cooker with cooking spray. Put the water, rice, and onion in the slow cooker, stirring to combine. Cook, covered, on low for 3 hours or on high for 1½ hours, or until the rice is fluffy and the water is absorbed. Transfer to a large bowl.

2. Add the remaining ingredients. Using two utensils, toss gently. Let stand for 15 minutes under a tented piece of aluminum foil to keep warm while the flavors blend. (Don't cover tightly. You don't want to steam the food.)

PER SERVING
Calories **361**
Total Fat **12.0 g**
  Saturated Fat **3.0 g**
  Trans Fat **0.0 g**
  Polyunsaturated Fat **4.0 g**
  Monounsaturated Fat **4.0 g**

Cholesterol **8 mg**
Sodium **440 mg**
Carbohydrates **52 g**
  Fiber **7 g**
  Sugars **5 g**
Protein **15 g**

Dietary Exchanges:
  **3 starch, 1 vegetable,
  ½ lean meat, 1½ fat**

FAST PREP!

SERVES 4; 1⅓ cups per serving

SLOW COOKER SIZE | SHAPE
3- to 4½-quart | round or oval

SLOW COOKING TIME
3 hours ON LOW, **OR**
1½ hours ON HIGH

Cooking spray
2 cups water
1 cup uncooked converted brown rice
1 medium onion, diced

——————— + ———————

2 cups arugula, coarsely chopped (2 ounces)
½ 15.5-ounce can no-salt-added chickpeas, rinsed and drained
½ cup crumbled low-fat blue cheese
½ cup pine nuts, dry-roasted
¼ cup chopped fresh basil
1 tablespoon finely chopped fresh rosemary or 1 teaspoon dried rosemary, crushed
2 teaspoons grated lemon zest
1 medium garlic clove, minced
¼ teaspoon salt

SERVES 4; ¾ cup vegetable mixture and ½ cup pasta per serving

SLOW COOKER SIZE | SHAPE
3- to 3½-quart | round or oval

SLOW COOKING TIME
6 to 7 hours ON LOW, **OR**
3 to 3½ hours ON HIGH

Cooking spray

6 ounces unpeeled eggplant, cut into 1-inch cubes (about 3 cups)

7 ounces grape tomatoes (about 1½ cups)

1 medium green bell pepper, cut into 1-inch squares

1 medium zucchini, halved lengthwise and cut crosswise into 1-inch slices

½ cup chopped onion

2 tablespoons water

2 teaspoons dried oregano, crumbled

1 teaspoon dried basil, crumbled

⅛ teaspoon crushed red pepper flakes

✛

1 tablespoon balsamic vinegar

¼ teaspoon salt

4 ounces dried whole-grain penne (about 1⅓ cups)

16 kalamata olives, coarsely chopped

¾ cup shredded low-fat mozzarella cheese

2 tablespoons shredded or grated Parmesan cheese

Rustic Two-Cheese Ratatouille

This meatless one-dish meal provides both fiber—7 grams of it—and the heady flavors of Italian herbs and kalamata olives.

1. Lightly spray the slow cooker with cooking spray. Put the eggplant, tomatoes, bell pepper, zucchini, onion, water, oregano, basil, and red pepper flakes in the slow cooker, stirring to combine. Cook, covered, on low for 6 to 7 hours or on high for 3 to 3½ hours, or until the bell pepper is very soft. Stir in the vinegar and salt.

2. About 20 minutes before serving, prepare the pasta using the package directions, omitting the salt. Drain well in a colander.

3. Serve the eggplant mixture over the pasta. Top with the olives, mozzarella, and Parmesan.

COOK'S TIPS

The flavor of the kalamata olives is more pronounced if they're served on top of, rather than stirred into, the eggplant mixture.

The flesh of an eggplant darkens quickly once it is exposed to the air, so cut the eggplant just before cooking it.

PER SERVING
Calories **245**
Total Fat **8.0 g**
  Saturated Fat **2.0 g**
  Trans Fat **0.0 g**
  Polyunsaturated Fat **1.0 g**
  Monounsaturated Fat **4.5 g**

Cholesterol **9 mg**
Sodium **595 mg**
Carbohydrates **34 g**
  Fiber **7 g**
  Sugars **7 g**
Protein **12 g**

Dietary Exchanges:
  1½ starch, 2 vegetable, 1 lean meat, 1 fat

Veggies and Pasta with Blue Cheese

This one-dish wonder is packed with slow-roasted veggies, whole-grain penne, and creamy blue cheese, plus a hint of fennel. All you need to do before turning on the slow cooker is slice the vegetables.

SERVES 4; 1¼ cups per serving

SLOW COOKER SIZE | SHAPE
5- to 7-quart | round or oval

SLOW COOKING TIME
4½ to 5 hours ON LOW, **OR**
2 hours 15 minutes to 2½ hours ON HIGH

1. Lightly spray the slow cooker with cooking spray. Put the bell peppers, squash, and onion in the slow cooker. Sprinkle with the fennel seeds. Drizzle with the oil. Don't stir. Cook, covered, on low for 4½ to 5 hours or on high for 2 hours 15 minutes to 2½ hours, or until the onion is soft.
2. About 20 minutes before the vegetables finish cooking, prepare the pasta using the package directions, omitting the salt. Drain well in a colander.
3. Stir the garlic and salt into the cooked bell pepper mixture. Gently stir in the pasta, blue cheese, and basil.

Cooking spray

1 medium red bell pepper, cut into 1-inch squares

1 medium green bell pepper, cut into 1-inch squares

1 medium yellow summer squash, cut lengthwise into 8 wedges and crosswise into 1-inch pieces

1 medium onion, cut into 8 wedges

¼ to ½ teaspoon dried fennel seeds

1 tablespoon olive oil

———— + ————

4 ounces dried whole-grain penne (about 1⅓ cups)

1 medium garlic clove, minced

¼ teaspoon salt

¾ cup crumbled low-fat blue cheese

¼ cup chopped fresh basil

PER SERVING
Calories **227**
Total Fat **8.0 g**
  Saturated Fat **3.0 g**
  Trans Fat **0.0 g**
  Polyunsaturated Fat **1.0 g**
  Monounsaturated Fat **3.5 g**

Cholesterol **11 mg**
Sodium **435 mg**
Carbohydrates **30 g**
  Fiber **6 g**
  Sugars **6 g**
Protein **10 g**

Dietary Exchanges:
  1½ starch, 2 vegetable, 1 lean meat, 1 fat

SERVES 4; 2 enchiladas per serving

SLOW COOKER SIZE | SHAPE
3- to 4½-quart | round or oval

SLOW COOKING TIME
3 to 4 hours ON LOW, **OR**
2 to 2½ hours ON HIGH

8 6-inch corn tortillas

FILLING

1 14.5-ounce can no-salt-added black beans, rinsed and drained

2 cups coarsely chopped kale, any large stems discarded

1 cup fresh or frozen whole-kernel corn

4 ounces shredded low-fat mozzarella cheese or 1 ounce crumbled queso fresco or Cotija

2 medium green onions, thinly sliced

2 medium garlic cloves, minced

1 teaspoon ground cumin

1 teaspoon chili powder

½ teaspoon smoked paprika (sweet or hot)

8 ounces tomatillos, papery husks discarded, rinsed, drained, and coarsely chopped

1 4-ounce can diced green chiles, drained

¼ cup fat-free, low-sodium vegetable broth, such as on page 50

— ✛ —

2 tablespoons queso fresco or Cotija

2 tablespoons sliced black olives, drained

2 tablespoons chopped fresh cilantro

Beans and Greens Enchiladas

These protein-packed enchiladas are full of deliciousness—including a hidden treasure of peppery kale. They're topped with a mild chile sauce and melted cheese to round out the classic Mexican flavors. Cooking the enchiladas in broth helps them stay moist.

1. Place the tortillas on a clean work surface. In a medium bowl, stir together the filling ingredients. Spoon about ¼ cup of the filling onto the center of each tortilla. Roll up jelly-roll style and place with the seam side down in the slow cooker. You may need to stack the enchiladas if you've already arranged a single layer in the bottom of the slow cooker.

2. Spoon the tomatillos and green chiles over the enchiladas. Pour the broth over all. Cook, covered, on low for 3 to 4 hours or on high for 2 to 2½ hours, or until the enchiladas are heated through. Transfer to serving plates. Sprinkle the queso fresco over the enchiladas. Garnish with the olives and cilantro.

PER SERVING
Calories **306**
Total Fat **6.0 g**
  Saturated Fat **1.5 g**
  Trans Fat **0.0 g**
  Polyunsaturated Fat **1.0 g**
  Monounsaturated Fat **1.5 g**

Cholesterol **13 mg**
Sodium **425 mg**
Carbohydrates **47 g**
  Fiber **10 g**
  Sugars **8 g**
Protein **19 g**

Dietary Exchanges:
  2½ starch,
  2 vegetable,
  1½ lean meat

SLOW COOKER SIZE | SHAPE
4- to 5-quart | round or oval

SLOW COOKING TIME
4 to 4½ hours ON LOW, **OR**
2 hours to 2 hours 15 minutes ON HIGH

Cooking spray

1 tablespoon canola or corn oil

1 medium green bell pepper, chopped

6 ounces button mushrooms, sliced

1 small onion, diced

1½ cups meatless spaghetti sauce (lowest sodium available)

2 medium tomatoes, diced

1 cup fat-free cottage cheese

½ cup snipped fresh parsley

2 large egg whites

2 teaspoons dried oregano, crumbled

¼ teaspoon dried fennel seeds (optional)

4 ounces dried whole-grain rotini (about 1⅓ cups)

¼ cup shredded low-fat mozzarella cheese

2 tablespoons shredded or grated Parmesan cheese

———— ✛ ————

¼ cup shredded low-fat mozzarella cheese

2 tablespoons shredded or grated Parmesan cheese

Layered Pasta Casserole

No need to cook the pasta ahead of time for this hunger-buster cheese-and-veggie–packed meal. Just add the pasta straight from the box or bag and let the slow cooker work its magic!

1. Lightly spray the slow cooker with cooking spray. Set aside.
2. In a large nonstick skillet, heat the oil over medium-high heat, swirling to coat the bottom. Cook the bell pepper, mushrooms, and onion for 3 minutes, or until the onion is soft, stirring frequently. Remove from the heat. Stir in the spaghetti sauce and tomatoes. Set aside.
3. In a medium bowl, stir together the cottage cheese, parsley, egg whites, oregano, and fennel.
4. In the slow cooker, layer the casserole as follows: one-third (about 1⅓ cups) of the bell pepper mixture, half the pasta, half the cottage cheese mixture, ¼ cup mozzarella cheese, and 2 tablespoons Parmesan. Make another layer each of one-third of the bell pepper mixture, the remaining pasta, and the remaining cottage cheese mixture. Spoon the final one-third of the bell pepper mixture over all. Cook, covered, on low for 4 to 4½ hours or on high for 2 hours to 2 hours 15 minutes, or until the pasta is tender.
5. Sprinkle with the remaining ¼ cup mozzarella and 2 tablespoons Parmesan. Turn off the slow cooker. Let the casserole stand, uncovered, for 15 minutes so the flavors blend, the pasta absorbs additional moisture, and the cheeses melt.

PER SERVING
Calories **357**
Total Fat **11.5 g**
　Saturated Fat **3.0 g**
　Trans Fat **0.0 g**
　Polyunsaturated Fat **2.5 g**
　Monounsaturated Fat **4.5 g**
Cholesterol **22 mg**
Sodium **559 mg**
Carbohydrates **45 g**
　Fiber **8 g**
　Sugars **15 g**
Protein **19 g**

Dietary Exchanges:
　2 starch, 3 vegetable, 2 lean meat, ½ fat

Italian Artichoke-Stuffed Bell Peppers

A highly satisfying entrée, these attractive bell peppers are filled with bulgur mixed with artichokes, provolone cheese, tomatoes, and fresh basil.

SERVES 4; 1 stuffed bell pepper per serving

SLOW COOKER SIZE | SHAPE
3½- to 5-quart | round or oval

SLOW COOKING TIME
4 to 6 hours ON LOW, **OR**
2 to 3 hours ON HIGH

1. Put the bulgur in a large bowl. Pour ¾ cup boiling water over the bulgur. Let stand, covered, for 30 minutes, or until the water is absorbed and the bulgur is tender. Fluff with a fork.
2. Meanwhile, in a medium nonstick skillet, heat the oil over medium heat, swirling to coat the bottom. Cook the onion for 2 minutes, stirring frequently.
3. Stir in the zucchini. Cook for 1½ minutes, stirring constantly.
4. Stir in the garlic and fennel seeds. Cook for 30 seconds, stirring constantly. Stir into the bulgur.
5. Gently stir in the artichokes, tomato, and basil. Gently stir in the provolone. Spoon the filling into the bell peppers, mounding as necessary.
6. Place the bell peppers in the slow cooker. Pour in enough of the ½ to ¾ cup water to cover the bottom of the slow cooker. Cook, covered, on low for 4 to 6 hours or on high for 2 to 3 hours, or until the peppers are tender and the filling is hot. Transfer to plates. Sprinkle with the Parmesan. Let stand for 5 minutes, or until the Parmesan has melted.

½ cup uncooked fine- or medium-grind quick-cooking bulgur

¾ cup boiling water

1 teaspoon olive oil

1 medium onion, chopped

1 cup diced zucchini

2 medium garlic cloves, minced

1 teaspoon dried fennel seeds, crushed

1 cup frozen artichokes, thawed, patted dry, and coarsely chopped

1 cup chopped tomato

½ cup loosely packed chopped fresh basil

2 ounces low-fat provolone, diced (about ½ cup)

4 large red bell peppers, tops, seeds, and ribs discarded

½ to ¾ cup water

+

1 tablespoon shredded or grated Parmesan cheese

PER SERVING
Calories **214**
Total Fat **5.0 g**
  Saturated Fat **2.0 g**
  Trans Fat **0.0 g**
  Polyunsaturated Fat **0.5 g**
  Monounsaturated Fat **1.5 g**

Cholesterol **9 mg**
Sodium **185 mg**
Carbohydrates **34 g**
  Fiber **11 g**
  Sugars **11 g**
Protein **10 g**

Dietary Exchanges:
1 starch, 4 vegetable, 1 fat

SERVES 4; 1 cup lentils and ½ cup quinoa per serving

SLOW COOKER SIZE | SHAPE
3- to 4½-quart | round or oval

SLOW COOKING TIME
4 hours ON LOW, **OR**
2 hours ON HIGH

Cooking spray

1 tablespoon canola or corn oil

1 medium onion, diced

3 cups fat-free, low-sodium vegetable broth, such as on page 50

1 cup dried lentils, sorted for stones and shriveled lentils, rinsed, and drained

1 medium red bell pepper, diced

½ teaspoon curry powder

⅛ to ¼ teaspoon crushed red pepper flakes

———— **+** ————

½ cup snipped fresh cilantro

1 tablespoon grated peeled gingerroot

½ teaspoon salt

2 cups water

½ cup uncooked quinoa, rinsed well under cold running water and drained

Gingered Lentils and Quinoa

Ginger, curry powder, and red pepper flakes punch up the mild flavor of lentils, served here on a bed of quinoa.

1. Lightly spray the slow cooker with cooking spray. Set aside.
2. In a medium nonstick skillet, heat the oil over medium-high heat, swirling to coat the bottom. Cook the onion for 4 to 5 minutes, or until beginning to richly brown, stirring frequently. Transfer to the slow cooker.
3. Stir in the broth, lentils, bell pepper, curry powder, and red pepper flakes. Cook, covered, on low for 4 hours or on high for 2 hours, or until the lentils are tender. Stir in the cilantro, gingerroot, and salt.
4. About 15 minutes before the lentils finish cooking, in a small saucepan, bring the water to a boil over high heat. Stir in the quinoa. Reduce the heat and simmer, covered, for 10 to 12 minutes, or until the water is absorbed and the quinoa is tender. Transfer to a fine-mesh strainer. Drain well. Shake off any excess liquid. Spoon onto plates. Spoon the lentils on top.

PER SERVING
Calories **312**
Total Fat **5.0 g**
  Saturated Fat **0.5 g**
  Trans Fat **0.0 g**
  Polyunsaturated Fat **1.5 g**
  Monounsaturated Fat **2.5 g**

Cholesterol **0 mg**
Sodium **338 mg**
Carbohydrates **51 g**
  Fiber **9 g**
  Sugars **8 g**
  Protein **18 g**

Dietary Exchanges:
  3 starch, 1 vegetable, 1 lean meat

Greek Lentils

With its Greek seasoning blend, oregano, feta cheese, and lemon zest, this easy one-pot meal will almost make you think you're cruising the Mediterranean Sea!

FAST PREP!

SERVES 6; 1 cup per serving

SLOW COOKER SIZE | SHAPE
3- to 4½-quart | round or oval

SLOW COOKING TIME
5 to 6 hours ON LOW, **OR**
2½ to 3 hours ON HIGH

1. In the slow cooker, stir together the broth, lentils, carrots, onion, seasoning blend, oregano, lemon zest, salt, and pepper. Cook, covered, on low for 5 to 6 hours or on high for 2½ to 3 hours, or until the liquid is absorbed and the lentils are tender.
2. Just before serving, stir in the spinach. Sprinkle the feta over each serving.

COOK'S TIP
If you have trouble finding salt-free Greek seasoning blend, you can use a brand that contains salt, but be sure to omit the ¼ teaspoon of salt called for in the recipe.

4 cups fat-free, low-sodium vegetable broth, such as on page 50

2 cups dried lentils, sorted for stones and shriveled lentils, rinsed, and drained

2 medium carrots, shredded (about 1 cup)

1 medium onion, chopped

1 teaspoon salt-free Greek seasoning blend, crumbled

1 teaspoon dried oregano, crumbled

1 teaspoon grated lemon zest

¼ teaspoon salt

¼ teaspoon pepper

———— + ————

4 ounces spinach, torn into bite-size pieces (about 4 cups)

¼ cup crumbled fat-free feta cheese

PER SERVING

Calories **248**	Cholesterol **0 mg**	Dietary Exchanges:
Total Fat **1.0 g**	Sodium **267 mg**	**2½ starch, 1 vegetable,**
Saturated Fat **0.0 g**	Carbohydrates **43 g**	**2 lean meat**
Trans Fat **0.0 g**	Fiber **16 g**	
Polyunsaturated Fat **0.5 g**	Sugars **6 g**	
Monounsaturated Fat **0.0 g**	Protein **19 g**	

Black and Red Bean Chili with Peppery Sour Cream

This two-bean chili gets additional splashes of color from grape tomatoes and yellow bell pepper. The unusual sour cream topping is an integral part of the dish—be sure to give it a try.

SERVES 6; 1 cup chili and 2 tablespoons sour cream per serving

SLOW COOKER SIZE | SHAPE
3- to 4½-quart | round or oval

SLOW COOKING TIME
8 hours ON LOW, **OR**
4 hours ON HIGH

1. Lightly spray the slow cooker with cooking spray. Set aside.
2. Fill a large saucepan three-fourths full of water. Bring to a boil over high heat. Stir in the beans. Reduce the heat and simmer for 15 minutes. Pour into a colander and rinse. Pour into the slow cooker.
3. Stir in the water, tomatoes, bell pepper, onion, poblanos, chili powder, cumin, sugar, garlic, salt, and oregano. Cook, covered, on low for 8 hours or on high for 4 hours. Stir in the lime juice.
4. Meanwhile, in a small bowl, whisk together the sour cream, oil, and hot-pepper sauce. Cover and refrigerate until serving time.
5. Ladle the chili into bowls. Spoon a dollop of the sour cream mixture onto each serving.

COOK'S TIP

For improved flavor and texture, cover and refrigerate the chili overnight in an airtight container, or for up to two days. Reheat in a large saucepan, covered, over medium heat for 10 minutes, or until heated through. Meanwhile, prepare the sour cream mixture. Top the chili as directed.

Cooking spray

½ cup dried pinto beans, sorted for stones and shriveled beans, rinsed, and drained

½ cup dried black beans, sorted for stones and shriveled beans, rinsed, and drained

3 cups water

10 ounces whole grape tomatoes (about 2 cups)

1 medium yellow bell pepper, chopped

1 medium onion, chopped

2 medium poblano peppers, seeds and ribs discarded, chopped

2 teaspoons chili powder

1½ teaspoons ground cumin

1½ teaspoons sugar

2 medium garlic cloves, minced

¾ teaspoon salt

¾ teaspoon dried oregano, crumbled

————— + —————

2 tablespoons fresh lime juice

¾ cup fat-free sour cream

1 tablespoon olive oil (extra virgin preferred)

2 to 3 teaspoons mild Louisiana-style hot-pepper sauce

PER SERVING
Calories **198**
Total Fat **3.0 g**
  Saturated Fat **0.5 g**
  Trans Fat **0.0 g**
  Polyunsaturated Fat **0.5 g**
  Monounsaturated Fat **1.5 g**
Cholesterol **5 mg**
Sodium **342 mg**
Carbohydrates **34 g**
  Fiber **7 g**
  Sugars **9 g**
  Protein **10 g**
Dietary Exchanges:
1½ **starch**, 2 **vegetable**,
½ **lean meat**

SERVES 4; 1 cup bean
    mixture and ⅔ cup rice
    per serving

SLOW COOKER SIZE | SHAPE
3-quart | round or oval

SLOW COOKING TIME

3½ to 4 hours ON LOW, **OR**

1 hour 45 minutes to
    2 hours ON HIGH

Cooking spray

1 tablespoon canola or
    corn oil and 2 teaspoons
    canola or corn oil,
    divided use

1 large onion, diced

1 large yellow bell pepper,
    chopped

1 15.5-ounce can no-salt-
    added dark kidney
    beans, rinsed and
    drained

1 8-ounce can no-salt-
    added tomato sauce

1 cup water

2 tablespoons sugar

1½ teaspoons ground
    coriander

1 teaspoon ground cumin

½ teaspoon ground
    cardamom

½ teaspoon ground ginger

½ teaspoon salt

⅛ teaspoon ground cloves
    or allspice

⅛ teaspoon cayenne

——————— ✦ ———————

½ cup uncooked instant
    brown rice

¼ teaspoon ground
    turmeric

⅓ cup dried apricot halves,
    diced

2 medium green onions,
    finely chopped

¼ cup finely chopped
    pecans, dry-roasted

East Indian Spiced Beans with Apricot Rice

The mélange of spices in this dish provides stellar flavor. Serve the deep-red beans over the crunchy apricot-flecked brown rice, or switch places and put the rice on top.

1. Lightly spray the slow cooker with cooking spray. Set aside.
2. In a large nonstick skillet, heat 1 tablespoon oil over medium-high heat. Cook the onion for 3 minutes, or until soft, stirring frequently. Transfer the mixture to the slow cooker.
3. Stir in the bell pepper, beans, tomato sauce, water, sugar, coriander, cumin, cardamom, ginger, salt, cloves, and cayenne. Cook, covered, on low for 3½ to 4 hours or on high for 1 hour 45 minutes to 2 hours, or until the onion is very soft.
4. About 15 minutes before serving, prepare the rice using the package directions, adding the turmeric and omitting the salt and margarine. Remove from the heat. Gently stir in the apricots, green onions, pecans, and the remaining 2 teaspoons oil. Serve the beans over the rice or the rice over the beans.

COOK'S TIPS

Coriander is considered both an herb and a spice because its leaves, known as cilantro, and seeds are both used as seasonings. The seeds have a mild taste reminiscent of a combination of lemon and sage and are often used in Indian dishes. Store ground coriander in a cool, dark place. It will stay fresh for about four to six months.

Cardamom A member of the ginger family, cardamom adds a wonderfully sweet and pungent flavor to foods. Because cardamom is one of the more expensive spices, and one that you may not use regularly, you can assure a fresh product and probably save money by purchasing a small quantity at a store that sells spices in bulk.

PER SERVING		Cholesterol **0 mg**	Dietary Exchanges:
Calories **345**		Sodium **322 mg**	1½ **starch, 3 vegetable,**
Total Fat **11.5 g**		Carbohydrates **53 g**	**1 fruit, 2 fat**
Saturated Fat **1.0 g**		Fiber **14 g**	
Trans Fat **0.0 g**		Sugars **21 g**	
Polyunsaturated Fat **3.5 g**		Protein **11 g**	
Monounsaturated Fat **6.5 g**			

Mexican Stuffed Squash

Portion control is easy with these squash "boats." Two of the yummy boats, filled with brown rice, black beans, and pickled jalapeño slices, are just the right size for a serving.

SERVES 4; 2 squash halves per serving

SLOW COOKER SIZE | SHAPE
4- to 6-quart | round or oval

SLOW COOKING TIME
5 to 6 hours ON LOW, **OR**
2½ to 3 hours ON HIGH

1. Lightly spray the slow cooker with cooking spray. Set aside.
2. Cut the squash in half lengthwise. Using a teaspoon, scrape the seeds and pulp into a small bowl, leaving a ¼-inch border of the shell all the way around.
3. In a large nonstick skillet, heat the oil over medium-high heat, swirling to coat the bottom. Cook the reserved squash seeds and pulp and the onion for 3 to 4 minutes, or until the onion is soft, stirring frequently. Remove from the heat. Stir in the rice, beans, jalapeños, and cumin. Spoon into the squash cavities.
4. Pour the water into the slow cooker. Add the squash. Sprinkle with the tomato. Cook, covered, on low for 5 to 6 hours or on high for 2½ to 3 hours, or until the squash boats are tender when pierced with a fork.
5. Sprinkle, in order, with the salt, cilantro, and Cheddar. Turn off the slow cooker. Let stand, uncovered, for 15 minutes so the flavors blend and the cheese melts.

Cooking spray

4 medium yellow summer squash

1 teaspoon canola or corn oil

½ medium onion, diced

1 cup frozen brown rice, thawed

½ 15.5-ounce can no-salt-added black beans, rinsed and drained

¼ cup pickled jalapeño slices, drained and finely chopped

1 teaspoon ground cumin

¼ cup water

1 medium Italian plum (Roma) tomato, diced

—————— + ——————

⅛ teaspoon salt

¼ cup snipped fresh cilantro

¾ cup shredded low-fat sharp Cheddar cheese

PER SERVING
Calories **178**
Total Fat **3.5 g**
  Saturated Fat **1.0 g**
  Trans Fat **0.0 g**
  Polyunsaturated Fat **0.5 g**
  Monounsaturated Fat **1.0 g**

Cholesterol **4 mg**
Sodium **411 mg**
Carbohydrates **27 g**
  Fiber **6 g**
  Sugars **8 g**
  Protein **12 g**

Dietary Exchanges:
  1 starch, 2 vegetable,
  1 lean meat

1 pound dried black beans, sorted for stones and shriveled beans, rinsed, and drained

4 cups water

1 14.5-ounce can no-salt-added diced tomatoes, undrained

1 large green bell pepper, chopped

1 medium onion, diced

1 tablespoon plus 1 teaspoon ground cumin

2 teaspoons dried minced garlic

2 medium dried bay leaves

1 teaspoon olive oil

3 drops red hot-pepper sauce

¼ teaspoon salt

+

1½ cups uncooked instant brown rice

3 tablespoons snipped fresh cilantro

⅓ cup chopped red onion (optional)

Cuban-Style Black Beans and Rice

Plenty of cumin, bay leaves, onion, and garlic—and not much salt— seasons this hearty, protein-packed dish. Serve a crisp leafy green salad with a light citrus vinaigrette to complete the meal.

1. Fill a large saucepan three-fourths full of water. Bring to a boil over high heat. Stir in the beans. Return to a boil. Reduce the heat and simmer for 15 minutes. Pour the beans into a colander and rinse. Pour into the slow cooker.

2. Stir in the water, tomatoes with liquid, bell pepper, onion, cumin, garlic, bay leaves, oil, hot-pepper sauce, and salt. Cook, covered, on high for 4 to 6 hours. Discard the bay leaves.

3. About 20 minutes before serving time, prepare the rice using the package directions, omitting the salt and margarine. Spoon the rice into bowls. Ladle the bean mixture on top. Sprinkle with the cilantro and red onion.

COOK'S TIP

The first slow cooker was actually the classic bean pot, a clay or ceramic vessel that protected beans from a fire-fed oven's high heat. Still perfect for cooking any variety of dried beans, slow cookers yield beans that tend to be creamier than their canned counterparts. Slow-cooked beans can be better for you, too, because you get to control the amount of added sodium.

PER SERVING
Calories **400**
Total Fat **3.0 g**
  Saturated Fat **0.5 g**
  Trans Fat **0.0 g**
  Polyunsaturated Fat **1.0 g**
  Monounsaturated Fat **1.0 g**

Cholesterol **0 mg**
Sodium **128 mg**
Carbohydrates **75 g**
  Fiber **17 g**
  Sugars **12 g**
Protein **20 g**

Dietary Exchanges:
  4½ starch,
  1 vegetable,
  2 lean meat

Red-Bean Spaghetti

This chunky, hearty bean mixture is great on pasta and is also very tasty over brown rice.

SERVES 5; ¾ cup bean mixture and ¾ cup spaghetti per serving

SLOW COOKER SIZE | SHAPE
3- to 4½-quart | round or oval

SLOW COOKING TIME
6 to 8 hours ON LOW plus 30 to 45 minutes ON HIGH, **OR**

3 to 4 hours ON HIGH plus 30 to 45 minutes ON HIGH

1. In the slow cooker, stir together the mushrooms, beans, tomatoes with liquid, bell pepper, onion, garlic, oregano, cumin, salt, and red pepper flakes. Cook, covered, on low for 6 to 8 hours or on high for 3 to 4 hours.
2. If using the low setting, change it to high. Quickly stir in the zucchini and tomato paste and re-cover the slow cooker. Cook for 30 to 45 minutes, or until the zucchini is tender-crisp.
3. About 15 minutes before serving time, prepare the spaghetti using the package directions, omitting the salt. Drain well in a colander. Serve with the bean mixture spooned on top.

2 cups chopped button mushrooms

1 15.5-ounce can no-salt-added dark red kidney beans, rinsed and drained

1 14.5-ounce can no-salt-added diced tomatoes, undrained

½ cup chopped green bell pepper

¼ cup finely chopped onion

2 medium garlic cloves, minced

1 teaspoon dried oregano, crumbled

½ teaspoon ground cumin

½ teaspoon salt

¼ teaspoon crushed red pepper flakes

———— + ————

1½ cups chopped zucchini

¼ cup no-salt-added tomato paste

8 ounces dried whole-grain spaghetti

PER SERVING
Calories **279**
Total Fat **1.5 g**
  Saturated Fat **0.0 g**
  Trans Fat **0.0 g**
  Polyunsaturated Fat **0.5 g**
  Monounsaturated Fat **0.5 g**

Cholesterol **0 mg**
Sodium **232 mg**
Carbohydrates **55 g**
  Fiber **14 g**
  Sugars **8 g**
  Protein **14 g**

Dietary Exchanges:
  3 starch, 2 vegetable

SLOW COOKER SIZE | SHAPE
3- to 4½-quart | round or oval

SLOW COOKING TIME
1 hour to 1 hour 10 minutes ON LOW, **OR**

45 minutes ON HIGH

16 ounces frozen stir-fry vegetables (such as broccoli, onions, and bell peppers), thawed (seasoning packet discarded)

12 ounces frozen meatless crumbles, thawed

2 teaspoons soy sauce (lowest sodium available)

2 teaspoons toasted sesame oil

2 medium garlic cloves, minced

1 teaspoon minced peeled gingerroot

1 teaspoon plain rice vinegar or white wine vinegar

1 8-ounce spaghetti squash, rinsed and patted dry

½ cup unsalted crushed peanuts, dry-roasted

¼ cup coarsely chopped cilantro (optional)

Spaghetti Squash Noodle Bowl

If you have the time, slow cooking is a great way to soften the pulp of a hard-shelled winter squash and give it a roasted flavor. For faster preparation, use a microwave to cook the squash while the Asian-flavored vegetable mixture finishes cooking in the slow cooker.

1. In the slow cooker, stir together the stir-fry vegetables, meatless crumbles, soy sauce, sesame oil, garlic, gingerroot, and vinegar. Cook, covered, on low for 1 hour to 1 hour 10 minutes or on high for 45 minutes, or until the vegetables are tender and the mixture is heated through.

2. About 30 minutes before the stir-fry vegetable mixture is cooked, pierce the squash several times with a sharp knife to help the steam escape while it cooks. Microwave the squash on 80 percent power (medium high) for 10 to 15 minutes, or until soft. If your microwave doesn't have a turntable, then microwave the squash for 5-minute increments, rotating it after each increment. Transfer the squash to a cutting board. Let stand for 10 minutes to cool just slightly. Cut in half lengthwise with a sharp knife. Using a spoon, scoop out and discard the seeds. Using a fork, scrape the squash pulp lengthwise to release the strands, which resemble spaghetti. Twirl the fork to break the strands. Transfer them to bowls. Spoon the vegetable mixture over the squash. Sprinkle with the peanuts and cilantro.

COOK'S TIP
If you have time, you can use the slow cooker to prepare the spaghetti squash strands in advance. The squash will have more of a roasted flavor if prepared in the slow cooker. Using a sharp knife, pierce the squash several times to help the steam escape while it cooks. Transfer the squash to the slow cooker. Pour in 1 cup of water. Cook, covered, on

PER SERVING
Calories **307**
Total Fat **13.0 g**
  Saturated Fat **1.5 g**
  Trans Fat **0.0 g**
  Polyunsaturated Fat **4.0 g**
  Monounsaturated Fat **5.5 g**

Cholesterol **0 mg**
Sodium **421 mg**
Carbohydrates **30 g**
  Fiber **11 g**
  Sugars **7 g**
  Protein **28 g**

Dietary Exchanges:
  1½ starch, 2 vegetable, 3 lean meat, 1 fat

low for 4 to 5 hours or on high for 2 to 3 hours, or until the squash feels slightly soft when grasped with tongs. Transfer the squash to a cooling rack or work surface. Let it cool for about 30 minutes. Follow the instructions on page 228 to cook the vegetable mixture as well as halve, clean, and scrape out the spaghetti-like squash strands. Cover and refrigerate the strands for up to four days. About 10 minutes before the vegetable mixture is cooked, microwave the strands on 100 percent power (high) for 3 to 5 minutes to reheat them.

SERVES 5; 1½ cups per serving

SLOW COOKER SIZE | SHAPE
3- to 4½-quart | round or oval

SLOW COOKING TIME
8 to 10 hours ON LOW plus 30 minutes ON LOW, **OR**

5 to 6 hours ON HIGH plus 30 minutes ON HIGH

1 cup dried cannellini, navy, or baby lima beans, sorted for stones and shriveled beans, rinsed, and drained

5 cups fat-free, low-sodium vegetable broth, such as on page 50

1 teaspoon dried sage

2 medium garlic cloves, minced

¼ teaspoon salt

⅛ teaspoon pepper

＋

1 medium turnip, peeled and cut into ½-inch cubes, or 1 medium red potato, cut into ½-inch cubes

1 small sweet potato, cut into ½-inch cubes

1 small red bell pepper, cut into ½-inch cubes

1 small onion, chopped

2 teaspoons olive oil

¼ teaspoon salt

⅛ teaspoon pepper

1 14.5-ounce can no-salt-added diced tomatoes, undrained

Bean and Roasted Vegetable Stew

It's so worth the extra step of roasting the vegetables for this stew. They play a key role in providing the stew's incredibly deep flavor.

1. Fill a small saucepan three-fourths full of water. Bring to a boil over high heat. Stir in the beans. Return to a boil. Reduce the heat and simmer for 15 minutes. Pour into a colander and rinse. Pour into the slow cooker.

2. Stir in the broth, sage, garlic, ¼ teaspoon salt, and ⅛ teaspoon pepper. Cook, covered, on low for 8 to 10 hours or on high for 5 to 6 hours, or until the beans are tender.

3. About 1 hour 15 minutes before the beans are done, preheat the oven to 400°F.

4. Place the turnip, sweet potato, bell pepper, and onion in a large baking pan. Drizzle with the oil. Sprinkle with the remaining ¼ teaspoon salt and ⅛ teaspoon pepper. Toss to coat. Spread the vegetables in a single layer.

5. Roast the vegetables for 25 minutes. Stir. Roast for 15 minutes, or until the vegetables are browned and tender.

6. Quickly stir the vegetables and tomatoes with liquid into the beans and re-cover the slow cooker. Cook for 30 minutes.

PER SERVING
Calories **225**
Total Fat **2.0 g**
  Saturated Fat **0.5 g**
  Trans Fat **0.0 g**
  Polyunsaturated Fat **0.0 g**
  Monounsaturated Fat **1.5 g**

Cholesterol **0 mg**
Sodium **338 mg**
Carbohydrates **40 g**
  Fiber **9 g**
  Sugars **8 g**
Protein **12 g**

Dietary Exchanges:
  2 starch, 2 vegetable, 1 lean meat

Louisiana Vegetable Stew

You'll never miss the meat in this thick, spicy stew from bayou country. All you need to add is a small whole-grain roll to soak up all this southern goodness.

In the slow cooker, stir together all the ingredients. Cook, covered, on low for 5½ to 6½ hours or on high for 3 to 3½ hours.

COOK'S TIP

For the best flavor, you almost always should add dried herbs and seasonings at the beginning of the slow cooking time. Fresh herbs are usually added toward the end. The flavor of some seasonings can diminish during slow cooking, so get in the habit of tasting your dish before serving. (Remember to avoid lifting the lid while the dish cooks because doing so lowers the temperature in the slow cooker.) If the seasonings—except salt and seasonings that include salt—aren't strong enough, you can add more.

PER SERVING
Calories **252**
Total Fat **1.5 g**
  Saturated Fat **0.5 g**
  Trans Fat **0.0 g**
  Polyunsaturated Fat **0.5 g**
  Monounsaturated Fat **0.5 g**

Cholesterol **0 mg**
Sodium **316 mg**
Carbohydrates **50 g**
  Fiber **8 g**
  Sugars **7 g**
  Protein **10 g**

Dietary Exchanges:
  2½ starch, 2 vegetable

FAST PREP!

SERVES 5; 1⅔ cups per serving

SLOW COOKER SIZE | SHAPE
4- to 6-quart | round or oval

SLOW COOKING TIME
5½ to 6½ hours ON LOW, **OR**
3 to 3½ hours ON HIGH

1 15.5-ounce can no-salt-added red beans, rinsed and drained

1 14.5-ounce can no-salt-added diced tomatoes, undrained

1¾ cups fat-free, low-sodium vegetable broth, such as on page 50

1½ cups frozen sliced okra, thawed

1 medium green bell pepper, finely chopped

1 medium onion, finely chopped

1 cup uncooked brown rice (not instant)

1 cup water

1 teaspoon extra-spicy salt-free all-purpose seasoning blend

½ teaspoon salt

3 to 5 drops red hot-pepper sauce, or to taste

SLOW COOKER SIZE | SHAPE
3- to 4½-quart | round
or oval

SLOW COOKING TIME
8 to 10 hours ON LOW, **OR**
5 to 6 hours ON HIGH

¾ cup dried cranberry
beans, sorted for stones
and shriveled beans,
rinsed, and drained

1 large sweet potato,
peeled and diced (about
2 cups)

2 cups fat-free, low-sodium
vegetable broth, such as
on page 50

1 14.5-ounce can no-salt-
added diced tomatoes,
undrained

1 medium onion, chopped

1 medium red or yellow bell
pepper, chopped

2 tablespoons no-salt-
added tomato paste

2 medium garlic cloves,
minced

1 tablespoon plus
1½ teaspoons chili
powder

1 tablespoon ground cumin

1 teaspoon dried oregano,
crumbled

¾ teaspoon salt

⅛ teaspoon cayenne

—————— ✦ ——————

3 tablespoons fresh lime
juice (from about
2 medium limes)

2 medium green onions,
thinly sliced

¼ cup chopped fresh
cilantro

Cranberry Bean and Sweet Potato Chili

A scrumptious trio of savory, sweet, and spicy flavors, this hearty chili is perfect to make in the fall and winter when you're looking for a warm bowl of comfort food. It's finished with a splash of lime juice and a sprinkle of green onions and cilantro to brighten up the taste after a long, slow simmer.

1. Fill a small saucepan three-fourths full of water. Bring to a boil over high heat. Stir in the beans. Return to a boil. Reduce the heat and simmer for 15 minutes. Pour the beans into a colander and rinse and drain them. Pour into the slow cooker. Stir in the sweet potato, broth, tomatoes with liquid, onion, bell pepper, tomato paste, and garlic.

2. In a small bowl, stir together the chili powder, cumin, oregano, salt, and cayenne. Stir half the chili powder mixture into the bean mixture in the slow cooker. Set the remaining chili powder mixture aside.

3. Cook, covered, on low for 8 to 10 hours or on high for 5 to 6 hours, or until the beans are tender. Stir in the lime juice and reserved chili powder mixture. Sprinkle each serving with the green onions and cilantro.

COOK'S TIP

Cranberry beans, sometimes called Roman beans or borlotti beans, are beige with reddish-brown stripes. Unfortunately, these stripes disappear when the beans are cooked. Cranberry beans have a creamy texture and mild flavor. They're delicious in soups, salads, pasta dishes, or chili. If you can't find them, use dried pinto beans.

PER SERVING			
Calories **259**	Cholesterol **0 mg**	Dietary Exchanges:	
Total Fat **1.5 g**	Sodium **409 mg**	2½ **starch,**	
Saturated Fat **0.0 g**	Carbohydrates **52 g**	3 **vegetable,**	
Trans Fat **0.0 g**	Fiber **16 g**	½ **lean meat**	
Polyunsaturated Fat **0.5 g**	Sugars **12 g**		
Monounsaturated Fat **0.0 g**	Protein **12 g**		

Thai Vegetable Curry

A creamy sauce of lite coconut milk spiked with green curry paste blankets brightly colored vegetables in this tofu-based curry.

SERVES 4; 1½ cups per serving

SLOW COOKER SIZE | SHAPE
3- to 4½-quart | round or oval

SLOW COOKING TIME
5 to 7 hours ON LOW plus 10 minutes ON HIGH, **OR**
2½ to 3½ hours ON HIGH plus 10 minutes ON HIGH

1. In a small skillet, heat the oil over medium heat, swirling to coat the bottom. Cook the onion for 3 minutes, or until beginning to soften, stirring frequently. Stir in the garlic and gingerroot. Cook for 1 minute, stirring constantly. Transfer to the slow cooker.

2. Top the onion mixture with one layer each, in order, of the sweet potato, cauliflower, bell pepper, and tofu. Don't stir.

3. In a small bowl, whisk together the coconut milk, soy sauce, and curry paste. Pour into the slow cooker. Don't stir. Cook, covered, on low for 5 to 7 hours or on high for 2½ to 3½ hours.

4. If using the low setting, change it to high. Quickly add the broccoli (don't stir) and re-cover the slow cooker. Cook for 10 minutes, or until the broccoli is tender.

5. Meanwhile, put the cornstarch in a small bowl. Pour in the water, whisking to dissolve. Set aside.

6. Using a slotted spoon, transfer the vegetable mixture to a serving bowl, being careful to keep the tofu cubes intact.

7. Pour the cooking liquid into a medium saucepan. Bring to a boil over medium-high heat. Gradually whisk in about half the cornstarch mixture. Bring to a boil, still over medium-high heat, whisking constantly. Whisk in the remaining cornstarch mixture 1 teaspoon at a time until the desired consistency. Boil for 1 minute, whisking constantly. Pour the sauce over the tofu and vegetables. Serve sprinkled with the cilantro.

COOK'S TIP

Thai green curry paste is a combination of chiles, herbs, and spices and is highly aromatic, flavorful, and very spicy. You can probably find it in the Asian section of your supermarket, or look in Asian grocery stores or online. If you like your curry hot, feel free to add more.

1 teaspoon canola or corn oil

1 large onion, cut into 1-inch squares (about 1½ cups)

4 medium garlic cloves, minced

2 teaspoons minced peeled gingerroot

1 sweet potato (about 9 ounces), peeled and cut into 1-inch cubes

1½ cups 1-inch cauliflower florets

1 medium red bell pepper, cut into 1-inch squares (about 1½ cups)

1 12.3-ounce package light extra-firm tofu, drained, patted dry, and cut into 1-inch cubes

1 13.5- to 13.75-ounce can lite coconut milk

1 teaspoon soy sauce (lowest sodium available)

½ teaspoon Thai green curry paste, or to taste

———— + ————

9 ounces frozen broccoli cuts, thawed

1½ tablespoons cornstarch

1½ tablespoons water

⅓ cup snipped fresh cilantro

PER SERVING

Calories **244**	Cholesterol **0 mg**	Dietary Exchanges:
Total Fat **8.0 g**	Sodium **176 mg**	**1 starch, 1 vegetable,**
Saturated Fat **3.5 g**	Carbohydrates **33 g**	**1 lean meat, 1 fat**
Trans Fat **0.0 g**	Fiber **7 g**	
Polyunsaturated Fat **1.0 g**	Sugars **10 g**	
Monounsaturated Fat **1.5 g**	Protein **12 g**	

Parmesan Polenta with Roasted Vegetables

An array of vegetables provides color and texture when spooned over creamy polenta. Keep in mind that it needs a quick stir every half-hour.

SERVES 4; 1 cup vegetables and ½ cup polenta per serving

SLOW COOKER SIZE | SHAPE
1½- to 2½-quart | round

SLOW COOKING TIME
1½ to 2 hours ON HIGH

1. Lightly spray the slow cooker with cooking spray. Set aside.
2. In a small saucepan, whisk together the evaporated milk, ½ cup half-and-half, the polenta, margarine, salt, and pepper. Cook over medium-high heat for 4 minutes, or until the mixture comes to a boil, whisking constantly to prevent lumps from forming. Boil for 1 minute, whisking constantly.
3. Pour the polenta into the slow cooker. Cook, covered, on high for 1 to 1½ hours, quickly stirring and re-covering the slow cooker every 30 minutes.
4. About 30 minutes before the polenta is ready, preheat the oven to 425°F.
5. Meanwhile, without peeling, cut the eggplant into 1-inch cubes. Place the eggplant, zucchini, and onion in a single layer on a baking sheet. Lightly spray them with cooking spray.
6. Roast the vegetables for 8 minutes. Stir. Roast for 5 minutes. Arrange the tomatoes on the baking sheet, keeping the vegetables in a single layer. Roast for 3 minutes, or until the vegetables are tender.
7. Just before serving, stir the remaining ¼ cup half-and-half and the Parmesan into the polenta. Spoon the polenta onto a deep serving platter. Spoon the vegetables on top.

Cooking spray

12 ounces canned fat-free evaporated milk

½ cup fat-free half-and-half

⅓ cup coarse polenta, coarse corn grits, or coarse cornmeal

1 tablespoon light tub margarine

¼ teaspoon salt

¼ teaspoon pepper

— + —

1 medium eggplant (about 1 pound)

1¾ cups sliced zucchini (about ¼ inch thick)

1 medium onion, cut into 8 wedges

3 medium Italian plum (Roma) tomatoes, quartered

¼ cup fat-free half-and-half

⅓ cup shredded or grated Parmesan cheese

PER SERVING
Calories **243**
Total Fat **4.0 g**
  Saturated Fat **1.5 g**
  Trans Fat **0.0 g**
  Polyunsaturated Fat **0.5 g**
  Monounsaturated Fat **1.5 g**

Cholesterol **8 mg**
Sodium **440 mg**
Carbohydrates **40 g**
  Fiber **7 g**
  Sugars **21 g**
Protein **16 g**

Dietary Exchanges:
  ½ **starch, 1 fat-free milk, 3 vegetable, ½ lean meat**

SLOW COOKER SIZE | SHAPE
3- to 4½-quart | round or oval

SLOW COOKING TIME
7 to 9 hours ON LOW, **OR**
3½ to 4½ hours ON HIGH

1 cup dried chickpeas, sorted for stones and shriveled peas, rinsed, and drained

1 teaspoon olive oil

1 large onion, cut into 1-inch squares (about 1½ cups)

3 medium carrots, cut into 1-inch pieces (about 1½ cups)

4 medium garlic cloves, minced

1 tablespoon snipped fresh thyme and 1 tablespoon snipped fresh thyme, divided use

1½ teaspoons paprika and 1½ teaspoons paprika, divided use

¼ teaspoon salt and ¼ teaspoon salt, divided use

¼ teaspoon pepper and ¼ teaspoon pepper, divided use

8 ounces unpeeled small red potatoes, each cut into 4 wedges (6 wedges if large) (about 1½ cups)

8 ounces rutabaga, cut into 1-inch cubes (about 1½ cups)

1 large red bell pepper, cut into 1-inch squares

3 cups fat-free, low-sodium vegetable broth, such as on page 50

Chickpea and Vegetable Stew

It takes only a little smoky roasted red bell pepper sauce to add a lot of flavor to this satisfying stew of chickpeas and veggies. For extra creaminess, top each serving with a dollop of fat-free plain yogurt.

1. Fill a small saucepan with water. Bring to a boil over high heat. Stir in the chickpeas. Return to a boil. Reduce the heat and simmer for 15 minutes. Pour into a colander and rinse. Pour into the slow cooker. Set aside.

2. In a medium nonstick skillet, heat the oil over medium-high heat, swirling to coat the bottom. Cook the onion for 3 minutes, or until soft and lightly browned on the edges, stirring frequently. Stir in the carrots. Cook for 30 seconds, stirring constantly. Stir in the garlic. Cook for 30 seconds, stirring constantly. Spoon over the chickpeas. Sprinkle with 1 tablespoon thyme, 1½ teaspoons paprika, ¼ teaspoon salt, and ¼ teaspoon pepper.

3. Top, in order, with one layer each of the potatoes, rutabaga, and bell pepper. Sprinkle with the remaining 1 tablespoon thyme, 1½ teaspoons paprika, ¼ teaspoon salt, and ¼ teaspoon pepper. Pour the broth over all, making sure the chickpeas are covered. (Don't worry if the vegetables aren't covered.) Don't stir. Cook, covered, on low for 7 to 9 hours or on high for 3½ to 4½ hours, or until the chickpeas are tender but still slightly firm and the vegetables are tender.

4. Meanwhile, in a food processor or blender, process the roasted peppers, 2 tablespoons yogurt (if using), and the garlic until smooth. Transfer to a small bowl. If you make this mixture 2 hours or more before the stew is ready, cover and refrigerate it. If less than 2 hours, set it aside.

5. Using a slotted spoon, transfer the stew to bowls. Spoon enough cooking liquid over the stew to moisten it. Garnish with the sprigs of fresh thyme. Spoon the sauce over the stew. Spoon a dollop of the remaining ¼ cup plus 2 tablespoons of yogurt onto each serving.

———— + ————

½ cup roasted red bell peppers (about 4 ounces), drained if bottled

2 tablespoons fat-free plain yogurt (optional) and ¼ cup plus 2 tablespoons fat-free plain yogurt, divided use

½ medium garlic clove, minced

Sprigs of fresh thyme

PER SERVING
Calories **220**
Total Fat **3.0 g**
  Saturated Fat **0.5 g**
  Trans Fat **0.0 g**
  Polyunsaturated Fat **1.0 g**
  Monounsaturated Fat **1.0 g**

Cholesterol **0 mg**
Sodium **123 mg**
Carbohydrates **40 g**
  Fiber **10 g**
  Sugars **12 g**
Protein **10 g**

Dietary Exchanges:
2 starch, 2 vegetable

SERVES 8; 1 cup curry and
½ cup rice per serving

SLOW COOKER SIZE | SHAPE
4- to 6-quart | round or
oval

SLOW COOKING TIME
9 to 10 hours ON LOW, **OR**
4½ to 5 hours ON HIGH

1 tablespoon olive oil

3 tablespoons curry
powder

1 teaspoon crushed red
pepper flakes

1 cup chopped onion

2 cups fat-free, low-sodium
vegetable broth, such as
on page 50

2 medium potatoes,
such as russet (about
8½ ounces each), peeled
and cut into ½-inch
cubes

2 15.5-ounce cans no-salt-
added chickpeas, rinsed
and drained

1 14.5-ounce can no-salt-
added diced tomatoes,
undrained

2 medium carrots, cut
crosswise into ¼-inch
slices (about 1 cup)

2 tablespoons uncooked
instant, or quick-
cooking, tapioca

3 medium garlic cloves,
minced

½ teaspoon salt

½ teaspoon pepper

＋

3 cups uncooked instant
brown rice

2½ cups fat-free, low-
sodium vegetable broth,
such as on page 50

Spicy Vegetable Curry

Protein-rich chickpeas and a variety of vegetables combine in this
stewlike dish, which uses enough curry powder and crushed red
pepper flakes to grab your attention!

1. In a small nonstick skillet, heat the oil over medium-high heat,
   swirling to coat the bottom. Cook the curry powder and red
   pepper flakes for 30 seconds, or until they start to brown and
   are aromatic, stirring constantly. Stir in the onion. Cook for
   1 minute, stirring constantly. Transfer to the slow cooker.
2. Stir in 2 cups broth, the potatoes, chickpeas, tomatoes with
   liquid, carrots, tapioca, garlic, salt, and pepper. Cook, covered,
   on low for 9 to 10 hours or on high for 4½ to 5 hours, or until the
   potatoes and carrots are tender.
3. Just before serving time, prepare the rice using the package
   directions, omitting the salt and margarine and substituting the
   remaining 2½ cups broth for the water.
4. Serve the curry on the rice.

PER SERVING
Calories **346**
Total Fat **4.0 g**
  Saturated Fat **0.5 g**
  Trans Fat **0.0 g**
  Polyunsaturated Fat **0.5 g**
  Monounsaturated Fat **2.0 g**

Cholesterol **0 mg**
Sodium **231 mg**
Carbohydrates **66 g**
  Fiber **9 g**
  Sugars **5 g**
Protein **11 g**

Dietary Exchanges:
  **4 starch, 1 vegetable,
  ½ lean meat**

Chickpea, Cucumber, and Tomato Salad with Feta

Firm, filling, and full of fiber, chickpeas star in this salad, which is lightly dressed with a dill-infused vinaigrette.

SERVES 4; 1½ cups per serving

SLOW COOKER SIZE | SHAPE
1½- to 2½-quart | round or oval

SLOW COOKING TIME
6 to 8 hours ON LOW, **OR**
3 to 4 hours ON HIGH

1. Fill a small saucepan three-fourths full of water. Bring to a boil over high heat. Stir in the chickpeas. Return to a boil. Reduce the heat and simmer for 15 minutes. Pour into a colander and rinse. Pour into the slow cooker. Pour in 3 cups water. Cook, covered, on low for 6 to 8 hours or on high for 3 to 4 hours, or until the chickpeas are tender but still slightly firm. Drain in a colander. Rinse under cold running water to cool. Transfer to a large bowl.

2. While the chickpeas are cooking, in a food processor or blender, process the remaining ⅓ cup water, the vinegar, dillweed, oil, mustard, and garlic until smooth. If you make this dressing 2 hours or more before the chickpeas are ready, cover and refrigerate it. If less than 2 hours, set it aside.

3. Stir the tomatoes, cucumber, green onions, and ¼ cup feta together with the chickpeas, tossing gently to combine. Pour in ½ cup dressing, tossing to lightly coat. Discard the remaining dressing or save for another use. Spoon the salad onto plates. Sprinkle with the chopped egg whites and yolk and the remaining ¼ cup feta.

1 cup dried chickpeas, sorted for stones and shriveled peas, rinsed, and drained

3 cups water

_____ + _____

⅓ cup water

3 tablespoons red wine vinegar

2 tablespoons snipped fresh dillweed

2 teaspoons olive oil (extra virgin preferred)

1 teaspoon Dijon mustard

1 medium garlic clove

_____ + _____

2 small tomatoes, chopped (about 1¼ cups)

1 medium cucumber, diced (about 1¼ cups)

½ cup sliced green onions (green and white parts)

¼ cup low-fat feta cheese and ¼ cup low-fat feta cheese, divided use

2 hard-cooked eggs, 1 yolk discarded, chopped

PER SERVING
Calories **267**
Total Fat **8.5 g**
 Saturated Fat **2.5 g**
 Trans Fat **0.0 g**
 Polyunsaturated Fat **2.0 g**
 Monounsaturated Fat **3.0 g**

Cholesterol **53 mg**
Sodium **321 mg**
Carbohydrates **34 g**
 Fiber **9 g**
 Sugars **8 g**
 Protein **16 g**

Dietary Exchanges:
 2 starch, 1 vegetable, 1½ lean meat

SERVES 4; 3 ounces tofu and ½ cup rice per serving

SLOW COOKER SIZE | SHAPE
3- to 4½-quart | oval or round

SLOW COOKING TIME
4 to 6 hours ON LOW, **OR**
1½ to 2 hours ON HIGH

1 cup diced onion

8 ounces no-salt-added tomato sauce

½ cup lite coconut milk

½ cup fat-free, low-sodium vegetable broth, such as on page 50

1 tablespoon fresh lemon juice

1 teaspoon garam masala

2 medium garlic cloves, minced

1 teaspoon minced peeled gingerroot

½ teaspoon salt

½ teaspoon ground turmeric

½ teaspoon ground cumin

12 ounces light firm tofu, drained and patted dry, cut into 1-inch cubes

———— ✛ ————

1 cup uncooked instant brown rice

2 tablespoons chopped fresh cilantro or basil

Tofu Tikka Masala

Tofu is bathed in a creamy, spice-infused tomato sauce in this classic Indian dish. Serve with sautéed spinach as a beautiful color complement to the orange of the tikka masala, which comes from the turmeric.

1. In the slow cooker, stir together the onion, tomato sauce, coconut milk, broth, lemon juice, garam masala, garlic, gingerroot, salt, turmeric, and cumin.
2. Gently stir in the tofu. Cook, covered, on low for 4 to 6 hours or on high for 1½ to 2 hours.
3. About 20 minutes before serving time, prepare the rice using the package directions, omitting the salt and margarine. Put the rice in bowls.
4. Spoon the tofu mixture over the rice. Sprinkle with the cilantro.

PER SERVING
Calories **188**
Total Fat **4.0 g**
  Saturated Fat **1.0 g**
  Trans Fat **0.0 g**
  Polyunsaturated Fat **1.5 g**
  Monounsaturated Fat **0.5 g**

Cholesterol **0 mg**
Sodium **346 mg**
Carbohydrates **28 g**
  Fiber **3 g**
  Sugars **5 g**
Protein **11 g**

Dietary Exchanges:
  1 starch, 2 vegetable, 1 lean meat

Vegetable Stew with Cornmeal Dumplings

Sweet butternut squash and cornbread-like dumplings make this stew so good that even the kids will enjoy eating their veggies.

1. In the slow cooker, stir together the squash, mushrooms, tomatoes with liquid, broth, carrot, celery, onion, oregano, pepper, and salt. Cook, covered, on low for 7 to 8 hours or on high for 3½ to 4 hours.
2. Just before the end of the cooking time, prepare the dumplings. In a medium bowl, stir together the flour, cornmeal, baking powder, and Italian seasoning.
3. In a small bowl, whisk together the egg, milk, and oil. Pour into the flour mixture, stirring with a fork until just combined but no flour is visible. Set aside.
4. When the stew is ready, quickly stir in the parsley. Drop four equal portions of the dumpling batter on top of the stew. Re-cover the slow cooker. If using the low setting, change it to high. Cook for 50 minutes, or until a wooden toothpick inserted in the centers of the dumplings comes out clean. (Don't remove the lid while cooking the dumplings.)

COOK'S TIP
The dumpling batter will spread when you drop it on the stew, so you don't need to worry about making the portions a particular thickness.

PER SERVING
Calories **280**
Total Fat **8.5 g**
  Saturated Fat **1.5 g**
  Trans Fat **0.0 g**
  Polyunsaturated Fat **1.0 g**
  Monounsaturated Fat **5.5 g**
Cholesterol **47 mg**
Sodium **337 mg**
Carbohydrates **45 g**
  Fiber **6 g**
  Sugars **7 g**
Protein **8 g**

Dietary Exchanges:
  2½ starch,
  2 vegetable, 1 fat

FAST PREP! ⏱

SERVES 4; 1 cup stew and 1 dumpling per serving

SLOW COOKER SIZE | SHAPE
3- to 4½-quart | round or oval

SLOW COOKING TIME
7 to 8 hours ON LOW plus 50 minutes ON HIGH, **OR**
3½ to 4 hours ON HIGH plus 50 minutes ON HIGH

3 cups chopped peeled butternut squash (about 1 pound)

6 ounces button mushrooms, sliced (about 2 cups)

1 14.5-ounce can no-salt-added diced tomatoes with basil, garlic, and oregano, undrained

1½ cups fat-free, low-sodium vegetable broth, such as on page 50

1 medium carrot, chopped

1 medium rib of celery, chopped

1 teaspoon dried minced onion

½ teaspoon dried oregano, crumbled

½ teaspoon pepper

¼ teaspoon salt

———— ✦ ————

½ cup all-purpose flour

⅓ cup yellow cornmeal

1 teaspoon baking powder

½ teaspoon dried Italian seasoning, crumbled

1 large egg

2 tablespoons fat-free milk

2 tablespoons olive oil

¼ cup snipped fresh parsley

Vegetables and Side Dishes

243 Honey-Roasted Vegetables ⏱

244 Roasted Red Potatoes with Lemon and Green Onions ⏱

246 Lemon-Garlic Artichokes with Lemon Dipping Sauce

247 Autumn Apple-Pear Sauce ⏱

248 Barley Casserole ⏱

249 Chipotle Baked Beans

250 Balsamic-Glazed Beets with Toasted Walnuts

251 Shredded Brussels Sprouts with Almonds

253 Braised Broccoli Rabe with Cherry Tomatoes

254 Sweet and Tangy Red Cabbage ⏱

255 Pomegranate Carrots

256 Crock-Roasted Carrots and Parsnips with Cumin-Yogurt Sauce ⏱

257 Braised Cauliflower with Crisp Garlic Crumbs

258 Cheese Lover's Mac-and-Cheese ⏱

260 Collard Greens with Turkey Bacon

261 Sicilian Eggplant Caponata ⏱

262 Cheesy Basil Grits ⏱

263 Lentil and Bell Pepper Salad with Lemon-Orange Dressing ⏱

264 Simple Mashed Sweet Potatoes ⏱

265 Acorn Squash Wedges with Walnuts

268 Maple-Glazed Quinoa ⏱

269 Pumpkin-Sage Risotto

270 Wild Rice with Harvest Vegetables ⏱

271 Vegetable and Mixed-Rice Pilaf ⏱

Honey-Roasted Vegetables

A touch of honey and the subtle flavor of thyme accent this dish and bring out the natural flavors of the vegetables.

FAST PREP!

SERVES 8; ½ cup per serving

SLOW COOKER SIZE | SHAPE
4- to 5-quart | round or oval

SLOW COOKING TIME
5 to 6 hours ON LOW, **OR**
2½ to 3 hours ON HIGH

1. In the slow cooker, make one layer each, in order, of the carrots, onions, red potatoes, and sweet potatoes. Sprinkle with the thyme, pepper, and salt. Add the water. Don't stir. Cook, covered, on low for 5 to 6 hours or on high for 2½ to 3 hours.
2. Just before serving, in a small bowl, whisk together the honey and lemon juice. Drizzle over the vegetables.

COOK'S TIP

So that all the veggies in this dish can slow cook together successfully, layer them, placing the carrots (and parsnips), which cook more slowly, on the bottom of the cooker, where they will get the most concentrated heat. The sweet potatoes slow cook more quickly than the other vegetables in this dish, so they go on top.

4 medium carrots, parsnips, or a combination (about 8 ounces total), cut crosswise into 1-inch pieces

8 whole boiling onions, or 1 medium onion, cut into 8 wedges

8 unpeeled red potatoes (about 2 ounces each), halved

2 medium sweet potatoes (about 8 ounces each), quartered

1 tablespoon snipped fresh thyme

½ teaspoon pepper

⅛ teaspoon salt

2 tablespoons water

———— + ————

1 tablespoon honey

2 teaspoons fresh lemon juice

PER SERVING
Calories **118**
Total Fat **0.0 g**
  Saturated Fat **0.0 g**
  Trans Fat **0.0 g**
  Polyunsaturated Fat **0.0 g**
  Monounsaturated Fat **0.0 g**

Cholesterol **0 mg**
Sodium **104 mg**
Carbohydrates **28 g**
  Fiber **4 g**
  Sugars **8 g**
Protein **3 g**

Dietary Exchanges:
  1½ starch, 1 vegetable

SERVES 4; 4 potato halves
 per serving

SLOW COOKER SIZE | SHAPE
3- to 4½-quart | round
 or oval

SLOW COOKING TIME
6 hours ON LOW, **OR**
3 hours ON HIGH

Cooking spray

8 2-ounce red potatoes,
 halved crosswise

½ medium onion, thinly
 sliced

½ teaspoon garlic powder

½ teaspoon dried oregano,
 crumbled

1 tablespoon olive oil

———————— + ————————

2 medium green onions,
 finely chopped

2 tablespoons water

1 to 2 teaspoons grated
 lemon zest

1 tablespoon fresh lemon
 juice

⅛ teaspoon salt

1½ teaspoons olive oil
 (extra virgin preferred)

Roasted Red Potatoes with Lemon and Green Onions

If you're looking for a versatile dish, you've found it. Ideal as a side dish, these flavorful potatoes also work well as an appetizer. They're easy to make and super easy to serve, and they're equally delicious warm or at room temperature.

1. Lightly spray the slow cooker with cooking spray. Put the potatoes, onion, garlic powder, oregano, and 1 tablespoon oil in the slow cooker, tossing to coat. (Be sure the potatoes are covered with the mixture.) Cook, covered, on low for 6 hours or on high for 3 hours, or until the potatoes are tender when pierced with a fork.

2. Turn off the slow cooker. Using a slotted spoon, transfer the potatoes to a shallow pan, such as a pie pan, leaving the drippings in the slow cooker. Stir the remaining ingredients into the drippings. Spoon over the potatoes, stirring gently to coat. Let stand for at least 10 minutes so the flavors blend and the potatoes are cool enough to eat.

PER SERVING
Calories **138**
Total Fat **5.0 g**
 Saturated Fat **0.5 g**
 Trans Fat **0.0 g**
 Polyunsaturated Fat **0.5 g**
 Monounsaturated Fat **3.5 g**

Cholesterol **0 mg**
Sodium **97 mg**
Carbohydrates **21 g**
 Fiber **3 g**
 Sugars **3 g**
 Protein **2 g**

Dietary Exchanges:
 1½ starch, 1 fat

SERVES 4; 1 artichoke and
1½ tablespoons sauce

SLOW COOKER SIZE | SHAPE
4- to 4½-quart | round
or oval

SLOW COOKING TIME
8 to 10 hours ON LOW, **OR**
4 to 5 hours ON HIGH

4 medium artichokes
(about 9 ounces each)

4 small garlic cloves,
crushed

1 small lemon, cut into
4 wedges

━━━━━━ + ━━━━━━

3 tablespoons fresh lemon
juice (from 1 large
lemon)

⅛ teaspoon salt

⅛ teaspoon pepper

3 tablespoons olive oil
(extra virgin preferred)

1 tablespoon chopped fresh
parsley

Lemon-Garlic Artichokes with Lemon Dipping Sauce

Infused with garlic and citrus, these artichokes become a succulent side dish when they cook low and slow.

1. Working with one artichoke at a time, cut away and discard the top third of the artichoke and cut off the bottom of the stem. Pull back the outer leaves to loosen them. Remove the tough leaves close to the stem and any of the tougher outer leaves. Using kitchen shears, cut off the spiny tops of the leaves. Using a small spoon or melon baller, scoop out and discard the pale yellow inner leaves and the fuzzy center choke. Insert a garlic clove and a lemon wedge into the center of the artichoke. Transfer to the slow cooker. Repeat with the remaining artichokes, garlic, and lemon wedges. Pour water into the slow cooker to a depth of about 2 inches.

2. Cook, covered, on low for 8 to 10 hours or on high for 4 to 5 hours, or until the artichokes are tender (the bottoms can be pierced with the tip of a sharp knife). Discard the garlic clove and lemon wedge in the center of each artichoke before serving.

3. About 10 minutes before serving time, in a small bowl, whisk together the lemon juice, salt, and pepper. Slowly whisk in the oil. Whisk in the parsley. Serve the artichokes with the dipping sauce.

COOK'S TIP

Eating Artichokes To eat an artichoke, pull off the outer leaves one at a time. Grip the top of each leaf and place the fleshy part in your mouth (you can dip the fleshy part in the dipping sauce first), using your teeth to scrape off the soft pulp. Eat the pulp and discard the rest of the leaf. When the leaves are finished, you can cut up the heart (that was covered by the choke) and the stem, which is an extension of the heart, and enjoy them with the dipping sauce.

PER SERVING		
Calories **141**	Cholesterol **0 mg**	Dietary Exchanges:
Total Fat **10.5 g**	Sodium **170 mg**	**2 vegetable, 2 fat**
Saturated Fat **1.5 g**	Carbohydrates **12 g**	
Trans Fat **0.0 g**	Fiber **6 g**	
Polyunsaturated Fat **1.5 g**	Sugars **1 g**	
Monounsaturated Fat **7.5 g**	Protein **3 g**	

Autumn Apple-Pear Sauce

When the produce stands are packed with the autumnal harvest of both apples and pears, you don't need to pick just one. Use your favorite variety of each in this wonderfully aromatic side dish, which teams well with entrées such as baked chicken breasts and roast beef. Even try this sauce as a complement to whole-wheat pancakes for breakfast on crisp fall mornings.

In the slow cooker, stir together all the ingredients. Cook, covered, on low for 5 hours or on high for 3 hours, or until the fruit is very tender. If you wish, mash the sauce to the desired consistency, keeping in mind that the sauce will thicken as it cools.

COOK'S TIP

We used McIntosh apples and Anjou pears, but you can use any varieties you like for this recipe. You can even make the sauce using only apples or only pears if you prefer. Whatever you decide to use, you'll want 3 to 3½ pounds of fruit.

FAST PREP!

SERVES 6; ½ cup per serving

SLOW COOKER SIZE | SHAPE
3- to 4½-quart | round or oval

SLOW COOKING TIME

5 hours ON LOW, **OR**

3 hours ON HIGH

4 large apples (about 1½ pounds total), peeled and cut into 1-inch chunks

4 large pears (about 1¾ pounds total), peeled and cut into 1-inch chunks

2 tablespoons sugar

1 tablespoon fresh lemon juice

⅛ teaspoon ground cinnamon

Pinch of ground nutmeg

PER SERVING
Calories **134**
Total Fat **0.5 g**
  Saturated Fat **0.0 g**
  Trans Fat **0.0 g**
  Polyunsaturated Fat **0.0 g**
  Monounsaturated Fat **0.0 g**

Cholesterol **0 mg**
Sodium **1 mg**
Carbohydrates **36 g**
  Fiber **5 g**
  Sugars **26 g**
Protein **1 g**

Dietary Exchanges:
  2½ fruit

SERVES 10; ½ cup per serving

SLOW COOKER SIZE | SHAPE
   3- to 4½-quart | round or oval

SLOW COOKING TIME

6 to 8 hours ON LOW, **OR**

3½ to 4 hours ON HIGH

8 ounces baby bella mushrooms, sliced (2½ to 3 cups)

2 cups low-sodium spicy mixed-vegetable juice

1 cup fat-free, low-sodium vegetable broth, such as on page 50

1 cup uncooked pearl barley (not quick cooking or instant)

1 cup chopped onion

2 teaspoons Worcestershire sauce (lowest sodium available)

3 medium garlic cloves, minced

1 teaspoon dried basil, crumbled

¼ teaspoon pepper

———— + ————

3 tablespoons plus 1 teaspoon slivered almonds, dry-roasted and coarsely chopped

Barley Casserole

A terrific dish for a potluck, this casserole features often-overlooked barley, one of the world's oldest grains. Mixed-vegetable juice, Worcestershire sauce, and pepper bump up the flavor of this easy-as-can-be dish.

In the slow cooker, stir together all the ingredients except the almonds. Cook, covered, on low for 6 to 8 hours or on high for 3½ to 4 hours, or until the barley is tender. Sprinkle each serving with 1 teaspoon almonds.

PER SERVING
Calories **108**
Total Fat **1.5 g**
   Saturated Fat **0.0 g**
   Trans Fat **0.0 g**
   Polyunsaturated Fat **0.5 g**
   Monounsaturated Fat **0.5 g**

Cholesterol **0 mg**
Sodium **42 mg**
Carbohydrates **21 g**
   Fiber **4 g**
   Sugars **3 g**
Protein **4 g**

Dietary Exchanges:
   1 starch, 1 vegetable

Chipotle Baked Beans

These unorthodox baked beans will be the hit of the next party or picnic. They pack a pleasing punch, courtesy of heat from chipotle peppers canned in adobo sauce.

SERVES 12; ½ cup per serving

SLOW COOKER SIZE | SHAPE
3- to 4½-quart | round or oval

SLOW COOKING TIME
8 hours ON LOW plus 2 to 4 hours ON LOW

1. Fill a large saucepan three-fourths full of water. Bring to a boil over high heat. Stir in the beans. Return to a boil. Reduce the heat and simmer for 15 minutes. Pour into a colander and rinse. Pour into a large bowl.
2. Stir the onion, orange juice concentrate, molasses, tomato paste, ¼ cup water, garlic, chipotle, and mustard into the beans. Transfer to the slow cooker. Cook, covered, on low for about 8 hours. Quickly check to see whether the beans look like they're getting too dry. They aren't intended to be at all soupy, but if you like a bit more liquid, stir in several tablespoons of water. Re-cover the slow cooker. Cook for 2 to 4 hours. When the beans are done, stir in the salt. Serve garnished with the cilantro.

2 cups dried navy beans, sorted for stones and shriveled beans, rinsed, and drained

1 large Vidalia, Maui, Oso Sweet, or other sweet onion, chopped

½ cup frozen orange juice concentrate, thawed

½ cup molasses (dark preferred)

¼ cup no-salt-added tomato paste

¼ cup water

2 large garlic cloves, minced

2 teaspoons chipotle pepper canned in adobo sauce, or to taste, finely chopped

2 teaspoons dry mustard

+

¼ teaspoon salt

¼ cup snipped fresh cilantro

COOK'S TIP

You can put the cooked beans directly into the slow cooker instead of back in the bowl, but the inside of the slow cooker will get less messy—and you can more easily combine all the ingredients—if you use the bowl.

PER SERVING
Calories **184**
Total Fat **1.0 g**
  Saturated Fat **0.0 g**
  Trans Fat **0.0 g**
  Polyunsaturated Fat **0.5 g**
  Monounsaturated Fat **0.0 g**

Cholesterol **0 mg**
Sodium **71 mg**
Carbohydrates **38 g**
  Fiber **9 g**
  Sugars **14 g**
Protein **8 g**

Dietary Exchanges:
  2½ starch

SERVES 4; ½ cup per serving

SLOW COOKER SIZE | SHAPE
1½- to 2½-quart | round or oval

SLOW COOKING TIME
3½ to 6 hours ON LOW, **OR**
2 to 3 hours ON HIGH

1¼ pounds beets (3 medium to large) peeled, halved, and cut into 1-inch wedges

¼ cup water

+

⅓ cup balsamic vinegar

¼ teaspoon firmly packed light or dark brown sugar

¼ cup chopped walnuts, dry-roasted

Balsamic-Glazed Beets with Toasted Walnuts

As it reduces, balsamic vinegar thickens and becomes sweeter (though it does smell pungent), making it an addictively tasty, syrupy glaze for fresh beets. Serve the beets as a side dish or use a smaller amount on salads.

1. Put the beets in the slow cooker. Pour in the water. Cook, covered, on low for 3½ to 6 hours or on high for 2 to 3 hours, or until the beets are tender when pierced with a fork.
2. Meanwhile, in a small saucepan, stir together the vinegar and brown sugar. Bring to a boil over medium-high heat. Boil for 2 to 3 minutes, or until syrupy, stirring frequently (you will begin to see the bottom of the pan as you stir). Using a slotted spoon, transfer the beets to a serving bowl.
3. Drizzle the vinegar mixture over the beets. Sprinkle with the walnuts. Serve warm or at room temperature.

COOK'S TIP

Peel the beets using a vegetable peeler and wear disposable gloves to avoid having your hands turn red as you peel.

PER SERVING
Calories **108**
Total Fat **5.0 g**
  Saturated Fat **0.5 g**
  Trans Fat **0.0 g**
  Polyunsaturated Fat **3.5 g**
  Monounsaturated Fat **0.5 g**

Cholesterol **0 mg**
Sodium **79 mg**
Carbohydrates **15 g**
  Fiber **3 g**
  Sugars **11 g**
Protein **3 g**

Dietary Exchanges:
  2 vegetable, ½ other carbohydrate, 1 fat

Shredded Brussels Sprouts with Almonds

A slow simmer makes these brussels sprouts tender and flavorful—but leaches out a lot of their color. We think you'll hardly notice that once you experience the flavor and crunch of this side dish, which is rich in vitamin C.

1. In a large nonstick skillet, heat the oil over medium-high heat, swirling to coat the bottom. Cook the onion and carrot, covered, for 6 minutes, or until tender, stirring occasionally. Stir in the garlic. Cook for 1 minute. Transfer to the slow cooker.
2. Stir in the brussels sprouts, broth, salt, and pepper. Cook, covered, on high for 2 hours. Turn off the slow cooker. Just before serving, stir in the almonds and vinegar.

COOK'S TIP

Use the coarse side of a box grater or the thin slicing blade of a food processor to shred the brussels sprouts.

SERVES 4; heaping ½ cup per serving

SLOW COOKER SIZE | SHAPE
1½- to 2½-quart | round or oval

SLOW COOKING TIME
2 hours ON HIGH

2 teaspoons olive oil
1 small onion, thinly sliced
1 small carrot, diced
1 medium garlic clove, minced
10 ounces brussels sprouts, trimmed and shredded
½ cup fat-free, low-sodium vegetable broth, such as on page 50, or fat-free, low-sodium chicken broth, such as on page 48
¼ teaspoon salt
Pinch of pepper

+

2 tablespoons slivered almonds, dry-roasted
½ teaspoon red wine vinegar

PER SERVING
Calories **88**
Total Fat **4.0 g**
  Saturated Fat **0.5 g**
  Trans Fat **0.0 g**
  Polyunsaturated Fat **1.0 g**
  Monounsaturated Fat **2.5 g**
Cholesterol **0 mg**
Sodium **180 mg**
Carbohydrates **11 g**
  Fiber **4 g**
  Sugars **4 g**
Protein **4 g**
Dietary Exchanges:
  2 vegetable, 1 fat

Braised Broccoli Rabe with Cherry Tomatoes

Cooking broccoli rabe until it is very tender softens its slightly bitter flavor, so the slow cooker is a good choice when preparing this staple of Italian cuisine.

SERVES 4; ½ cup per serving

SLOW COOKER SIZE | SHAPE
3-quart | round or oval

SLOW COOKING TIME

3½ to 4 hours ON LOW plus 30 minutes ON HIGH, **OR**

1½ hours to 2 hours ON HIGH plus 30 minutes ON HIGH

2 teaspoons olive oil

2 medium garlic cloves, thinly sliced

1 pound broccoli rabe, tough stems discarded, leaves and florets cut into 2-inch pieces (about 6 cups)

½ cup fat-free, low-sodium chicken broth, such as on page 48

⅛ teaspoon salt

⅛ teaspoon crushed red pepper flakes

—————— + ——————

1 cup cherry tomatoes

1. In a small skillet, heat the oil over medium-high heat, swirling to coat the bottom. Cook the garlic for 2 minutes, or until lightly browned, stirring constantly. Transfer to the slow cooker.
2. Stir in the broccoli rabe, broth, salt, and red pepper flakes. Cook, covered, on low for 3½ to 4 hours or on high for 1½ to 2 hours, or until the broccoli rabe is tender.
3. If using the low setting, change it to high. Quickly stir in the tomatoes and re-cover the slow cooker. Cook for 30 minutes, or until the tomatoes are softened. Using a slotted spoon, transfer the mixture to plates.

COOK'S TIP

This dish makes a delicious vegetarian meal for two when served over whole-grain pasta and sprinkled with a small amount of shredded or grated Parmesan cheese. (Be sure to use vegetable broth instead of chicken broth.) Unlike when you serve the broccoli rabe as a side dish, here you will want to spoon the cooking liquid over the pasta to add moisture and flavor.

PER SERVING

Calories **69**
Total Fat **2.5 g**
  Saturated Fat **0.5 g**
  Trans Fat **0.0 g**
  Polyunsaturated Fat **0.5 g**
  Monounsaturated Fat **1.5 g**

Cholesterol **0 mg**
Sodium **118 mg**
Carbohydrates **9 g**
  Fiber **1 g**
  Sugars **3 g**
Protein **5 g**

Dietary Exchanges:
  2 vegetable, ½ fat

SERVES 8; ½ cup per serving

SLOW COOKER SIZE | SHAPE
3- to 4½-quart | round or oval

SLOW COOKING TIME
5 to 7 hours ON LOW, **OR**
2½ to 3½ hours ON HIGH

1 medium head red cabbage (about 1½ pounds), coarsely shredded (about 7 cups)

1 medium tart apple, such as Honey Crisp, Granny Smith, or Cortland, cut into medium slices

½ cup diced onion

3 tablespoons cider vinegar

2 tablespoons dark brown sugar

2 tablespoons unsweetened dried cranberries

2 tablespoons water

¼ teaspoon salt

¼ teaspoon pepper

Sweet and Tangy Red Cabbage

Dried cranberries temper the snap of cider vinegar in this jewel-toned side dish. Try it with lean pork roast or pork chops.

In the slow cooker, stir together all the ingredients. Cook, covered, on low for 5 to 7 hours or on high for 2½ to 3½ hours.

COOK'S TIP

For quick and easy slicing, discard any tough outer cabbage leaves. Quarter the head and discard the core. Use the thin-slicing blade of a food processor, or cut the quarters crosswise into very thin strips.

PER SERVING
Calories **59**
Total Fat **0.0 g**
  Saturated Fat **0.0 g**
  Trans Fat **0.0 g**
  Polyunsaturated Fat **0.0 g**
  Monounsaturated Fat **0.0 g**

Cholesterol **0 mg**
Sodium **170 mg**
Carbohydrates **15 g**
  Fiber **3 g**
  Sugars **10 g**
Protein **1 g**

Dietary Exchanges:
  1 vegetable, ½ other carbohydrate

Pomegranate Carrots

You'll be so taken with how the well-balanced combination of ingredients—pomegranate juice, Dijon mustard, rice vinegar, ginger, and honey—makes these carrots come alive with flavor that you probably won't mind their change in color.

SERVES 6; scant ½ cup per serving

SLOW COOKER SIZE | SHAPE
3- to 4½-quart | round or oval

SLOW COOKING TIME
4 to 4½ hours ON HIGH

1. Place the carrots in the slow cooker. Set aside.
2. In a small nonstick skillet, heat the oil over medium-high heat, swirling to coat the bottom. Cook the onion for 3 to 4 minutes, or until soft, stirring frequently. Stir in the garlic. Cook for 30 seconds, stirring constantly. Gently stir into the carrots.
3. In a small bowl, whisk together the remaining ingredients except the parsley. Pour into the slow cooker. Cook, covered, on high for 4 to 4½ hours, or until the carrots are tender-crisp. Just before serving, garnish with the parsley.

1 pound baby carrots (halved lengthwise if extra large)

1 teaspoon olive oil

½ cup chopped onion

1 medium garlic clove, minced

¼ cup 100% pomegranate juice

2 tablespoons Dijon mustard

2 tablespoons honey

2 teaspoons plain rice vinegar

1 teaspoon grated peeled gingerroot

_____ + _____

1 tablespoon snipped fresh parsley

PER SERVING
Calories **78**
Total Fat **1.5 g**
  Saturated Fat **0.0 g**
  Trans Fat **0.0 g**
  Polyunsaturated Fat **0.0 g**
  Monounsaturated Fat **0.5 g**

Cholesterol **0 mg**
Sodium **157 mg**
Carbohydrates **17 g**
  Fiber **3 g**
  Sugars **12 g**
Protein **1 g**

Dietary Exchanges:
1 vegetable, ½ other carbohydrate

SERVES 6; ½ cup vegetables
and 1 tablespoon sauce
per serving

SLOW COOKER SIZE | SHAPE
1½- to 2½-quart | round
or oval (preferred)

SLOW COOKING TIME
5 to 7 hours ON LOW, **OR**
2½ to 3½ hours ON HIGH

12 ounces medium carrots,
each halved crosswise,
then quartered
lengthwise (cut into
sixths if large) (strips
should be ½ to ¾ inch
thick)

12 ounces medium
parsnips, each halved
crosswise, then
quartered lengthwise
(cut into sixths if large)
(strips should be ½ to ¾
inch thick)

¼ cup fat-free, low-sodium
chicken broth, such as
on page 48

— ✛ —

⅓ cup fat-free plain yogurt

1 tablespoon fat-free milk

1 teaspoon ground cumin
(dry-roasted preferred)

Dash of pepper

1 tablespoon snipped fresh
parsley

Crock-Roasted Carrots and Parsnips with Cumin-Yogurt Sauce

The key to success with this dish is to select carrots and parsnips of approximately equal size and cut them into pieces of similar size and shape so they will cook evenly at the same rate. Serve this dish with roasted meat or poultry.

1. In the slow cooker, make one layer of the carrots, then of the parsnips. Pour in the broth. Don't stir. Cook, covered, on low for 5 to 7 hours or on high for 2½ to 3½ hours, or until the vegetables are just tender and lightly browned on the edges that touch the sides of the crock.

2. Just before serving time, in a small bowl, whisk together the yogurt, milk, cumin, and pepper. Set aside.

3. Using tongs, transfer the vegetables to plates. Sprinkle with the parsley. Drizzle with the sauce.

COOK'S TIP

Many people dry-roast whole spices to intensify their flavor. It is common in Indian cooking to also dry-roast ground spices, as in this recipe.

PER SERVING
Calories **76**
Total Fat **0.5 g**
  Saturated Fat **0.0 g**
  Trans Fat **0.0 g**
  Polyunsaturated Fat **0.0 g**
  Monounsaturated Fat **0.0 g**

Cholesterol **0 mg**
Sodium **60 mg**
Carbohydrates **17 g**
  Fiber **4 g**
  Sugars **7 g**
Protein **2 g**

Dietary Exchanges:
  1 starch, 1 vegetable

Braised Cauliflower with Crisp Garlic Crumbs

Showering cauliflower with crunchy garlic-infused crumbs makes it irresistible!

SERVES 8; ½ cup per serving

SLOW COOKER SIZE | SHAPE
3- to 4½-quart | round or oval

SLOW COOKING TIME
2 hours ON HIGH

1. In the slow cooker, cook the cauliflower and broth, covered, on high for 2 hours, or until the cauliflower is tender.
2. About 10 minutes before the cauliflower is ready, put the bread crumbs in a medium nonstick skillet. Drizzle with the oil. Using your fingers, combine until the crumbs are coated. Stir in the garlic, salt, and pepper. Cook over medium heat for 5 minutes, or until lightly browned, stirring frequently. Remove from the heat. Stir in the parsley. Set aside.
3. Using a slotted spoon, transfer the cauliflower to plates. Sprinkle with the crumb mixture.

1 medium head of cauliflower (about 1½ pounds), cut into 1½-inch florets

½ cup fat-free, low-sodium vegetable broth, such as on page 50, or fat-free, low-sodium chicken broth, such as on page 48

— + —

2 slices whole-wheat bread (lowest sodium available), processed to crumbs, or 1½ cups plain whole-wheat panko (Japanese-style bread crumbs)

1 tablespoon olive oil

2 medium garlic cloves, minced

¼ teaspoon salt

⅛ teaspoon pepper

2 tablespoons snipped fresh parsley

PER SERVING
Calories **42**
Total Fat **2.0 g**
  Saturated Fat **0.5 g**
  Trans Fat **0.0 g**
  Polyunsaturated Fat **0.0 g**
  Monounsaturated Fat **1.5 g**

Cholesterol **0 mg**
Sodium **120 mg**
Carbohydrates **5 g**
  Fiber **1 g**
  Sugars **1 g**
Protein **2 g**

Dietary Exchanges:
  1 vegetable, ½ fat

SERVES 6; ½ cup per
serving

SLOW COOKER SIZE | SHAPE
3- to 4½-quart | round
or oval

SLOW COOKING TIME
3 to 4 hours ON LOW, **OR**
1½ to 2 hours ON HIGH

12 ounces fat-free
evaporated milk

1 tablespoon all-purpose
flour

⅛ teaspoon cayenne

⅛ teaspoon smoked
paprika (sweet or hot)

⅛ teaspoon pepper

1/16 teaspoon salt

4 ounces dried whole-
wheat pasta (about
1 cup)

1 cup fat-free milk

4 ounces low-fat Cheddar
cheese, shredded

2 tablespoons shredded or
grated Parmesan cheese

2 tablespoons shredded
Asiago cheese

Cheese Lover's Mac-and-Cheese

This beloved classic is a breeze to make in the slow cooker—throw
a few ingredients into the cooker and let it create a creamy delight.
The undertones of two peppers and paprika perk up a trio of cheeses
to make this over-the-top side dish the one that you turn to over and
over again.

In the slow cooker, whisk together the evaporated milk, flour,
cayenne, paprika, pepper, and salt. (You can also shake together
these ingredients in a jar or container with a tight-fitting lid and
pour into the slow cooker.) Stir in the pasta and milk. Using the
back of a spoon, gently stir and press the macaroni into the milk
to coat. Sprinkle the cheeses over all. Cook, covered, on low for
3 to 4 hours or on high for 1½ to 2 hours, or until the pasta is
tender. You can stir once, halfway through the cooking time—for
both low and high settings—to distribute the moisture if desired
(but this step isn't absolutely necessary).

PER SERVING
Calories **183**
Total Fat **3.0 g**
  Saturated Fat **1.5 g**
  Trans Fat **0.0 g**
  Polyunsaturated Fat **0.0 g**
  Monounsaturated Fat **0.5 g**

Cholesterol **11 mg**
Sodium **210 mg**
Carbohydrates **25 g**
  Fiber **2 g**
  Sugars **9 g**
  Protein **15 g**

Dietary Exchanges:
  **1½ starch, 1 fat-free
  milk, 1 lean meat**

SLOW COOKER SIZE | SHAPE
3- to 4½-quart | round
or oval

SLOW COOKING TIME
7 to 8 hours ON LOW, **OR**
3½ to 4 hours ON HIGH

3 slices smoked turkey
    bacon
2 teaspoons canola or corn
    oil
1 medium onion, halved
    and thinly sliced
1 large garlic clove, minced
⅓ cup fat-free, low-sodium
    chicken broth, such as
    on page 48
1 pound collard greens,
    large stems discarded,
    chopped (about 10
    cups)
⅛ teaspoon crushed red
    pepper flakes

Collard Greens with Turkey Bacon

Smoky and earthy, long-simmered collard greens are a Southern staple. If you want to enjoy these greens in authentic Down South fashion, serve them with catfish and brown rice drizzled with some of the cooking liquid.

1. In a Dutch oven, cook the bacon over medium-high heat for 4 minutes, or until well browned, turning occasionally. Transfer the bacon to a plate.

2. Reduce the heat to medium. Pour in the oil, swirling to coat the bottom. Cook the onion for 3 minutes, or until almost soft, stirring frequently. Stir in the garlic. Cook for 1 minute, or until fragrant, stirring constantly. Pour in the broth. Cook for 2 minutes, or until boiling, scraping the bottom and side to dislodge any browned bits. Add the collard greens, in batches if necessary. Cook for 2 minutes, or just until wilted, stirring occasionally. (Stovetop cooking reduces the volume of the greens so they can actually fit in the slow cooker.) Transfer the mixture to the slow cooker.

3. Coarsely chop the bacon. Add the bacon and red pepper flakes to the collard greens mixture in the slow cooker.

4. Cook, covered, on low for 7 to 8 hours or on high for 3½ to 4 hours, or until the greens are very tender.

COOK'S TIP
To quickly remove the tough stems of collards, working with one leaf at a time, hold the stem end with one hand, pinch the stem with the other hand, and quickly pull down to strip away the leaf.

PER SERVING
Calories **82**
Total Fat **3.5 g**
    Saturated Fat **0.5 g**
    Trans Fat **0.0 g**
    Polyunsaturated Fat **1.0 g**
    Monounsaturated Fat **2.0 g**

Cholesterol **8 mg**
Sodium **216 mg**
Carbohydrates **9 g**
    Fiber **5 g**
    Sugars **3 g**
Protein **4 g**

Dietary Exchanges:
    2 vegetable, 1 fat

Sicilian Eggplant Caponata

You can enjoy this caponata in several ways: as a vegetable side dish, ladled over whole-grain pasta or polenta (see the Cook's Tip on page 262), as a vegetarian main dish for four, or spread lightly on thin pieces of toasted baguettes for bruschetta for 20. Add a sprinkling of Parmesan cheese when using the caponata as a main dish or bruschetta.

1. Lightly spray the slow cooker with cooking spray. Using half of each ingredient, make one layer each, in order, of the tomatoes, eggplant, onion, celery, and garlic in the slow cooker. Sprinkle with half each of the tapioca, sugar, and salt. Repeat. Don't stir.
2. In a small bowl, whisk together the tomato paste and vinegar. Pour into the slow cooker. Cook, covered, on low for 4 hours or on high for 2 hours. Quickly stir the vegetables and re-cover the slow cooker. Cook on low for 3 to 4 hours or on high for 1 to 2 hours, or until the vegetables are tender.
3. Stir in the olives and capers. Change the setting to warm or turn off the slow cooker. For maximum flavor, let the caponata cool for about 30 minutes, or until room temperature. Just before serving, sprinkle with the parsley.

COOK'S TIP
Refrigerate any leftovers in an airtight container for up to two days. Let them come to room temperature before serving.

FAST PREP!

SERVES 10; ½ cup per serving

SLOW COOKER SIZE | SHAPE
3- to 4½-quart | round or oval

SLOW COOKING TIME
4 hours ON LOW plus 3 to 4 hours ON LOW, **OR**
2 hours ON HIGH plus 1 to 2 hours ON HIGH

Cooking spray
1½ pounds Italian plum (Roma) tomatoes, seeded and chopped
1 1-pound unpeeled eggplant, cut into ½-inch cubes
1½ cups chopped Vidalia, Maui, Oso Sweet, or other sweet onion
2 medium ribs of celery, cut crosswise into ¼-inch slices
2 medium garlic cloves, minced
1 tablespoon uncooked instant, or quick-cooking, tapioca
2 teaspoons sugar
¼ teaspoon salt
¼ cup no-salt-added tomato paste
3 tablespoons red wine vinegar

———— + ————

5 medium pimiento-stuffed green olives, finely chopped
1 tablespoon capers, drained, halved if large
½ cup snipped fresh parsley or chopped fresh basil (optional)

PER SERVING
Calories **50**
Total Fat **0.5 g**
    Saturated Fat **0.0 g**
    Trans Fat **0.0 g**
    Polyunsaturated Fat **0.0 g**
    Monounsaturated Fat **0.0 g**
Cholesterol **0 mg**
Sodium **143 mg**
Carbohydrates **11 g**
    Fiber **3 g**
    Sugars **6 g**
Protein **2 g**
Dietary Exchanges:
    2 vegetable

SERVES 6; ½ cup per serving

SLOW COOKER SIZE | SHAPE
3- to 4½-quart | round or oval

SLOW COOKING TIME
4 hours ON LOW, **OR**
2 hours ON HIGH

Cooking spray

3 cups water

1 cup uncooked grits (not instant or quick-cooking)

½ teaspoon garlic powder

———— **+** ————

⅛ teaspoon salt

¼ cup shredded or grated Parmesan cheese or finely shredded part-skim mozzarella

2 tablespoons chopped fresh basil

1 medium fresh jalapeño, seeds and ribs discarded, finely chopped

1 small tomato, seeded and diced

1 tablespoon olive oil (extra virgin preferred)

Cheesy Basil Grits

A little southern, a little Mediterranean, and a little south of the border, these grits qualify as comfort food wherever they're served. Keep in mind that you'll need to stir the grits several times as they cook to creamy goodness.

1. Lightly spray the slow cooker with cooking spray.
2. In the slow cooker, stir together the water, grits, and garlic powder. Cook, covered, on low for 4 hours or on high for 2 hours, or until the grits are creamy and tender, stirring every hour on low or every 30 minutes on high. Be sure to quickly stir and re-cover each time.
3. Spoon the grits into a shallow serving dish. Sprinkle in the order listed with the remaining ingredients except the oil. Drizzle with the oil.

COOK'S TIP

Leftover Grits Ever wonder what to do with leftover grits? The answer is simple—make polenta for a great side dish! Cover and refrigerate the cooked grits for up to two days, then cut into wedges. To microwave one serving, place a wedge on a microwaveable plate. Microwave, covered, on 100 percent power (high) for 20 to 30 seconds, or until heated through.

PER SERVING
Calories **133**
Total Fat **3.5 g**
  Saturated Fat **1.0 g**
  Trans Fat **0.0 g**
  Polyunsaturated Fat **0.5 g**
  Monounsaturated Fat **2.0 g**

Cholesterol **2 mg**
Sodium **110 mg**
Carbohydrates **23 g**
  Fiber **2 g**
  Sugars **1 g**
Protein **4 g**

Dietary Exchanges:
  1½ **starch,** ½ **fat**

Lentil and Bell Pepper Salad with Lemon-Orange Dressing

Lentils are nutritious and inexpensive but become visually appealing only when surrounded by colorful ingredients, such as the baby spinach, yellow and orange bell peppers, cherry tomatoes, and blackish-purple olives that brighten this salad. Adding the tangy citrus dressing to the lentils while they are still warm assures maximum flavor absorption.

1. In the slow cooker, stir together the water and lentils. Cook, covered, on low for 2½ to 3½ hours or on high for 1 hour 15 minutes to 1 hour 45 minutes, or until the lentils are just tender but still hold their shape.
2. Meanwhile, in a small bowl, whisk together the orange juice concentrate, lemon zest, lemon juice, oil, mustard, garlic, salt, and pepper. Set the dressing aside.
3. When the lentils are ready, drain well in a colander. Transfer to a large bowl. Pour ⅓ cup dressing over the lentils, lightly tossing to coat. Let stand for 15 minutes so the flavors blend.
4. Add the spinach, bell peppers, tomatoes, and olives to the lentils, tossing gently to combine, and adding 1 to 2 tablespoons of the extra dressing if the salad seems too dry.

COOK'S TIP
Extra-Virgin Olive Oil More expensive than regular olive oil (but well worth the cost), extra-virgin olive oil is best to use in cold dishes so you can taste the deep richness and fruitiness of its flavor to the fullest.

FAST PREP!

SERVES 8; ½ cup per serving

SLOW COOKER SIZE | SHAPE
1½- to 2½-quart | round or oval

SLOW COOKING TIME
2½ to 3½ hours ON LOW, **OR**
1 hour 15 minutes to 1 hour 45 minutes ON HIGH

3 cups water
1 cup dried brown lentils (about 8 ounces), sorted for stones and shriveled lentils, rinsed, and drained

———— + ————

3 tablespoons frozen orange juice concentrate, thawed
1 teaspoon grated lemon zest
⅓ cup fresh lemon juice
1 teaspoon olive oil (extra virgin preferred)
½ teaspoon Dijon mustard
1 medium garlic clove, minced
⅛ teaspoon salt
⅛ teaspoon pepper
1 ounce baby spinach (about 1 cup), coarsely chopped
¾ cup diced yellow bell pepper
¾ cup diced orange bell pepper
⅔ cup cherry tomatoes, halved
¼ cup kalamata olives, halved

PER SERVING
Calories **132**
Total Fat **2.0 g**
  Saturated Fat **0.0 g**
  Trans Fat **0.0 g**
  Polyunsaturated Fat **0.5 g**
  Monounsaturated Fat **1.5 g**

Cholesterol **0 mg**
Sodium **126 mg**
Carbohydrates **23 g**
  Fiber **4 g**
  Sugars **6 g**
Protein **8 g**

Dietary Exchanges:
  1½ **starch**, ½ **lean meat**

SERVES 6; generous ½ cup per serving (plus 2 cups reserved for Sweet Potato Bread Pudding, page 312)

SLOW COOKER SIZE | SHAPE
3- to 4½-quart | round

SLOW COOKING TIME
6 to 8 hours ON LOW

3 pounds sweet potatoes, peeled, cut crosswise into ½-inch slices

¼ cup firmly packed light brown sugar

¾ teaspoon ground cinnamon

¼ teaspoon ground nutmeg

⅓ cup unsweetened apple juice

Simple Mashed Sweet Potatoes

This is one of the easiest ways to prepare mashed sweet potatoes—no potato masher required!

1. In the slow cooker, make a layer of half the sweet potatoes. Sprinkle with half each of the brown sugar, cinnamon, and nutmeg. Repeat. Pour the apple juice over all. Don't stir. Cook, covered, on low for 6 to 8 hours.
2. Just before serving, use the back of a large spoon to mash the sweet potatoes against the side of the crock until the desired consistency. Spoon 2 cups of the sweet potatoes into an airtight container and refrigerate them to use later for Sweet Potato Bread Pudding (page 312).

PER SERVING
Calories **100**
Total Fat **0.0 g**
  Saturated Fat **0.0 g**
  Trans Fat **0.0 g**
  Polyunsaturated Fat **0.0 g**
  Monounsaturated Fat **0.0 g**

Cholesterol **0 mg**
Sodium **51 mg**
Carbohydrates **24 g**
  Fiber **3 g**
  Sugars **9 g**
Protein **1 g**

Dietary Exchanges:
  1½ **starch**

Acorn Squash Wedges with Walnuts

Achieving an attractive browned finish to slow-cooked food usually isn't easy, but that isn't a problem here. The cut sides of acorn squash wedges lie on top of skillet-browned onions and brown as they slow cook; then the onions are incorporated into a brown-sugar-and-walnut sauce to top the squash. "Browning" never looked better!

1. Lightly spray the slow cooker with cooking spray. Set aside.
2. In a large nonstick skillet, heat 1 teaspoon oil over medium-high heat, swirling to coat the bottom. Cook the onion for 3 to 4 minutes, or until beginning to lightly brown, stirring frequently. Transfer to the slow cooker.
3. Stir in the water, walnuts, cinnamon, and nutmeg.
4. Arrange each squash wedge with a cut side down on top of the onion mixture, making sure that a cut side of each squash wedge touches the onion mixture. Cook, covered, on low for 4 hours or on high for 2 hours, or until the squash is tender when pierced with a fork.
5. Place the squash wedges on plates. Stir the remaining ingredients into the onion mixture. Spoon over the squash.

SERVES 4; 1 squash wedge and 2 tablespoons sauce per serving

SLOW COOKER SIZE | SHAPE
3- to 4-quart | round or oval

SLOW COOKING TIME
4 hours ON LOW, **OR**
2 hours ON HIGH

Cooking spray
1 teaspoon canola or corn oil
1 medium onion, diced
¼ cup water
2 tablespoons chopped walnuts
¾ teaspoon ground cinnamon
¼ teaspoon ground nutmeg
1 large acorn squash (about 1½ pounds), seeds and strings discarded, cut into 4 wedges

———— + ————

1 tablespoon plus 1 teaspoon firmly packed dark brown sugar
1 tablespoon light tub margarine
1 teaspoon vanilla extract
⅛ teaspoon salt
2 teaspoons canola or corn oil

PER SERVING
Calories **150**
Total Fat **7.0 g**
  Saturated Fat **0.0 g**
  Trans Fat **0.0 g**
  Polyunsaturated Fat **3.0 g**
  Monounsaturated Fat **3.0 g**

Cholesterol **0 mg**
Sodium **102 mg**
Carbohydrates **22 g**
  Fiber **3 g**
  Sugars **10 g**
Protein **2 g**

Dietary Exchanges:
  1½ starch, 1 fat

Acorn Squash Wedges
with Walnuts, page 265

SERVES 8; ½ cup per
serving

SLOW COOKER SIZE | SHAPE
1½- to 2½-quart | round
or oval

SLOW COOKING TIME

2½ to 3½ hours ON LOW, **OR**

1 hour 15 minutes to 1 hour
45 minutes ON HIGH

2 cups water

1 cup uncooked quinoa,
rinsed well under cold
running water and
drained

1 medium carrot, diced

2 tablespoons dark raisins
or sweetened dried
cranberries

1 tablespoon pure maple
syrup

¼ teaspoon maple extract

Maple-Glazed Quinoa

By using maple extract to supplement pure maple syrup, you get
more intense flavor without added calories.

In the slow cooker, stir together all the ingredients. Cook,
covered, on low for 2½ to 3½ hours or on high for 1 hour
15 minutes to 1 hour 45 minutes, or until the water is absorbed
and the quinoa is tender. Fluff with a fork before serving.

COOK'S TIP

Quinoa (KEEN-wah), an ancient grain native to the Andes, contains
complete protein, as well as contributing iron and calcium. Toss quinoa
with dry-roasted pine nuts and fresh herbs, chill it to combine with fruit
for a salad, or serve it as a breakfast cereal.

PER SERVING
Calories **97**
Total Fat **1.5 g**
  Saturated Fat **0.0 g**
  Trans Fat **0.0 g**
  Polyunsaturated Fat **0.5 g**
  Monounsaturated Fat **0.5 g**

Cholesterol **0 mg**
Sodium **10 mg**
Carbohydrates **18 g**
  Fiber **2 g**
  Sugars **5 g**
Protein **3 g**

Dietary Exchanges:
  1 starch

Pumpkin-Sage Risotto

Canned pumpkin adds a luscious reminder of fall to this risotto, which is made extra creamy with arborio rice and fat-free half-and-half.

1. In a small skillet, heat the oil over medium heat, swirling to coat the bottom. Cook the shallots for 2 minutes, or until beginning to soften, stirring constantly.
2. Stir in the garlic and chopped sage. Cook for 30 seconds, stirring constantly.
3. Stir in the rice. Cook for 2 minutes, stirring constantly. Transfer to the slow cooker.
4. Stir in the pumpkin. Pour in the broth, stirring until combined. Cook, covered, on low for 3½ to 4½ hours or on high for 1 hour 45 minutes to 2 hours 15 minutes, or until the rice is tender but with a slight bite and almost all the liquid is absorbed but is still creamy. Transfer to a large bowl.
5. Stir in the half-and-half, salt, and pepper. Serve the risotto garnished with the sage leaves or sprigs.

COOK'S TIP

Make sure you cook arborio rice in oil for at least 2 minutes so the hull will begin to soften and the rice will stay creamy as it slow cooks. To preserve that creaminess, serve risotto as soon as possible after it has finished cooking. However, if your slow cooker has a warm setting, you can use it to let the risotto stand for up to 30 minutes.

SERVES 8; ½ cup per serving

SLOW COOKER SIZE | SHAPE
1½- to 2½-quart | round or oval

SLOW COOKING TIME
3½ to 4½ hours ON LOW, **OR**
1 hour 45 minutes to 2 hours 15 minutes ON HIGH

1 teaspoon olive oil
⅓ cup minced shallots or onions
1 medium garlic clove, minced
2 tablespoons chopped fresh sage
1 cup uncooked arborio rice
1 cup canned solid-pack pumpkin (not pie filling)
3 cups fat-free, low-sodium chicken broth, such as on page 48

————— + —————

¼ cup fat-free half-and-half
¼ teaspoon salt
⅛ teaspoon pepper
Leaves or sprigs of fresh sage

PER SERVING
Calories **110**
Total Fat **0.5 g**
  Saturated Fat **0.0 g**
  Trans Fat **0.0 g**
  Polyunsaturated Fat **0.0 g**
  Monounsaturated Fat **0.5 g**

Cholesterol **0 mg**
Sodium **103 mg**
Carbohydrates **23 g**
  Fiber **2 g**
  Sugars **2 g**
Protein **4 g**

Dietary Exchanges:
  1½ **starch**

SERVES 12; ½ cup per serving

SLOW COOKER SIZE | SHAPE
3- to 4-quart | round or oval

SLOW COOKING TIME
5 to 6 hours ON LOW

2½ cups fat-free, low-sodium vegetable broth, such as on page 50, or fat-free, low-sodium chicken broth, such as on page 48

1½ cups chopped peeled butternut squash (about 8 ounces, already peeled and seeded)

1 cup uncooked wild rice, rinsed and drained

1 medium leek (white and light green parts), sliced crosswise (about 1 cup)

1 cup frozen whole-kernel corn, thawed

½ teaspoon dried summer savory, crumbled

¼ teaspoon salt

¼ teaspoon pepper

✦

¼ cup snipped fresh parsley

¼ cup chopped pecans, dry-roasted

Wild Rice with Harvest Vegetables

Butternut squash, corn, and parsley provide a nice contrast to dark wild rice in this side that is elegant enough for a holiday family gathering.

1. In the slow cooker, stir together the broth, squash, rice, leek, corn, summer savory, salt, and pepper. Cook, covered, on low for 5 to 6 hours, or until the liquid is absorbed and the rice is tender.

2. Just before serving, stir in the parsley and pecans.

COOK'S TIPS

Dry-Roasting Nuts on the Stovetop One way to dry-roast nuts is on the stovetop. Spread the nuts in a single layer in a skillet and dry-roast them over medium heat for 3 to 4 minutes, or until they're just fragrant, stirring frequently. Watch carefully so they don't burn. Remove them from the skillet immediately so they don't continue to cook. For how to dry-roast nuts in the oven, see the Cook's Tip on page 303.

Dried Savory Milder than winter savory, summer savory has a thymelike scent and a faint bitter, almost minty flavor. Summer savory can be used in side dishes, as in this recipe, as well as in meat dishes, bean dishes, stuffing, and soups. Both summer and winter savory are available in the spice aisle of grocery stores.

PER SERVING
Calories **97**
Total Fat **2.0 g**
  Saturated Fat **0.0 g**
  Trans Fat **0.0 g**
  Polyunsaturated Fat **0.5 g**
  Monounsaturated Fat **1.0 g**

Cholesterol **0 mg**
Sodium **64 mg**
Carbohydrates **18 g**
  Fiber **2 g**
  Sugars **2 g**
Protein **3 g**

Dietary Exchanges:
  1 starch

Vegetable and Mixed-Rice Pilaf

This pilaf is filled with fresh vegetables, so you get two side dishes in one! Just add a simple grilled or roasted main course, and your meal is complete.

1. In the slow cooker, stir together the mushrooms, asparagus, carrots, and onion. Add the oil, stirring to coat.
2. Stir in the brown rice and wild rice. Stir in the broth, water, garlic, basil, thyme, seasoning blend, and salt. Cook, covered, on low for 5 to 6 hours or on high for 3 to 3½ hours.
3. Just before serving, sprinkle the pilaf with the parsley. Drizzle with the lemon juice. Using a fork, stir to combine the ingredients and fluff the rice.

COOK'S TIP

Wild rice is a marsh grass, not actually a type of rice, but nevertheless is considered a grain. Clean wild rice by rinsing it well. When the rice is cooked, it should be slightly chewy and will have a nutty flavor.

PER SERVING
Calories **105**
Total Fat **1.0 g**
  Saturated Fat **0.0 g**
  Trans Fat **0.0 g**
  Polyunsaturated Fat **0.5 g**
  Monounsaturated Fat **0.5 g**

Cholesterol **0 mg**
Sodium **102 mg**
Carbohydrates **21 g**
  Fiber **3 g**
  Sugars **2 g**
Protein **4 g**

Dietary Exchanges:
1 starch, 1 vegetable

FAST PREP! ⏱

SERVES 8; scant ⅔ cup per serving

SLOW COOKER SIZE | SHAPE
3- to 4-quart | round or oval

SLOW COOKING TIME
5 to 6 hours ON LOW, **OR**
3 to 3½ hours ON HIGH

3 to 4 ounces button mushrooms, sliced (about 1 cup)

6 ounces asparagus spears, trimmed and cut into 2-inch pieces (about 1 cup)

2 medium carrots, sliced

½ medium onion, chopped

1 teaspoon olive oil

½ cup uncooked brown rice (not instant)

½ cup uncooked wild rice, rinsed and drained

1¾ cups fat-free, low-sodium vegetable broth, such as on page 50

1 cup water

2 medium garlic cloves, minced

1 teaspoon dried basil, crumbled

½ teaspoon dried thyme, crumbled

½ teaspoon salt-free all-purpose seasoning blend

¼ teaspoon salt

       +

1 tablespoon snipped fresh Italian (flat-leaf) parsley

2 teaspoons fresh lemon juice

Sauces and More

273   Chunky Tomato Sauce with Green Olives

274   Meaty Mushroom Pasta Sauce

275   Thick and Rich Root Beer Barbecue Sauce

276   Caramelized Onions ⏱

277   Caramelized Onion-Mushroom Gravy

278   Pickled Beets ⏱

279   Pear and Dried Cherry Chutney ⏱

280   Zesty Tomato-Apple Chutney ⏱

281   Wine-Spiked Cranberry Sauce ⏱

282   Strawberry and Dried Fig Spread

283   Eggplant and Basil Mediterranean Salsa

Chunky Tomato Sauce with Green Olives

You'll enjoy this sauce so much that you won't want to limit it to your favorite whole-grain pasta—try it over barley or quinoa for a change. Be sure to add the olives and basil just before serving for more pronounced flavors.

SERVES 4; ½ cup per serving

SLOW COOKER SIZE | SHAPE
1½ to 2½-quart | round or oval

SLOW COOKING TIME
6 hours ON LOW, **OR**
3 hours ON HIGH

1. Lightly spray the slow cooker with cooking spray. Set aside.
2. In a large nonstick skillet, heat 1 teaspoon oil over medium-high heat, swirling to coat the bottom. Cook the bell pepper and onion for 3 minutes, or until the onion is soft, stirring frequently. Stir in the garlic. Cook for 30 seconds, stirring constantly. Transfer to the slow cooker.
3. Stir in the Italian plum and grape tomatoes, sugar, and red pepper flakes. Cook, covered, on low for 6 hours or on high for 3 hours, or until the onion is very soft.
4. Just before serving, stir in the olives, basil, and remaining 1 tablespoon oil.

Cooking spray

1 teaspoon olive oil

1 medium green bell pepper, chopped

½ cup finely chopped onion

3 medium garlic cloves, minced

8 ounces Italian plum (Roma) tomatoes, halved lengthwise and cut crosswise into ¼-inch slices

8 ounces grape tomatoes

1 teaspoon sugar

⅛ teaspoon crushed red pepper flakes (optional)

+

8 small pimiento-stuffed green olives, finely chopped

2 to 3 tablespoons chopped fresh basil

1 tablespoon olive oil (extra virgin preferred)

COOK'S TIP

This sauce is the perfect amount for a small household, but it doubles well. Use a 3- to 3½-quart slow cooker and the same timing.

PER SERVING
Calories **92**
Total Fat **6.0 g**
  Saturated Fat **1.0 g**
  Trans Fat **0.0 g**
  Polyunsaturated Fat **0.5 g**
  Monounsaturated Fat **4.0 g**

Cholesterol **0 mg**
Sodium **176 mg**
Carbohydrates **10 g**
  Fiber **2 g**
  Sugars **6 g**
Protein **2 g**

Dietary Exchanges:
2 vegetable, 1 fat

SERVES 12; ⅔ cup per serving

SLOW COOKER SIZE | SHAPE
4- to 6-quart | round or oval

SLOW COOKING TIME
8 to 10 hours ON LOW, **OR**
4 to 6 hours ON HIGH

Cooking spray
2 teaspoons olive oil
1 pound ground skinless turkey breast
1 pound extra-lean ground beef
2 medium onions, chopped
4 medium garlic cloves, minced
8 ounces button mushrooms, thinly sliced
⅔ cup snipped fresh parsley
1 tablespoon dried Italian seasoning, crumbled
½ teaspoon pepper
¼ teaspoon salt
4 8-ounce cans no-salt-added tomato sauce
1 cup dry red wine (regular or nonalcoholic)

Meaty Mushroom Pasta Sauce

Once you smell the tantalizing aroma coming from the slow cooker, you're going to know that this sauce will taste great. Because the recipe makes about two quarts of sauce, you can either serve it to a group for a casual party or use some tonight on whole-grain pasta and freeze some for another meal, perhaps served over soft polenta.

1. Lightly spray the slow cooker and a large skillet with cooking spray. Set the slow cooker aside.
2. Heat the oil in the skillet over medium-high heat, swirling to coat the bottom. Cook the turkey for 3 minutes, or until it turns white, stirring occasionally.
3. Stir in the beef. Cook for 3 to 5 minutes, or until the turkey and beef are browned on the outside and no longer pink in the center, stirring occasionally to turn and break up the turkey and the beef.
4. Stir in the onions and garlic. Cook for 5 minutes, stirring occasionally. Transfer to the slow cooker.
5. Stir in the mushrooms, parsley, Italian seasoning, pepper, and salt. Stir in the tomato sauce and wine. Cook, covered, on low for 8 to 10 hours or on high for 4 to 6 hours.

COOK'S TIP
Use a wide spatula, such as a pancake turner, in each hand to make turning and separating the ground turkey and ground beef into small pieces faster and easier.

PER SERVING
Calories **161**
Total Fat **3.0 g**
  Saturated Fat **1.0 g**
  Trans Fat **0.0 g**
  Polyunsaturated Fat **0.5 g**
  Monounsaturated Fat **1.5 g**

Cholesterol **44 mg**
Sodium **109 mg**
Carbohydrates **10 g**
  Fiber **2 g**
  Sugars **6 g**
  Protein **19 g**

Dietary Exchanges:
  2 vegetable,
  2½ very lean meat

Thick and Rich Root Beer Barbecue Sauce

Root beer is a great "multitasking" ingredient in this sauce. It imparts sweetness and a deep, clovelike molasses flavor as well as adding a heady aroma during cooking. Use this version on grilled poultry and meats, just as you would an ordinary barbecue sauce.

1. Lightly spray the slow cooker with cooking spray. Set aside.
2. In a large nonstick skillet, heat the oil over medium-high heat, swirling to coat the bottom. Cook the onion for 3 minutes, or until soft, stirring frequently. Transfer to the slow cooker.
3. Pour 1½ cups root beer into the skillet. Bring to a boil, still over medium-high heat. Boil for 6 minutes, or until the root beer is reduced to ½ cup. Pour into the slow cooker.
4. Stir in the bell pepper, tomato paste, brown sugar, vinegar, Worcestershire sauce, cumin, and salt. Cook, covered, on low for 4½ to 5 hours or on high for 2 hours 15 minutes to 2½ hours, or until the sauce has thickened. For a thinner consistency, stir in the remaining ¼ cup root beer or water. Stir in the gingerroot.

SERVES 6; ¼ cup per serving

SLOW COOKER SIZE | SHAPE
1½ to 2½-quart | round or oval

SLOW COOKING TIME
4½ to 5 hours ON LOW, **OR**
2 hours 15 minutes to 2½ hours ON HIGH

Cooking spray
1 teaspoon canola or corn oil
1 large onion, finely chopped
1½ cups diet root beer
1 medium red bell pepper, diced
1 6-ounce can no-salt-added tomato paste
¼ cup firmly packed dark brown sugar
¼ cup cider vinegar
1 tablespoon Worcestershire sauce (lowest sodium available)
1 teaspoon ground cumin
¼ teaspoon salt

———— + ————

¼ cup diet root beer or water, if needed
1 tablespoon grated peeled gingerroot

PER SERVING
Calories **74**
Total Fat **1.0 g**
  Saturated Fat **0.0 g**
  Trans Fat **0.0 g**
  Polyunsaturated Fat **0.5 g**
  Monounsaturated Fat **0.5 g**

Cholesterol **0 mg**
Sodium **224 mg**
Carbohydrates **16 g**
  Fiber **1 g**
  Sugars **13 g**
Protein **1 g**

Dietary Exchanges:
  1 other carbohydrate

FAST PREP!

SERVES 5; ¼ cup per
 serving

SLOW COOKER SIZE | SHAPE
1½- to 2½-quart | round
 or oval

SLOW COOKING TIME
5 to 8 hours ON LOW, **OR**
2½ to 4 hours ON HIGH

8 ounces onions, halved
 lengthwise and cut
 crosswise into ⅜-inch
 slices
½ teaspoon olive oil
Pinch of sugar

Caramelized Onions

Slow cooking onions until they're deep brown and caramelized gives them a deep, rich, slightly sweet flavor that complements many entrées and side dishes. Spoon them over chicken breasts, pork chops, steak, or turkey burgers, or skip the sausage and top your pizza with them. They also are very good when stirred into cooked brown rice or whole-wheat couscous or tossed with cooked vegetables, such as green beans, broccoli, or potatoes. Keep in mind that you'll need to do a quick stir every hour or so as the onions cook.

In a large bowl, toss together the onions, oil, and sugar to coat. Transfer to the slow cooker. Cook, covered, on low for 5 to 8 hours or on high for 2½ to 4 hours, or until the onions are golden brown, quickly stirring and re-covering every 1 to 2 hours to brown evenly. Unless you're making the Caramelized Onion-Mushroom Gravy (page 277), transfer the onions to an airtight container and refrigerate for up to one week or freeze in an airtight freezer container for up to three months.

PER SERVING
Calories **22**
Total Fat **0.5 g**
 Saturated Fat **0.0 g**
 Trans Fat **0.0 g**
 Polyunsaturated Fat **0.0 g**
 Monounsaturated Fat **0.5 g**

Cholesterol **0 mg**
Sodium **2 mg**
Carbohydrates **4 g**
 Fiber **1 g**
 Sugars **2 g**
Protein **1 g**

Dietary Exchanges:
 1 vegetable

Caramelized Onion-Mushroom Gravy

We've added fat-free, low-sodium chicken broth, sliced button mushrooms, and seasonings to the Caramelized Onions on page 276 to make a perfect gravy with no last-minute fuss; spoon it over dishes that you'd usually top with chicken gravy.

SERVES 10; ¼ cup per serving

SLOW COOKER SIZE | SHAPE
1½- to 2½-quart | round or oval

SLOW COOKING TIME

3 to 4 hours ON LOW plus 5 to 10 minutes ON HIGH, **OR**

1½ to 2 hours ON HIGH plus 5 to 10 minutes ON HIGH*
*These times don't include making the Caramelized Onions.

1 recipe hot Caramelized Onions (page 276)

+

2 cups fat-free, low-sodium chicken broth, such as on page 48

4 ounces sliced button mushrooms

1 teaspoon dried sage

⅛ teaspoon salt

⅛ teaspoon pepper

+

2 tablespoons cornstarch

2 tablespoons water

1. Have the caramelized onions ready in the slow cooker. Stir the broth, mushrooms, sage, salt, and pepper into the hot onions. Cook, covered, on low for 3 to 4 hours or on high for 1½ to 2 hours, or until the gravy comes to a full boil.

2. If using the low setting, change it to high. Put the cornstarch in a small bowl. Pour in the water, whisking to dissolve. Quickly stir about ¾ of the cornstarch mixture into the gravy and re-cover the slow cooker. Cook for 5 minutes. For a thicker gravy, stir in the remaining cornstarch mixture, re-cover the slow cooker, and cook for 5 minutes more, or until the desired consistency.

COOK'S TIP

If you want to have plenty of onions for the gravy and other uses, double the recipe on page 276 and use a 2- to 3½-quart round or oval slow cooker. Cook for 3½ to 4½ hours on low or 1 hour 45 minutes to 2 hours 15 minutes on high.

PER SERVING
Calories **22**
Total Fat **0.5 g**
  Saturated Fat **0.0 g**
  Trans Fat **0.0 g**
  Polyunsaturated Fat **0.0 g**
  Monounsaturated Fat **0.0 g**

Cholesterol **0 mg**
Sodium **38 mg**
Carbohydrates **4 g**
  Fiber **1 g**
  Sugars **1 g**
Protein **1 g**

Dietary Exchanges:
  1 vegetable

FAST PREP! ⏱

SERVES 6; ⅓ cup per
  serving

SLOW COOKER SIZE | SHAPE
  1½- to 2½-quart | round
  or oval

SLOW COOKING TIME
6 to 7 hours ON LOW, **OR**
3 to 3½ hours ON HIGH

1 cup water

½ cup cider vinegar

3 tablespoons honey

¼ teaspoon salt

¼ teaspoon black
  peppercorns

3 medium beets (about
  1 pound total), trimmed,
  peeled, and cut into
  ⅛- to ³⁄₁₆-inch slices

1 medium Vidalia, Maui,
  Oso Sweet, or other
  sweet onion, halved and
  thinly sliced

1 cinnamon stick (about
  3 inches long)

1 medium dried bay leaf

Pickled Beets

Beets are anything but boring when they are pickled in a delightful combination of sweet and sour. Enjoy them hot or cold as a condiment to perk up entrées, and be sure to save some to use as a colorful addition to salads.

1. In a small bowl, stir together the water, vinegar, honey, salt, and peppercorns. Set aside.
2. In the slow cooker, make a layer of half the beets. Top with a layer of half the onion. Place the cinnamon stick and bay leaf on the onion. Repeat the layers of beets and onion.
3. Pour the vinegar mixture over the beet mixture. Don't stir. Cook, covered, on low for 6 to 7 hours or on high for 3 to 3½ hours, or until the beets are tender and the onion is soft.
4. Discard the cinnamon stick, bay leaf, and peppercorns. Serve the beets hot or transfer to a glass or other stainproof container and refrigerate, covered, for 6 to 8 hours to serve cold. The refrigerated beets will keep for up to one week.

COOK'S TIP

For recipes using onions that aren't browned on the stovetop before being slow cooked, you may prefer sweet onions, such as Vidalia, Maui, or Oso Sweet, to white or yellow onions if you want milder flavor.

PER SERVING
Calories **72**
Total Fat **0.0 g**
  Saturated Fat **0.0 g**
  Trans Fat **0.0 g**
  Polyunsaturated Fat **0.0 g**
  Monounsaturated Fat **0.0 g**

Cholesterol **0 mg**
Sodium **152 mg**
Carbohydrates **17 g**
  Fiber **2 g**
  Sugars **15 g**
Protein **1 g**

Dietary Exchanges:
  **2 vegetable, ½ other
  carbohydrate**

Pear and Dried Cherry Chutney

Take a break from salsas and sauces and serve a chutney instead. This tangy-sweet fruity creation is perfect served either hot or cold with grilled or roasted pork or poultry dishes.

FAST PREP!

SERVES 4; ¼ cup per serving

SLOW COOKER SIZE | SHAPE
3- to 4½-quart | round or oval

SLOW COOKING TIME
4 hours ON LOW, **OR**
2 hours ON HIGH

Cooking spray
1 medium Anjou or Bartlett pear, chopped
¼ cup unsweetened dried cherries
2 tablespoons finely chopped red onion
1 tablespoon water

— + —

1 tablespoon sugar
1 tablespoon red wine vinegar

1. Lightly spray a 2-cup heatproof glass measuring cup with cooking spray. Put the pear, cherries, onion, and water in the measuring cup (no stirring needed). Place in the slow cooker. Cook, covered, on low for 4 hours or on high for 2 hours, or until the onion is very soft.

2. Stir the sugar and vinegar into the pear mixture. Spread in a shallow pan, such as a pie pan, and let cool for about 20 minutes, or until thickened. Serve at room temperature or transfer to an airtight container and refrigerate for about 1 hour to serve chilled.

COOK'S TIP

You might wonder why you need a medium-size slow cooker to make only one cup of chutney. It's because the handle of the measuring cup takes up too much space to fit into a smaller crock.

PER SERVING
Calories **68**
Total Fat **0.0 g**
  Saturated Fat **0.0 g**
  Trans Fat **0.0 g**
  Polyunsaturated Fat **0.0 g**
  Monounsaturated Fat **0.0 g**
Cholesterol **0 mg**
Sodium **1 mg**
Carbohydrates **17 g**
  Fiber **2 g**
  Sugars **12 g**
Protein **1 g**
Dietary Exchanges:
  1 fruit

SERVES 16; ¼ cup per serving

SLOW COOKER SIZE | SHAPE
3- to 4-quart | round or oval

SLOW COOKING TIME
6 to 7 hours ON LOW, **OR**
3½ to 4 hours ON HIGH

Cooking spray

2½ cups Italian plum (Roma) tomatoes, seeded and finely chopped

2½ cups finely chopped semi-tart apples, such as Jonagold, Braeburn, or Gala

1 large red bell pepper, finely chopped

½ cup finely chopped Vidalia, Maui, Oso Sweet, or other sweet onion

¼ cup dried currants

1 medium fresh jalapeño, seeds and ribs discarded, minced

3 tablespoons cider vinegar

3 tablespoons honey

1 tablespoon plus 1 teaspoon uncooked instant, or quick-cooking, tapioca

2 teaspoons grated peeled gingerroot

¼ teaspoon salt

Zesty Tomato-Apple Chutney

Fruits and vegetables unite in this versatile chutney. Serve it as a relish to accompany curries or double the serving size (and the nutritionals) to serve eight as a side dish with roast poultry or pork tenderloin. For an appetizer for 32 guests, spread room-temperature chutney on whole-grain, low-sodium crostini and garnish with a nibble of low-fat sharp Cheddar cheese.

Lightly spray the slow cooker with cooking spray. Put all the ingredients in the slow cooker, stirring to combine. Cook, covered, on low for 6 to 7 hours or on high for 3½ to 4 hours, quickly stirring once halfway through. Serve the chutney hot or transfer it to an airtight container and let it cool to room temperature, about 30 minutes. Refrigerate any leftovers in the container for up to two days.

COOK'S TIP
If you have a microplane, use it to make quick work of grating fresh peeled gingerroot.

PER SERVING
Calories **43**
Total Fat **0.0 g**
  Saturated Fat **0.0 g**
  Trans Fat **0.0 g**
  Polyunsaturated Fat **0.0 g**
  Monounsaturated Fat **0.0 g**

Cholesterol **0 mg**
Sodium **39 mg**
Carbohydrates **11 g**
  Fiber **1 g**
  Sugars **8 g**
Protein **1 g**

Dietary Exchanges:
  ½ **other carbohydrate**

Wine-Spiked Cranberry Sauce

You'll think you're eating mulled wine transformed into a cranberry sauce when you experience this condiment alongside your holiday turkey or any other roasted meats.

In the slow cooker, stir together all the ingredients except the wine. Stir in the wine. Cook, covered, on low for 4 to 6 hours or on high for 2 to 3 hours, or until the cranberries have popped and are tender. To serve the day you make the sauce, pour it into a medium bowl, cover the bowl, and refrigerate for at least 2 to 3 hours. To serve later, pour it into an airtight container and refrigerate until needed. The sauce is at its best if you make it within three days of serving, but it will stay fresh for up to one week.

FAST PREP!

SERVES 10; ¼ cup per serving

SLOW COOKER SIZE | SHAPE
1½- to 2½-quart | round or oval

SLOW COOKING TIME
4 to 6 hours ON LOW, **OR**
2 to 3 hours ON HIGH

12 ounces fresh or frozen cranberries, thawed if frozen

⅓ cup sugar

1½ teaspoons ground cinnamon

¼ teaspoon ground nutmeg

¼ teaspoon ground cardamom

⅛ teaspoon ground cloves

Pinch of ground allspice

½ cup dry red wine (regular or nonalcoholic)

PER SERVING
Calories **54**
Total Fat **0.0 g**
  Saturated Fat **0.0 g**
  Trans Fat **0.0 g**
  Polyunsaturated Fat **0.0 g**
  Monounsaturated Fat **0.0 g**

Cholesterol **0 mg**
Sodium **1 mg**
Carbohydrates **12 g**
  Fiber **2 g**
  Sugars **8 g**
Protein **0 g**

Dietary Exchanges:
½ **fruit,** ½ **other carbohydrate**

SLOW COOKER SIZE | SHAPE
3- to 4½-quart | round or oval

SLOW COOKING TIME

4 hours ON LOW plus 20 minutes ON HIGH, **OR**

2 hours ON HIGH plus 20 minutes ON HIGH

Cooking spray

2 cups fresh or frozen unsweetened strawberries, hulled if fresh, thawed if frozen (about 8 ounces)

8 dried figs, chopped

3 tablespoons sugar

1 tablespoon water

½ teaspoon ground cinnamon

⅛ to ¼ teaspoon ground allspice

———————— **+** ————————

2 teaspoons cornstarch

1 tablespoon water

1 teaspoon vanilla extract

Strawberry and Dried Fig Spread

You already know that fruit spread is great on toast, so now go for the unexpected! Top a baked sweet potato for a refreshing side, spread some over fat-free cream cheese on low-fat whole-grain crackers for a snack, or spoon it over poached or baked fruit for a delicious dessert.

1. Lightly spray a 2-cup heatproof glass measuring cup with cooking spray. Put the strawberries, figs, sugar, 1 tablespoon water, the cinnamon, and allspice in the measuring cup (no stirring needed). Place in the slow cooker. Cook, covered, on low for 4 hours or on high for 2 hours, or until the figs are very soft.

2. Put the cornstarch in a small bowl. Add the remaining 1 tablespoon water and the vanilla, stirring to dissolve. Quickly stir into the strawberry mixture, breaking up any large pieces of fruit while stirring, and re-cover the slow cooker. If using the low setting, change it to high. Cook for 20 minutes, or until slightly thickened.

3. Carefully remove the measuring cup. Transfer the strawberry mixture to a shallow pan, such as a pie pan. Cover and refrigerate for at least 1 hour to cool completely. Refrigerate leftovers in an airtight container for up to one month.

PER SERVING
Calories **88**
Total Fat **0.5 g**
  Saturated Fat **0.0 g**
  Trans Fat **0.0 g**
  Polyunsaturated Fat **0.0 g**
  Monounsaturated Fat **0.0 g**

Cholesterol **0 mg**
Sodium **2 mg**
Carbohydrates **22 g**
  Fiber **3 g**
  Sugars **17 g**
Protein **1 g**

Dietary Exchanges:
  2 fruit

Eggplant and Basil Mediterranean Salsa

Call it a cooked salsa, a caponata, or simply an eggplant topping, but whatever you call it, be sure to make this when you want compliments. It's delicious served with whole-grain pita wedges or on thin slices of lightly toasted whole-grain baguette.

SERVES 6; ¼ cup per serving

SLOW COOKER SIZE | SHAPE
3- to 4½-quart | round or oval

SLOW COOKING TIME
4 hours ON LOW, **OR**
2 hours ON HIGH

Cooking spray
1 teaspoon canola or corn oil
¼ medium eggplant (about 4 ounces), unpeeled, diced (about 1 cup)
5 ounces grape tomatoes (about 1 cup)
1 medium banana pepper, chopped, or ½ medium yellow or red bell pepper, chopped
1 tablespoon water
½ teaspoon dried oregano, crumbled
½ teaspoon garlic powder
¼ teaspoon fennel seeds, crushed (optional)

———— + ————

2 tablespoons capers, drained, halved if large
1 tablespoon chopped fresh basil
1 teaspoon red wine vinegar

1. Lightly spray a heatproof 2-cup glass measuring cup with cooking spray. Set aside.
2. In a large nonstick skillet, heat the oil over medium-high heat, swirling to coat the bottom. Cook the eggplant for 3 minutes, or until beginning to lightly brown, stirring frequently. Remove the skillet from the heat.
3. Stir in the tomatoes, banana pepper, water, oregano, garlic powder, and fennel seeds. Transfer the mixture to the measuring cup. Place in the slow cooker. Cook, covered, on low for 4 hours or on high for 2 hours, or until the eggplant is soft.
4. Carefully remove the cup from the slow cooker. Spoon the eggplant mixture into a shallow pan, such as a pie pan, and let stand for about 30 minutes, or until room temperature. Gently fold in the capers, basil, and vinegar, keeping the vegetables intact. Serve at room temperature for peak flavors.

PER SERVING
Calories **21**
Total Fat **1.0 g**
 Saturated Fat **0.0 g**
 Trans Fat **0.0 g**
 Polyunsaturated Fat **0.5 g**
 Monounsaturated Fat **0.5 g**
Cholesterol **0 mg**
Sodium **89 mg**
Carbohydrates **3 g**
 Fiber **1 g**
 Sugars **1 g**
Protein **1 g**
Dietary Exchanges:
 Free

Breads and Breakfast Dishes

285   Spiced Banana Bread

286   Steamed Pumpkin Bread

288   Blueberry-Lemon Muffins ⏱

289   Apricot-Cinnamon Granola ⏱

291   PB&O Breakfast ⏱

292   Nutty Breakfast Grits with Pears ⏱

293   Cinnamon Quinoa with Peaches ⏱

294   Greek Frittata with Spinach, Goat Cheese, and Roasted Red Bell Peppers

296   Apple-Maple Oatmeal ⏱

297   Breakfast Hash Brown Casserole

Spiced Banana Bread

Yes, you can use your slow cooker as a mini oven to bake tasty quick breads! The trick is to place the loaf pan on a rack or several balls of aluminum foil to raise it off the bottom of the slow cooker so your bread will "bake" evenly.

1. Lightly spray an 8½ x 4½ x 2½-inch loaf pan with cooking spray. Set aside.
2. In a large bowl, stir together the flour, sugars, baking powder, nutmeg, baking soda, and salt.
3. In a medium bowl, whisk together the remaining ingredients except the pecans. Add to the flour mixture, stirring until the flour mixture is just moistened, but no flour is visible. Don't overmix; the batter should be slightly lumpy. Spoon into the loaf pan, gently smoothing the top. Sprinkle with the pecans.
4. Place a metal rack with short legs, such as a pressure cooker rack, or three or four 12 x 6-inch sheets of aluminum foil crumpled into balls in the slow cooker. Put the loaf pan on top. Cook, covered, on high for 2½ hours, or until a wooden toothpick inserted in the center comes out clean.
5. Let the bread stand for 5 minutes. Using a metal spatula, loosen it from the pan. Turn out onto a cooling rack and let cool completely, about 1 hour. For the best results, wrap the cake in plastic wrap and let the flavors blend overnight.

SERVES 16; 1 slice per serving

SLOW COOKER SIZE | SHAPE
5- to 6-quart | oval

SLOW COOKING TIME
2½ hours ON HIGH

Cooking spray
1¾ cups white whole-wheat flour
⅓ cup firmly packed dark brown sugar
⅓ cup granulated sugar
2 teaspoons baking powder
½ teaspoon ground nutmeg
¼ teaspoon baking soda
⅛ teaspoon salt
1 cup very ripe mashed bananas (about 2 medium)
4 large egg whites
⅓ cup low-fat buttermilk
¼ cup canola or corn oil
1 teaspoon vanilla, butter, and nut flavoring or vanilla extract
¼ cup finely chopped pecans, dry-roasted

PER SERVING
Calories **141**
Total Fat **5.0 g**
   Saturated Fat **0.5 g**
   Trans Fat **0.0 g**
   Polyunsaturated Fat **1.5 g**
   Monounsaturated Fat **3.0 g**
Cholesterol **0 mg**
Sodium **109 mg**
Carbohydrates **21 g**
   Fiber **2 g**
   Sugars **11 g**
Protein **3 g**
Dietary Exchanges:
   1½ other carbohydrate, 1 fat

SERVES 16; 1 slice per serving

SLOW COOKER SIZE | SHAPE
7-quart | oval

SLOW COOKING TIME
2 to 2½ hours ON HIGH

Cooking spray
6 cups water
½ cup all-purpose flour
½ cup whole-wheat flour
½ cup cornmeal
1 teaspoon baking soda
1 teaspoon ground cinnamon
½ teaspoon ground allspice
¼ teaspoon salt
⅓ cup unsweetened dried cranberries
⅓ cup chopped walnuts
¾ cup canned solid-pack pumpkin (not pie filling)
¾ cup low-fat buttermilk
2 large egg whites
¼ cup dark or light molasses

Steamed Pumpkin Bread

Pumpkin, dried cranberries, walnuts, and spices update a traditional steamed brown bread recipe. The result is moist and delicious.

1. Lightly spray a 9 x 5 x 3-inch ovenproof glass loaf pan with cooking spray. Place a metal rack with short legs, such as a pressure cooker rack, or three or four 12 x 6-inch sheets of aluminum foil crumpled into balls in the slow cooker.
2. In a large saucepan, bring the water to a boil over high heat.
3. Meanwhile, in a large bowl, stir together the flours, cornmeal, baking soda, cinnamon, allspice, and salt. Stir in the cranberries and walnuts. Make a well in the center.
4. In a medium bowl, whisk together the pumpkin, buttermilk, egg whites, and molasses. Pour into the well. Stir just until the flour mixture is moistened, but no flour is visible. Don't overmix. Pour into the loaf pan, gently smoothing the top. Cover tightly with aluminum foil. Secure with kitchen twine.
5. Place the pan on the rack or crumpled foil in the slow cooker. Pour the boiling water down the side of the crock until the water reaches midway up the side of the pan. Cook, covered, on high for 2 to 2½ hours, or until a wooden toothpick inserted in the center of the bread comes out clean. Carefully transfer the pan to a cooling rack. Discard the foil. Let the bread cool in the pan for 10 minutes. Turn out onto the cooling rack. Serve the bread warm.

PER SERVING
Calories **87**
Total Fat **2.0 g**
  Saturated Fat **0.5 g**
  Trans Fat **0.0 g**
  Polyunsaturated Fat **1.5 g**
  Monounsaturated Fat **0.5 g**
Cholesterol **1 mg**
Sodium **139 mg**
Carbohydrates **16 g**
  Fiber **2 g**
  Sugars **5 g**
Protein **3 g**
Dietary Exchanges:
  1 starch

SERVES 4; 1 muffin per
serving

SLOW COOKER SIZE | SHAPE
6-quart | oval

SLOW COOKING TIME
2 to 2½ hours ON HIGH

Cooking spray

½ cup white whole-wheat
flour

2 tablespoons sugar/sugar
substitute blend and
2 teaspoons sugar/sugar
substitute blend

½ teaspoon baking powder

⅛ teaspoon baking soda

⅛ teaspoon salt

⅓ cup low-fat plain yogurt

2 tablespoons canola or
corn oil

1 large egg white

½ teaspoon grated lemon
zest

¼ cup fresh or frozen
unsweetened blueberries
and 3 tablespoons fresh
or frozen unsweetened
blueberries, divided
use (no need to thaw if
frozen)

Blueberry-Lemon Muffins

Craving something sweet, but don't want to buy a sugary, store-bought baked good or heat up the kitchen? These muffins are a surprisingly delicious treat you can enjoy without the guilt.

1. Place six 12 x 6-inch sheets of aluminum foil crumpled into balls in the slow cooker.
2. Lightly spray 4 straight-sided 6-ounce ramekins or custard cups with cooking spray. Insert a paper bake cup into each ramekin. Lightly spray the bake cups with cooking spray.
3. In a medium bowl, stir together the flour, sugar blend, baking powder, baking soda, and salt. Make a well in the center.
4. In a small bowl, whisk together the remaining ingredients except the blueberries until well blended. Pour into the well. Stir until the flour mixture is just moistened but no flour is visible. Don't overmix; the batter should be lumpy.
5. Using a rubber scraper, carefully fold ¼ cup blueberries into the batter. Spoon into the bake cups to fill about three-quarters full. Sprinkle the remaining 3 tablespoons blueberries over the muffins.
6. To make sure they're level, carefully press the ramekins into the foil balls in the slow cooker. Place a clean kitchen towel over the top of the slow cooker. Put the lid on top of the towel (to prevent condensation from dripping onto the muffins). Cook, covered, on high for 2 to 2½ hours, or until a wooden toothpick inserted in the centers of the muffins comes out clean.
7. Remove the muffins (in the bake cups) from the ramekins. Transfer to a cooling rack and let cool. Serve warm or at room temperature.

COOK'S TIP
Because the slow cooker takes a while to heat up and the batter doesn't solidify right away, you need the ramekins to help the bake cups hold the batter in and produce a more attractively shaped muffin.

PER SERVING
Calories **179**
Total Fat **7.5 g**
  Saturated Fat **0.5 g**
  Trans Fat **0.0 g**
  Polyunsaturated Fat **2.0 g**
  Monounsaturated Fat **4.5 g**

Cholesterol **1 mg**
Sodium **191 mg**
Carbohydrates **21 g**
  Fiber **2 g**
  Sugars **12 g**
Protein **4 g**

Dietary Exchanges:
1½ starch, 1 fat

Apricot-Cinnamon Granola

Making granola in the slow cooker produces an evenly browned, crisp cereal. This version is filled with good-for-you oats, flax seed, wheat germ, bran, and nuts. Be sure to make this recipe when you're going to be at home so you can stir the granola every 30 minutes.

1. In the slow cooker, stir together the oats, bran cereal, flax seed, wheat germ, sunflower seeds, walnuts, cinnamon, and nutmeg. Set aside.
2. In a medium glass measuring cup, whisk together the honey and oil. Microwave on 100 percent power (high) for 40 seconds to 1 minute, or until the honey is melted. Stir in the vanilla and almond extracts. Pour over the oat mixture, stirring until moistened.
3. Cook, with the lid slightly ajar, on high for 1½ hours, stirring every 30 minutes. Change the slow cooker setting to low. Cook, with the lid slightly ajar, for 1 to 1½ hours, or until the mixture is golden brown, stirring every 30 minutes. Watch carefully during the last 30 minutes to avoid overbrowning.
4. Stir in the apricots. Spread the granola on a large rimmed baking sheet. Let stand for 2 hours, or until completely cool. Store in an airtight container at room temperature for up to one month.

COOK'S TIP
Cooking the granola on high at the beginning gets the browning started, and finishing on low with the lid partially open reduces the moisture.

FAST PREP!

SERVES 14; ½ cup per serving

SLOW COOKER SIZE | SHAPE
3- to 4½-quart | round or oval

SLOW COOKING TIME
1½ hours ON HIGH plus 1 to 1½ hours ON LOW

4 cups uncooked rolled oats (not instant)
1½ cups wheat bran cereal (not flakes)
½ cup ground flax seed
½ cup toasted wheat germ
½ cup raw shelled sunflower seeds
½ cup chopped walnuts
1 tablespoon ground cinnamon
½ teaspoon ground nutmeg
½ cup honey
3 tablespoons canola or corn oil
2 teaspoons vanilla extract
1 teaspoon almond extract

—————— ✦ ——————

½ cup dried apricots, chopped

PER SERVING
Calories **250**
Total Fat **11.5 g**
   Saturated Fat **1.0 g**
   Trans Fat **0.0 g**
   Polyunsaturated Fat **5.5 g**
   Monounsaturated Fat **4.0 g**

Cholesterol **0 mg**
Sodium **20 mg**
Carbohydrates **38 g**
   Fiber **7 g**
   Sugars **15 g**
Protein **7 g**

Dietary Exchanges:
   2 starch, ½ fruit, 2 fat

PB&O Breakfast

Having trouble getting the kids to eat a healthy breakfast? Serve peanut butter and banana oatmeal that has slow cooked overnight and watch them chow down!

1. Lightly spray the slow cooker with cooking spray. Put the water, milk, oats, brown sugar, 1 teaspoon cinnamon, and the vanilla in the slow cooker, stirring to combine. Cook, covered, on low for 7½ to 8 ½ hours.
2. At serving time, stir in the peanut butter until well blended. Spoon into bowls. Top with the banana slices. Sprinkle the cinnamon over all.

COOK'S TIPS

Cover and refrigerate leftover oatmeal for up to three days. To reheat a single serving, spoon 1 cup oatmeal into a small microwaveable bowl. Microwave, covered, on 100 percent power (high) for 1 to 2 minutes, or until heated through, stirring once halfway through, and adding 1 to 2 tablespoons fat-free milk as needed for the desired consistency. (The oatmeal will have thickened in the refrigerator.)

Steel-cut Oats Whenever a slow cooker recipe calls for steel-cut oats, also known as Irish oats or pinhead oats, it is important to use them, not rolled oats. Steel-cut oats can withstand the long cooking time without getting mushy.

FAST PREP!

SERVES 8; 1 cup oatmeal and ½ banana per serving

SLOW COOKER SIZE | SHAPE
4- or 5-quart | round

SLOW COOKING TIME
7½ to 8½ hours ON LOW

Cooking spray

6 cups water

2 cups fat-free milk

2 cups uncooked steel-cut oats

¼ cup firmly packed light brown sugar

1 teaspoon ground cinnamon

1 teaspoon vanilla extract

——————— + ———————

¾ cup low-sodium smooth peanut butter

4 large bananas, sliced crosswise

Ground cinnamon to taste

PER SERVING
Calories **420**
Total Fat **15.5 g**
 Saturated Fat **2.5 g**
 Trans Fat **0.0 g**
 Polyunsaturated Fat **4.5 g**
 Monounsaturated Fat **6.5 g**

Cholesterol **1 mg**
Sodium **39 mg**
Carbohydrates **60 g**
 Fiber **11 g**
 Sugars **23 g**
Protein **15 g**

Dietary Exchanges:
 2 starch, 1 fruit,
 1 other carbohydrate,
 1 lean meat, 1 fat

SERVES 6; ⅔ cup grits and ¼ cup topping per serving

SLOW COOKER SIZE | SHAPE
3- to 4½-quart | round or oval

SLOW COOKING TIME
3 hours ON LOW, **OR**
1½ hours ON HIGH

Cooking spray
1 quart water
1 cup uncooked grits (not instant or quick-cooking)
¼ teaspoon salt

———— ✦ ————

¼ cup sugar
2 tablespoons light tub margarine
1½ teaspoons vanilla extract
½ teaspoon almond extract
1 medium pear, diced
¼ cup slivered almonds, dry-roasted and coarsely chopped
2 tablespoons unsweetened dried cranberries, finely chopped

Nutty Breakfast Grits with Pears

Think out of the box the next time you want hot cereal for breakfast: serve sweet grits prepared in a not-so-traditional way. Fresh pear combined with almonds and dried cranberries makes a crunchy topping that contrasts nicely with the creamy grits. The grits don't have to cook very long, but they will need to be stirred several times so they cook evenly and don't have lumps.

1. Lightly spray the slow cooker with cooking spray. Pour in the water. Stir in the grits and salt. Cook, covered, on low for 3 hours or on high for 1½ hours, or until the grits are creamy and tender, quickly stirring every hour if using the low setting or every 30 minutes if using the high setting. Re-cover the slow cooker after each stirring.

2. Add the sugar, margarine, and vanilla and almond extracts, stirring until the margarine has melted. Spoon into bowls.

3. In a small bowl, stir together the pear, almonds, and cranberries. Spoon over the grits.

COOK'S TIP
If you have leftovers, refrigerate the grits and the topping in separate airtight containers for up to two days. For one serving, stir 3 to 4 tablespoons of fat-free milk into the grits. Reheat the grits in a small saucepan over medium heat for 3 to 4 minutes, or until heated through, stirring frequently. Top with the pear mixture.

PER SERVING
Calories **191**
Total Fat **4.0 g**
  Saturated Fat **0.0 g**
  Trans Fat **0.0 g**
  Polyunsaturated Fat **1.0 g**
  Monounsaturated Fat **2.5 g**

Cholesterol **0 mg**
Sodium **133 mg**
Carbohydrates **37 g**
  Fiber **3 g**
  Sugars **12 g**
Protein **3 g**

Dietary Exchanges:
  1½ **starch, 1 fruit,**
  ½ **fat**

Cinnamon Quinoa with Peaches

A bowl of hot quinoa topped with sweetened fat-free half-and-half and peaches makes a nutritious, protein-rich breakfast. The quinoa doesn't need tending to while it cooks, allowing you to get yourself and the kids ready for the day while the slow cooker does the work.

1. Lightly spray the slow cooker with cooking spray. Pour in the water. Stir in the quinoa and cinnamon. Cook, covered, on low for 2 hours or on high for 1 hour, or until the water is absorbed and the quinoa is tender.

2. Just before the quinoa is ready, in a small bowl, stir together the half-and-half, sugar, and vanilla until the sugar has dissolved.

3. Spoon the quinoa into bowls. Top with the peaches. Pour in the half-and half mixture. Sprinkle with the pecans.

FAST PREP!

SERVES 6; ½ cup quinoa, ¼ cup peaches, ¼ cup half-and-half, and 1 tablespoon almonds per serving

SLOW COOKER SIZE | SHAPE
3-quart | round

SLOW COOKING TIME
2 hours ON LOW, **OR**
1 hour ON HIGH

Cooking spray

2½ cups water

1 cup uncooked quinoa, rinsed well under cold running water and drained

½ teaspoon ground cinnamon

———— ✛ ————

1½ cups fat-free half-and-half

¼ cup sugar

1½ teaspoons vanilla extract

2 cups frozen unsweetened peach slices, thawed and sliced or diced

¼ cup plus 2 tablespoons chopped pecans, dry-roasted and coarsely chopped

PER SERVING
Calories **245**
Total Fat **7.0 g**
 Saturated Fat **0.5 g**
 Trans Fat **0.0 g**
 Polyunsaturated Fat **2.5 g**
 Monounsaturated Fat **3.5 g**

Cholesterol **0 mg**
Sodium **65 mg**
Carbohydrates **42 g**
 Fiber **4 g**
 Sugars **17 g**
Protein **10 g**

Dietary Exchanges:
 2 starch, 1 fruit, 1 lean meat, ½ fat

SERVES 6; 1 wedge per serving

SLOW COOKER SIZE | SHAPE
3- to 4½-quart | round (preferred) or oval

SLOW COOKING TIME
2½ to 3 hours ON LOW

Cooking spray
4 large eggs
4 large egg whites
⅓ cup low-fat milk
½ teaspoon dried oregano, crumbled
¼ teaspoon salt
¼ teaspoon pepper
10 ounces frozen chopped spinach, thawed, drained, and squeezed until very dry
½ cup bottled roasted red bell peppers, drained, patted dry, and chopped
3 ounces soft goat cheese, crumbled
2 small green onions, thinly sliced

Greek Frittata with Spinach, Goat Cheese, and Roasted Red Bell Peppers

Surprise! You can make brunch in a slow cooker. This veggie-packed frittata is infused with Mediterranean flavors. Invite your friends over, toss a fresh fruit salad, toast some whole-grain country bread, and you're ready for an almost effortless get-together.

1. Lightly spray the slow cooker with cooking spray.
2. In a large bowl, whisk together the eggs, egg whites, milk, oregano, salt, and pepper. Stir in the remaining ingredients. Pour into the slow cooker.
3. Cook, covered, on low for 2½ to 3 hours, or until set (the frittata doesn't jiggle when the slow cooker is gently shaken). Using a wide spatula, gently lift the frittata out of the slow cooker. Transfer to a cutting board. Let stand for 5 minutes before slicing.

COOK'S TIP
Don't be alarmed by the liquid in the slow cooker when the frittata is done—and don't drain it off. By letting it stand, you give the liquid time to absorb into the frittata, preserving its moisture and flavor.

PER SERVING
Calories **121**
Total Fat **6.5 g**
  Saturated Fat **3.0 g**
  Trans Fat **0.0 g**
  Polyunsaturated Fat **1.0 g**
  Monounsaturated Fat **2.0 g**

Cholesterol **131 mg**
Sodium **286 mg**
Carbohydrates **4 g**
  Fiber **2 g**
  Sugars **2 g**
Protein **11 g**

Dietary Exchanges:
  2 lean meat

SERVES 6; 1 cup per serving

SLOW COOKER SIZE | SHAPE
3- to 4½-quart | round
or oval

SLOW COOKING TIME
6 to 7 hours ON LOW

Cooking spray

4¾ cups water

1½ cups uncooked steel-cut
oats

1 large tart apple (about
8 ounces), such as
Granny Smith, peeled
and chopped (about
1⅓ cups)

¼ cup pure maple syrup

1 teaspoon ground
cinnamon

1 teaspoon vanilla extract

⅛ teaspoon salt

Apple-Maple Oatmeal

You can put these ingredients into your slow cooker in no time at all right before bed. Waking up to a hot, cinnamon-scented breakfast will definitely get your day off to a great start!

Lightly spray the slow cooker with cooking spray. Put all the ingredients in the slow cooker, stirring to combine. Cook, covered, on low for 6 to 7 hours, or until the oats are tender and the water is absorbed.

COOK'S TIP

If you have leftovers, reheat in a small saucepan over medium-low heat, stirring occasionally and adding a small amount of water if the mixture seems too thick.

PER SERVING
Calories **215**
Total Fat **3.0 g**
  Saturated Fat **0.0 g**
  Trans Fat **0.0 g**
  Polyunsaturated Fat **1.0 g**
  Monounsaturated Fat **1.0 g**

Cholesterol **0 mg**
Sodium **56 mg**
Carbohydrates **41 g**
  Fiber **9 g**
  Sugars **12 g**
  Protein **6 g**

Dietary Exchanges:
  2 starch, 1 fruit

Breakfast Hash Brown Casserole

Company coming for brunch? Rev up the slow cooker early, then relax with a cup of coffee and your morning paper until your guests arrive.

SERVES 6; 1 cup per serving

SLOW COOKER SIZE | SHAPE
3- to 4½-quart | round or oval

SLOW COOKING TIME
4½ to 5 hours ON LOW, **OR**
2 hours 15 minutes to 2½ hours ON HIGH

1. Lightly spray the slow cooker with cooking spray. Set aside.
2. In a medium nonstick skillet, heat 1 teaspoon oil over medium-high heat, swirling to coat the bottom. Cook the sausage for 1 to 2 minutes, or until browned, stirring frequently to break up the larger pieces. Set aside.
3. Put the hash browns, onion, and bell pepper in the slow cooker, stirring to combine and smoothing the top.
4. In a medium bowl, whisk together the egg substitute, milk, oregano, pepper, ⅛ teaspoon salt, the cayenne, and remaining 1 tablespoon plus 2 teaspoons oil. Pour over the hash brown mixture. Sprinkle the sausage on top.
5. Cook, covered, on low for 4½ to 5 hours or on high for 2 hours 15 minutes to 2½ hours, or until a knife inserted in the center of the casserole comes out clean. Turn off the slow cooker. Sprinkle the casserole with the remaining ⅛ teaspoon salt and the Cheddar. Let stand, uncovered, for 30 minutes for peak flavors and texture.

Cooking spray

1 teaspoon canola or corn oil and 1 tablespoon plus 2 teaspoons canola or corn oil, divided use

1 3.5-ounce sweet Italian turkey sausage, casing discarded

1 pound frozen fat-free diced hash browns (lowest sodium available), thawed

1 large onion, diced

1 large green or red bell pepper, diced

1 cup egg substitute

¼ cup fat-free milk

½ teaspoon dried oregano, crumbled

½ teaspoon pepper (coarsely ground preferred)

⅛ teaspoon salt

⅛ teaspoon cayenne (optional)

—— + ——

⅛ teaspoon salt

½ cup shredded low-fat sharp Cheddar cheese

COOK'S TIPS

Don't skip the standing time; it's very important. The casserole will be a bit dry and the seasonings won't be blended in when you test it for doneness, but the liquid from the other ingredients will soak into the potatoes and create the desired texture during the standing time.

To quickly thaw the hash browns, place them in a large colander and run them under cold water for about 20 seconds (it will take a little longer if your colander is small). Shake off the excess water.

PER SERVING
Calories **185**
Total Fat **7.0 g**
  Saturated Fat **1.0 g**
  Trans Fat **0.0 g**
  Polyunsaturated Fat **1.5 g**
  Monounsaturated Fat **4.0 g**

Cholesterol **16 mg**
Sodium **360 mg**
Carbohydrates **19 g**
  Fiber **2 g**
  Sugars **4 g**
Protein **11 g**

Dietary Exchanges:
  1 starch, 1 vegetable, 1 lean meat, ½ fat

Desserts

299   Decadent Chocolate Pudding Cake

300   Mini Mint-Chocolate Cheesecakes

302   Carrot Cake

303   Apple Jumble Crumble

305   Strawberry, Rhubarb, and Peach Crumble

306   Pears with Raspberry-Orange Sauce

307   Sweet Mango Sticky Rice

308   Sugar Plum Pears

309   Dried-Fruit Compote with Pomegranate Juice

311   Apples with Almond-Apricot Sauce

312   Sweet Potato Bread Pudding

313   Tapioca Pudding with Blueberries

314   Pumpkin-Pecan Crisp

Decadent Chocolate Pudding Cake

Indulge your sweet tooth and let your taste buds experience a little bit of paradise with every bite of this ooey, gooey chocolate creation. This recipe uses part whole-wheat flour, unsweetened dark cocoa powder, fat-free milk, and canola oil as substitutes for less-healthy ingredients.

1. Lightly spray the slow cooker with cooking spray. Set aside.
2. In a medium bowl, stir together the flours, sugar, 2 tablespoons cocoa powder, and the baking powder. Whisk in the milk, oil, and vanilla until smooth. Spoon the batter into the slow cooker, spreading to cover the bottom.
3. In a small bowl, stir together the brown sugar and remaining 3 tablespoons cocoa powder. Sprinkle over the batter.
4. Pour the boiling water over the batter. Don't stir. Cook, covered, on high for 2 hours, or until a wooden toothpick inserted in the center comes out almost clean. Let stand, uncovered, in the slow cooker for 30 minutes. Spoon into small bowls and top with the bananas, whipped topping, and pecans.

COOK'S TIP

Spoon any leftover pudding cake (without the toppings) into an airtight container. Refrigerate for up to one day. To reheat an individual portion, spoon ½ cup of the pudding cake into a small microwaveable dish. Microwave on 100 percent power (high) for 20 to 25 seconds, or until warm. Top with the banana, whipped topping, and pecans.

FAST PREP!

SERVES 8; ½ cup cake, ¼ banana, 2 tablespoons whipped topping, and 1 teaspoon pecans per serving

SLOW COOKER SIZE | SHAPE
3- to 4½-quart | round or oval

SLOW COOKING TIME
2 hours ON HIGH

Cooking spray
½ cup all-purpose flour
½ cup whole-wheat flour
⅓ cup sugar
2 tablespoons unsweetened dark cocoa powder and 3 tablespoons unsweetened dark cocoa powder, divided use
1½ teaspoons baking powder
½ cup fat-free milk
1 tablespoon canola or corn oil
1½ teaspoons vanilla extract
⅓ cup firmly packed light brown sugar
1½ cups boiling water

——————— + ———————

2 medium bananas, each cut crosswise into 8 slices
1 cup refrigerated fat-free aerosol whipped topping
3 tablespoons chopped pecan pieces, dry-roasted

PER SERVING
Calories **200**
Total Fat **4.5 g**
  Saturated Fat **0.5 g**
  Trans Fat **0.0 g**
  Polyunsaturated Fat **1.0 g**
  Monounsaturated Fat **2.5 g**

Cholesterol **0 mg**
Sodium **86 mg**
Carbohydrates **40 g**
  Fiber **3 g**
  Sugars **23 g**
Protein **4 g**

Dietary Exchanges:
1½ other carbohydrate, 1 fat

SERVES 4; 1 mini
cheesecake per serving

SLOW COOKER SIZE | SHAPE
6-quart | oval

SLOW COOKING TIME
1 hour to 1 hour 15 minutes
ON LOW

Cooking spray

2 tablespoons crushed
low-fat graham cracker
crumbs (about 2 small
rectangles)

1 teaspoon olive oil

2½ ounces fat-free cream
cheese, softened

1½ ounces light cream
cheese, softened

3 tablespoons
unsweetened Dutch-
process cocoa powder

2½ tablespoons sugar

1 large egg or ¼ cup egg
substitute

4 ounces fat-free sour
cream

½ teaspoon mint extract

4 sprigs of fresh mint

Mini Mint-Chocolate Cheesecakes

The batter cooks low and slow to create creamy, dreamy
cheesecakes with a hint of mint. Each bakes in its own ramekin so
you have perfect portion control for this irresistible delight.

1. Place a metal rack with short legs, such as a pressure cooker
   rack, or 4 layers of paper towels in the bottom of the slow
   cooker. If you don't have a rack, take a sheet of aluminum foil
   that's 3 feet in length and fold it in half lengthwise. Fold in half
   lengthwise again. Twist the foil to create a "rope." Coil the rope
   at the bottom of the slow cooker.

2. Pour 1 cup water into the slow cooker. Cook, covered, on low
   while preparing the cheesecake batter.

3. Lightly spray 4 custard cups (½-cup size) with cooking spray. In
   a small bowl, stir together the graham cracker crumbs and oil.
   Spoon 1½ teaspoons of the mixture into each of the custard cups.
   Using your fingertips, gently press the mixture to form a crust.

4. In a medium mixing bowl, using an electric mixer on medium-
   high speed, beat the cream cheeses, cocoa powder, and sugar for
   3 minutes, or until light and fluffy. Add the egg. Beat on medium
   speed until combined. Add the sour cream and mint extract. Beat
   for 30 seconds, or until combined.

5. Pour the batter into the custard cups, smoothing the tops with
   the back of a spoon. Place the cups in the slow cooker. If using
   the twisted foil to line the bottom, press the cups into the foil to
   make sure they are level. Place a clean kitchen towel over the top
   of the slow cooker. Put the lid on top of the towel. Cook, covered,
   on low for 1 hour to 1 hour 15 minutes, or until the centers of the
   cheesecakes are set (don't jiggle when the cups are gently shaken).

6. Transfer the cups to a cooling rack. Let cool for 30 minutes.
   Cover each cup with plastic wrap and refrigerate for at least
   2 hours. Garnish with the sprigs of mint.

PER SERVING
Calories **161**
Total Fat **5.5 g**
  Saturated Fat **2.0 g**
  Trans Fat **0.0 g**
  Polyunsaturated Fat **0.5 g**
  Monounsaturated Fat **2.0 g**

Cholesterol **62 mg**
Sodium **227 mg**
Carbohydrates **19 g**
  Fiber **1 g**
  Sugars **12 g**
Protein **8 g**

Dietary Exchanges:
  **1 other carbohydrate,
  1 lean meat, ½ fat**

SERVES 12; 1 slice per serving

SLOW COOKER SIZE | SHAPE
6-quart | oval

SLOW COOKER TIME
2½ to 3 hours ON HIGH

Cooking spray
¾ cup all-purpose flour
½ cup sugar
1 teaspoon pumpkin pie spice
¾ teaspoon baking soda
¼ teaspoon baking powder
⅛ teaspoon salt
¾ cup grated carrots
⅓ cup unsweetened applesauce
1 large egg
1 tablespoon fat-free milk
¼ cup chopped pecans, dry-roasted

Carrot Cake

It's the combination of grated carrots, applesauce, and the slow cooking process itself that produces the moist goodness of this loaf cake.

1. Lightly spray an 8½ x 4½ x 2½-inch loaf pan with cooking spray. Cut parchment paper or wax paper to fit the bottom of the pan. Place the paper in the pan. Lightly spray the paper with cooking spray. Set aside.
2. In a large bowl, stir together the flour, sugar, pumpkin pie spice, baking soda, baking powder, and salt. Stir the carrots into the flour mixture until coated.
3. In a small bowl, whisk together the applesauce, egg, and milk. Stir into the flour mixture just until the batter is moistened but no flour is visible. Don't overmix. Stir in the pecans. Pour the batter into the pan, gently smoothing the top. Transfer the pan to the slow cooker. Cook, covered, on high for 2½ to 3 hours, or until a wooden toothpick inserted in the center comes out clean.
4. Carefully transfer the pan to a cooling rack. Let stand for 10 minutes. Invert the cake onto a plate. Let stand for 30 minutes, or until cooled completely.

COOK'S TIP
Anytime a recipe calls for using a loaf pan or other baking dish in a slow cooker, be sure to check the fit before mixing your batter. Generally, oval slow cookers and loaf pans without protruding handles work best.

PER SERVING
Calories **89**
Total Fat **2.0 g**
 Saturated Fat **0.5 g**
 Trans Fat **0.0 g**
 Polyunsaturated Fat **0.5 g**
 Monounsaturated Fat **1.0 g**

Cholesterol **16 mg**
Sodium **123 mg**
Carbohydrates **16 g**
 Fiber **1 g**
 Sugars **10 g**
 Protein **2 g**

Dietary Exchanges:
 **1 other carbohydrate,
 ½ fat**

Apple Jumble Crumble

When you just want a bowl of warm, sweet, delicious goodness, this jumble crumble will satisfy that craving. The dessert comes together quickly and needs absolutely no attention while it slow cooks. Talk about easy!

1. Lightly spray the slow cooker with cooking spray. Put the apples with a cut side down in the slow cooker. Sprinkle with the lemon juice and flavoring.
2. In a medium bowl, stir together the brown sugar, oatmeal, flour, cinnamon, and nutmeg. Sprinkle over the apples.
3. Sprinkle the pecans and raisins over the brown sugar mixture. Drizzle with the margarine.
4. Cook, covered, on low for 3 hours 15 minutes to 3½ hours or on high for 1½ hours to 1 hour 45 minutes, or until the apples are tender. Turn off the slow cooker. Let stand, uncovered, for 15 minutes for peak texture and flavor.

COOK'S TIP

Dry-roasting nuts intensifies their flavor. Spread the nuts in a single layer in a baking pan or on a rimmed baking sheet. Roast at 350°F for 5 to 7 minutes, or until golden brown. Transfer the nuts to a plate so they don't burn. Let stand to cool. See the tip on page 270 if you would rather dry-roast nuts on the stovetop.

See the tip on page 270

FAST PREP!

SERVES 6; ½ cup per serving

SLOW COOKER SIZE | SHAPE
3-quart | round or oval

SLOW COOKING TIME
3 hours 15 minutes to 3½ hours ON LOW, **OR**
1½ hours to 1 hour 45 minutes ON HIGH

Cooking spray

3 medium apples, halved, then cut lengthwise into ½-inch slices

1 tablespoon fresh lemon juice

1 teaspoon vanilla, butter, and nut flavoring or vanilla extract

¼ cup firmly packed dark brown sugar

¼ cup uncooked quick-cooking oatmeal

¼ cup white whole-wheat flour

¾ teaspoon ground cinnamon

¼ teaspoon ground nutmeg

½ cup chopped pecans, dry-roasted

2 tablespoons dark raisins

3 tablespoons light tub margarine, melted

PER SERVING
Calories **209**
Total Fat **9.5 g**
　Saturated Fat **0.5 g**
　Trans Fat **0.0 g**
　Polyunsaturated Fat **2.5 g**
　Monounsaturated Fat **5.0 g**

Cholesterol **0 mg**
Sodium **49 mg**
Carbohydrates **31 g**
　Fiber **4 g**
　Sugars **21 g**
Protein **2 g**

Dietary Exchanges:
1 fruit, 1 other carbohydrate, 2 fat

Strawberry, Rhubarb, and Peach Crumble

With its sweet-tart filling and crunchy topping, this crumble is a wonderful introduction to rhubarb for those unfamiliar with this springtime treat.

FAST PREP! ⏱

SERVES 10; ½ cup per serving

SLOW COOKER SIZE | SHAPE
5- to 7-quart | round or oval

SLOW COOKING TIME
30 minutes ON HIGH plus 2 to 3 hours ON LOW

1. Lightly spray the slow cooker with cooking spray. Set aside.
2. In a very large bowl, gently but thoroughly stir together the peaches, rhubarb, strawberries, sugar, cornstarch, tapioca, and 1 tablespoon orange zest, separating any peach slices still frozen together. Transfer to the slow cooker. Cook, covered, on high for 30 minutes.
3. Meanwhile, put the remaining ingredients in a small bowl. Using a fork, stir together until crumbly. Set aside.
4. When the filling is cooked, quickly sprinkle with the topping. Re-cover the slow cooker, leaving the lid slightly ajar. Change the setting to low. Cook for 2 to 3 hours, or until the fruit is tender.

COOK'S TIPS

If you remove the peaches from the freezer and set them aside while you prep the rhubarb and strawberries, they will be partially thawed to just the right point.

You can dry-roast the walnuts and toast the coconut at the same time. Preheat the oven to 350°F. Spread the nuts and the coconut in a single layer in a shallow baking pan. Bake for 5 to 10 minutes, or until the nuts are fragrant and the coconut is golden brown, stirring several times. Transfer the mixture to a medium plate to stop the cooking. Let stand for about 10 minutes, or until cool.

Cooking spray

1 pound frozen unsweetened peach slices, set aside to partially thaw

1 pound fresh rhubarb, cut diagonally into ½-inch slices

1 quart fresh strawberries, hulled and halved, quartered if very large

⅓ cup sugar

2 tablespoons cornstarch

2 tablespoons uncooked instant, or quick-cooking, tapioca

1 tablespoon coarsely shredded or grated orange zest

— + —

½ cup uncooked quick-cooking oatmeal

¼ cup whole-wheat pastry flour or all-purpose flour

¼ cup chopped walnuts, dry-roasted

1 tablespoon plus 1 teaspoon firmly packed light brown sugar

3 tablespoons canola or corn oil

2 tablespoons unsweetened flaked coconut, toasted

1 tablespoon coarsely shredded orange zest

PER SERVING

Calories **187**	Cholesterol **0 mg**	Dietary Exchanges:
Total Fat **7.5 g**	Sodium **4 mg**	**1 fruit, 1 other**
Saturated Fat **1.0 g**	Carbohydrates **29 g**	**carbohydrate, 1½ fat**
Trans Fat **0.0 g**	Fiber **4 g**	
Polyunsaturated Fat **3.0 g**	Sugars **14 g**	
Monounsaturated Fat **3.0 g**	Protein **3 g**	

SERVES 4; 1 pear and
1½ tablespoons sauce
per serving

SLOW COOKER SIZE | SHAPE
3- to 4½-quart | round

SLOW COOKING TIME
5 to 6 hours ON LOW, **OR**
2½ to 3 hours ON HIGH

Cooking spray

4 medium, firm pears,
peeled, stems left on

¼ cup dry white wine
(regular or nonalcoholic)

2½ tablespoons sugar

———— **+** ————

½ cup raspberries

1 teaspoon vanilla extract

½ teaspoon grated orange
zest

Fresh mint leaves
(optional)

Pears with Raspberry-Orange Sauce

If you really want to impress, serve this dessert the next time you
have dinner guests—or make it for your family tonight as a special
surprise! Each person gets a whole cooked pear resting on ruby-red
sauce. Serve this dessert in clear wine goblets or dessert bowls for
dramatic effect.

1. Lightly spray the slow cooker with cooking spray. Put the pears
   with the stem end up in the slow cooker. Pour the wine over the
   pears. Sprinkle with the sugar. Cook, covered, on low for 5 to
   6 hours or on high for 2½ to 3 hours, or until just tender when
   pierced with a fork.

2. Using a slotted spoon, carefully transfer the pears with the stem
   end up to a large plate, leaving the liquid in the crock. Set the
   pears aside.

3. Gently stir the raspberries, vanilla, and orange zest into the
   cooking liquid. Let stand, uncovered, for 1 hour, or until the
   sauce is slightly thickened. Spoon the sauce into bowls. Place the
   pears on the sauce. Garnish with mint.

PER SERVING
Calories **155**
Total Fat **0.5 g**
  Saturated Fat **0.0 g**
  Trans Fat **0.0 g**
  Polyunsaturated Fat **0.0 g**
  Monounsaturated Fat **0.0 g**

Cholesterol **0 mg**
Sodium **3 mg**
Carbohydrates **38 g**
  Fiber **7 g**
  Sugars **26 g**
Protein **1 g**

Dietary Exchanges:
  2½ **fruit**

Sweet Mango Sticky Rice

This variation of a popular Thai dessert is made with short-grain sweet rice, also known as Thai sweet rice or glutinous rice, cooked in mango juice and lite coconut milk. Coconut extract adds extra flavor and sweetness without additional calories or saturated fat.

Put the rice in the slow cooker. Stir in the mango juice, 1 cup coconut milk, the sugar, and the coconut extract. Cook, covered, on low for 3 to 4 hours or on high for 1½ to 2 hours, or until the rice is tender and slightly creamy and the liquid is absorbed. Transfer to a large bowl. Slowly and gently stir in the remaining ⅔ cup coconut milk. Let stand for 1 hour, or until room temperature. Spoon into bowls, making a small mound for each serving. Serve topped with the mango slices.

COOK'S TIP

Look for Thai sweet rice in Asian markets and some supermarkets. If you prefer, you can substitute fragrant jasmine rice. It's a long-grain rice and will create a slightly different texture, but the results still will be excellent.

FAST PREP!

SERVES 8; ¼ cup plus 2 tablespoons rice and ¼ mango per serving

SLOW COOKER SIZE | SHAPE
1- to 1½-quart | round or oval

SLOW COOKING TIME
3 to 4 hours ON LOW, **OR**
1½ to 2 hours ON HIGH

1 cup uncooked sweet rice or jasmine rice

1⅓ cups 100% mango juice or pineapple juice

1 cup lite coconut milk

2 tablespoons sugar

½ teaspoon coconut extract

+

⅔ cup lite coconut milk

2 medium mangoes, sliced

PER SERVING
Calories **198**
Total Fat **3.0 g**
  Saturated Fat **2.0 g**
  Trans Fat **0.0 g**
  Polyunsaturated Fat **0.5 g**
  Monounsaturated Fat **0.5 g**

Cholesterol **0 mg**
Sodium **20 mg**
Carbohydrates **42 g**
  Fiber **2 g**
  Sugars **21 g**
Protein **2 g**

Dietary Exchanges:
  1½ **starch,** 1½ **fruit,** ½ **fat**

FAST PREP!

SERVES 8; ½ cup per serving

SLOW COOKER SIZE | SHAPE
3- to 4½-quart | round

SLOW COOKING TIME
3½ hours ON LOW plus 15 minutes ON HIGH, **OR**
1 hour 45 minutes ON HIGH plus 15 minutes ON HIGH

Cooking spray

3 medium, firm pears, cut lengthwise into ½-inch slices

¼ cup dry white wine (regular or nonalcoholic)

3 tablespoons sugar

2 tablespoons chopped crystallized ginger

———— + ————

3 small red plums or medium purple plums, cut lengthwise into ½-inch slices

2 teaspoons grated lemon zest

1 teaspoon vanilla extract

Sugar Plum Pears

Slow cooking firm pears for a while and later adding fresh plums lets the different fruits retain their distinct flavors and textures in this slightly syrupy dessert.

1. Lightly spray the slow cooker with cooking spray. Put the pears, wine, sugar, and ginger in the slow cooker, stirring to combine. Cook, covered, on low for 3½ hours or on high for 1 hour 45 minutes, or until the pears are just tender.

2. Quickly add the plums, lemon zest, and vanilla, gently stirring to coat, and re-cover the slow cooker. If using the low setting, change it to high. Cook, covered, for 15 minutes.

3. Transfer the pear mixture to a large pan, such as a 13 x 9 x 2-inch glass baking dish. Arrange the fruit in a single layer. Let cool completely, about 30 minutes. The plums will slightly cook and thicken the sauce as they cool.

PER SERVING
Calories **87**
Total Fat **0.0 g**
  Saturated Fat **0.0 g**
  Trans Fat **0.0 g**
  Polyunsaturated Fat **0.0 g**
  Monounsaturated Fat **0.0 g**

Cholesterol **0 mg**
Sodium **1 mg**
Carbohydrates **21 g**
  Fiber **3 g**
  Sugars **15 g**
Protein **1 g**

Dietary Exchanges:
1 fruit, ½ other carbohydrate

Dried-Fruit Compote with Pomegranate Juice

Sweet and fragrant, this compote will stand on its own as a dessert, or you can stretch the number of servings by spooning it over fat-free vanilla ice cream. The compote is also excellent as an accompaniment to roast pork or chicken. You can even top it with dollops of fat-free plain yogurt to break the breakfast routine.

1. In the slow cooker, stir together the juice, apricots, plums, raisins, brown sugar, and cinnamon stick.
2. Put the allspice and cloves in a tea ball or in the center of a 4-inch square piece of cheesecloth. If using the cheesecloth, bring the ends together to make a bag. Tie it securely with kitchen twine. Add to the slow cooker. Cook, covered, on low for 5 hours or on high for 3 hours, or until the fruit is soft and plump. Discard the bag of spices and the cinnamon stick.
3. Stir in the orange zest. Serve the compote warm, let it cool for about 1 hour to serve at room temperature, or cover and refrigerate it for 3 to 4 hours to serve chilled.

COOK'S TIP

If you prefer, substitute ¼ teaspoon ground cinnamon, ⅛ teaspoon ground allspice, and a pinch of ground cloves for the cinnamon stick, whole allspice, and whole cloves (no tea ball or cheesecloth bag needed).

FAST PREP!

SERVES 10; ½ cup per serving

SLOW COOKER SIZE | SHAPE
3- to 4½-quart | round or oval

SLOW COOKING TIME
5 hours ON LOW, **OR**
3 hours ON HIGH

3 cups 100% pomegranate juice

2 cups dried apricot halves (about 11 ounces)

1½ cups dried plums (about 8 ounces)

1 cup golden raisins (about 4¾ ounces)

⅓ cup firmly packed light brown sugar

1 cinnamon stick (about 3 inches long)

½ teaspoon whole allspice

¼ teaspoon whole cloves

——————— + ———————

1 teaspoon grated orange zest

PER SERVING
Calories **224**
Total Fat **0.0 g**
  Saturated Fat **0.0 g**
  Trans Fat **0.0 g**
  Polyunsaturated Fat **0.0 g**
  Monounsaturated Fat **0.0 g**
Cholesterol **0 mg**
Sodium **18 mg**
Carbohydrates **58 g**
  Fiber **4 g**
  Sugars **47 g**
Protein **2 g**
Dietary Exchanges:
  4 fruit

Apples with Almond-Apricot Sauce

Baked apples are always a treat, but coring whole apples can be a hassle. Just buy larger apples and cut them in half! Then all you have to do is scoop out the easily accessible core, add the sweet toppings, and let your slow cooker take it from there.

1. Lightly spray the slow cooker with cooking spray. Pour in the water. Add the apple halves with the cut side up.
2. In a small bowl, stir together the remaining ingredients except the margarine. Spoon onto each apple half. Top each with 1 teaspoon margarine. Cook, covered, on low for 2 to 2½ hours or on high for 1 hour to 1 hour 15 minutes, or until just tender. Be careful not to overcook; the apples will continue to cook while cooling.
3. Carefully transfer the apples to plates, leaving the sauce in the slow cooker. Stir the sauce. Spoon over the apples. Let cool completely, about 30 minutes. The sauce will thicken slightly while cooling.

COOK'S TIP

If you let the apples overcook, they will become mushy.

FAST PREP!

SERVES 4; ½ apple and 1 tablespoon sauce per serving

SLOW COOKER SIZE | SHAPE
4- to 6-quart | round or oval

SLOW COOKING TIME
2 to 2½ hours ON LOW, **OR**
1 hour to 1 hour 15 minutes ON HIGH

Cooking spray

2 tablespoons water

2 large apples (about 8 ounces each), halved and cored

¼ cup chopped almonds

2 tablespoons chopped dried apricots

2 tablespoons firmly packed dark brown sugar

¼ teaspoon ground ginger or ground allspice

½ teaspoon ground cinnamon

½ teaspoon vanilla extract

1 tablespoon plus 1 teaspoon light tub margarine

PER SERVING
Calories **149**
Total Fat **5.0 g**
  Saturated Fat **0.5 g**
  Trans Fat **0.0 g**
  Polyunsaturated Fat **1.0 g**
  Monounsaturated Fat **3.0 g**

Cholesterol **0 mg**
Sodium **34 mg**
Carbohydrates **27 g**
  Fiber **4 g**
  Sugars **21 g**
Protein **2 g**

Dietary Exchanges:
1 fruit, 1 other carbohydrate, 1 fat

SERVES 16; one ½-inch slice per serving

SLOW COOKER SIZE | SHAPE
6- to 7-quart | oval (removable crock needed)

SLOW COOKING TIME
3 to 4 hours ON HIGH

Cooking spray

2 cups cooked and mashed sweetened sweet potatoes with spices, such as from Simple Mashed Sweet Potatoes (page 264)

1½ cups unsweetened vanilla almond milk

3 large egg whites

¼ cup dark raisins

2 tablespoons lightly packed light or dark brown sugar

½ teaspoon ground cinnamon

⅛ teaspoon ground nutmeg

1 whole-wheat baguette (lowest sodium available), crust removed, cut into ¾-inch cubes to measure 6 cups, dried overnight (reserve any extra for another use)

5 to 6 cups boiling water

Sweet Potato Bread Pudding

Using sweet potatoes ups the nutritional benefit of ever-popular bread pudding.

1. Lightly spray a 9 x 5 x 3-inch ovenproof glass loaf pan with cooking spray. Place a metal rack with short legs, such as a pressure cooker rack, or four 12 x 6-inch sheets of aluminum foil crumpled into balls in the slow cooker. Set aside.

2. In a large bowl, whisk together the sweet potatoes, milk, egg whites, raisins, brown sugar, cinnamon, and nutmeg. Add the bread cubes, folding until well coated. Spoon the mixture into the loaf pan. Cover tightly with aluminum foil, using kitchen twine to keep it secure. Place the loaf pan on the rack or crumpled foil in the slow cooker. The pan needs to be level and about ½ inch above the water. Pour the boiling water down the side of the crock until the water reaches midway up the side of the loaf pan.

3. Cook, covered, on high for 3 to 4 hours, or until the internal temperature registers at least 190°F on an instant-read thermometer and a knife inserted in the middle of the pudding comes out clean.

4. Carefully transfer the removable crock to a cooling rack. Let the bread pudding stand, still in the hot water, for at least 15 minutes.

5. Carefully remove the loaf pan from the crock. Cut the pudding into slices and transfer to plates. Serve warm.

PER SERVING
Calories **77**
Total Fat **1.0 g**
  Saturated Fat **0.0 g**
  Trans Fat **0.0 g**
  Polyunsaturated Fat **0.0 g**
  Monounsaturated Fat **0.0 g**

Cholesterol **0 mg**
Sodium **92 mg**
Carbohydrates **15 g**
  Fiber **1 g**
  Sugars **7 g**
Protein **3 g**

Dietary Exchanges:
  1 starch

Tapioca Pudding with Blueberries

Cooking homemade pudding on the stovetop can be tricky and tedious because the milk scorches easily and constant stirring is required. Fortunately, switching to a slow cooker solves both problems—and you don't need to feel guilty about enjoying this dessert, because it supplies a full serving of fruit for each diner.

FAST PREP!

SERVES 8; ½ cup tapioca, ½ cup blueberries, and 2 tablespoons whipped topping per serving

SLOW COOKER SIZE | SHAPE
2½- to 3-quart | round

SLOW COOKING TIME
1 hour to 1 hour 15 minutes ON HIGH plus 1 hour to 1 hour 15 minutes ON HIGH

2 cups fat-free milk

2 cups fat-free half-and-half

½ cup egg substitute

⅓ cup sugar

¼ cup plus 2 tablespoons uncooked instant, or quick-cooking, tapioca

2 teaspoons grated orange zest

2 teaspoons vanilla extract

¾ teaspoon ground cinnamon

— + —

4 cups blueberries

1 cup refrigerated fat-free aerosol whipped topping

1. In the slow cooker, whisk together the milk, half-and-half, egg substitute, sugar, tapioca, orange zest, vanilla, and cinnamon. Cook, covered, on high for 1 hour to 1 hour 15 minutes. Quickly stir the pudding and re-cover the slow cooker. Cook for 1 hour to 1 hour 15 minutes, or until the pudding is slightly thickened.

2. Carefully transfer the removable crock from the slow cooker to a cooling rack. Let stand, uncovered, for 20 to 30 minutes to cool. (If the slow cooker doesn't have a removable crock, spoon the tapioca into a large bowl for cooling.)

3. Spoon half the blueberries into 8 ramekins, custard cups, or wineglasses. Spoon the tapioca over the blueberries. Sprinkle with the remaining blueberries. If serving warm, top each serving with a dollop of whipped topping just before serving. To serve chilled, cover and refrigerate the tapioca for at least 2 hours. Just before serving, top with the whipped topping.

PER SERVING
Calories **178**
Total Fat **0.5 g**
  Saturated Fat **0.0 g**
  Trans Fat **0.0 g**
  Polyunsaturated Fat **0.0 g**
  Monounsaturated Fat **0.0 g**

Cholesterol **1 mg**
Sodium **118 mg**
Carbohydrates **38 g**
  Fiber **2 g**
  Sugars **25 g**
Protein **8 g**

Dietary Exchanges:
  1 fruit, 1 fat-free milk, ½ other carbohydrate

SERVES 8; ½ cup pumpkin mixture and 1 tablespoon topping

SLOW COOKER SIZE | SHAPE
3- to 4½-quart | round or oval (removable crock needed)

SLOW COOKING TIME
2½ to 3 hours ON LOW

Cooking spray

1 15-ounce can solid-pack pumpkin (not pie filling)

1½ cups low-fat milk

2 large eggs

2 large egg whites

¼ cup sugar/sugar substitute blend

2 tablespoons all-purpose flour

1¼ teaspoons pumpkin pie spice

1 teaspoon vanilla extract

⅛ teaspoon salt

TOPPING

¼ cup uncooked rolled oats

¼ cup chopped pecans

1 teaspoon canola or corn oil

1 tablespoon plus 1 teaspoon sugar/sugar substitute blend

½ teaspoon ground cinnamon

Pumpkin-Pecan Crisp

This dessert tastes like you're eating pumpkin pie without the crust. It has an addictively delicious, crunchy oat-and-nut topping instead. It's perfect for any fall or winter get-together when you want an autumnal dessert that doesn't take up oven space.

1. Lightly spray the slow cooker with cooking spray.

2. In a large bowl, whisk together the pumpkin, milk, eggs, egg whites, ¼ cup sugar blend, flour, pumpkin pie spice, vanilla, and salt. Pour into the slow cooker. Cook, covered, on low for 2½ to 3 hours, or until the center is set (the custard doesn't jiggle when the slow cooker is gently shaken). Remove the crock from the slow cooker as soon as the custard is done to prevent overcooking.

3. To make the topping, about 15 minutes before the custard is finished cooking, lightly spray a 12 x 12-inch sheet of aluminum foil with cooking spray. Place on a flat, heatproof surface.

4. Put the oats, pecans, and oil in a small bowl. Using your fingers, combine the oats and pecans with the oil until evenly coated.

5. In a small dish, stir together the remaining 1 tablespoon plus 1 teaspoon sugar blend and the cinnamon. Set aside.

6. In a medium nonstick skillet, cook the oat mixture over medium heat for 4 minutes, or until toasted and fragrant, stirring frequently. Reduce the heat to low. Stir in the sugar blend mixture. Cook for about 1 minute, or until the sugar blend mixture melts and coats the oat mixture, watching carefully so it doesn't burn, stirring constantly. Immediately transfer the topping onto the aluminum foil and spread it to cool.

7. To serve, spoon the pumpkin custard into bowls. Sprinkle with the topping. Serve the custard warm or at room temperature. It will take about 45 minutes to cool to room temperature.

PER SERVING
Calories **147**
Total Fat **5.0 g**
  Saturated Fat **1.0 g**
  Trans Fat **0.0 g**
  Polyunsaturated Fat **1.0 g**
  Monounsaturated Fat **2.5 g**

Cholesterol **49 mg**
Sodium **90 mg**
Carbohydrates **18 g**
  Fiber **3 g**
  Sugars **12 g**
Protein **6 g**

Dietary Exchanges:
  1 other carbohydrate, 1 fat

Index

A

apples
  Apple Jumble Crumble, 303
  Apple-Maple Oatmeal, 296
  Apples with Almond-Apricot Sauce, *310*, 311
  Autumn Apple-Pear Sauce, 247
Apricot-Cinnamon Granola, 289
artichokes
  Artichoke-Lemon Chicken, 131
  Artichoke-Spinach "Mini Wraps," 36
  Flank Steak with Artichoke Ratatouille, 175
  Italian Artichoke-Stuffed Bell Peppers, 219
  Lemon-Garlic Artichokes with Lemon Dipping Sauce, 246
Arugula and Nutty Brown Rice Toss, 213
Asparagus-and-Sole Rolls, 97

B

bananas
  PB&O Breakfast, *290*, 291
  Spiced Banana Bread, 285
barley
  Barley Casserole, 248
  Barley Risotto with Mushrooms and Spinach, 208
  Beef Barley Soup with Vegetables, 85
  Double-Mushroom and Barley Soup, 55
  Mexican-Style Barley and Black Beans, 206
beans
  Bean and Roasted Vegetable Stew, 230
  Bean Florentine Soup, 74
  Beans and Greens Enchiladas, 216, *217*
  Black and Red Bean Chili with Peppery Sour Cream, *222*, 223
  Black Bean and Jalapeño Soup, 81
  Chicken and Bean Soup with Lemon and Basil, 65
  Chicken and Fresh Fennel Cassoulet, 121
  Chicken with Black Beans and Sweet Potatoes, 140
  Chickpea, Cucumber, and Tomato Salad with Feta, 239
  Chickpea and Vegetable Stew, 236–37
  Chipotle Baked Beans, 249
  Chunky Chili con Carne, 176
  Country Cassoulet, 183
  Cranberry Bean and Sweet Potato Chili, 232
  Crunchy Barbecue-Flavored Chickpeas, 37
  Cuban-Style Black Beans and Rice, 226
  Curried Garlic-Bean Spread, 27
  East Indian Spiced Beans with Apricot Rice, 224
  Five-Way Cincinnati-Style Chili, 178
  Jamaican Bean and Vegetable Soup, 72, *73*
  Mexican Stuffed Squash, 225
  Mexican-Style Barley and Black Beans, 206
  Nutty Brown Rice and Arugula Toss, 213
  Pork-and-Beans Chili, 196
  Red-Bean Spaghetti, 227
  Smoky Red Bell Pepper Hummus, 28–29
  Spicy Vegetable Curry, 238
  Turkey Cassoulet with Gremolata, 155
  Tuscan Pork and Beans, 188
  White Chicken Chili, 135
beef
  Asian Lettuce Wraps, 174
  Balsamic Beef Borscht, 87
  Beef and Bell Pepper Gyros with Tzatziki Sauce, *162*, 163
  Beef and Brew Stew, 177
  Beef Barley Soup with Vegetables, 85
  Beef Goulash with Lemon, 182
  Beef Stew with Fresh Mango, 179, *180–81*
  Beef Vindaloo, 170, *171*
  Brisket with Exotic-Mushroom and Onion Gravy, 164–65
  Cabernet-Simmered Beef Roast with Rosemary, 166–67
  Chunky Chili con Carne, 176
  Coffee Kettle Pot Roast, 169
  Country Cassoulet, 183
  Countryside Beef and Garden Vegetable Soup, 86
  Dark-Roasted Beef Broth, 49
  Five-Way Cincinnati-Style Chili, 178
  Flank Steak Fajitas, 173
  Flank Steak with Artichoke Ratatouille, 175
  Hot Stuffed Peppers, 158
  Indonesian Beef with Couscous, 168
  Korean Beef Soup, 88
  Meaty Mushroom Pasta Sauce, 274
  Molasses-Glazed Beef and Veggie Meat Loaf, 184
  Open-Face Empanadas, 35
  Picadillo Beef, 185
  Sauerbraten, 172
  Sherried Steak-and-Mushroom Soup, 89
  Swiss Steak with Melting Tomatoes and Onions, 161
beets
  Balsamic-Glazed Beets with Toasted Walnuts, 250
  Pickled Beets, 278
beverages
  Chai Tea, 43
  Hot Pomegranate-Cherry Cider, 40
  Mulled Pineapple-Citrus Punch, 41
  Warm and Spicy Tomato Punch, 42
Blueberry-Lemon Muffins, 288
Bread Pudding, Sweet Potato, 312
breads
  Spiced Banana Bread, 285
  Steamed Pumpkin Bread, 286, *287*
Broccoli-Potato Soup, Creamy, 54
Broccoli Rabe, Braised, with Cherry Tomatoes, *252*, 253
broth
  Chicken Broth, 48
  Dark-Roasted Beef Broth, 49
  Harvest Vegetable Broth, 50
Brussels Sprouts, Shredded, with Almonds, 251

C

Cabbage, Sweet and Tangy Red, 254
cakes
  Carrot Cake, 302
  Decadent Chocolate Pudding
    Cake, 299
carrots
  Carrot Cake, 302
  Crock-Roasted Carrots and
    Parsnips with Cumin-Yogurt
    Sauce, 256
  Pomegranate Carrots, 255
Catfish, Creole, 95
cauliflower
  Braised Cauliflower with Crisp
    Garlic Crumbs, 257
  Cauliflower-Crust Pizza with
    Vegetable Topping and Balsamic
    Glaze, 203, 204–5
  Cream of Cauliflower Soup, 52
Chai Tea, 43
cheese
  Cheese Lover's
    Mac-and-Cheese,
    258, 259
  Cheesy Basil Grits, 262
  Layered Pasta Casserole, 218
  Mini Mint-Chocolate Cheesecakes,
    300, 301
  Rustic Two-Cheese Ratatouille,
    214
  White and Greens Lasagna,
    209–10, 211
chicken
  Artichoke-Lemon Chicken, 131
  Athens Chicken Pinwheels on
    Pasta, 128–29
  Cajun-Sauced Drumsticks, 144
  Chicken, Mushrooms, and Pearl
    Onions in Red Wine, 139
  Chicken and Bean Soup with
    Lemon and Basil, 65
  Chicken and Brown Rice Soup with
    Blue Cheese Crumbles, 62
  Chicken and Dumplings, 126–27
  Chicken and Fresh Fennel
    Cassoulet, 121
  Chicken and Tomato Stew with
    Kalamata Olives, 141
  Chicken Broth, 48
  Chicken Cacciatore, 145
  Chicken Pho, 68
  Chicken Sofrito, 147
  Chicken Tortilla Soup, 69

Chicken with Autumn Vegetables,
    122–23, 123
Chicken with Black Beans and
    Sweet Potatoes, 140
Country Chicken Noodle Soup, 67
Curry-Rubbed Chicken, 137
Garlic Chicken with Honey-Lemon
    Sauce, 134
Herbed Chicken Soup with
    Arugula, 64
Mediterranean Chicken, 130
Mole Chicken Tacos,
    146
Moroccan Chicken Thighs with
    Raisin-and-Carrot Couscous,
    132, 133
Pad Thai with Chicken, 142, 143
Pepper-Pineapple Chicken, 136
Rosemary Chicken with Bell
    Peppers, 138
Saucy Boneless Chicken "Wings,"
    32, 33
Shrimp and Chicken Paella, 115
Slow-Roasted Tarragon Chicken,
    124–25
Spicy Chicken and Corn Soup, 66
Thai Coconut-Chicken Soup, 63
White Chicken Chili,
    135
chili
  Beer Barrel Turkey Chili, 157
  Black and Red Bean Chili with
    Peppery Sour Cream, 222, 223
  Chunky Chili con Carne, 176
  Cranberry Bean and Sweet Potato
    Chili, 232
  Five-Way Cincinnati-Style Chili,
    178
  Pork-and-Beans Chili, 196
  White Chicken Chili,
    135
chocolate
  Decadent Chocolate Pudding
    Cake, 299
  Mini Mint-Chocolate Cheesecakes,
    300, 301
chutney
  Pear and Dried Cherry Chutney,
    279
  Zesty Tomato-Apple Chutney, 280
Clam and Cod Chowder, 61
cod
  Citrus Cod, 96
  Cod and Clam Chowder, 61

Mediterranean Fish Stew with
    Rouille, 112, 113
Collard Greens with Turkey Bacon,
    260
corn
  Corn and Wild Rice Soup, 56, 57
  Spicy Chicken and Corn Soup, 66
Cornish Hen, Peach-Glazed, for Two,
    159
Crab and Red Bell Pepper Soup, 60
Cranberry Sauce, Wine-Spiked, 281

E

eggplant
  Baba Ghanoush, 26
  Eggplant and Basil Mediterranean
    Salsa, 283
  Rustic Two-Cheese Ratatouille,
    214
  Sicilian Eggplant Caponata, 261
eggs. See Frittata

F

Fig, Dried, and Strawberry Spread,
    282
fish
  Creole Catfish, 95
  Fish Amandine in Foil, 94
  Lemony Fish and Vegetable Stew,
    91
  Shrimp-and-Fish Bayou Gumbo,
    118
  see also specific fish names
Frittata, Greek, with Spinach,
    Goat Cheese, and Roasted
    Red Bell Peppers, 294, 295
fruit
  Dried-Fruit Compote with
    Pomegranate Juice, 309
  see also specific fruits

G

grains. See specific grains
Granola, Apricot-Cinnamon, 289
greens
  Beans and Greens Enchiladas, 216,
    217
  Salad Greens with Lime and Herb
    Pulled Pork, 195
  White and Greens Lasagna,
    209–10, 211
  see also specific greens
grits
  Cheesy Basil Grits, 262

Nutty Breakfast Grits with Pears, 292
Shrimp and Grits, 119
Gyros, Beef and Bell Pepper, with Tzatziki Sauce, *162*, 163

H
Halibut, Coconut Curry, with Green Beans and Roasted Red Bell Peppers, 98, *99*
Healthy For Good™
   Add Color, 15–16
   Be Well, 17–18
   Eat Smart, 14–15
   Move More, 16–17

K
Kale and Red Quinoa Soup, 82, *83*

L
Lamb Steaks, Garlicky, with Green Olive and Tomato Relish, 201
lentils
   Curried Lentil and Vegetable Soup, 80
   Gingered Lentils and Quinoa, 220
   Greek Lentils, 221
   Lentil and Bell Pepper Salad with Lemon-Orange Dressing, 263
   Moroccan Lentil Soup, 79
   Persian Red Lentil Soup, 78
   Turkey Sausage and Lentil Soup, 70
Lettuce Wraps, Asian, 174

M
Mahi Mahi Tacos, 92, *93*
mangoes
   Beef Stew with Fresh Mango, 179, *180–81*
   Jerk Pork Loin with Mango Salsa, 189
   Sweet Mango Sticky Rice, 307
meatballs
   Smoked Turkey Meatballs, 31
   Southwestern Turkey Meatballs, 156
meatless crumbles
   "Baked" Potatoes Stuffed with Blue Cheese and Meatless Crumbles, 207
   Black-Eyed Pea Soup with Meatless Crumbles, 84

Cauliflower-Crust Pizza with Vegetable Topping and Balsamic Glaze, 203, *204–5*
Spaghetti Squash Noodle Bowl, 228–29, *229*
meat loaf
   Molasses-Glazed Beef and Veggie Meat Loaf, 184
   Turkey Meat Loaf with Creamy Chicken Gravy, 150
Muffins, Blueberry-Lemon, 288
mushrooms
   Barley Casserole, 248
   Barley Risotto with Mushrooms and Spinach, 208
   Brisket with Exotic-Mushroom and Onion Gravy, 164–65
   Caramelized Onion-Mushroom Gravy, 277
   Chicken, Mushrooms, and Pearl Onions in Red Wine, 139
   Double-Mushroom and Barley Soup, 55
   Layered Pasta Casserole, 218
   Meaty Mushroom Pasta Sauce, 274
   Sherried Steak-and-Mushroom Soup, 89
mussels
   Cioppino with White Wine, 111
   Mediterranean Fish Stew with Rouille, 112, *113*

N
noodles
   Chicken Pho, 68
   Country Chicken Noodle Soup, 67
   Korean Beef Soup, 88
   Pad Thai with Chicken, 142, *143*

O
oats
   Apple-Maple Oatmeal, 296
   Apricot-Cinnamon Granola, 289
   PB&O Breakfast, *290*, 291
onions
   Caramelized Onion-Mushroom Gravy, 277
   Caramelized Onions, 276
   French Onion Soup, 45

P
Parsnips and Carrots, Crock-Roasted, with Cumin-Yogurt Sauce, 256

pasta
   Athens Chicken Pinwheels on Pasta, 128–29
   Cheese Lover's Mac-and-Cheese, 258, *259*
   Italian Vegetable and Pasta Soup, 58
   Layered Pasta Casserole, 218
   Red-Bean Spaghetti, 227
   Sicilian Tuna Farfalle, 110
   Veggies and Pasta with Blue Cheese, 215
   White and Greens Lasagna, 209–10, *211*
peaches
   Cinnamon Quinoa with Peaches, 293
   Pork Tenderloin with Cherry and Peach Salsa, *190*, 191
   Strawberry, Rhubarb, and Peach Crumble, *304*, 305
peanuts & peanut butter
   Cinnamon-Honey Peanuts, 39
   PB&O Breakfast, *290*, 291
pears
   Autumn Apple-Pear Sauce, 247
   Gingered Pear and Apricot Dip, 30
   Nutty Breakfast Grits with Pears, 292
   Pear and Dried Cherry Chutney, 279
   Pears with Raspberry-Orange Sauce, 306
   Sugar Plum Pears, 308
peas
   Black-Eyed Pea Soup with Meatless Crumbles, 84
   Smoky Split Pea Soup, 75, *76–77*
Pecans, Cajun-Spiced, 38
peppers
   Hot Stuffed Peppers, 158
   Italian Artichoke-Stuffed Bell Peppers, 219
   Lentil and Bell Pepper Salad with Lemon-Orange Dressing, 263
   Rustic Two-Cheese Ratatouille, 214
   Smoky Red Bell Pepper Hummus, 28–29
pineapple
   Mulled Pineapple-Citrus Punch, 41
   Pepper-Pineapple Chicken, 136

Pistachio and Pumpkin Seed Snack Mix, 24, *25*

Pizza, Cauliflower-Crust, with Vegetable Topping and Balsamic Glaze, 203, *204–5*

Plum Pears, Sugar, 308

Polenta, Parmesan, with Roasted Vegetables, *234,* 235

Pomegranate-Cherry Cider, Hot, 40

pork
    Alsatian Pork-and-Potato Casserole, 187
    Cuban-Style Pork with Orange, 186
    Four-Seed Pork Loin, 193
    German Schnitzel, 200
    Jerk Pork Loin with Mango Salsa, 189
    Pork-and-Beans Chili, 196
    Pork and Butternut Stew, 192
    Pork and Water Chestnut Mini Phyllo Tarts, 34
    Pork Carnitas, 194
    Pork Chops with Grape Tomatoes and Fresh Basil, 197, *198–99*
    Pork Tenderloin with Cherry and Peach Salsa, *190,* 191
    Salad Greens with Lime and Herb Pulled Pork, 195
    Tuscan Pork and Beans, 188

potatoes
    Alsatian Pork-and-Potato Casserole, 187
    "Baked" Potatoes Stuffed with Blue Cheese and Meatless Crumbles, 207
    Breakfast Hash Brown Casserole, 297
    Creamy Potato-Broccoli Soup, 54
    Roasted Red Potatoes with Lemon and Green Onions, 244, *245*
    Tilapia with Lemon Potatoes, 106
    see also sweet potatoes

pudding
    Sweet Potato Bread Pudding, 312
    Tapioca Pudding with Blueberries, 313

pumpkin
    Pumpkin-Pecan Crisp, 314
    Pumpkin-Sage Risotto, 269
    Steamed Pumpkin Bread, 286, *287*
    Sweet and Spicy Pumpkin Soup, 46, *47*
    Pumpkin Seed and Pistachio Snack Mix, 24, *25*

Q

quinoa
    Cinnamon Quinoa with Peaches, 293
    Gingered Lentils and Quinoa, 220
    Kale and Red Quinoa Soup, 82, *83*
    Maple-Glazed Quinoa, 268

R

Raspberry-Orange Sauce, Pears with, 306

recipes, about, 20–21

Rhubarb, Strawberry, and Peach Crumble, *304,* 305

rice
    Chicken and Brown Rice Soup with Blue Cheese Crumbles, 62
    Corn and Wild Rice Soup, 56, *57*
    Cuban-Style Black Beans and Rice, 226
    East Indian Spiced Beans with Apricot Rice, 224
    Mexican Stuffed Squash, 225
    Nutty Brown Rice and Arugula Toss, 213
    Pumpkin-Sage Risotto, 269
    Shrimp and Chicken Paella, 115
    Shrimp Jambalaya, 114
    Sweet Mango Sticky Rice, 307
    Vegetable and Mixed-Rice Pilaf, 271
    Wild Rice with Harvest Vegetables, 270
    Zucchini and Tomato Risotto, 212

Root Beer Barbecue Sauce, Thick and Rich, 275

S

salads
    Chickpea, Cucumber, and Tomato Salad with Feta, 239
    Lentil and Bell Pepper Salad with Lemon-Orange Dressing, 263

salmon
    Jerk Salmon with Orange-Brown Sugar Glaze, 102
    Mojito Salmon, 101
    Salmon Fillets with Pineapple-Melon Relish, 100
    Salmon with Cucumber-Dill Aïoli, 103

Salsa, Eggplant and Basil Mediterranean, 283

sandwiches. *See* Gyros

sauces & gravy
    Autumn Apple-Pear Sauce, 247
    Caramelized Onion-Mushroom Gravy, 277
    Cherry Barbecue Sauce, 32
    Chunky Tomato Sauce with Green Olives, 273
    Meaty Mushroom Pasta Sauce, 274
    Red Ranch Sauce, 32
    Thick and Rich Root Beer Barbecue Sauce, 275
    Wine-Spiked Cranberry Sauce, 281

sausages (turkey)
    Beer Barrel Turkey Chili, 157
    Breakfast Hash Brown Casserole, 297
    Hot Stuffed Peppers, 158
    Low-Country Boil with Shrimp and Smoked Turkey Sausage, 116, *117*
    Turkey Meat Loaf with Creamy Chicken Gravy, 150
    Turkey Sausage and Lentil Soup, 70

shellfish
    Cioppino with White Wine, 111
    Cod and Clam Chowder, 61
    Crab and Red Bell Pepper Soup, 60
    Mediterranean Fish Stew with Rouille, 112, *113*
    see also shrimp

shrimp
    Low-Country Boil with Shrimp and Smoked Turkey Sausage, 116, *117*
    Shrimp and Chicken Paella, 115
    Shrimp-and-Fish Bayou Gumbo, 118
    Shrimp and Grits, 119
    Shrimp Jambalaya, 114

slow cookers
    benefits of, 10
    cooking guidelines, 12–13
    how they work, 11

Sole-and-Asparagus Rolls, 97

soups, list of recipes, 44

spinach
    Artichoke-Spinach "Mini Wraps," 36
    Barley Risotto with Mushrooms and Spinach, 208
    Bean Florentine Soup, 74
    Greek Frittata with Spinach, Goat Cheese, and Roasted Red Bell Peppers, 294, *295*
    Greek Lentils, 221

Split Pea Soup, Smoky, 75, *76–77*
squash
  Acorn Squash Wedges with
    Walnuts, 265, *266–67*
  Butternut Squash Bisque, 51
  Mexican Stuffed Squash, 225
  Pork and Butternut Stew, 192
  Spaghetti Squash Noodle Bowl,
    228–29, *229*
  Veggies and Pasta with Blue
    Cheese, 215
  see also pumpkin; zucchini
stews
  Bean and Roasted Vegetable Stew,
    230
  Beef and Brew Stew, 177
  Beef Goulash with Lemon, 182
  Beef Stew with Fresh Mango, 179,
    180–81
  Chicken and Tomato Stew with
    Kalamata Olives, 141
  Chickpea and Vegetable Stew,
    236–37
  Cioppino with White Wine, 111
  Lemony Fish and Vegetable Stew,
    91
  Louisiana Vegetable Stew, 231
  Mediterranean Fish
    Stew with Rouille, 112, *113*
  Pork and Butternut Stew, 192
  Shrimp-and-Fish Bayou Gumbo,
    118
  Turkey and Sweet Potato Stew,
    151
  Vegetable Stew with Cornmeal
    Dumplings, 241
  see also chili
Strawberry, Rhubarb, and Peach
  Crumble, *304*, 305
Strawberry and Dried Fig Spread,
  282
sweet potatoes
  Chicken with Black Beans and
    Sweet Potatoes, 140
  Cranberry Bean and Sweet Potato
    Chili, 232
  Simple Mashed Sweet Potatoes,
    264
  Sweet Potato Bread Pudding, 312
  Turkey and Sweet Potato Stew,
    151

T
tacos
  Mahi Mahi Tacos, 92, *93*
  Mole Chicken Tacos, 146
Tapioca Pudding with Blueberries,
  313
Tarts, Pork and Water Chestnut Mini
  Phyllo, 34
Tea, Chai, 43
tilapia
  Cioppino with White Wine, 111
  Lime-Infused Tilapia, *104,* 105
  Tilapia with Lemon Potatoes, 106
tofu
  Thai Vegetable Curry,
    233
  Tofu Tikka Masala, 240
tomatoes
  Chicken and Tomato Stew with
    Kalamata Olives, 141
  Chickpea, Cucumber, and Tomato
    Salad with Feta, 239
  Chunky Tomato Sauce with Green
    Olives, 273
  Fresh Tomato Soup with Goat
    Cheese and Basil, 53
  Pork Chops with Grape Tomatoes
    and Fresh Basil, 197, *198–99*
  Sun-Dried Tomato, Kalamata, and
    Tuna Tapenade, 23
  Swiss Steak with Melting
    Tomatoes and Onions, 161
  Warm and Spicy Tomato Punch, 42
  Zesty Tomato-Apple Chutney, 280
  Zucchini and Tomato Risotto, 212
Trout, Whole Rosemary, 107
tuna
  Sicilian Tuna Farfalle, 110
  Spanish-Style Tuna, 109
  Sun-Dried Tomato, Kalamata, and
    Tuna Tapenade, 23
  Super-Simple Asian Tuna, 108
turkey
  Barbecue-Spiced Turkey Breast,
    149
  Beer Barrel Turkey Chili, 157
  Hot Stuffed Peppers, 158
  Meaty Mushroom Pasta Sauce, 274
  Pulled Turkey Tostadas with
    Cucumber Guacamole, *152,*
    153–54

Smoked Turkey and Rice Soup
  with Fresh Sage, 71
Smoked Turkey Meatballs, 31
Southwestern Turkey Meatballs,
  156
Turkey and Sweet Potato Stew,
  151
Turkey Breast with Gravy, 148
Turkey Cassoulet with Gremolata,
  155
Turkey Meat Loaf with Creamy
  Chicken Gravy, 150
see also sausages (turkey)

V
vegetables
  Bean and Roasted Vegetable Stew,
    230
  Chicken with Autumn Vegetables,
    122–23, *123*
  Chickpea and Vegetable Stew,
    236–37
  Countryside Beef and Garden
    Vegetable Soup, 86
  Harvest Vegetable Broth, 50
  Honey-Roasted Vegetables, 243
  Italian Vegetable and Pasta Soup,
    58
  Jamaican Bean and Vegetable
    Soup, 72, *73*
  Louisiana Vegetable Stew, 231
  Parmesan Polenta with Roasted
    Vegetables, *234*, 235
  Ribollita, 59
  Spicy Vegetable Curry, 238
  Thai Vegetable Curry, 233
  Vegetable and Mixed-Rice Pilaf,
    271
  Vegetable Stew with Cornmeal
    Dumplings, 241
  Wild Rice with Harvest
    Vegetables, 270
  see also specific vegetables

Z
zucchini
  Rustic Two-Cheese Ratatouille,
    214
  Zucchini and Tomato Risotto, 212

Copyright © 2012, 2018 by the American Heart Association

Previous edition published in the United States in 2012.

Published in the United States by Harmony Books, an imprint of the Crown Publishing Group, a division of Penguin Random House LLC, New York.

crownpublishing.com

Harmony Books is a registered trademark and the Circle colophon is a trademark of Penguin Random House LLC.

An earlier edition of this work was published by Clarkson Potter/Publishers, an imprint of the Crown Publishing Group, a division of Penguin Random House LLC, in 2012.

Your contributions to the American Heart Association support research that helps make publications like this possible. For more information, call 1-800-AHA-USA1 (1-800-242-8721) or contact us online at heart.org.

Library of Congress Cataloging-in-Publication Data

Title: American Heart Association healthy slow cooker cookbook.

Other titles: Healthy slow cooker cookbook | Slow cooker cookbook

Description: Second edition. | New York : Harmony, [2018] | Series: American heart association | Includes index.

Identifiers: LCCN 2018006860 (print) | LCCN 2018007601 (ebook) | ISBN 9780553448054 (ebook) | ISBN 9780553448047 (paperback)

Subjects: | BISAC: COOKING / Health & Healing / General. | COOKING / Methods / Cookery for One. | COOKING / Methods / Quick & Easy.

Classification: LCC RM237.7 (ebook) | LCC RM237.7 .A47 2018 (print) | DDC 641.5/63—dc23

LC record available at https://lccn.loc.gov/2018006860

ISBN 978-0-553-44804-7

Ebook ISBN 978-0-553-44805-4

Printed in China

Design by Sonia Persad

Photographs by Lauren Volo

1 2 3 4 5 6 7 8 9

Second Edition